GW00367513

3555081300

University of Stirling Library, FK9 4LA
Tel. 01786 - 467220

POPULAR LOAN

This item is likely to be in heavy demand.
Please **RETURN** or **RENEW** no later
than the last date stamped below.

ETHNOSYNTAX

WITHDRAWN

from

STIRLING UNIVERSITY LIBRARY

M Z
3.3
ENF

POPLOAN

87350.
7/03

ETHNOSYNTAX

Explorations in Grammar and Culture

Edited by
N. J. Enfield

OXFORD
UNIVERSITY PRESS

OXFORD
UNIVERSITY PRESS

Great Clarendon Street, Oxford OX2 6DP

Oxford University Press is a department of the University of Oxford.
It furthers the University's objective of excellence in research, scholarship,
and education by publishing worldwide in

Oxford New York

Auckland Bangkok Bogotá Buenos Aires Cape Town
Chennai Dar es Salaam Delhi Hong Kong Istanbul Karachi
Kolkata Kuala Lumpur Madrid Melbourne Mexico City Mumbai
Nairobi São Paulo Shanghai Singapore Taipei Tokyo Toronto

with an associated company in Berlin

Oxford is a registered trade mark of Oxford University Press
in the UK and in certain other countries

Published in the United States
by Oxford University Press Inc., New York

© Editorial matter and organization Nick Enfield 2002
© The chapters their authors 2002

The moral rights of the author have been asserted
Database right Oxford University Press (maker)

First published 2002

All rights reserved. No part of this publication may be reproduced,
stored in a retrieval system, or transmitted, in any form or by any means,
without the prior permission in writing of Oxford University Press,
or as expressly permitted by law, or under terms agreed with the appropriate
reprographics rights organization. Enquiries concerning reproduction
outside the scope of the above should be sent to the Rights Department,
Oxford University Press, at the address above

You must not circulate this book in any other binding or cover
and you must impose the same condition on any acquirer

British Library Cataloguing in Publication Data

Data available

Library of Congress Cataloging in Publication Data

Data applied for

ISBN 0-19-924906-7

1 3 5 7 9 10 8 6 4 2

Typeset in Times
by Peter Kahrel, Lancaster
Printed in Great Britain
on acid-free paper by
T. J. International Ltd.,
Padstow, Cornwall

CONTENTS

ACKNOWLEDGEMENTS

This book owes its existence to the patience, enthusiasm, and generosity of many. Each of the contributors have made the editor's work much easier and more enjoyable than it might have been, through their cooperation, support, and advice. Cliff Goddard in particular has generously made time for consultation at many critical moments, from inception through to completion of the work.

A number of contributors presented earlier versions of their chapters at a workshop on 11 July 1998, as part of the Australian Linguistic Institute, University of Queensland, St Lucia, Brisbane. Mary Laughren and other organizers of the Institute made the workshop not only possible, but smooth and enjoyable. Presenters were Burridge, Diller and Khanittanan, Enfield, Goddard, Pawley, Simpson, and Wierzbicka, as well as Jean Harkins. Chafe was present, but did not give a paper. Langacker, Newman, and Rumsey were unable to attend. The success of the workshop owes much to those who attended and participated in many valuable discussions. These include, in particular, Joan Bresnan, Penny Lee, and Eve Sweetser, who kindly chaired sessions, as well as Avery Andrews, Gerrit Dimendaal, Bill Foley, Randy LaPolla, Chris Manning, David Nash, Sally Rice, Arie Verhagen, and many others who contributed by raising important questions and making useful and stimulating comments. I would especially like to acknowledge the contributions that Jean Harkins and Randy LaPolla have made.

In early stages of this project, I received valuable encouragement from Felix Ameka, Nick Evans, John Lucy, and David Wilkins. As the project was being finalized, Steve Levinson provided much appreciated advice. To these five I am extremely grateful, and I regret not having been able to elicit contributions from them.

Finally, John Davey at Oxford has been a perfect gentleman.

N. J. E.

Nijmegen
February 2002

NOTES ON THE CONTRIBUTORS

KATE BURRIDGE completed her undergraduate training in Linguistics and German at the University of Western Australia, followed by three years of postgraduate study at the University of London. Kate completed her Ph.D. in 1983 on syntactic change in medieval Dutch, and taught at the Polytechnic of Central London before joining the Department of Linguistics at La Trobe University in 1984, where she is now an Associate Professor. Her main areas of research are grammatical change in Germanic languages, the Pennsylvania German spoken by Anabaptist communities in Canada, the notion of linguistic taboo, and the structure and history of English. She is the author of numerous books, including *Syntactic Change in Germanic* (Benjamins 1993), *Euphemism and Dysphemism: Language Used as Shield and Weapon* (OUP 1991, co-authored with Keith Allan), and *English in Australia and New Zealand—An Introduction to its History, Structure, and Use* (OUP 1998, co-authored with Jean Mulder). Kate is a member of the Australian Academy of Humanities.

WALLACE CHAFE is Professor Emeritus of Linguistics at the University of California at Santa Barbara. He has worked with Native American languages of the Iroquoian and Caddoan families, and has been involved in attempts to understand language from functional and cognitive perspectives. He has studied differences between spoken and written language, as well as applications of linguistics to literature. His most recent book was *Discourse, Consciousness, and Time* (Chicago University Press 1994). At present he is engaged in a long-term project to produce text collections, a dictionary, and a grammar of the Seneca language. He is also currently investigating the role of laughter in ordinary speech.

ANTHONY V. N. DILLER has been promoting Thai language and cultural studies at the Australian National University, Canberra, and has taught in Thailand, Canada, and the USA. He has published widely on topics in synchronic and diachronic grammar of Thai and the Tai language family, including research on grammaticalization, sociolinguistics, and the relation between the two. Current interests focus on cognitive, sociocultural, and historical interactions in linguistic research.

N. J. ENFIELD is a member of the scientific staff at the Max Planck Institute for Psycholinguistics, Nijmegen. He has conducted fieldwork in mainland Southeast Asia (especially Laos) for over ten years, and is the author of *Linguistic Epidemiology: Semantics and Grammar of Language Contact in Mainland Southeast Asia* (Routledge 2002). He is interested in a multidisciplinary approach to semiotic phenomena. Recent publications include work on topics in the grammar of Southeast Asian languages, areal linguistics, semantics, pragmatics, co-speech gesture, and linguistic anthropology (including 'The theory of cultural logic', *Cultural Dynamics*, 12.1, 2000, '"Lip-pointing"—a discussion of form and function with reference to data from Laos', *Gesture*, 1.2, 2002, and 'Semantic analysis of body parts in emotion terminology', *Pragmatics and Cognition*, 10.1-2, 2002).

CLIFF GODDARD is an Associate Professor in Linguistics at the University of New England, Australia. His interests include cross-cultural semantics and pragmatics, language description, and typology. He has written a grammar and dictionary of Yankunytjatjara, an indigenous language of Central Australia, and more recently has been working on Malay (Bahasa Melayu), the national language of Malaysia. His most recent book is *Semantic Analysis* (OUP 1998). With Anna Wierzbicka, he is co-editor of *Semantic and Lexical Universals* (Benjamins 1994) and *Meaning and Universal Grammar* (Benjamins 2002).

WILAIWAN KHANITTANAN established Thai as a foreign language at the University of Sydney, has authored Thai learning materials and currently teaches linguistics at Thammasat University, Bangkok. Her research publications include works in Thai sociolinguistics and descriptive and comparative–historical studies of Saek, Phu-Thai, Phake, Khamti, and other Tai languages.

JOHN NEWMAN is Senior Lecturer in Linguistics at Massey University, New Zealand. His research interests range over cognitive linguistics, corpus linguistics, historical linguistics, and phonology. Recent publications of his in the area of cognitive linguistics include a monograph *Give: A Cognitive Linguistic Study* (Mouton de Gruyter 1996) and an edited volume *The Linguistics of Giving* (Benjamins 1997). An edited volume *The Linguistics of Sitting, Standing, and Lying* will appear soon. His publications in phonology include a book chapter 'Footnotes to a History of Cantonese: Accounting for the Phonological Irregularities' (in *The Comparative Method Reviewed*, M. Durie and M. Ross (eds.), OUP 1996) and an undergraduate textbook *Coursebook in Feature Geometry* (Lincom Europa 1997). He is also an advocate and practitioner of online teaching in linguistics.

ANDREW PAWLEY is Professor of Linguistics, Research School of Pacific and Asian Studies, Australian National University, Canberra. He is interested in the nature of idiomatic command of a language, and does lexicographical, grammatical, and historical research, mainly on Austronesian and Papuan languages. His publications include 'Two puzzles for linguistic theory: nativelike selection and nativelike fluency' (with Frances Syder) (in J. Richards and R. Schmidt (eds.), *Language and Communication*, Longman 1983), 'Encoding events in Kalam and English: different logics for reporting experience' (in R. Tomlin (ed.), *Coherence and Grounding in Discourse*, Benjamins 1987), 'A language which defies description by ordinary means (in W. Foley (ed.), *The Role of Theory in Language Description*, Mouton de Gruyter 1993), and 'The one clause at a time hypothesis; (in H. Riggenbach (ed.), *Perspectives on Fluency*, University of Michigan Press 2000).

ANNA WIERZBICKA is Professor of Linguistics at the Australian National University, and a Fellow of the Australian Academy of the Humanities, of the Academy of Social Sciences of Australia, and of the Russian Academy of Sciences. She has lectured extensively at universities in Europe, America, and Asia and is the author of numerous books, including *Cross-Cultural Pragmatics* (Mouton de Gruyter 1991), *Semantics: Primes and Universals* (OUP 1996), *Emotions Across Languages and Cultures: Diversity and Universals* (CUP 1999), and *What Did Jesus Mean? Explaining the Sermon on the Mount and the Parables in Simple and Universal Human Concepts* (OUP 2001). Her work spans a number of disciplines, including anthropology, psychology, cognitive science, philosophy, and religious studies as well as linguistics, and has been published in many journals across all these disciplines.

PART I

Ethnosyntax: Theory and Scope

1

Ethnosyntax: Introduction

N. J. ENFIELD

Grammar is thick with cultural meaning. Encoded in the semantics of grammar we find cultural values and ideas, we find clues about the social structures which speakers maintain, we find evidence, both historically relevant and otherwise, of the social organization of speech communities. We find complex morphosyntactic systems, such as honorific inflection and agreement in Japanese, dedicated to the expression of social deixis (Prideaux 1990; Shibatani 1990). We find systems of nominal classification encoding a range of distinctions of cultural importance, their very existence possibly even revealing the kind of society speakers maintain (Craig 1986). We find that variation in the grammatical resources used within a single social system is sensitive to fundamental sociocultural distinctions such as gender and kinship relations, as observed in the sometimes extensive differences in grammar of men's and women's speech (Dunn 2000), or in the grammar of auxiliary languages such as 'avoidance styles' (Dixon 1971). We find different grammatical systems coexisting and interacting in culturally mediated ways, as in situations of diglossia, bilingualism, and code-switching arising from complex social conditions (Ferguson 1964: 433; Gumperz and Wilson 1971). We find grammatical constructions directly encoding cultural values of a given group of speakers, as for example in a range of grammatical devices in Russian expressing 'emotionality', 'non-rationality', 'non-agentivity', and 'moral passion' (Wierzbicka 1992).

This list of ways in which culture is entwined in grammar could go on and on (for a smorgasbord of examples, see Hymes 1964). It is intended that 'ethno-syntax'—broadly defined as the study of connections between the cultural knowledge, attitudes, and practices of speakers, and the morphosyntactic resources they employ in speech—should encompass this diverse range of grammar–culture effects. This field of research asks not just how culture and grammar may be connected, but also how they may be interconstitutive, through overlap and interplay

For generous and helpful comments on various drafts of this Introduction, I am grateful to the following people: Penny Brown, Kate Burridge, Tony Diller, Dominique Estival, Nick Evans, Helen Fraser, Cliff Goddard, Geoffrey Haig, Randy LaPolla, Penny Lee, Steve Levinson, Chris Manning, Andy Pawley, Alastair Pennycook, Alan Rumsey, Gunter Senft, Jane Simpson, Catherine Travis, Anna Wierzbicka, an anonymous referee (R2), and, especially, another anonymous referee (R1). I also acknowledge helpful input from Melissa Bowerman, Bill Foley, John Lucy, and David Wilkins. None are responsible for shortcomings.

between people's cultural practices and preoccupations and the grammatical structures they habitually employ. This may make reference to the semantics of grammar, or to ways in which the use or productivity of grammatical resources are constrained or licensed by culture.

This introductory chapter has two aims: first, to identify the range of ethnolinguistic phenomena treated in various contributions to this volume (without aiming to survey the potential scope of ethnosyntax as a field of research); and second, to discuss a number of methodological and theoretical issues of importance to research on the grammar–culture interface. The chapter is structured as follows. Section 1.1 provides brief background on selected work directly relevant to the focus of this book. Section 1.2 discusses a range of phenomena which come under the rubric of 'ethnosyntax', and which are dealt with in various contributions to the volume. An initial distinction, referred to by a number of contributors (e.g. Goddard, Rumsey, and Simpson), is between 'narrow' and 'broad' senses of the term. The 'narrow sense' refers to the direct encoding of cultural meaning in the semantics of morphosyntax—i.e. where a semantic explication of a grammatical construction could reveal a 'cultural script' (Wierzbicka, this volume). The 'broad sense' encompasses a much wider range of possible relations between grammar and culture, including semantic and pragmatic consequences of 'typicality' (as culturally defined), socially indexical significance of grammatical choices, culturally determined patterns of use of certain grammatical features, and interaction between culture and grammatical description. Phenomena which bridge the 'broad' and 'narrow' categories, and which may even provide an explanatory link between them, involve the role of culture in semantic and grammatical change.

Fundamental questions of theory and methodology inevitably arise when one attempts to demonstrate links between grammar and culture, and these are discussed in Section 1.3. The two main problems are, first, settling on methods of describing grammar and culture, and second, finding independent support for putative grammar–culture links.

Finally, Section 1.4 gives a brief overview of the volume, and Section 1.5 concludes.

1.1. BACKGROUND

Many have intuited that there is a connection between linguistic structures on one hand, and patterns of thought of speakers, on the other.[1] Patterns of thought are seldom clearly separated in that literature from patterns of culture, given that for many, culture is defined as *collective* patterns of thought. Thus, for Sapir (1994:

---

[1] Important sources include Boas 1911, Sapir 1949, 1994, Hoijer 1953, 1964, Whorf 1956, Lee 1959, Hymes 1961, 1964, 1966, Mathiot 1964, Landar 1966, Blount 1974, Hale 1986, Grace 1987, Rumsey 1990, Hill and Mannheim 1992, Lucy 1992*a*, Wierzbicka 1992, D'Andrade 1995, Gumperz and Levinson 1996, Lee 1996, Duranti 1997, Foley 1997, Pütz and Verspoor 2000, Niemeier and Dirven 2000, among others.

36), for example, it is *consensus* and *sanction* with regard to the meanings of things that defines culture. Sapir adopted the then emerging American structuralist approach to grammatical description, ascribing a greater and more complex order to the systematic structuring in language of human experience (cf. Sapir 1949). Like Boas before him, Sapir recognized that there may be influence of culture upon language. He later stressed that culture was not about 'what people did' *per se*, but about the *meaning* of what they did (Sapir 1994). Further, like Boas, Sapir saw the influences of culture on language as being mostly in the lexicon, and less in the grammar. An extensive literature in ethnosemantics has since explored this area (see D'Andrade 1995 and references therein).

Whorf (1956) took further the notion that language could influence habitual patterns of thought, stressing the systematic relationship between language and cognition, and putting forward his 'principle of linguistic relativity', by which 'users of markedly different grammars are pointed by the grammars toward different types of observations', thus arriving at 'somewhat different views of the world' (Whorf 1956: 221). Exactly what Whorf intended has been a matter of discussion ever since (Lucy 1992*a*; Gumperz and Levinson 1996; Lee 1996, 2000; Goddard in press), and how this relates specifically to 'culture', rather than 'thought' *per se*, remains open to interpretation.[2] Whorf's work is important in the context of this book, since it was Whorf who turned attention to the more subtle realms of morphosyntax.

There is abundant literature describing past and present approaches to the relationship between grammar and culture (see n. 1), and no review is necessary here. In the rest of this section, I restrict discussion to two important authors on the grammar–culture relationship—Anna Wierzbicka and Ken Hale—who have largely been overlooked in recent reviews.

Wierzbicka (1979) coined the term 'ethnosyntax', using it exclusively in the 'narrow' sense (see s. 1.2.1 below). She claimed that it is possible to show 'in a rigorous and verifiable way' that 'every language embodies in its very structure a certain world view, a certain philosophy' (Wierzbicka 1979: 313).[3] Rather than focusing on 'a few arbitrary lexical items', she examined grammatical constructions, arguing that '[s]ince the syntactic constructions of a language embody and codify certain language-specific meanings and ways of thinking, the syntax of a language must determine to a considerable extent this language's cognitive profile' (Wierzbicka 1979: 313; see s. 1.2.1 below). Wierzbicka's work is conspicuously absent from the otherwise excellent recent reviews of linguistic anthropology referred to above. Many scholars are put off by a simple universalist claim at the heart of her approach—namely, that all languages have a directly translatable primitive semantic core, and it is at this level that linguistic and cultural analysis

---

[2] Note the primacy assigned to culture in a recent definition of linguistic relativity as 'the idea that culture, *through* language, affects the way we think' (Gumperz and Levinson 1996: 1).

[3] Wierzbicka's work on ethnosyntax is discussed in detail in this volume, with reference to a number of examples, by Cliff Goddard. Thus, I do not discuss details in this introduction.

is to be done. But to ignore her work on this basis is unjustified. One may refrain from making the same theoretical commitments, yet still engage with the rich and careful descriptions of grammar and culture that Wierzbicka has produced over more than twenty years (see Wierzbicka 1979, 1988, 1991, 1992, 1997, 1998).

A second researcher of importance to the theme of this volume is Ken Hale, whose 1966 paper 'Kinship reflections in syntax' inspired an important body of research on 'kin-tax' in Australian languages, not often referred to outside specialist contexts (Hercus and White 1973; Heath, Merlan, and Rumsey 1982; Dench 1987; Wilkins 1988, 1993). The purpose of Hale's paper was to show that principles of kinship organization, which are of course firmly within the realm of culture, can and do play a role in syntactic rules. He showed with evidence from Arrernte and Lardil that agnation (i.e. patrilineal descent) and generation harmony (a relationship holding between those of alternate, but not adjacent, generations) are referred to in the 'structural description' of a syntactic rule of compound noun-phrase reduction. He concluded as follows (Hale 1966: 324):

> It is not unusual among the languages of the world for the grammatical apparatus devoted to personal deixis to mark categories relating to sociologically defined notions. Also, given the importance of classificatory kinship in Australian societies, it is not surprising to find that certain central features of the kinship system are reflected in the pronominal paradigm. This being so, it is reasonable to expect that a syntactic rule which mentions pronominal categories in its structural description might also make reference to one or more aspects of the kinship system. As we have seen, this expectation is correct.

A later study (Hale 1986) looks at the relationship between semantic categories and two distinct senses of 'world view'. Hale's 'World View-1' refers to 'the central propositions or postulates in a people's theory of how things are in the world' (Hale 1986: 233), and Hale stresses that these cultural 'propositions' are established independent of language. Nevertheless, relationships between 'World View-1' and language can be found. (See s. 1.3.5 below for further discussion of Hale's position.) Hale describes 'two fundamental themes in Warlpiri philosophy'—the 'eternal logic' (the logic of 'cyclical perpetuity, or unbroken circles', including themes such as the 'persistence of entities through transformation' and the 'unity of the actual and the potential') and the 'logic of complementarity' (or the 'unity of the opposites'). He then attempts to 'relate [these themes] to aspects of the Warlpiri language' (Hale 1986: 235), giving a range of supporting examples in lexical and grammatical semantics, including 'actual/potential' metonymy (O'Grady 1960; Evans 1997), distinctive ways of referring to manufacture (not as 'making' but as 'transforming' or 'fixing'), themes in sacred myth, aspects of kinship nomenclature, and patterns of antonymy.

Hale's 'World View-2' is defined as 'the "analysis of phenomena" embodied in the system of lexico-semantic themes or motifs which function as integral components in a grammar' (Hale 1986: 234), and which is therefore common to all speakers of the language. Warlpiri speakers, qua speakers of Warlpiri, elaborate a 'fundamental theory of relations' (p. 242), involving 'the definition of spatial, temporal, and identity relations in terms of "central" versus "non-central" (or "terminal") coincidence' (p. 238). This abstract theme in the world view of Warlpiri speakers 'manifests itself in the meanings of certain grammatical elements' in the language (p. 238). Hale provides data from 'six areas of Warlpiri grammar'—local cases, directional enclitics, finite complementizers, infinitival complementizers, tense/aspect markers, and depictive and translative predicates—concluding that 'a fundamental abstract semantic opposition of central versus non-central coincidence is at work' and that 'it is to be observed with particular clarity and purity in the grammar of Warlpiri' (Hale 1986: 252). I refer the reader to Hale's paper for data and detailed discussion.

1.2. FORMS OF ETHNOSYNTAX: A RANGE OF CULTURE–GRAMMAR CONNECTIONS

To cover the full scope of candidates for ethnosyntax phenomena would be beyond the limits of this introductory chapter, and probably premature. It is hoped that this book may lead to further efforts in defining the range of phenomena which may come under the ethnosyntax rubric. This part focuses largely on phenomena which are discussed in contributions to this volume, beginning with a distinction between 'narrow' and 'broad' senses of the term 'ethnosyntax', the former corresponding to Wierzbicka's original sense, the latter having a broadened and more diverse scope. After discussion of a number of distinct 'broad sense' phenomena, the section finishes with a discussion of language change, in which a linkage between 'broad' and 'narrow' senses of ethnosyntax can be observed.

1.2.1. *'Narrow' and 'broad' senses of ethnosyntax*

Wierzbicka's original sense of the term 'ethnosyntax' refers to the direct encoding of cultural ideas in the semantics of morphosyntax, and this is referred to here as ethnosyntax in the 'narrow' sense. This 'narrow sense' does not include any grammatical phenomenon in which a *semantic* analysis would not reveal some 'statement' of a notion specific to the culture of speakers. For example, in the present volume, Wierzbicka argues that the semantics of certain English causative constructions embody primary Anglo values of independence and autonomy in personal interaction. Elsewhere, she has argued that important cultural values of Russian speakers are encoded directly in a host of grammatical devices such as diminutives, infinitive constructions, and reflexive constructions (Wierzbicka 1992: ch. 12). Her original work on 'ethno-syntax' (Wierzbicka 1979) includes a masterful study of subtle variations of semantic detail in grammatical constructions encoding 'bodily actions and events' in a number of European languages, as well as Japanese. Semantic analyses of different languages reveal different 'philosophies' regarding the involvement of individuals in bodily events and actions.

Similarly, but from a different descriptive tradition, Langacker (1994) has argued that 'direct symbolization of culture-specific conceptions' can be found in grammatical devices. Based on his view of grammatical semantics fundamentally centring on experientially based prototypes, Langacker claims that while cognitive models that come into play in prototype semantics 'are themselves quite abstract, and may in large measure be universal and pre-cultural', it remains 'evident that cultural factors play some role in either shaping the models or determining their extension to non-prototypical instances' (Langacker 1994: 44; cf. Lakoff 1987; Newman 1996, this volume; Palmer 1996). He gives examples (from Tuggy 1979) of honorific meanings encoded in Tetelcingo Nahuatl morphosyntax, and cites a 'controlled' versus 'uncontrolled' distinction in Chipewyan classificatory verb stems which is 'claimed to have a larger cultural relevance' for speakers (Rushforth and Chisholm 1991; cf. Rice 1998; Newman, this volume).

Going beyond examples of this kind, there are 'broad sense' phenomena. These include morphosyntactic categories and constructions which do not themselves encode culture-specific 'statements' in their semantics, but which may nevertheless show culture-specific patterns of distribution and use, or other culture-related effects. Morphosyntactic devices which are not necessarily culture-specific in semantic terms—such as switch-reference systems and classifier constructions—may nevertheless be *used* differently, where those differences have culture-specific motivations. Thus, culture-specific uses of such non-culture-specific devices may relate to the pragmatic effects of different 'cultural premises' (Enfield, this volume), or to culture-specific semantics of the lexical items involved.[4]

We now turn to some 'broad sense' phenomena which are treated in contributions to this volume, namely 'typicality' effects, the social indexicality of grammatical choices, and the effects of cultural institutions taking an interest in grammar.

1.2.1.1. Typicality effects

Repeated experiences of complex phenomena result in *typifications* (Schutz 1970) or *schemas/frames/scenarios* (Holland and Quinn 1987), which may guide our interpretations of the semantics of complex grammatical constructions. My own contribution to this volume takes as its starting point an observation made in literature on verb serialization (Durie 1997; Bruce 1988), that certain combinations of morphemes in serial constructions are deemed by speakers to be unacceptable, not because they are anomalous in some structural way, but because they describe events which do not qualify as 'event types'. The most interesting feature of this interplay between grammar and culture is not the apparent inadmissibility of certain combinations, but the overall semantic behaviour of the complex constructions. When certain combinations are culturally typical, they can become enriched metonymically, evoking the default details defined by a given culturally normal

---

[4] David Wilkins has suggested distinctions along these lines in correspondence with contributors to this book. See contributions by Goddard and Rumsey for further discussion.

event type. This corresponds to the principle in Gricean pragmatics whereby one does not mention details wherever details need not be mentioned (Grice's 'Maxim of Quantity No. 2', 1975: 45; Levinson's 'I-Principle', 2000: 37). Thus, given two scenes of equivalent objective/perceptual complexity, but of different typicality status, speakers produce descriptions of different morphosyntactic complexity.

Constructions showing certain levels of syntactic, and therefore conceptual, complexity are more usually acceptable (i.e. considered more 'grammatical') when they describe culturally typical or easily imaginable scenarios. Thus, the former of the following sentences is more acceptable, and certainly more easily processed:[5]

(*a*) Did you hear that the guy who the police were looking for's red Cortina got stolen?

(*b*) Will they deny that a nun who your shopkeeper was chatting up's large settee got replicated?

Clark and Malt (1984: 203) similarly point out that in comprehension of a hard-to-process utterance, if a certain meaning seems highly likely to be intended in the context, then one is likely not to bother going through with fully resolving the difficult processing task. They give the example of Wason and Reich's (1979) 'verbal illusion' *No head injury is too trivial to ignore*, and point to the background assumptions or 'heuristic procedures' used in figuring out what 'must' be meant. It can take a while to figure out that this sentence means 'All head injuries are to be ignored, including the most trivial ones'. What is not explicitly discussed in such accounts is that these heuristics are often *cultural* (Levinson 1995: 240; Enfield 2000*a*: 39), and that describing them is a matter of ethnography.

Langacker (1994) discusses the problem of culture-related constraints on accessibility to morphosyntactic resources under the heading of '*distributional* impact of cultural knowledge', by which 'a specific cultural practice or belief motivates the otherwise unexpected membership of some entity in a conceptually grounded category of grammatical significance' (Langacker 1994: 39). He argues that 'quite a number of grammatical phenomena are in one way or another sensitive to cultural expectations. They somehow reflect culturally determined conceptions of what constitutes a *familiar scenario*, a *canonical situation*, or a *normal course of events*' (Langacker 1994: 39–40, original emphasis). Langacker (1994) discusses one example concerning the distribution of verb stems in Cupeño (Uto-Aztecan). He reports Hill's (1969) argument that verbs in the 'zero stem' class (as opposed to those that take either the *-in* suffix or the *-yax* suffix) make 'natural' predications, describing 'the normal behaviour of animals, plants, inanimate objects, and the weather', '[most] natural processes, as well as states of mind', and the everyday activities which Hill describes as 'good solid Cupeño cultural behaviour' (1969: 352)—these include 'make acorn mush', 'make a basket', 'shoot arrows', and

---

[5] I thank Avery Andrews for pointing this out.

'relate tribal history'. Langacker (1994: 43) also discusses violations of the 'co-ordinate structure constraint' in English (e.g. *What did Bill go to the store and buy?*), which are permissible when the underlying 'scenario' instantiates the 'natural course of events' (Lakoff 1986: 153) (unlike, say **What did Sally mow the lawn and fix?*). Similar is the contrast between definite articles and 'zero articles' in expressions like *She went to (the) school/church/university/bed/hospital/sea/town/ etc.* (Levinson 2000: 147). Presence of the article results in a simple 'go to goal of motion' reading, while ellipsis of *the* evokes a much richer culturally defined scenario in each case (compare *John went to prison* versus *John went to the prison*).

Another case of typicality having an effect on grammar is the common restriction on productivity of noun incorporation. The constraint on using certain noun–verb combinations in incorporating structures relates to the cultural 'normalness' of the concepts (signified by the given noun and verb) being routinely associated in daily life. Mithun gives an example from Chukchi, in which 'fuel-gathering, wood-cutting, and tent-breaking' are 'unitary, name-worthy activities' which appear in noun-incorporating compounds, yet 'brushwood-plucking, boat-loading, and tent-loading are not, so they are expressed by separate V's and N's' (Mithun 1984: 861).

A final example concerns an apparently increased tolerance for 'extensions' beyond the strict semantic specifications of certain productive grammatical constructions in cases where the extension is 'licensed' by a culturally provided scenario. For example, in English, a clash between the direct causation suggested by the frame 'V NP$_1$ OFF NP$_2$' and indirect causation in a scene being described is tolerated when the scenario is 'licensed' by virtue of being a culturally established one—thus, one may be *booed off the stage*, but not **fidgeted off the stage*.[6]

Constraints in the productivity and interpretation of morphosyntactic devices, contingent upon the 'normal course of events' as culturally defined, are evidently widespread and pervasive. However, they have not so far been the focus of concentrated cross-linguistic research (see Enfield, this volume).

1.2.1.2. Social indexicality and 'emblematicity' of grammar

Productive morphosyntactic features can have conscious cultural value, such that mastery in use is encouraged and deliberately maintained for aesthetic or other cultural reasons.[7] Examples include grammatical structures with expressive or creative import, such as expletive infixation in Australian English (*fan-bloody-tastic*), or the productive systems of expressive rhyming reduplication found across languages of mainland South-East Asia (Diffloth 1979). In Lao, for example,

---

[6] I thank Melissa Bowerman for pointing this out.
[7] On the level of whole systems, diglossia (Ferguson 1964) is a good example—the ability of some speakers to handle the 'high' register better than other speakers can correlate with significant social facts.

there is a pattern of expressive reduplication involving complex rules of reduplication and vowel mutation (e.g. where *nam⁰.hòòm³* 'perfume' derives *nam⁰.hòòm³-nam⁰.hèèm³* 'perfume and that sort of stuff'). This is a productive grammatical system which all Lao speakers are aware of and can recognize and comprehend. And unlike, say, the verbal tense-aspect-modality system, not all speakers have equal command of expressive morphosyntax, and indeed individual skill in using it is recognized.

Such morphosyntactic rules are consciously and creatively employed, in a manner roughly analogous to art, dance, or music. As Hale (1998: 204) has put it:

Some forms of verbal art—verse, song, or chant—depend crucially on morphological and phonological, even syntactic, properties of the language in which [they are] formed. In such cases, the art could not exist without the language, literally.

Burridge and Allan (1998) discuss 'secret languages' (such as 'Pig Latin', 'Eggy Peggy', and 'Upp-upp'), which involve manipulation or remodelling of a language by means of affixation and/or morphophonological permutation (cf. Kirshenblatt-Gimblett 1976). They show that not only can these grammatical devices be used to index and/or verify cultural identity, but they can be used to exclude out-groupers, citing the example of Romani 'camouflaging suffixes' which can modify local languages, making them unintelligible to non-in-group members.

Also relevant here are 'sociosyntax' phenomena such as the syntactic variables which distinguished various Harlem gangs from 'lames' (non-gang-members), including expletive subject *it* in presentational sentences (*It's a policeman in that unmarked car*), or auxiliary inversion in embedded questions (*He asked me could I go there*; Labov 1972, cited in Chambers 1995: 92–3). Wolfram and Fasold (1974: 164) describe grammatical variables in non-standard varieties of English, such as multiple negation (*We ain't never had no trouble about none of us pulling out no knife*), and copula deletion (*He busy right now*). The contribution to this volume by Diller and Khanittanan describes some of the sociocultural correlates with grammatical alternatives in Thai.

1.2.1.3. Syntax from the native's perspective

Cultural institutions may affect grammatical structure through the efforts of grammarians themselves, via the academic culture of linguistic science. Pennycook rightly describes linguistics as 'a very particular cultural form' (Pennycook 1994: 125). Accordingly, grammatical description is constrained by culture-specific assumptions, objectives, expectations, superstitions, and taboos. It is, among other things, an art. Cultural preoccupations of modern grammarians include deference to scientific principles like parsimony of description, logical argumentation, and the aim for neat generalizations; awareness of the special attention paid within the culture to those who publish important counter-examples or unusual data, or make strong and/or controversial claims; career ambition; the tension between a desire to follow an original approach, to adopt a fashionable research agenda, or to discover the truth; and so on (cf. Harris 1980, 1987; Murray 1994; Pennycook 1994: 114 ff.). And grammatical traditions in radically different cultures may indeed be radically different in form. There is no better demonstration of this than a comparison of the standard modern linguistic grammar with the ancient Sanskrit grammar of *Pāṇini* (Katre 1987). Our training in the culture of grammarians has a coercive effect on how we gather and analyse linguistic data, how we write about it, and how we interpret what we read about it. This issue is further explored by Diller and Khanittanan (this volume), the only contributors who take the term 'ethnosyntax' to mean 'syntax from the native's point of view' (i.e. analogous to terms like 'ethnopsychology' and 'ethnobiology'). Andy Pawley, also, touches on this issue in an 'afterthought' to his chapter. He argues that traditions of normative grammar can cause grammarians not even to *notice* some facts about grammatical structures in real language use.

An area of grammarians' practice strongly tied to culture is the notion of 'grammaticality' (and/or 'acceptability'), a problem also explored by Diller and Khanittanan (this volume). Syntacticians traditionally rely on a binary distinction between 'grammatical' and 'ungrammatical' utterances—those which are 'part of the grammar' and those which are not—and yet we are all acquainted with that expansive middle ground in which an adjustment to the 'unmarked' context can make an otherwise 'ungrammatical' utterance perfectly good. Kay (1996: 112) rejects *Sybil had John fall off the couch*, yet he himself shows that the string is fine in the right context. The causative verb *have* requires its lower verb to be agentive, but the lower verb *fall*, rather than *entailing* non-agentivity, merely *implies* non-agentivity, since people do not typically fall on purpose. This typification is easily overridden by a licensing (albeit marked) cultural context—theatre—in which people *do* fall on purpose. The 'ungrammaticality' of Kay's starred sentence is of a completely different order from, say, that of **Couch John Sybil off had fall the.*[8] My own contribution to this volume discusses a case in which sentences judged by speakers as odd, and even unacceptable, due to 'logical' problems, are later produced spontaneously by the same speakers. It turns out that the 'logic' involved in many grammaticality or acceptability judgements makes reference to what is culturally normal. A culturally atypical scenario can successfully elicit a supposedly 'ungrammatical' structure.

The culture of grammarians can not only affect the way language is *described*, but this culture-mediated description can also turn around and affect the language itself, via 'self-fulfilling prophecy' effects of prescriptive grammar, often associated with social modernization, nationalism, and the politically motivated official language standardization that inevitably goes with it (Lucy 1996: 59–63; Fish-

---

[8] Work on 'verb class semantics', such as that in Dowty 1979, Foley and Van Valin 1984, Frawley 1992: ch. 4 and references therein, is a good example of an area in which the culturally normal plays a central role in whether and/or how various combination are interpreted.

man 1997). Diller (1988, 1993) has documented changes that Thai has undergone, resulting directly from language engineering inspired by a combination of influences from Sanskrit and Western grammar, selectively appropriated by authorities with essentially political aims. This has resulted in an expanded classifier system, a more developed system of speech-act particles and various politeness-marking forms, elaborated systems of overt subordination or adjunction (complementizers, 'prepositions'), and reduced deictic and pronominal systems, among other things. A final example of modernization affecting grammar is the global spread of an impersonal sentence type modelled on the English passive construction, usually due to translation of news, instruction manuals, or educational textbooks of foreign origin (Blake 2001).

1.2.2. *Culture, pragmatics, and semantic change*

The 'broad' and 'narrow' senses of ethnosyntax are not exclusive. One important way in which they are linked is in the semanticization (in grammar) of pragmatic inferences based on cultural logic (Wilkins 1991; Enfield 2000*a*, 2002), one mechanism, perhaps the main one, by which 'narrow' phenomena (i.e. cultural semantics in grammar) emerge out of 'broad' phenomena (i.e. culturally mediated patterns of use or interpretation of grammar). These mechanisms can provide accounts for 'linkage' in psychologically based explanations of why grammar is structured as it is (Clark and Malt 1984; Hall 1992; see s. 1.3.3 below for discussion). Pragmatic inferences drive the processes of semantic change known as 'grammaticalization', and account for how particular grammatical resources come to exist in the first place (Traugott and Heine 1991; Hopper and Traugott 1993). Semantic change involves, first, a stage where a meaning *p* of an expression regularly gives rise, via pragmatic inference, to an interpretation *q*, then secondly, a stage where *q* becomes wholly conventionalized as an alternative *meaning* of the expression (i.e. the expression becomes polysemous; Evans and Wilkins 2000: 549–50; Enfield 2002: 28–30). Once two separate meanings are conventionalized, they may diverge, and the semantic connection between the new signs may become tenuous (despite their being signified by a single phonological form).

Where culture comes into play in this process is in providing culture-specific premises driving the pragmatic inferences which eventually harden to become semantically encoded in morphosyntax. It is routinely claimed that pragmatic inferences—such as those behind the metonymic shifts that *go* and *since* have undergone in English—are made upon 'general' (i.e. universal, non culture-specific) cognitive principles (e.g. Sweetser 1990). But *culture-specific* principles can also play a hand (Keesing 1979: 27; Evans and Wilkins 2000: 550, 580–5). Inferential processes are based on premises found in our cultural currency. As Levinson (1995: 240) has argued, the premises culture provides may be viewed as heuristics for figuring out the intentions behind others' words and actions. Those who share the same common ground—i.e. the same 'cultural premises'—will naturally make the same kinds of inferences (cf. Hutchins 1980; Levinson 1995; Enfield 2000a, this volume).

1.3. METHODOLOGICAL ISSUES

The study of grammar and culture confronts a host of thorny methodological and theoretical problems. The investigator must (a) adopt a sound approach to semantic description, (b) adopt a sound approach to cultural description, and (c) have a sound and plausible way of showing the relationship between these. Among existing approaches to the language–culture relationship, there are differing views as to what counts as an adequate demonstration of a putative culture–grammar relationship. I concentrate here on five issues that are most important in the context of this book: the description of grammar, the description of culture, characterizing the linkage between grammar and culture, the question of linguistic relativity, and the risk of circularity in argumentation.

1.3.1. *Describing grammar*

In research on the grammar–culture relationship, one cannot work at the level of overarching generalizations of a language's grammatical 'type'. Rather, one must examine specific morphosyntactic structures and/or resources and make explicit hypotheses as to their meanings. As Wierzbicka notes (1979: 378), 'a formal, rigorous analysis of meanings grammaticalized in different languages is a necessary prerequisite for any systematic study of correlations between linguistic and extra-linguistic aspects of culture' (see also Langacker, this volume). The same point is made by Mathiot (1979: pp. ix–x), who says that 'without a better substantive knowledge than we presently have of the meanings communicated through language, any further enquiry into the relation of language to the rest of culture runs the danger of being vacuous' (cited in Wilkins 1993: 91).

To assess the relationship between culture and grammar one's approach to the latter needs especially to ask what a given morphosyntactic resource or construction *means*. Three approaches which prioritize meaning in the description of grammar are especially relevant in this context. First, 'cognitive grammar' (Langacker 1987, 1990, 1991) gives priority to conceptual and 'imagic' aspects of the grammatical organization of meaning. The approach assigns semantics to grammatical resources in much the same way as it does to lexical items (see Langacker, this volume).[9] A second approach is 'construction grammar', as originated by Fillmore and

[9] Palmer (1996) has recently argued that cognitive linguistics—the broader movement in which Langacker's Cognitive Grammar is situated—'can be applied directly to language and culture' (1996: 4), since the approach 'centres on linguistic imagery, which is largely defined by culture' (1996: 290). Palmer argues that by incorporating recent developments in cognitive linguistics into the continuing development of cognitive anthropology, we can 'reconstitut[e] linguistic anthropology as an imagery-centred, cultural theory of language that weaves some bright new cognitive strands into the historical tapestry of our field' (Palmer 1996: 296).

colleagues (Fillmore 1988; Fillmore, Kay, and O'Connor 1988; Goldberg 1995, 1997), which regards the semantics of constructions as essentially equivalent to the semantics of lexical items, given that the semantics of productive constructions can be demonstrated *not* to be derived or 'projected' from constituent parts, and furthermore that constructions—like words—can be polysemous (Goldberg 1997: 163–5). Third, a semantic approach to grammar developed by Wierzbicka and colleagues maintains that 'there is no fundamental gulf between grammatical semantics and lexical semantics' (Goddard 1998: 320; see Wierzbicka 1988). In the view of these three modern traditions, the central task of grammatical description is to provide explicit definitions of meanings encoded in grammatical structure.

One area of research among more formal approaches to syntax which has actively begun to acknowledge and incorporate a great deal of cultural information into its account is the field of natural language processing. Researchers engaged in the mind-boggling work of trying to get computers to process natural language have long grappled with problems of grammatical (and lexical) ambiguity (cf. Deemter and Peters 1995; Hirst 1987; *inter alia*). Real speakers can effortlessly disambiguate strings like *John had Bill removed from the organization after he figured out what was going on* or *Moving furniture can hurt your back*, by referring to the context and to an enormous catalogue of background knowledge, both 'public' (known to be shared by some general population), and 'private' (known to be shared among given individuals). Much of this 'knowledge base' (Buvač 1995) is nothing other than culture.

To begin asking questions about the relation of grammar and culture, one must at least adopt a view of grammatical constructions as meaningful. While not without its merits, a purely formal approach to grammar can be of little aid to linguistic anthropology (other than to those who study the cultural practices of grammarians; see s. 1.2.1.3 above).

1.3.2. *Describing culture*

Culture has been defined in very many ways, the most important general positions being 'culture is knowledge', 'culture is symbols', and 'culture is action' (see Duranti 1997: ch. 2; Layton 1997 for recent overviews). Despite routine portrayal of the many approaches to cultural description as conflicting alternatives, they are often not fundamentally incompatible at all—it usually boils down to a difference of opinion as to what is *interesting*.[10] In turn, within the realm of 'culture', however it is conceived, there are different levels one can focus on in relation to language— one may be interested in widely adopted 'values', in the on-the-ground patterns of inter- and intra-societal organization, or in the abstract structures which underlie

---

[10] This is often linked to preoccupations with sociopolitically distinct 'research agendas' and the cliques that cohere around them and their charismatic and/or politically influential leaders (Murray 1994).

and regulate sociocultural arrangements. What is important is that in adopting a view of some aspect of culture in the context of its relation to grammar, given that the two are both fundamentally semiotic in nature, one needs a way of describing cultural *meanings* such that they can be coherently related to grammatical meanings. Cultural description is not easy, but I would steadfastly oppose suggestions that linguists 'leave [problems of culture] to the anthropologists' (Trudgill 1997: 358), as if linguists cannot, or should not, venture into such ground. To the contrary, linguists are practitioners of anthropology in one of its major forms, and ought to embrace this fact by considering the relevance to their work of the broader range of social and semiotic phenomena.

A significant stumbling block is the issue of 'cultures' (as opposed to 'culture'), and whether it is possible at all to characterize 'a culture', and/or to generalize about its members, their practices, values, and/or beliefs. D'Andrade argues that the idea of a culture as a complex whole is 'an article of faith, since no one ever offered an empirical demonstration of any culture's structure' (1995: 249). Indeed, it is today a matter of routine to eschew the idea that we can speak of 'cultures' at all. Bickel (2000: 164), for example, says that 'any notion of "THE culture of x" is highly suspicious if at all viable'. (Cf. Wierzbicka 1997: 17–22, Brown in press for different views.)

The very mention of an overarching object such as 'Australian culture' or 'Russian culture' regularly elicits a shrill response. Interestingly, linguists who feel most strongly about the mere mention of 'this culture' or 'that culture' are often those most ready to defend the discreteness of 'languages' and the legitimacy of making generalizations about their structure. Yet D'Andrade's point about the lack of any empirical demonstration of 'a culture' can be made about 'languages' too. Linguists deal with words and constructions which appear to be part of the common ground, or 'idiolectal intercalibration' (Hockett 1987: 106–7, 157–8) of some (theoretically) definable group, but it remains the case that we never encounter or describe a thing we may call 'the language'. We successfully proceed with linguistic description *as if* we were describing aspects of a coherent whole. It is possible—with care—to similarly proceed with cultural description.

Generalizations along the lines of 'egalitarianism is important and/or significant in Anglo Australian culture' are common, and are often taken to imply reference to some coherent whole 'Anglo Australian culture'. But there is no necessary connection between a claim that a particular cultural idea has currency across a large definable group, and a conclusion that this must be the tip of a monolithic iceberg we will call 'the culture'. A 'monolithic' view and a 'generalization' view are logically distinct. Assuming that exhaustive characterization of 'a culture' that is real and/or relevant for all individuals who identify and/or are identified as members is not possible, let us instead consider what a cultural 'generalization' might amount to.

Claims such as 'egalitarianism is part of Anglo Australian culture' can be interpreted in a number of ways. For example:

(*a*) Egalitarianism exists in Anglo Australian society.

(*b*) Anglo Australians hold egalitarian values (regardless of the truth of (*a*)).

(*c*) A certain community of people may be defined by their knowledge that there may be assumed, among (Anglo) Australians, a popular belief that egalitarian values are widely held by (Anglo) Australians (regardless of the truth of (*a–b*)).

Making generalizations about 'cultures' is highly problematic if the claim is that 'the culture' itself is empirically definable, in an *extensional* sense, and that the description is of some structure 'in the world'. Neither (*a*) nor (*b*) is viable. However, it is possible to approach cultural generalizations as descriptions of *ideas* about social identities, and about what is collectively assumed to be 'normal'—or, more precisely, what is assumed to be assumed to be normal (as in (*c*)). Crucially, the sense of 'normal' here can be at some remove from what *actually is* normal (however that is defined). Accordingly, Green treats 'normal belief' as a technical term, defined as follows: 'If everybody believes that everybody believes that it is normal to believe P, then belief in P is a normal belief, EVEN IF NOBODY ACTUALLY BELIEVES P' (Green 1995: 13, original emphasis). It is the stereotype *ideas* themselves, mythical or not, that are important in accounting for cultural logic, and emotional disagreements over whether it is valid to generalize about human groups or 'cultures' usually arise out of confusion as to whether the generalization intended is *extensional* (hardly tenable) or *intensional* (more like it; cf. Green 1995: 13)—i.e. whether the stereotype claims to describe the facts or whether it claims to describe some context-based default premises for cultural logic, which must be *known about*, but not necessarily *committed to* (cf. also Putnam 1975: 249 ff.).

The idea is akin to the 'maxims' which guide our interpretations of linguistic utterances in context (Grice 1975). A maxim such as 'avoid obscurity' is not a rule to be obeyed—we grapple daily with the obscurity (intentional or not) of our social associates. Rather, it is a *working assumption* for interpreting others' actions (and with respect to which one knows that one's own actions will be interpreted). And when the facts run against this assumption, it is the very presence of the assumption which makes the marked scenario marked. Cultural stereotypes work in exactly the same way.

Apart from the issue of stereotypes, there remains the problem of 'heteroglossia' (Bakhtin 1981: 262–3, 288–300) and analogous variation in culture. No two people's common ground, linguistic and/or otherwise, overlaps perfectly with the common ground of any other two. While members of communities do show many commonalities, there are further levels of commonality and structured relations, both 'nested' within distinct communities (Clark 1996), and extending between culturally quite distinct communities (Leach 1964). In *any* social setting, individuals maintain multiple identifications, and master, passively and/or actively, multiple linguistic and cultural systems. This is not a reason to abandon cultural description, but it does mean that care must be taken (Enfield 2000*a*: 54–7).

1.3.3. *Linkage*

Scholars concerned with the problem of *explaining* grammatical structure have pointed to the theoretical and methodological need not merely to identify correlations (e.g. between a putative psychological or cultural constraint and a grammatical construction of a certain kind), but also to offer plausible causal mechanisms by which observed correlations can be supported. In their discussion of possible 'psychological constraints on language', Clark and Malt (1984) offer four ideal properties that any proposed constraint should possess—'empirical grounding', 'structure independence', 'theoretical coherence', and 'linkage', the latter being 'probably the most challenging' (Clark and Malt 1984: 201). They note (1984: 198) that most commonly an account of the linkage between a 'psychological process' and a structured feature of language will involve mechanisms of linguistic change, or linguistic creation (i.e. of pidgins and creoles). Accordingly, historical processes provide the strongest support of linkage between descriptively correlated grammatical and cultural facts, as reported in the contributions to this volume by Burridge and Simpson. Section 1.2.2 above discussed the process whereby morphosyntactic constructions and categories can emerge out of the use of cultural assumptions as premises in the pragmatic inferential processes which drive semantic change.

In his discussion of what constitutes 'explanation' in linguistics, Hall (1992: 37) says that psycholinguistics is 'indispensable'. In the present context, this is correct in as far as cultural and social facts can be reduced to psychological facts (which I think they probably can, cf. Enfield 2000a). Some important concepts in psycholinguistics—including 'common ground' (Clark 1996: 332 ff.), 'heuristic strategies' (Clark and Malt 1984: 203), 'scripts' and 'schemas' (Mandler 1984), 'context' (Buvač 1995; Green 1995)—in fact are squarely matters of culture, but they are usually described with terms like 'local knowledge', 'prototypes', 'stereotypicality', even 'common sense'. Indeed, psycholinguistics in its current form expresses little interest in ethnography. But the kind of material presented in this book shows that psycholinguistics can broaden the scope of what counts as 'psychological' (this obviously includes the subject matter of 'psychological anthropology' and 'cultural psychology'; Shweder and LeVine 1984; Holland and Quinn 1987; Stigler, Shweder, and Herdt 1990; Schwartz, White, and Lutz 1992; Strauss and Quinn 1997; *inter alia*).

1.3.4. *Linguistic relativity*

The term 'linguistic relativity' refers to that famous principle developed by scholars such as Humboldt, Sapir, and Whorf, which asserts, for example, that '[c]oncepts of "time" and "matter" are not given in substantially the same form by experience to all men but depend upon the nature of the language or languages through the use of which they have been developed' (Whorf 1956: 158). An important point about Whorf's idea of linguistic relativity is that the 'influence' of language on thought was not viewed as a function of isolated, or indeed isolable aspects of a linguistic system, but associated with 'the ways of analysing and reporting experience which have become fixed in the language as integrated "fashions of speaking" and which cut across the typical grammatical classifications' (Whorf 1956: 158). By some, this principle has been taken to be a 'hypothesis', testable via isolation of linguistic facts on the one hand, and non-linguistic facts on the other, followed by empirical demonstration of a correlation between the two (Lucy 1992*a*, 1992*b*). Others have regarded this 'hypothesis' view as a misconstrual of what was originally intended, namely a *principle* (Hill and Mannheim 1992; Lee 1996, 2000). Lee (1996: 78) points out that the 'deliberate operational separation of language and thought in order to accommodate theoretical preconditions for empirical investigation' erroneously presupposes that this separation is possible at all. While Lee mentions only 'thought' here, it is clear that her comments are meant to apply also to 'culture'. For Hill and Mannheim (1992: 382), similarly, the 'separation of "language" and "nonlanguage" such that these can be then "related" one to another' is problematic. As far as they are concerned, the 'notion of the "linguistic" versus the "nonlinguistic" eludes contemporary cultural anthropologists' (cf. Enfield 2000*b*). This has obvious methodological consequences for ethnosyntax.[11]

While the principle of linguistic relativity is of course relevant to our present concerns, the study of ethnosyntax need not be specifically concerned with *comparing* languages and seeing how the differences may relate to corresponding cultural differences. 'Cultural' does not *entail* 'culture-specific'—that is, as long as you believe in *some* cultural universals. But this of course does not mean that ethnosyntax should not be a comparative enterprise. Studies in ethnosyntax can and should be comparative, as Lucy (1992*a*, 1996) has recently emphasized. (See contributions to this volume by Wierzbicka, Newman, and Langacker.) Explicit comparison between particular languages and cultures is obviously a most effective method, especially where they differ in minor, but specific ways, throwing the more subtle linguistic and/or cultural differences into sharper relief.

However, it may not necessarily be the primary aim of a particular study in ethnosyntax to address linguistic diversity *per se*. If solid argumentation based on extensive linguistic and ethnographic data can be used to establish a connection between cultural and grammatical facts, this is not intrinsically weakened by the lack of comparative contrast with another language and culture (*pace* Lucy 1992*a*). Nothing entails that a given cultural preoccupation *will* show some manifestation in grammar. For one thing, certain grammatical developments in languages may be licensed or constrained by different existing typological profiles (cf. Aikhenvald and Dixon 1998: 254; Enfield 2001: 284–7). Conversely, if a similar morphosyntactic feature is attested among unrelated speech communities, to what extent can we

---

[11] Unfortunately, the two sides to this debate, typified by Lee on one hand, and Lucy on the other, are often wrongly treated as competing or even conflicting alternatives. In many respects they are not in conflict, and indeed the achievements of each approach complement those of the other.

expect these groups to share some associated cultural preoccupation? Most would agree that the answer is 'not necessarily at all', as John Newman shows in his contribution to this volume, referring to a morphosyntactic parallel between Nahuatl and Zulu which has no obvious corresponding cultural parallel. But this is not a simple problem. First, as Lee (1996) has stressed, such grammatical/behavioural phenomena need to be examined not in isolation, but as elements of large-scale fashions of speaking (Whorf 1956). Second, it is not necessarily the case that the existence of a given grammatical feature will have a cultural explanation anyway. Third, the same grammatical feature in two languages could logically be the outcome of processes relating to *different* cultural phenomena. (For further discussion of these points, see the contributions to this volume by Chafe, Newman, and Pawley.)

Another reason that an ethnosyntax claim is not necessarily a relativist claim is that—*theoretically*—a relationship between particular cultural and grammatical phenomena might well apply universally. After all, most would expect there to be universals in both language and culture. Consider the morphosyntactic effects of the substantival hierarchy (i.e. the hierarchy of accessibility of different nominal types, such as pronouns versus full noun phrases, to certain grammatical phenomena such as ergative case-marking; Silverstein 1976), where indeed it appears that a universal pattern in conceptualization (i.e. the relative focus of interest and attention on the members of the interaction dyad, other people, animates, inanimates, and so on) gives rise to a system with some morphosyntactic effect in most if not all languages.[12] Can we interpret a conceptual schema like the substantival hierarchy as *cultural*? The same could be asked of many other universal functions of grammar, such as the global need to distinguish semantic roles in asymmetrical transitive expressions. The particular method of making this functional distinction in a given language (e.g. by case-marking, cross-referencing, and/or constituent order) is certainly common ground among speakers in the given speech community, and so therefore may (trivially?) be regarded as 'cultural'. Consider John Newman's note (this volume) that while there is great variation in the way languages model the syntax of 'give' expressions on the grammar of prototypical transitive expressions, apparently none treat the 'giver' argument morphosyntactically as a direct object. Is this due to a general, cognitive constraint, a universal cultural one, or somehow both?

1.3.5. *Characterization of the language–culture connection: circularity?*

Finally, we may consider more closely a point touched upon early in the previous section, regarding the distinction between a 'hypothesis' approach to the language–culture relationship (in which a putative correlation between operationally distinct phenomena is tested experimentally) and a 'principle' approach (which

---

[12] See papers in Goody (1995) for explorations of the thesis that human intelligence is fundamentally oriented towards dyadic interaction.

aims to characterize the relationship between language and culture based on an initial assumption of their fundamentally inseparable nature). If one takes the first view (cf. Lucy 1992*a*, 1992*b*, 1996), then there emerges the danger of a certain kind of circular argumentation. Indeed, one of Lucy's most emphatic points is the methodological need for studies in linguistic relativity to avoid this. In trying to separately describe facts about morphosyntactic resources available to speakers, *as distinct from* facts of a cultural nature about those speakers, and relate these two together, it is naturally unacceptable to adopt genuinely circular argumentation. One could not use a linguistic feature as evidence for some cultural feature and then claim that this cultural feature correlates with the linguistic feature, thus 'establishing' a culture–grammar link. A connection between culture and language would have been assumed in the first place, since the linguistic feature was admitted as evidence for the cultural feature. Yet the connection in question was what the analysis was supposed to demonstrate. Hale also wants to avoid this, arguing that 'establishing a connection or relation between a philosophical postulate and a principle of grammar requires that the two be established independently' (Hale 1986: 233). So, two options are (*a*) to avoid the 'linguocentrism' of the argument by using only non-linguistic evidence to establish claims about culture—what we may call the 'non-linguistic evidence' position—or (*b*) to assume from the outset a principle of language–culture relatedness, and explore its various manifestations, rather than try to 'prove' it—what we may call the 'fashions of speaking' position.

If claimed to be the only way to explore the culture–grammar relationship, the 'non-linguistic evidence' position goes too far. Logically, in order to avoid the circularity described above, it is necessary that the evidence for establishing a cultural fact be *independent* of the relevant linguistic phenomena, but not necessarily *non-linguistic*. In other words, it need not be independent of *language* as a whole, but rather of *the particular linguistic phenomenon under discussion*.[13] One consequence of a decision to rule out any use of linguistic evidence in cultural description would be a seriously impoverished ethnography. Lucy of course recognizes that to reject linguocentrism 'is not to say that vocabulary items do not reflect non-linguistic culture or that discourse using language does not provide important evidence about cultural beliefs', but he suggests that 'from a methodological point of view, such materials cannot be persuasive by themselves in showing the broader effects of language' (Lucy 1996: 44). Thus, his objection is apparently not to linguocentrism *per se*, but simply to logical circularity, which may easily result from simple-minded argumentation involving linguistic evidence not independent of the phenomena being examined (cf. Enfield 2000*b* for further discussion).

From a 'fashions of speaking' position, the mere fact of using linguistic evidence in cultural description does *not* entail circularity. While just one piece of

---

[13] Clark and Malt (1986: 207) point out that facts about linguistic use can be considered independent of facts about linguistic structure (with respect to the proposed methodological requirement of 'structure independence').

linguistic evidence is naturally not convincing in making a claim about culture, it is possible to provide a wide variety of evidence from many areas of linguistic structure, including lexicon, morphosyntax, idiom, socialization routines, mechanisms of discourse and conversation, linguistic ideologies, and so on. If wide-ranging evidence from a number of such sources points towards a consistent conclusion, then linguistic evidence *can* be convincing in establishing generalizations about culture, without entailing circularity of an argument for language–culture relatedness. Hale (1986) argues that 'world view' (in one of his two senses; cf. s. 1.1, above) is observable in the semantic categories of language, namely in those cases where a 'theme' emerges throughout the language, and, specifically, where examples are found 'in parts of the grammar not otherwise intimately related' (Hale 1986: 238). This sense of 'world view' 'consists in the analysis [by speakers, NJE] of phenomena which is embodied in the system of lexico-semantic themes and semantic categories which function in any grammar (though in different ways and to different extents in distinct languages)' (1986: 237–8). This openly linguocentric position is entirely compatible with Whorf's (1956) notion of fashions of speaking (cf. Hasan 1984; Rumsey 1990; Lee 1996). Wilkins takes the same perspective, arguing with regard to the establishment of cultural meanings from the analysis of grammatical semantics that 'once tells us nothing, twice could be a coincidence, but three times starts to confirm a pattern of regularity' (Wilkins 1993: 84). Thus, linguistic evidence of cultural concerns becomes increasingly convincing as evidence from various areas of a language accumulates. What is crucial is sound semantic description and sound ethnography. This view acknowledges an inherent interconnectedness between language and culture, and sees the point of the exercise as an attempt to describe the ways in which this is manifest. The task of then establishing 'external' connections can test and provide further support to the grammar–culture correlations described.

1.4. OVERVIEW

This book is divided into three parts. The first part concerns theoretical and methodological questions of the scope of ethnosyntax (as both a set of phenomena and a field of research). Part II focuses on the cultural significance of grammatical semantics, while Part III is concerned with culture-mediated patterns of use of grammatical resources, and their diachronic effects. The twelve contributions cross-cut and overlap in many ways, and a different organization for the volume could have been just as appropriate. Each of the chapters includes detailed discussion of linguistic and ethnographic data, with a broad cross-linguistic and cross-cultural coverage, and each chapter engages with theoretical and methodological issues.

Languages discussed in detail in this book represent a range of linguistic types from around the world. These include Papuan languages Ku Waru (Rumsey) and Amele (Newman), Australian languages Warumungu and Warlpiri (Simpson), Indo-European languages German (Wierzbicka), Russian (Goddard, Wierzbicka), varieties of English (Pawley, Wierzbicka), Pennsylvania German (Burridge), the Austronesian language Maori (Newman), Tai languages Lao (Enfield) and Thai (Diller and Khanittanan), Native American languages Koasati, Nahuatl, and Chipewyan (Newman), Mixtec (Langacker), and the Northern Iroquoian group (Chafe), as well as Japanese and Zulu (Newman). The grammatical phenomena investigated also cover broad ground, including person and pronominal systems (Chafe, Newman, Pawley, Rumsey), modal and directional auxiliaries (Burridge, Simpson), locative constructions (Langacker), causative constructions (Wierzbicka), 'serial verb' structures (Enfield), features of 'give' expressions (Newman), existential and positional constructions (Rumsey), control and other properties of complementation (Diller and Khanittanan, Goddard).

Thematically, most contributions are not restricted to one or other of the so-called 'broad' or 'narrow' senses of ethnosyntax, although some are concerned to directly address this distinction (Rumsey, Goddard, Simpson). Several contributions pay particular attention to the historical dimension of culture–grammar relatedness (Burridge, Chafe, Simpson, Wierzbicka). Simpson, in particular, is concerned to address the methodological importance of historical data in establishing a culture–grammar link. Some contributions emphasize the role of sound semantic description (Langacker, Wierzbicka), while others concentrate on the socially situated usage and productivity of grammatical devices (Enfield, Rumsey). A number of contributions focus on questions of how culture is best described (Enfield, Goddard, Simpson, Wierzbicka). For Burridge and Chafe, available ethnographic data are relied upon to support statements about culture with relevance to the linguistic analyses provided. The theoretical scope of the volume is uniquely enriched by Goddard's contribution, which asks how Peircean semiotic distinctions found in different aspects of grammar are relevant to the characterization of a culture–grammar relationship. His efforts are valuable in a field vexed by confusion (or entire absence) of basic distinctions between different semiotic functions. A final angle which most contributions take is to offer cross-linguistic comparison as a means for focusing the research question (see in particular Chafe, Goddard, Langacker, Rumsey, Simpson, and Wierzbicka). Newman's approach is particularly illustrative of the merits of cross-linguistic comparison, drawing from his long-standing interest in the cross-linguistic structuring of an essentially stable semantic domain, namely 'giving'. This turns out to be a productive focus for cross-linguistic work.

1.5. CONCLUDING REMARKS

The scholar who claims to have demonstrated a causal or non-arbitrary link between linguistic and non-linguistic phenomena is prone to criticism. Clark and Malt (1984) outline a set of stringent methodological requirements, arguing that few if any claims to have 'explained' linguistic structure with reference to psychological constraints constitute 'strong arguments' according to their ideals. Even so, they argue, exploratory attempts at explanation can be extremely valuable, in that they suggest places to look further for the ideal 'strong arguments'. Such exploratory attempts 'may have their most important value as provocateurs: they goad us to look for strong psychological rationales for universal features of language' (Clark and Malt 1984: 211). Contributors to this book on the one hand show caution (see especially Langacker, Pawley, Simpson). Langacker warns that apparent grammatical differences between two languages, which we may want to associate with cultural differences between speakers of those languages, 'may be less profound and less extensive than they might seem to be on first examination'. Newman similarly argues that while there are grammatical devices whose meaning/function would seem to be culture-specific, there are also cases where no such claim could be made. On the other hand, the very premiss of this book is that it is well worth exploring the idea that a language's morphosyntactic resources *are* related to the cultural knowledge, attitudes, and practices of its speakers. The results make ethnosyntax a rich and rewarding field of study. If 'strong psychological rationales' are what will explain universal features of language, then may this book encourage interested scholars to seek strong *cultural* rationales for the subtle (and not so subtle) ways in which languages *differ*.

REFERENCES

AIKHENVALD, ALEXANDRA Y., and DIXON, R. M. W. 1998. 'Evidentials and areal typology: a case study from Amazonia'. *Language Sciences*, 20.3: 241–57.

ALSINA, ALEX, BRESNAN, JOAN, and SELLS, PETER (eds.). 1997. *Complex Predicates*. Palo Alto, Calif.: Stanford University Centre for the Study of Language and Information.

BAKHTIN, MIKHAIL M. 1981. *The Dialogic Imagination*. Austin: University of Texas Press.

BICKEL, BALTHAZAR. 2000. 'Grammar and social practice: on the role of culture in linguistic relativity'. In Niemeier and Dirven 2000, 161–92.

BLAKE, BARRY. 2001. 'Global trends in language'. *Linguistics*, 39.5: 1009–28.

BLOUNT, BEN G. (ed.) 1974. *Language, Culture and Society*. Cambridge, Mass.: Winthrop.

BOAS, FRANZ. 1911. 'Introduction'. In Franz Boas (ed.), *Handbook of American Indian Languages*. Lincoln: University of Nebraska Press, 1–79.

BROWN, PENELOPE. In press. 'Language as a model for culture: lessons from the cognitive sciences'. In R. Fox and B. King (eds.), *Anthropology beyond Culture*. Berg.

BRUCE, LES. 1988. 'Serialization: from syntax to lexicon'. *Studies in Language*, 12.1: 19–49.

BURRIDGE, KATE, and ALLAN, KEITH. 1998. 'The X-phemistic value of Romani in nonstandard speech'. In Y. Matras (ed.), *The Romani Element in Non-Standard Speech*. Sondersprachenforschung 4. Wiesbaden: Harrassowitz, 29–50.

BUVAČ, SAŠA. 1995. 'Resolving lexical ambiguity using a formal theory of context'. In van Deemter and Peters 1995: 101–24.

CHAMBERS, J. K. 1995. *Sociolinguistic Theory*. Oxford: Blackwell.

CLARK, HERBERT H. 1996. 'Communities, commonalities, and communication'. In Gumperz and Levinson 1996: 324–55.

——and MALT, BARBARA C. 1984. 'Psychological constraints on language: a commentary on Bresnan and Kaplan and on Givón'. In Walter Kintsch, James R. Miller, and Peter G. Polson (eds.), *Methods and Tactics in Cognitive Science*. Hillsdale, NJ: Lawrence Erlbaum, 191–214.

CRAIG, COLETTE GRINEVALD. 1986. 'Jacaltec noun classifiers: a study in language and culture'. In Colette Craig (ed.), *Noun Classes and Categorization*. Amsterdam: John Benjamins, 263–93.

D'ANDRADE, ROY. 1995. *The Development of Cognitive Anthropology*. Cambridge: Cambridge University Press.

DEEMTER, KEES VAN, and PETERS, STANLEY. 1995. *Semantic Ambiguity and Underspecification*. Stanford, Calif.: CSLI Publications.

DENCH, ALAN. 1987. 'Kinship and collective activity in the Ngayarda languages of Western Australia'. *Language in Society*, 16: 321–40.

DIFFLOTH, G. 1979. 'Expressive phonology and prosaic phonology in Mon-Khmer'. In Theraphan L. Thongkham *et al.* (eds.), *Studies in Mon-Khmer Phonetics and Phonology in Honour of Eugenie J. A. Henderson*. Bangkok: Chulalongkorn University Press, 49–59.

DILLER, ANTHONY. 1988. 'Thai syntax and "national grammar"'. *Language Sciences*, 10.2: 273–312.

——1993. 'Diglossic grammaticality in Thai'. In William A. Foley (ed.), *The Role of Theory in Language Description*. Berlin: Mouton de Gruyter, 393–420.

DIXON, R. M. W. 1971. 'A method of semantic description'. In Danny D. Steinberg and Leon A. Jakobovits (eds.), *Semantics: An Interdisciplinary Reader in Philosophy, Linguistics, and Psychology*. Cambridge: Cambridge University Press, 436–71.

DOWTY, DAVID R. 1979. *Word Meaning and Montague Grammar*. Dordrecht: Kluwer.

DUNN, MICHAEL. 2000. 'Chukchi women's language: a historical-comparative perspective'. *Anthropological Linguistics*, 42.3: 305–28.

DURANTI, ALLESANDRO. 1990. 'Politics and grammar: agency in Samoan political discourse'. *American Ethnologist*, 17.4: 646–66.

——1997. *Linguistic Anthropology*. Cambridge: Cambridge University Press.

DURIE, MARK. 1997. 'Grammatical structures in verb serialization'. In Alsina, Bresnan, and Sells 1997: 289–354.

ENFIELD, N. J. 2000*a*. 'The theory of cultural logic: how individuals combine social intelligence with semiotics to create and maintain cultural meaning'. *Cultural Dynamics*, 12.1: 35–64.

——2000*b*. 'On linguocentrism'. In Pütz and Verspoor 2000: 125–57.

——2001. 'On genetic and areal linguistics in Mainland Southeast Asia: parallel polyfunctionality of "acquire"'. In Alexandra Aikhenvald and R. M. W. Dixon (eds.), *Areal Diffusion and Genetic Inheritance*. Oxford: Oxford University Press, 255–90.

——2002. *Linguistic Epidemiology: Semantics and Grammar of Language Contact in Mainland Southeast Asia*. London: Routledge.

EVANS, NICHOLAS D. 1997. 'Sign metonymies and the problem of flora-fauna polysemy in Australian linguistics'. In Darrell Tryon and Michael Walsh (eds.), *Boundary Rider*. Canberra: Pacific Linguistics, 133–53.

——and WILKINS, DAVID P. 2000. 'In the mind's ear: the semantic extensions of perception verbs in Australian languages'. *Language*, 76.3: 546–92.

FERGUSON, CHARLES A. 1964. 'Diglossia'. In Hymes 1964: 429–39 (first pub. *Word* 15 (1959), 325–40).

FILLMORE, CHARLES J. 1988. 'The mechanisms of "construction grammar"'. *Berkeley Linguistics Society, Proceedings of the 14th Meeting.* Berkeley: Berkeley Linguistics Society, 35–55.

——KAY, PAUL, and O'CONNOR, MARY CATHERINE. 1988. 'Regularity and idiomaticity in grammatical constructions: the case of *let alone*'. *Language,* 64.3: 501–38.

FISHMAN, JOSHUA A. 1997. *In Praise of the Beloved Language: A Comparative View of Positive Ethnolinguistic Consciousness.* Berlin: Mouton de Gruyter.

FOLEY, WILLIAM A. 1997. *Anthropological Linguistics.* London: Blackwell.

——and VAN VALIN, ROBERT D. 1984. *Functional Syntax and Universal Grammar.* Cambridge: Cambridge University Press.

FRAWLEY, WILLIAM. 1992. *Linguistic Semantics.* Hillsdale, NJ: Lawrence Erlbaum.

GODDARD, CLIFF. 1998. *Semantic Analysis: A Practical Introduction.* New York: Oxford University Press.

——In press. 'Whorf meets Wierzbicka: variation and universals in language and thinking'. *Language Sciences.*

GOLDBERG, ADELE E. 1995. *Constructions: A Construction Grammar Approach to Argument Structure.* Chicago: University of Chicago Press.

——1997. 'Making one's way through the data'. In Alsina, Bresnan, and Sells 1997: 151–73.

GOODY, ESTHER N. (ed.) 1995. *Social Intelligence and Interaction.* Cambridge: Cambridge University Press.

GRACE, GEORGE. 1987. *The Linguistic Construction of Reality.* London: Croom Helm.

GREEN, GEORGIA M. 1995. 'Ambiguity resolution and discourse interpretation'. In van Deemter and Peters 1995: 1–26.

GRICE, H. PAUL. 1975. 'Logic and conversation'. In Peter Cole and Jerry L. Morgan (eds.), *Speech Acts.* New York: Academic Press, 41–58.

GUMPERZ, JOHN L., and LEVINSON, STEPHEN (eds.). 1996. *Rethinking Linguistic Relativity.* Cambridge: Cambridge University Press.

——and WILSON, ROBERT. 1971. 'Convergence and creolization: a case from the Indo-Aryan/Dravidian border in India'. In Dell Hymes (ed.), *Pidginization and Creolization of Languages*, 151–67. Cambridge: Cambridge University Press.

HALE, KENNETH L. 1966. 'Kinship reflections in syntax: some Australian languages'. *Word*, 22: 318–24.

——1986. 'Notes on world view and semantic categories: some Warlpiri examples'. In Pieter Muysken and Henk van Riemsdijk (eds.), *Features and Projections.* Dordrecht: Foris, 233–54.

——1998. 'On endangered languages and the importance of linguistic diversity'. In Lenore A. Grenoble and Lindsay J. Whaley (eds.), *Endangered Languages.* Cambridge: Cambridge University Press, 192–216.

HALL, CHRISTOPHER J. 1992. *Morphology and Mind: A Unified Approach to Explanation in Linguistics.* London: Routledge.

HARRIS, ROY. 1980. *The Language-Makers.* Ithaca, NY: Cornell University Press.

——1987. *The Language Machine.* London: Duckworth.

HASAN, RUQAIYA. 1984. 'What kind of a resource is language?' *The Australian Review of Applied Linguistics*, 7.1: 57–85.

HEATH, JEFFREY, MERLAN, FRANCESCA, and RUMSEY, ALAN (eds.) 1982. *The Languages of Kinship in Aboriginal Australia.* Sydney: University of Sydney Press.

HERCUS, LUISE, and WHITE, ISOBEL. 1973. 'Perception of kinship structure reflected in Adnjamathanha pronouns'. *Papers in Australian Linguistics*, 6. Canberra: Pacific Linguistics, 47–72.

HILL, JANE H. 1969. 'Volitional and non-volitional verbs in Cupeño'. *Papers from the Regional Meeting of the Chicago Linguistic Society*, 5: 348–56.

——and MANNHEIM, BRUCE. 1992. 'Language and world view'. *Annual Review of Anthropology*, 21: 381–406.

HIRST, GRAEME. 1987. *Semantic Interpretation and the Resolution of Ambiguity*. Cambridge: Cambridge University Press.

HOCKETT, CHARLES F. 1987. *Refurbishing our Foundations: Elementary Linguistics from an Advanced Point of View*. Amsterdam: John Benjamins.

HOIJER, HARRY. 1953. 'The relation of language to culture'. In A. L. Kroeber (ed.), *Anthropology Today*. Chicago: University of Chicago Press, 554–73.

——1964. 'Cultural implications of some Navaho linguistic categories'. In Hymes 1964: 142–48.

HOLLAND, DOROTHY, and QUINN, NAOMI (eds.). 1987. *Cultural Models in Language and Thought*. Cambridge: Cambridge University Press.

HOPPER, PAUL J., and TRAUGOTT, ELIZABETH CLOSS. 1993. *Grammaticalization*. Cambridge: Cambridge University Press.

HUTCHINS, EDWIN. 1980. *Culture and Inference: A Trobriand Case Study*. Cambridge, Mass.: Harvard University Press.

HYMES, DELL H. 1961. 'On typology of cognitive styles in language (with examples from Chinookan)'. *Anthropological Linguistics*, 3.1: 22–54.

——(ed.) 1964. *Language in Culture and Society: A Reader in Linguistics and Anthropology*. New York: Harper & Row.

——1966. 'Two types of linguistic relativity (with examples from Amerindian ethnography)'. In William Bright (ed.), *Sociolinguistics*. Proceedings of the UCLA Sociolinguistics Conference. The Hague: Mouton, 114–67.

KATRE, SUMITRA M. 1987. *Aṣṭādhyāyi of Pāṇini*. Austin: University of Texas Press.

KAY, PAUL. 1996. 'Intra-speaker relativity'. In Gumperz and Levinson 1996: 97–114.

KEESING, ROGER M. 1979. 'Linguistic knowledge and cultural knowledge: some doubts and speculations'. *American Anthropologist*, 81: 14–36.

KIRSHENBLATT-GIMBLETT, B. (ed.) 1976. *Speech Play*. Philadelphia: University of Pennsylvania Press.

LABOV, WILLIAM. 1972. *Language in the Inner City: Studies in the Black English Vernacular*. Philadelphia: University of Pennsylvania Press.

LAKOFF, GEORGE. 1986. 'Frame semantic control of the coordinate structure constraint'. In A. M. Farrell *et al.* (eds.), *Papers from the Parasession on Pragmatics and Grammatical Theory*. Chicago: Chicago Linguistic Society, 152–67.

——1987. *Women, Fire, and Dangerous Things: What Categories Reveal About the Mind*. Chicago: University of Chicago Press.

LANDAR, HERBERT. 1966. *Language and Culture*. New York: Oxford University Press.

LANGACKER, RONALD W. 1987. *Foundations of Cognitive Grammar*, i: *Theoretical Prerequisites*. Stanford, Calif.: Stanford University Press.

——1990. *Concept, Image, and Symbol: The Cognitive Basis of Grammar*. Berlin: Mouton de Gruyter.

——1991. *Foundations of Cognitive Grammar*, ii: *Descriptive Applications*. Stanford, Calif.: Stanford University Press.

LANGACKER, RONALD W. 1994. 'Culture, cognition, and grammar'. In Martin Pütz (ed.), *Language Contact and Language Conflict*. Amsterdam: John Benjamins, 25–53.

LAYTON, ROBERT. 1997. *An Introduction to Theory in Anthropology*. Cambridge: Cambridge University Press.

LEACH, EDMUND. 1964. *Political Systems of Highland Burma*. London: The Athlone Press (first pub. 1954).

LEE, DOROTHY D. 1959. 'Linguistic reflection of Wintu thought'. In Dorothy D. Lee (ed.), *Freedom and Culture*. Englewood Cliffs, NJ: Prentice-Hall, 21–30.

LEE, PENNY. 1996. *The Whorf Theory Complex: A Critical Reconstruction*. Amsterdam: Benjamins.

——2000. 'When is "Linguistic Relativity" Whorf's Linguistic Relativity?' In Pütz and Verspoor 2000: 45–68.

LEVINSON, STEPHEN C. 1995. 'Interactional biases in human thinking'. In Goody 1995: 221–60.

——2000. *Presumptive Meanings: The Theory of Generalized Conversational Implicature*. Cambridge, Mass.: MIT Press.

LUCY, JOHN. 1992a. *Language Diversity and Thought: A Reformulation of the Linguistic Relativity Hypothesis*. Cambridge: Cambridge University Press.

——1992b. *Grammatical Categories and Cognition: A Case Study of The Linguistic Relativity Hypothesis*. Cambridge: Cambridge University Press.

——1996. 'The scope of linguistic relativity'. In Gumperz and Levinson 1996: 37–69.

MANDLER, JEAN MATTER. 1984. *Stories, Scripts, and Scenes: Aspects of Schema Theory*. Hillsdale, NJ: Lawrence Erlbaum.

MATHIOT, MADELEINE. 1964. 'Noun classes and folk taxonomy in Papago'. In Hymes 1964: 154–61.

——(ed.) 1979. *Ethnolinguistics: Boas, Sapir and Whorf Revisited*. The Hague: Mouton.

MITHUN, MARIANNE. 1984. 'The evolution of noun incorporation'. *Language*, 60.4: 847–94.

MURRAY, STEPHEN O. 1994. *Theory Groups and the Study of Language in North America: A Social History*. Amsterdam: John Benjamins.

NEWMAN, JOHN. 1996. *Give: A Cognitive Linguistic Study*. Berlin: Mouton de Gruyter.

NIEMEIER, S., and DIRVEN, R. (eds.) 2000. *Evidence for Linguistic Relativity*. Amsterdam: John Benjamins.

O'GRADY, GEOFF. 1960. 'Comments on "More on lexicostatistics"'. *Current Anthropology*, 1: 338–9.

PALMER, GARY B. 1996. *Toward a Theory of Cultural Linguistics*. Austin: University of Texas Press.

PENNYCOOK, ALASTAIR. 1994. *The Cultural Politics of English as an International Language*. London: Longman.

PRIDEAUX, GARY D. 1970. *The Syntax of Japanese Honorifics*. The Hague: Mouton.

PUTNAM, HILARY. 1975. *Mind, Language, and Reality: Philosophical Papers*, vol. ii. Cambridge: Cambridge University Press.

PÜTZ, MARTIN, and VERSPOOR, MARJOLIJN (eds.). 2000. *Explorations in Linguistic Relativity*. Amsterdam: John Benjamins.

RICE, SALLY. 1998. 'Giving and taking in Chipewyan: the semantics of THING-marking classificatory verbs'. In John Newman (ed.), *The Linguistics of Giving*. Amsterdam: Benjamins, 97–134.

RUMSEY, ALAN. 1990. 'Wording, meaning, and linguistic ideology'. *American Anthropologist*, 92: 346–61.

RUSHFORTH, SCOTT, and CHISHOLM, JAMES S. 1991. *Cultural Persistence: Continuity in Meaning and Moral Responsibility among the Bearlake Athapaskans*. Tucson: University of Arizona Press.

SAPIR, EDWARD. 1949. *Selected Writings*. Berkeley and Los Angeles: University of California Press.

——1994. *The Psychology of Culture*, reconstructed and ed. by Judith T. Irvine. Berlin: Mouton de Gruyter.

SCHUTZ, ALFRED. 1970. *On Phenomenology and Social Relations*. Chicago: University of Chicago Press.

SCHWARTZ, THEODORE, WHITE, GEOFFREY M., and LUTZ, CATHERINE A. (eds.) 1992. *New Directions in Psychological Anthropology*. Cambridge: Cambridge University Press.

SHIBATANI, MASAYOSHI. 1990. *The Languages of Japan*. Cambridge: Cambridge University Press.

SHWEDER, RICHARD A., and LEVINE, ROBERT A. (eds.). 1984. *Culture Theory: Essays on Mind, Self, and Emotion*. Cambridge: Cambridge University Press.

SILVERSTEIN, MICHAEL. 1976. 'Hierarchy of features and ergativity'. In R. M. W. Dixon (ed.), *Grammatical Categories in Australian Languages*. Canberra: Australian Institute of Aboriginal Studies, 112–71.

STIGLER, JAMES W., SHWEDER, RICHARD A., and HERDT, GILBERT (eds.). 1990. *Cultural Psychology: Essays on Comparative Human Development*. Cambridge: Cambridge University Press.

STRAUSS, CLAUDIA, and QUINN, NAOMI. 1997. *A Cognitive Theory of Cultural Meaning*. Cambridge: Cambridge University Press.

SWEETSER, EVE. 1990. *From Etymology to Pragmatics*. Cambridge: Cambridge University Press.

TRAUGOTT, ELIZABETH CLOSS, and HEINE, BERND (eds.). 1991. *Approaches to Grammaticalization*. Amsterdam: Benjamins.

TRUDGILL, PETER. 1997. 'Typology and sociolinguistics: Linguistic structure, social structure and explanatory comparative dialectology'. *Folia Linguistica*, 23.3–4: 349–60.

TUGGY, DAVID. 1979. 'Tetelcingo Nahuatl'. In Ronald W. Langacker (ed.), *Studies in Uto-Aztecan Grammar*, ii: *Modern Aztec Grammatical Sketches*. Dallas: Summer Institute of Linguistics and University of Texas at Arlington, 1–140.

WASON, P. C., and REICH, C. C. 1979. 'A verbal illusion'. *Quarterly Journal of Experimental Psychology*, 31: 591–8.

WHORF, BENJAMIN LEE. 1956. *Language, Thought, and Reality*. Cambridge, Mass.: MIT Press.

WIERZBICKA, ANNA. 1979. 'Ethno-syntax and the philosophy of grammar'. *Studies in Language*, 3.3: 313–83.

——1988. *The Semantics of Grammar*. Amsterdam: John Benjamins.

——1991. *Cross-Cultural Pragmatics: The Semantics of Human Interaction*. Berlin: Mouton de Gruyter.

——1992. *Semantics, Culture, and Cognition*. New York: Oxford University Press.

——1997. *Understanding Cultures Through Their Key Words*. New York: Oxford University Press.

N. J. Enfield

WIERZBICKA, ANNA. 1998. *Emotions Across Languages and Cultures: Diversity and Universals*. Cambridge: Cambridge University Press.

WILKINS, DAVID P. 1988. 'Switch-reference in Mparntwe Arrernte: form, function, and problems of identity'. In Peter Austin (ed.), *Complex Sentence Constructions in Australian Languages*. Amsterdam: John Benjamins, 141–76.

——1991. 'The semantics, pragmatics and diachronic development of "Associated Motion" in Mparntwe Arrernte'. *Buffalo Working Papers in Linguistics*, 207–57.

——1993. 'Linguistic evidence in support of a holistic approach to traditional ecological knowledge'. In G. N. Williams and G. Baines (eds.), *Traditional Ecological Knowledge: Wisdom for Sustainable Development*. Canberra: CRES Publications, 71–93.

WOLFRAM, WALT, and FASOLD, RALPH W. 1974. *The Study of Social Dialects in American English*. Englewood Cliffs, NJ: Prentice-Hall.

2

Syntactic Enquiry as a Cultural Activity

ANTHONY V. N. DILLER and WILAIWAN KHANITTANAN

Can there be 'syntax' without 'ethno-'? Answers to this question will vary depending on how the two parts of the 'ethnosyntax' compound are construed. The sections that follow turn attention to these components, taking up a methodological issue in how 'ethno'- and 'syntax' intermesh in syntactic enquiry.

Note that this chapter differs in perspective from other contributions to this book that argue in one way or another that cultural factors found in a particular speech community can constrain, license, account for, or otherwise be associated with morphosyntactic rules or constructions of the language(s) spoken there. In contrast, what follows here digresses from this worthwhile pursuit by wondering, in addition, about cultural perspectives dominant in current forms of Western linguistic enquiry. We start then from the 'ethno-' of the professional observers rather than from the 'ethno-' of the observed. In particular, we raise questions about how institutionally situated norms of current linguistic practice can have some impact on syntactic discovery. The impacts we focus on relate to judging grammaticality and to assessing coreference where professionally institutionalized imagination and culturally situated tolerance for ambiguity affect how linguists succeed in their syntactic research.

2.1. TRACING LINGUISTIC ACCEPTABILITY

The particular intermeshing of 'ethno-' and 'syntax' taken up here relates to the empirical basis for syntactic enquiry, a topic recently surveyed in detail by Schütze (1996). Below we follow a perspective somewhat different from the mainly cognitive orientation of Schütze's useful overview. The suggestion here is that, in addition to more cognitive constraints on the interpretation of syntactic well-formedness, the working of cultural and institutionally based social factors in judgements of grammaticality/acceptability should be recognized and adequately probed. Given the present scope, we concentrate on summarizing some of the lead-

Grants from the Australian Research Council have made possible work reported here, which was also facilitated by the Thai National Research Council. Parts of this study were presented at the Fourth International Symposium on Language and Linguistics, Bangkok, January 1996, and at the Ethnosyntax Workshop during ALI98, Brisbane, July 1998. We are grateful to discussants at those presentations for useful comments.

ing issues and on presenting the background and implications of a particular case study dealing with Thai complement coreference.

It is important from the outset to emphasize that what we have in mind is not an attack on hypotheses of autonomous syntax *per se* nor a deconstruction of assumed innate syntactic principles/parameters embedded in a bioprogramme. The argument that follows here is agnostic with regard to that prospectus. That is, whether or not an autonomous syntactic component or set of modules etc. may ultimately be shown to account for core syntactic phenomena—or what these modules may look like—is not the issue at this point. The 'ethno-' envisioned here refers rather to questions of method—to uncovering the evidence that linguists require to examine different architectural possibilities and to verify or disprove syntactic hypotheses.

The argument here is that, in finding out about syntax, what is suggested by the 'ethno-' prefix may be operative and even unavoidable, but masquerades as institutionally based 'common sense' and thus escapes attention. The 'ethno-' we are interested in here is the 'ethno-' of the discovery process itself, not yet of the result. In short, the reading of 'ethnosyntax' developed here refers to sociocultural grounding of methods of syntactic enquiry.

To overlook this even in the English-only context can lead to difficulties but such grounding is apt to be of particular significance when dealing with language data whose cultural context differs markedly from what is familiar in Western speech communities. If language L under investigation in a syntactic enquiry is not English, the methodological 'ethno-' will involve cross-cultural perspectives of academic practice, especially of linguistics as currently conducted in Western academia, along with local cultural attitudes towards language and linguistic research characterizing native-speaking consultants for L. A preliminary issue, for example, would be just what sort of a variety 'L' is in sociolinguistic terms: the extent to which 'L' can be considered the sort of unified and standardized linguistic entity that Standard English may appear to be.

A further and more complex set of possibilities arises in the increasingly common professional context of trained linguists originally from non-Western backgrounds. As native speakers of L, but with Western-based professional expertise and outlook, these linguists may learn to reify and formulate their intuitions in ways isomorphic to how this typically occurs in the context of English-based research into formal syntax, stressing the particular norms of presentation acceptable in syntactic argumentation. But does this practice differ from that of more naive speakers of L confronted with the same data? If so, what is the significance to theory construction of the professionals' methodological isomorphism to the community of English-speaking linguists? This question becomes especially important as the search for syntactic universals comes to rely increasingly on subtle and precise grammaticality judgements pertaining to syntactic phenomena in languages like L. Here the intuitions of native L-speaking professional linguists become crucial to success in the research agenda.

To investigate this question in more specific terms, we next take up the institutional and cultural grounding of some critical linguistic sensibilities: assessments of situated acceptability and intuitive judgements of a more context-free notion of grammaticality. These are sensibilities that underwrite the way that 'starring behaviour' is typically deployed in current linguistic discussions. Apart from global issues of well-formedness, 'starring behaviour' is also used in current linguistic argumentation to refer to speakers' intuitions about coreference principles and coindexing, e.g. of bound empty categories. Argumentation relying on such evidence has played a central role in how linguistic theory has progressed over the past several decades.

2.2. ESTABLISHING ABNORMALITY

Questions of grammaticality and acceptability, along with parallel dichotomies like competence/performance, have for decades led to critical but inconclusive arguments relating to the nature, in linguistic theory, of discrete bifurcations as against gradience, fuzzy distinctions or category 'squishes'. Schütze's (1996: 62) review in effect distinguishes four theoretical positions widely debated at least since the early 1970s:

(i) the notion that breaking different types of grammatical rules can give rise to different sorts or degrees of perceived deviance;

(ii) the contention that grammaticality itself is a continuum function (e.g. Lakoff 1973);

(iii) the contention that non-discrete judgements of grammaticality may reflect non-discrete application of grammatical rules (Ross 1972);

(iv) the allegation that the 'starring behaviour' of native speakers—especially that of naive consultants—may confound acceptability and grammaticality and that speakers thus do not necessarily have an unproblematic direct access to their own grammatical rules.

The first complexity was noted by Chomsky (1965: ch. 4) in *Aspects of the Theory of Syntax*, where he developed a notion of 'degrees of grammaticalness' by considering types of particular constraints that might undergo violation. Particular interest was in what sorts of selectional constraints were being violated: syntactic or semantic. Included in Chomsky's exposition at that time:

(1)   strict subcategorization
       e.g. *John compelled.

(2)   selectional restrictions (forced metaphorical interpretation possible)
       e.g. *?Colourless green ideas sleep furiously

(3)   lexical category requirements
       e.g. *Sincerity may virtue the boy.

More obvious types of rule-breaking, such as in morphological agreement, basic constituent order, etc., could easily be added. The use of asterisks in linguistic discourse came to be common practice, although, as McCawley (1988: 3) observed for his own usage, 'they do not refer . . . just to a single undifferentiated kind of abnormality, nor to abnormality of a sentence regarded merely as a string of words'.

Degrees or subtypes of grammaticality and its violations have been the subject of much experimentation. Schütze (1996: 70–88) summarizes the extensive range of psycholinguistic enquiry focusing on data sets such as (1)–(3) above. However, in the immediate wake of the *Aspects* model, a combination of problems in experimental design led to certain quandaries. Problems included the intrusion of variables not originally considered, non-replicability of experiments and, especially, substantial adjustments and evolution in the linguistic models themselves, as espoused by professional linguists.

In time, psycholinguists tended to express the opinion that grammatical competence could not effectively be investigated with the rather stark experimental techniques that had been used at first. For example, derivational complexity predicted by linguistic models often failed to be confirmed by experimental techniques. Worse still, specific predictions of a model might be experimentally confirmed, only for the model to be revised and rejected in subsequent linguistic theorizing. Some spoke of an institutional or even cultural divide between linguistics and psychology.

Possible reasons for syntactic abnormality seemed far more complex than had been assumed. In spite of much effort, the consensus is that few findings of enduring significance for understanding a competence-based language faculty have been obtained experimentally—a position that Bever, Sanz, and Townsend (1998) have recently underscored. Perhaps partly for this reason, linguistics as an institutionalized discipline has tended to develop its own in-house rules. For research into syntactic rules on the part of many linguists, introspective judgements have remained the accepted normal investigative tool rather than experimental techniques or other quantitative approaches such as text counts.

2.3. CAN GRAMMATICALITY BE DETERMINED THROUGH WELL-FORMEDNESS JUDGEMENTS?

In view of the complicated nature of well-formedness, the tacit or intuitive knowledge required to assess these versions of grammaticality may be opaque to the native speaker, as Chomsky observed in 1965:

Although there is no way to avoid the traditional assumption that the speaker-hearer's linguistic intuition is the ultimate standard that determines the accuracy of the proposed grammar, linguistic theory or operational test, it must be emphasized . . . that this tacit knowledge may very well not be immediately available to the user of the language.   (1965: 21)

Two decades later, a development of the same message can be found:

In general, informant judgements do not reflect the structure of language directly; judgements of acceptability, for example, may fail to provide direct evidence as to grammatical status because of the intrusion of numerous other factors. (Chomsky 1986: 36)

Note that these views of Chomsky now raise at least two sorts of difficulties with informant judgements: (i) linguistic exemplars themselves may relate to different grammaticality criteria as in (1)–(3) etc. (e.g. violations of phrase-structure rules as against violations of strict subcategorization rules) and (ii) other factors may intrude (e.g. contextual felicity conditions, quantitative performance constraints).

This line of argument is vigorously taken over into a methodological critique of generative practice by Labov (1975: 14), who holds that 'intuitive data has been found increasingly faulty as a support for our theoretical constructions'. This is because 'the studies of introspective judgments carried out so far show that variation in this field is widespread, uncontrolled and chaotic' (1975: 6).

While Labov's reaction suggests a rejection of introspective data entirely, another approach is to examine it more critically. One key hypothesis, articulated in an early form by Bever (1970: 345), is that the automatic production of well-formed sentences is a linguistic operation located on a different cognitive plane from the more reflective ability to judge grammatical well-formedness. Ontogenetically, the former develops before the latter. Hakes (1980), for example, demonstrates that a child becomes competent in metalinguistic tasks such as judgements of synonymy and syntactic well-formedness after the development of competence in producing what adults judge to be well-formed utterances. Furthermore, this sequence reflects more general principles of cognitive development. Judging well-formedness, according to Hakes, is more like the type of reasoning seen in tasks requiring 'decentring' in the Piagetian sense. This includes judging the conservation of liquids. Linguistic and non-linguistic abilities may develop in parallel (see also discussion by Schütze 1996: 93).

Bialystok and Ryan (1986) and others further carry on this line of analysis, suggesting that even literacy and formal schooling may be implicated in metalinguistic judgements. What is the significance of this for evaluating the status of elicited grammaticality judgements? If judging syntactic well-formedness is indeed grounded in institutional and cultural experience of this sort, the 'ethno-' of ethnosyntax becomes difficult to evade.

2.4. GRAMMATICALITY JUDGEMENTS AS INSTITUTIONALLY SITUATED

Even given the developments sketched above, the strong tendency in most recent formal work in syntax has been to rely very heavily on well-formedness judgements, more often than not those of the single linguist-professional presenting a particular syntactic argument. One's own introspective sensibilities seem to be adequate for determining well-formedness or deviance of whatever examples are under consideration—not infrequently complex and contorted from the standpoint of what would be usual in real speech. One assumes that the linguist's professional expertise, operating as a professionally shared mode of 'common sense', will sort things out. Thus Chomsky (1992: 1) remains optimistic that as linguists 'we can distinguish the language from a conceptual system and from a system of pragmatic competence'.

In a variant of categorical starring, syntactic debate may actually relish ranked degrees of deviance and utilize them as an investigative tool, perhaps with sentences coded by symbols like ?, ?*, ??, etc. Direct appeal to such rankings then may be used to back up some syntactic argument, explaining why *X is worse than ?Y. Minkoff (2000) frames an argument on such 'gradations of unacceptability', seeking to elucidate the interaction of various anaphoric binding principles. Sometimes indeed a linguist may go so far as to star, and then unstar, the same sentence in the course of an argument as other factors are introduced; see Enfield's (this volume) discussion of such a sentence discussed by Kay (1996).

This tendency to accept 'starring behaviour' as a methodological primitive, even admitting all of the complexity noted above, would appear to rest on a form of tacit professional consensus. Relying on professional 'common sense' achieved through training, the syntactic theoretician can assume that problems with the status of evidence can be safely left to one side for the time being, even when judgements seem rather fine-tuned.

In a compelling and provocative chapter, Newmeyer (1983: ch. 2) defends this approach to the use of introspective data, setting up a sturdy defence to attacks such as Labov's above. He admits with Labov that 'speakers are . . . prone to give acceptability judgements that depart both from their linguistic competence and from their everyday use of language' (1983: 51). Newmeyer's defensive line is then to draw an 'absolutely clear' distinction between grammaticality and acceptability, echoing Chomsky's dictum above that grammaticality is not necessarily accessible to the intuitions of the native speaker.

Newmeyer admits (1983: 51 n. 2) that many formal linguists are 'sloppy' about indicating the grammaticality/acceptability distinction, especially when it comes to using an asterisk to conflate judgements of these two very different—to Newmeyer—categories of phenomena, recalling McCawley's overt practice mentioned above. Newmeyer also goes on to note that naive speakers may rank certain grammatical sentences as unacceptable. Also, they may give favourable judgements to presumably ungrammatical sentences that belong to stylistic registers that they do not control. These judgements then raise important questions of diglossic register variation to which we return below. The questions are paralleled by more general concerns with subforms of language (Sapir 1933) or 'heteroglossia' as developed by Bakhtin and linked to sociopolitical power; see Enfield (this volume).

Prefiguring the fuller treatment of Schütze (1996), Newmeyer sees attitudinal, cognitive, and pragmatic factors as potentially coming between naive speakers' grammars and their intuitions about grammaticality. But in the long run, Newmeyer's compelling contribution to solving the introspective problem lies in the follow-ing assumption: these methodological uncertainties can be dispelled by invoking professional common sense—an assumption inherent in much of Schütze's work as well. By relying on the informed and careful introspective judgements of the community of 'professional linguists' rather than those of 'linguistically naive speakers' (1983: 66) analysis can proceed on course. Although Newmeyer overt-ly states this principle only in passing, his critique everywhere relies on such a two-storeyed notion of linguistic sensibility. Otherwise, no reliability could be guaranteed for starring behaviour as a means of uncovering truly grammatical phenomena, as opposed to mere performance epiphenomena. Without the covert norms of professional common sense, grammatical argumentation of the sort cur-rently normal would become transparently unfalsifiable.

This being the case, what of the objective measurement of external data—for purposes here, the impartial recording and assembling of native speakers' patterns of starring behaviour? If it is only trained linguists who can be trusted to star cor-rectly, or else to interpret naive speakers' starring, then grammatical investigation can hardly foster a delusion of being entirely a positivistic 'science' based on some detached viewpoint. Grammatical enquiry rather comes to be an intersubjective set of acquired skills and tacitly agreed-on practices situated well within the culture of linguistic professionalism—the 'ethnos' giving rise to the assumed professional consensus. It thus falls within the scope of hermeneutic engagement associated with the humanistic disciplines.

2.5. IMAGINATION, INSTITUTIONAL TRAINING, AND JUDGEMENTS OF COREFERENCE

Nowhere does the subjective character of judging grammaticality show up more quintessentially than in the case of anaphora and coreference. Needless to say, these concepts have been crucial in the development of much recent linguistic pro-fessional debate. Formal approaches have been characterized by the postulation of various syntactically controlled empty categories or alternative mechanisms to explain the relevant phenomena. It is not our purpose here to survey details of these debates but rather to turn attention to the especially variegated texture of the gram-maticality judgements on which much of this work relies.

It would probably seem clear to most English-speaking linguists familiar with argumentation in this area, and especially to those practitioners who rely on their own native-speaker intuitions, that some judgements feel quite clear-cut and binary. Others feel less discrete and may be subject to 'asterisk fade': given extended con-sideration, a particular judgement may shift, as far as the practitioner's sensibility goes, from 'acceptable' to 'poor' or else from 'bad' to 'marginal' and even to 'OK'.

Apart from well-formedness judgements indicated through starring, in the case of anaphoric enquiries, coindexing applying to particular constructions can give rise to varied or shifting judgements. Those conducting experimental research in this area would probably concur that naive consultants vary considerably in their tolerance for ambiguity or their willingness to entertain alternative coreferential indexing. Even among practising linguists some differences can be discerned. For example, with reference to (4), Jackendoff (1997: 72) argues that unlike most passive complements with 'ask', this sentence exhibits categorical object control. This is for reasons concerned with Jackendoff's theoretical proposals regarding global semantic interpretation.

(4)   Bill asked Harry$_j$ [PRO$_j$ to be examined by the doctor].
(5)   Bill$_i$ asked Harry$_j$ [PRO$_{ij}$ to be examined by the doctor].

Other linguists may opt instead for subject control here, as though Harry was somehow in charge of things, or admit ambiguity as indexed in (5). Some linguists consulted even report an initial (4), followed by (5) on 'further consideration'. This consideration may involve the exercise of imagination, requiring a few extra seconds to activate, coupled with a professional tolerance for ambiguity in the matter of coreferential indexing. Naive consultants, on the other hand, tend to show less tolerance of this type and less willingness to exercise imagination appropriately. We infer that relevant tolerance and imagination are typically developed or at least enhanced in the course of linguistic training.

Regarding (4) and (5), Jackendoff's position is that 'control cannot be determined without first composing the relevant conceptual structure of the complement, which cannot be localized in a single lexical item or structural position' (1997: 72). This notion of control then is not strictly dependent on lexical properties of 'ask' taken alone abstractly, but requires interpretation of a more complex contextual sort. The role of context in interpretation is also present in Comrie's treatment of (6).

(6)   Otto$_i$ asked Helga$_j$ [PRO$_{ij}$ to leave the room].

As an active 'ask' complement, (6) was reported by Comrie (1984: 452) to produce a interpretative quandary similar to that of the passives, which normally show matrix subject control. Comrie notes that while all English speakers appear to accept object control for active complements, namely: . . . Helga$_j$ [PRO$_j$ . . ., some will additionally accept subject control. Hence the ambiguity indicated in (6). Comrie's solution is to suggest that 'both interpretations are latent for all speakers of English . . . but that the secondary interpretation tends to be masked unless context makes it plausible'.

Similarly, a combination of imagination and markedness characterizes Cutrer's (1993: 188) examination of 'ask' complements. She observes that pragmatic factors influence acceptability: 'the relative salience of the imagined contexts can override the unmarked . . . interpretation.'

Salience of imagined contexts can differ across consultants. Kuno (1987: 110 n. 3; 289) observes that 'speakers who can readily imagine . . . a situation' will exhibit anaphoric starring behaviour different from that of less imaginative speakers. Kuno's surmise at this point supports the contention that consultants vary significantly in imaginative abilities. In particular, professional linguists may come to acquire a more supple imagination of possible contexts for linguistic coreference configurations than is available for naive consultants, although both linguists and naive consultants might be expected to show considerable variation in this regard. The point of interest here is that at least some of the variation seems subjective in a way that relates to institutionally based training, as though such training could sharpen imaginative powers, allowing the professionals more privileged access to the bedrock of their innate competence. The profession, relying on a shared sort of institutionalized common sense regarding these intuitions, does not widely react to this state of affairs with much concern.

When professional linguists are pitted against naive native-speaking consultants, this general contrast becomes all the more salient. As Gordon and Hendrick observe:

One of the skills that linguistic training develops is facility at imagining contexts in which a sentence might be appropriate . . . In the case of coreference in name-pronoun sequences, this might involve imagining a context in which the initial pronoun could be interpreted as referring to an entity that has been mentioned already in discourse.   (1997: 352)

The observation above arose in the context of psycholinguistic investigation. Gordon and Hendrick (1997) designed a series of experiments to examine the extent to which coreference judgements of naive native-speaking subjects accorded with those of professional linguists. A key finding was that for constructions with certain configurations of referring expressions (following Principle C of Binding Theory), naive and professional assessments differed significantly. Gordon and Hendrick attributed this partly to the professional training of linguists, as above.

In this section we have concentrated on native English-speaking professionals and naive consultants. Next we turn to the more complex cross-cultural task of assessing judgements of syntactic acceptability in a non-English-speaking context.

2.6. ZERO ANAPHORA AND COREFERENCE IN THAI

In terms of importance to current syntactic theory, questions of zero anaphora in languages such as Thai, Lao, and Chinese are of particular interest, given that typologically they are inflection-free but admit rather general suppression of overt nominals. Recent generative approaches have sought to formulate a universal taxonomy of zero elements (e.g. pro, PRO, trace, and the like) and to establish cross-linguistic parameters to account for the distribution of zero elements. This project has seen over two decades of competing proposals and vigorous debate, summarized effectively with special implications for relatively isolating languages by Yan Huang (1995). Since important syntactic findings are often attributable to quite subtle distinctions, accurate comparative analyses are crucial for the universalist project. These in turn depend on fine-tuned judgements of grammaticality.

Assessing zero anaphora possibilities in these languages leads directly into issues of verb serialization, complementation, auxiliary-like modality, and other complex construction types. Well-formedness assessments for these constructions may relate to cultural predictability of events and as such are likely to be subject to culturally specific contextual conditions (see Enfield, this volume, for Lao examples; also Durie 1997: 329). In addition, critical abilities needed for effective analysis may involve culturally situated feelings about correctness and ambiguity. These factors may lead to differential inclinations on the part of consultants to exercise imagination in the typical test-like situation normally used in syntactic investigation, as we see below.

Most analyses of Thai have agreed that some instances of Thai syntactic zero involve coreferential subject interpretation. This type accords rather closely with what would be matrix-subject-controlled PRO ('big PRO') in standard generative frameworks. In English, these zero items occur in infinitival complements of intransitive predicates with semantics such as 'intend', 'try', 'begin', and the like. Thus in sentences like 'I intend to go', the matrix subject 'I' is interpreted as the subject of embedded verb 'go'. Furthermore, an utterance like 'I intend me to go' is odd in Standard English, showing that full coreferential embedded-subject pronouns are not acceptable in this particular construction. Similarly, full pronouns or nouns are not permitted directly after Thai counterparts of these verbs with such nominals functioning as subjects of embedded clauses. Also, for both languages, if the embedded subject differs from the matrix one, a different complement construction is required. Compare English: 'I intend for him to go'; and Thai switch-reference indicator *hây* (elsewhere a verb 'to give') discussed further below.

Moreover, Thai applies the constraints above to certain verbs such as *yà:k* 'to want', where English translational equivalents permit a different construction: one that allows overt pronouns or nouns in post-main-verb position functioning as complement-clause subjects. Thus for the equivalent of 'I want him to go', Thai would not admit a straightforward item-by-item translation. Required instead would be the switch-reference construction with extended collocation *yà:k + hây*, where marker *hây* enables either overt or covert non-coreferential complement-clause subject.

Depending partly on definition, some but not all serial verb construction types would exhibit coreference patterning and constraints similar to the above controlled or 'big PRO' type; see also Durie (1997). On the other hand, not all Thai zero anaphora is of this type. One or more additional types of zero element must also be recognized to account for freer or pragmatically controlled coreference possibilities. Here zero elements can be assumed in syntactic positions where overt nominals could occur as well. For verbs like *chuan* 'to invite' overt direct-object nominals can occur postverbally and they also can serve as subjects for following complement-clause verbs (cf. 'invite him to go'). In Thai this is one possibility, but overt nominals need not occur in these positions. They may be absent when reference is understood. Some researchers working in the generative tradition have used 'little pro' to code these positions and to distinguish them from the 'big PRO' sites mentioned above (Hoonchamlong 1991; see also discussion in Diller 1996). It is in the interpretation of anaphoric links in the latter constructions that shared background information and imagined context become especially important. Shared background in turn opens up questions of sociolinguistics and genre. Khanittanan (1988) has shown how spoken Thai and other informal varieties depend more on zero anaphora than do relatively autonomous written styles, where background cannot be taken as shared to the same extent.

As the several interpretations in (7) show, both PRO and pro can occur in the same utterance, with specifics of anaphoric indexing reflecting a number of semantic contrasts.

(7)   *khon   nán yà:k chuan pay dûay.*
        person that want invite go   also
        (i) [khon nán]$_i$ yà:k PRO$_i$ chuan pro$_j$ pay dûay.
             'That person wants to invite (me, us, etc.) to go too.'
        (ii) [khon nán]$_i$ pro$_j$ yà:k PRO$_j$ chuan pro$_i$ pay dûay.
             'That person (I, etc.) want to invite to go too.'
        (iii) *[khon nán]$_i$ pro$_j$ yà:k PRO$_i$ chuan pro$_j$ pay dûay.
             ('That person (I, etc.) want to invite (us, etc.) to go too.')
        (iv) [khon nán]$_i$ pro$_j$ yà:k hây pro$_i$ chuan pro$_j$ pay dûay.
             'That person (I, etc.) want to have invite (us, etc.) to go too.'

As the unacceptability of interpretation (iii) suggests, complex constraints apply. The subject of a simple *yà:k* complement clause must be coreferential with the matrix subject and is thus not pragmatically determined. To obtain an associated pragmatically determined switch-reference reading the element *hây* must be added, as in (iv), requiring very special context. For further analysis based on examples of this type, see Grima (1978).

As for cross-clausal anaphora, (8) shows interpretations for conjoined clauses with conjunctions such as *tàe:* 'but', *láe* 'and', etc. with zero-anaphora second-clause subject.

(8)   *khon   nán chuan tâng lǎ:y   khráng tàe: mây pay sàk-thi:*
        person that invite all   many time   but not go once
        (i) 'That person (we've) invited many times but he hasn't gone even once.'
        (ii) 'That person has invited (me) many times but (I've) not gone even once.'

In (8), interpretations (i) and (ii) establish that Thai coreference in this construction type is not syntactically controlled by a 'pivot' subject of a previous clause. Rather, in Thai, subjects of clauses conjoined with these conjunctions are pragmatically determined. Thus in regard to ellipsis of this type, Thai differs subtly but fundamentally from English, which does show cross-clausal subject control. In (8),

it is not preceding subject but rather two subtypes of preceding direct object, differing in specifics of topicality, that are coreferential with the following conjoined
non-overt subject. In (i) the leading NP is interpreted as fronted direct object, followed by zero subject for the first clause. In (ii), the leading NP is instead taken
as subject with direct object being a zero anaphor requiring contextual interpretation. Without further context, it might well refer to the speaker. Whatever the
reference, for (i) and (ii) context and common sense relating to the message in
its communicative context would assign the anaphoric link between first-clause
direct object and conjoined-clause ellipsed subject. This case thus differs crucially
from the *yà:k* complements discussed above, where anaphora is indeed based on
semantic and syntactic properties which cannot be overridden by context.

In many—probably most—cases of Thai cross-clausal anaphora, subjects are in
fact given coreferential interpretation, as in (9).

(9)   *khon   nán chuan tâng lǎ:y   khráng tàe: phû:t mây suphâ:p thúk khráng.*
        person that invite all   many time   but speak not polite   each time
        'That person has invited (us) many times but has spoken rudely each time.'

The interpretative outcome in (9) may relate to a common topic-chaining strategy in Thai narrative (Burusphat 1991). Methodologically this distribution should
sound a note of caution. If a syntactic argument were constructed on the basis of
samples like (9) alone, disregarding data like (8), an invalid case could be built
up for syntactic control of Thai cross-clausal anaphora. Without imagination and
experimentation on the part of analyst and consultants, Thai example (9) could
masquerade as a construction with just the same sort of anaphoric control as applies
to its English translation. Thus the important typological difference between Thai
and English in this matter would be obfuscated.

2.7. TEXT-BASED STUDIES OF THAI ZERO ANAPHORA

Generally speaking, there is substantial cross-speaker variation in assessing where
zero anaphora of the freer pragmatic type is appropriate in Thai and which particular anaphoric links are to be construed. Evers (1988), following a technique developed by Li and Thompson (1979) for Chinese, analysed a corpus of transcribed
Thai conversational materials and conducted completion experiments in which
transcribed texts were edited with blanks. Native-speaking consultants were then
invited to fill in 'missing' material, selecting between overt NPs, pronouns, or zero.
Evers reports a very significant degree of cross-speaker variability in terms of how
blanks were filled: for fifty subjects, no two responded in the same way, although
a few text sites involving topic chains were specified as zero by all subjects. Since
transcribed texts of material originating in the spoken genre were manipulated in a
test version written in Thai orthography, Evers's study also raises important methodological questions relating to diglossic variation across spoken and written genres and their related sensibilities.

Cross-speaker variability in a completion task is also confirmed by a study of Maneeroje (1986), in this case based on a recovery task applied to written Thai magazine texts. The study concentrated on subject, object, and prepositional object positions compared across clauses in different types of hypotactic relations (e.g. coordination, subordination). Distributionally, for the entire text corpus analysed, consultants concurred that about 50 per cent of the total possible anaphoric links were accomplished by zero, but differed as to specific items. For all categories other than trans-paragraph anaphora, zero in subject position was much preferred over overt nominal or pronominal anaphoric subjects when referents were contextually recoverable, with objects showing a less robust preference.

Across paragraphs, repeated full nouns were the preferred link, a trend confirmed in work by Burusphat (1991). This finding suggests that for Thai repetition of a full, but contextually recoverable, nominal could constitute in effect a paragraphing device. Interestingly, overt pronouns in all positions were rare, with a very low (6 per cent) overall occurrence for anaphoric linkage in Maneeroje's corpus. These factors taken together suggest the discourse-sensitive nature of at least some types of zero anaphora.

For writing of the earlier period before much impact of Western 'translationese', Khanittanan (1987: 56), Bamroongraks (1988), and others present convincing evidence that zero anaphora was widespread in many written genres and was used in positions where Thai normative grammar would now specify overt nominals.

As noted above, quite specific genre constraints continue to affect significantly the distribution of zero anaphora vs. overt nominals. Khanittanan (1994: 50) reports substantial differences between foreign and domestic TV broadcast news in the use of zero anaphora vs. overt NPs. The study shows a virtually categorical difference in how, in the mid-1990s, President Bill Clinton and Thai Prime Minister Chuan Leekphai were referred to anaphorically in news after they had been overtly introduced as topical actors. Clinton and other actors in the foreign news regularly received the Thai form *kháw*, a normal third person anaphoric pronoun, perhaps reflecting English source texts in 'he'. On the other hand, in over 100 news broadcasts in Khanittanan's sample, the Thai Prime Minister was never once referred to with this pronoun. Instead, he was referred to by a shortened form of his title (*na:yók*, the most frequent means), by zero anaphora (second most frequent), or by other means. The distribution may be partly related to translation from a Western-language source text in the case of foreign news, but there are sociolinguistic constraints at work as well. *Kháw* seems to border on disrespect when used of a high-status individual, especially one in the Thai cultural milieu.

The finding above recalls not only the low-frequency-pronominal facts reported by Maneeroje (1986) but also sociolinguistic work regarding pronominal avoidance, and hence increased zero anaphora, in certain types of Thai address and reference. Truwichian (1980), describing a preference for avoidance of overt self-reference terms by women speakers in some situations, establishes that zero anaphora may function as a means of suspending strong commitment to specific social relationships coded by overt pronouns and other self-reference forms. Probably no overt Thai pronoun is entirely devoid of sociolinguistic nuances and these nuances would certainly affect speakers' judgements about when to select zero anaphora over overt pronouns. It would be naive to ignore this complex pragmatic/ sociolinguistic background when turning to grammaticality judgements relating to zero in formal analyses of Thai.

Historically, interest in zero-anaphora phenomena in Thai goes back at least to the traditional Thai grammarian Phaya Upakitsilapasan (1979: 297), who analyses it mainly in terms of register difference. The spoken language, he says, is characterized by zero anaphora in positions where, in the written language, 'grammatical sentences' demand full nouns or pronouns. However, this is but a diglossic trend; even in Phaya Upakitsilapasan's own prose one finds frequent uses of zero anaphora where his own rules for 'grammatical sentences' would specify nouns or pronouns. Some modern written, especially quasi-oral, genres such as folklore narrative admit very high density of zero anaphors. These are especially common in narrative topic-chains where a single actor is the main focus of attention through a sequence of events (Burusphat 1991: 143).

Probably in part as a result of transplanting Western school norms during the formative period of Thai mass education, Thai equivalents of Western traditionalist doctrines like 'be clear, be concise, be correct' became entrenched and are still to be found in Thai schoolbooks. Sentences that are ambiguous (*kamkuam* in Thai) are widely viewed by educators to be defective and in need of correction, especially for the higher literary styles. The filling-in of zero anaphors would be one natural way to reduce ambiguity. Another way would be to propound single 'correct interpretations' for anaphoric linkages which might be observed to be freer (i.e. ambiguous) in spoken registers. The impact of changing norms and prescriptive attitudes of this type on Thai sensibilities as to well-formedness is analysed in more detail elsewhere (Khanittanan 1987; Diller 1993).

For purposes here, it is important to emphasize that the element of professional Thai practice that devalues or eschews ambiguity, by now a widespread and thoroughly indigenous attitude, is diametrically opposed to what we claimed is a typical result of Western linguistic training: the sharpening of imaginative power to savour ambiguities, e.g. in discerning different possible coreferential interpretations. The obvious prediction would follow that if traditionally inclined Thai educators served as linguistic consultants, reports of ambiguity would be minimalized; if Western-trained linguists were used instead, results would go in the opposite direction.

2.8. CONSTRUING ANAPHORIC LINKS IN THAI QUOTATIVE COMPLEMENTS

Against this background, we now turn to coreference judgements in a common type of Thai complement construction. A verb *wâ:*, originally meaning 'say', has been grammaticalized in Thai to the point where it functions as a complementizer, not only for verbs of expression, but also judgement, perception, cognition, and the like. In diachronic terms, perhaps some of the complexity apparent in grammaticality judgements for *wâ:* complements as discussed below might relate to different stages or degrees of grammaticalization, at present sensitive to sociolinguistic register differences or even variable across speakers.

Illustrated in (10) is such a *wâ:* complement, including a zero anaphor for the embedded subject—a construction commonly encountered in speech and writing. Note that the embedded subject's referent could also be coded overtly in the same position by a pronoun such as *kháw* 'he, she, they' or a fuller NP referring expression, although as noted in the previous section, those choices are not the quantitatively preferred ones. On the basis of this limited evidence, (10) appears have a zero element more like pro than PRO in standard generative terms.

(10)   *nuan khít wâ: ø tô'ng pay ro:ng-rian wan-ní:.*
        Nuan think that   must go school   today
        'Nuan thinks that (she) must go to school today.'

The problem is, to what can the zero anaphor ø in (10) refer? This question has led to an interesting disagreement found in two doctoral dissertations in Thai linguistics written by native speakers of similar educational and social background, each of whom had received professional training in Western institutional contexts. Hoonchamlong's (1991: 253 ff.) analysis includes a critique of configurational claims regarding zero elements in Pingkarawat (1989), who treats (10) as a case of syntactic binding.

One group of native speakers interviewed by Pingkarawat reports that this zero must be bound logophorically by its matrix subject and is thus not potentially ambiguous. On the contrary, for another group of native speakers—Hoonchamlong's group—a referent outside the sentence is allowed in similar examples. How are we to account for this rather basic disagreement between native speakers, including those with doctorates in linguistics? The case is not trivial, since it provides crucial evidence regarding configurational vs. pragmatic determination of coreference in this common Thai complement construction. The outcome of this determination would ultimately affect the project of framing a universal parametric typology and locating Thai within it.

To probe this particular complement construction further, one of us (WK) presented sentences including (11), (12), and (13) to three groups of native-speaking Thai consultants, all in Thai tertiary institutions, but with different professional backgrounds.

(11)   *dae:ng bò':k e: wâ: ø hěn.cay   dèk*
        Daeng tell   NAME that   sympathize-with children
        'Daeng told "A" that (she) sympathized with the children.'

(12)   *dae:ng bò':k e: wâ: ø khâw.khâ:ng dèk*
        Daeng tell   NAME that   take-side-of children
        'Daeng told "A" that (she) was siding with the children.'

(13)   *kháw bò':k dae:ng wâ: ø ca   pay . . .*
       3P   tell   NAME   that   IRREALIS go . . .
       'She told Daeng that (she) would go . . .'

The results strongly confirmed the sort of interpretative differences reported above by Evers, Maneeroje, and others and also reconfirmed the division found in the two doctoral investigations. The following variables were found to exert a strong effect on coreference assignments:

   (i)   naive consultant vs. professionally trained linguist;
  (ii)   vague task instructions vs. task instructions encouraging respondents to exercise imagination and to consider possible multiple contexts;
 (iii)   semantic content of predicates assessed in terms of plausibility in typical real-life applications.

Variables (i), (ii), and (iii) exerted synergistic effects. Naive consultants given minimal instructions relied on (iii), real-world semantic plausibility, to assign matrix subject control to (11) but object control to (12). Results for (13) were more mixed, with 23 naive consultants opting for subject control, 6 object control, but only 1 naive consultant reporting either possibility. It did not occur to any of the 45 naive consultants to report extra-sentential coreferential possibilities for (13), although no such prohibition was laid down in instructions and such links could easily be elicited under manipulated conditions.

Thai results relating to professional training are reminiscent of the findings for English of Gordon and Hendrick (1997), but for Thai the professional vs. naive breakdown is somewhat different. One Western-trained Thai linguist exercised more developed contextual imagination and reported more coreference possibilities for (11) than naive consultants did, including trans-sentential anaphoric coreference, i.e. of a topic in prior discourse. However, this trend was not categorical: three out of ten respondents with at least some training in linguistics would not accept any trans-sentential anaphoric coreference possibilities at all. A copy-writer in a mass-circulation news magazine concurred with this view.

The strong tendency then especially on the part of naive consultants was to deny ambiguity and to report a single coreferential link between an overt nominal appearing in the matrix clause and the zero embedded subject. If two overt nominals were present, then the most semantically plausible in terms of predicate content of the embedded clause would be selected categorically. Recall Jackendoff's discussion of 'ask' complements as in (4), where control could not, he claimed, be determined on the basis of a single lexical item or structural position, but rather depended on composing the relevant conceptual structure of the complement.

This coreferential assignment behaviour is particularly important in terms of syntactic discovery, as it suggests a possible 'masquerading' effect for coreference judgements in complements of this type. Pingkarawat's (1989) consultants, for example, apparently reported results for (10) that were interpreted as anaphoric control based on structural position (c-commanding subject NP of matrix clause) but it seems difficult to determine whether these judgements were 'syntactically based' or were instead relying on more semantic impressions of predicate meaning and real-world plausibility like those noted above. The crucial problem here is that different procedures produce the same type of superficial results. Only with more attention to experimental design and further testing could firmer conclusions be drawn.

2.9. CONCLUSION

We have seen above that grammaticality judgements provide a major source of empirical data used in syntactic research but their complex make-up, especially their cultural grounding, is seldom an overt concern. As McCawley (1985: 673) has phrased the problem:

The controversies about such data have generally failed to separate three quite distinct issues:

   (i) the accuracy with which such judgements can be made,
   (ii) the accuracy of the consultant's reports of his judgements, and
   (iii) the possibility of bias . . .

Note that issue (ii) is a serious one even when the investigator is his own consultant, regardless of issue (iii), since the investigator may really be judging something other than what he thinks he is judging; thus he may think he is dealing with grammaticality, but he may be reporting, say, his success in imagining a context in which the example would sound normal.

Now the ability McCawley refers to as 'success in imagination', as we have argued above, is likely to be affected by varied cultural processes since 'a context in which an example would sound normal' would surely be culturally, institutionally, and professionally determined at least in part. Sentences that might 'sound normal', say, in giving stage directions in a dramatic production or in scripting a science-fiction film might seem abnormal to someone lacking experience with those particular communicative subforms. As far as sensibilities go, imagination will have its limits, with the culturally bizarre merging into the unimaginable, reported as ungrammatical. In the Lao cultural context xylophones are not played lying down, but would Lao speakers be willing to imagine this possibility or express it? (See Enfield, this volume, for related discussion.)

Relevant here are both Western-based linguistic training and culturally specific attitudes towards language evaluation in speech communities where syntax is being investigated. The practices of concern here thus fall both within the 'ethno' of the contemporary linguistics research agenda and within the 'ethno' of whichever language community is being investigated.

Further, are we to assume that one could always keep these two cultural worlds arbitrarily separate, as though language L–culture L formed an 'exotic other' simply 'out there' to be clinically observed from a privileged and objective vantage point? The preceding argument has presented a case study indicating that this is an untenable oversimplification. Such an assumption obscures the status of empirical data crucial in syntactic argumentation. If linguistic research is to have a convincing basis, then cross-cultural interaction among these cultural spheres needs to be traced as well, as our case study has attempted to do in a preliminary way.

Concerning the contemporary linguistics research agenda, the preceding sections point to the value of a preliminary critique taking account of syntactic discovery procedures. The part of this account followed above relates especially to the issue of linguists acting as linguistic consultants in determining well-formedness and anaphoric coreference. We suggest that they typically undergo professional training and development that leads to an agile form of 'institutionalized imagination' which is then brought to bear in the syntactic judging process. This results in the starring behaviour typically used in professional argumentation. As we saw above, the work of Gordon and Hendrick (1997) indicates that this professional starring behaviour is at some variance from judgements of naive consultants. Finally, this mismatch or any other problems with the process—even the hardly infrequent disagreements among the professionals—are ameliorated through another part of the professional 'ethno-': covertly agreed-upon norms of institutionalized 'common sense'.

Concerning language communities under investigation, the preceding section took up Thai grammaticality judgements relating to coreference as an example. In a series of experiments, we examined coreference judgements in a type of complement construction across different groups of consultants. As in the English-only case, we found a contrast between naive consultants and professional Thai linguists, but there were important Thai–English differences also. As reported above, native Thai speakers familiar with the Western-oriented syntactic research agenda tended to exhibit a differential robustness in their professional exercise of imagination. However, even among linguist-consultants with Ph.D.s in linguistics from leading Western institutions, differences so important were observed as to cast doubt on the prospects for this standard method of enquiry ever to produce a definitive taxonomy of Thai zero elements.

For the Thai situation, those counted as 'naive' consultants also displayed judgements affected by an institutional context, but the relevant institution in their case is rather that of traditional Thai education. Consultants imbued with local cultural attitudes towards language education were found to avoid reporting ambiguous (*kamkuam*) interpretations almost categorically—in contrast to those with extensive training in linguistics. Instead the more naive consultants would favour unitary interpretations felt to be normatively correct (*thù:k-tô'ng*). Above all they would find it appropriate to rely on the semantics of complement predicate clauses and favour those coreferential links that give rise to culturally plausible real-world scenarios. Following local attitudes, the goal of indigenous Thai language education should be to protect the standard language from irrationality, impurity, and misuse. Probing it for potential ambiguities or attempting to imagine far-fetched contexts for decontextualized example sentences would run counter to these sensibilities.

Such linguistic sensibilities evoke more general attitudes in Thai schooling, where aims of education are widely seen as giving rise to results directly beneficial or 'useful' (*prayò:t*) in ways that are both meaningful and normatively correct. In this traditional viewpoint, theory (*thrítsadii*) simply for its own sake is difficult to reconcile with objectives more useful in practice (*pàtibàt*). In such a context, strange indeed would be a quest for syntactic universals to be deduced through recognizing subtle ambiguities and probing degrees of deviance in language. This oddness would be all the more salient if the exercise were aimed at the goal, hardly practical in a direct sense, of teasing out just how much of syntactic well-formedness is autonomous and configurational, rather than culturally situated in daily-life meanings and norms.

Garfinkel (1967: 32) has observed:

> [for] particular determinations in members' practices of consistency, planfulness, relevance or reproducibility of their practices . . . —from witchcraft to topology—results are acquired and assured only through particular, located organizations and artful practices.

Following Garfinkel's lead, we can raise critical questions and forge a way ahead for ethnosyntax projects, under the particular reading of that term that we have developed here. Relevant topics to trace through organizations and practices would include institutionalized imagination and its interpretative treatment, which we suggest accords with covert common-sense norms currently characterizing the profession of linguistics.

REFERENCES

BAMROONGRAKS, CHOLTICHA. 1988. 'Sukhothai Thai as a discourse-oriented language: evidence from zero noun phrases'. Ph.D. dissertation, University of Wisconsin, Madison.

BEVER, THOMAS G. 1970. 'The cognitive basis for linguistic structures'. In John R. Hayes (ed.), *Cognition and the Development of Language*. New York: John Wiley and Sons, 279–362.

——SANZ, MONSERRAT, and TOWNSEND, DAVID J. 1998. 'The emperor's psycholinguistics'. *Journal of Psycholinguistic Research*, 27.2: 261–84.

BIALYSTOK, ELLEN, and RYAN, ELLEN BOUCHARD. 1985. 'A metacognitive framework for the development of first and second language skills'. In Donna-Lynn Forrest-Presley, G. E. MacKinnon, and T. Gary Waller (eds.), *Metacognition, Cognition, and Human Performance*, i: *Theoretical Perspectives*. Orlando, Fla.: Academic Press, 207–52.

BURUSPHAT, SOMSONGE. 1991. *The Structure of Thai Narrative*. SIL and University of Texas at Arlington.

CHOMSKY, NOAM. 1965. *Aspects of the Theory of Syntax*. Cambridge, Mass.: MIT Press.

——1986. *Knowledge of Language: Its Nature, Origin, and Use*. New York: Praeger.

——1992. *A Minimalist Program for Linguistic Theory*. MIT Occasional Papers in Linguistics 1. Cambridge, Mass.: MIT Working Papers in Linguistics.

COMRIE, BERNARD. 1984. 'Subject and object control: syntax, semantics and pragmatics'. *Berkeley Linguistics Society*, 10: 450–64.

CUTRER, L. MICHELLE. 1993. 'Semantic and syntactic factors in control'. In Robert D. Van Valin, Jr. (ed.), *Advances in Role and Reference Grammar*. Amsterdam: John Benjamins, 167–96.

DILLER, A. 1993. 'Diglossic grammaticality in Thai'. In William A. Foley (ed.), *The Role of Theory in Linguistic Description*. Trends in Linguistics, Studies and Monographs 69. Berlin: Mouton de Gruyter, 393–420.

——1996. 'Linguistic zero in Asia: from Panini to Pro-drop'. In Somsonge Burusphat *et al.* (eds.), *Pan-Asiatic Linguistics, Proceedings of the Fourth International Symposium on Languages and Linguistics*, vol. i. Nakhon Pathom: Mahidol University, Institute of Language and Culture for Rural Development, 242–58.

DURIE, MARK. 1997. 'Grammatical structures in verb serialization'. In Alex Alsina, Joan Bresnan, and Peter Sells (eds.), *Complex Predicates*. Palo Alto, Calif.: Stanford University Centre for the Study of Language and Information, 289–354.

EVERS, BART. 1988. 'Noun phrase choice in Thai'. Honours thesis (linguistics), Australian National University, Canberra.

GARFINKEL, HAROLD. 1967. *Studies in Ethnomethodology*. Englewood Cliffs, NJ: Prentice-Hall.

GORDON, PETER C., and HENDRICK, RANDALL. 1997. 'Intuitive knowledge of linguistic co-reference'. *Cognition*, 62.3: 325–70.

GRIMA, JOHN A. JR. 1978. 'Categories of zero nominal reference and clausal structure in Thai'. Ph.D. dissertation, University of Michigan.

HAKES, DAVID T. 1980. *The Development of Metalinguistic Abilities in Children*. New York: Springer-Verlag.

HOONCHAMLONG, YUPHAPHANN. 1991. 'Some issues in Thai anaphora: a Government and Binding approach'. Ph.D. dissertation, University of Wisconsin, Madison.

HUANG, YAN. 1995. 'Null subjects and null objects in generative grammar'. *Linguistics*, 33.6: 1081–1123.

JACKENDOFF, RAY. 1997. *The Architecture of the Language Faculty*. Linguistic Inquiry Monograph 28. Cambridge, Mass.: MIT Press.

KAY, PAUL. 1996. 'Intra-speaker relativity'. In John Gumperz and Stephen Levinson (eds.), *Rethinking Linguistic Relativity*. Cambridge: Cambridge University Press, 97–114.

KHANITTANAN, WILAIWAN. 1987. 'Some aspects of language change in the linguistic usage of Kings Rama IV, Rama V and Rama VI'. *Proceedings of the International Conference on Thai Studies*, iii.1. Canberra: Australian National University, 53–70.

——1988. 'Thai written discourse: a change toward a more autonomous style'. In Cholticha Bamroongraks *et al.* (eds.), *International Symposium on Language and Linguistics, Faculty of Liberal Arts, Thammasat University*. Bangkok: Thammasat University Press, 120–8.

——1994. *Raingan wichai laksana phasa thi chai phan su'muanchon thorathat* [Research Report: Features of Language Used in Television Media]. Bangkok: National Research Council.

KUNO, SUSUMO. 1987. *Functional Syntax: Anaphora, Discourse and Empathy*. Chicago: University of Chicago Press.

LABOV, WILLIAM. 1975. 'What is a linguistic fact?' In Robert Austerlitz (ed.), *The Scope of American Linguistics*. Peter de Ridder, 77–133.

LAKOFF, GEORGE. 1973. 'Fuzzy grammar and the performance/competence terminology game'. In Claudia Corum *et al.* (eds.), *CLS Papers from the Ninth Regional Meeting*. Chicago: Chicago Linguistic Society, 271–91.

LI, CHARLES N., and THOMPSON, SANDRA. 1979. 'Third person pronouns and zero anaphora in Chinese discourse'. In T. Givón (ed.), *Discourse and Syntax*. Syntax and Semantics 12. New York: Academic Press, 311–35.

MCCAWLEY, JAMES D. 1988. *The Syntactic Phenomena of English*. Chicago: University of Chicago Press.

MANEEROJE, PRAPAPORN. 1986. 'Kan-chay rup thaen kham-nam phu'a bo'k khwam-to'-nu'ang nay kho'-khian phasa thay' [Nominal Avoidance Constructions Indicating Cohesion in Written Thai]. MA thesis, Chulalongkorn University, Bangkok.

MINKOFF, S.A. 2000. 'Principle D'. *Linguistic Inquiry*, 31.4: 583–608.

NEWMEYER, FREDERICK J. 1983. *Grammatical Theory, Its Limits and Its Possibilities*. Chicago: University of Chicago Press.

PINGKARAWAT, NAMTIP. 1989. 'Empty noun phrases and the theory of control, with special reference to Thai'. Ph.D. dissertation, University of Illinois, Urbana-Champaign.

ROSS, JOHN ROBERT. 1972. 'The category squish: endstation Hauptwort'. In Claudia Corum *et al.* (eds.), *CLS Papers from the Eighth Regional Meeting*. Chicago: Chicago Linguistic Society, 316–38.

SAPIR, EDWARD. 1933. 'Language'. In *Encyclopaedia of Social Sciences*, ix. 155–69.

SCHÜTZE, CARSON T. 1996. *The Empirical Base of Linguistics*. Chicago: University of Chicago Press.

TRUWICHIAN, AIM-ON. 1980. 'Address avoidance in Thai'. *Language and Linguistics: Journal of Humanities [Warasan Manutsayasat]* (Chiangmai University), 10.3: 31–9.

UPAKITSILAPASAN, PHAYA. 1979. *Lak phasa Thai* [Principles of the Thai Language]. Bangkok: Thai Watanaphanit (first pub. 1937).

3

Ethnosyntax, Ethnopragmatics, Sign-Functions, and Culture

CLIFF GODDARD

The main goal of this chapter is conceptual and theoretical: to articulate and discuss the concept of ethnosyntax from the standpoint of the natural semantic metalanguage (NSM) theory of Anna Wierzbicka and colleagues (1980, 1996a; Goddard and Wierzbicka 1994, in press).[1] I recognize two senses of the term 'ethnosyntax': a narrow sense referring to culture-related semantic content encoded in morphosyntax, and a broad sense encompassing a much wider range of phenomena in which grammar and culture may be related. The chapter begins with material which is relatively specific and concrete, and progresses in stages toward concerns which are broader and more abstract. Section 3.1 discusses ethnosyntax in the narrow sense, illustrating with a slightly reinterpreted version of some of Wierzbicka's classic work on 'fatalism' in Russian grammar. Section 3.2 discusses the relationship between ethnosyntax and ethnopragmatics, drawing on the NSM theory of cultural scripts. Section 3.3 argues for the importance of recognizing that language involves different kinds of sign-function—semantic (symbolic), iconic, indexical—and asks how we can deal with ethnosyntactic connections in the realm of iconic-indexical meaning. Section 3.4 broadens the focus further in an effort to situate ethnosyntax in a larger semiotic theory of culture, but argues that a semiotic concept of culture is not viable unless it adequately recognizes iconic and indexical, as well as semantic (symbolic), phenomena.

3.1. TWO SENSES OF ETHNOSYNTAX

The term 'ethnosyntax' was coined by Anna Wierzbicka in her 1979 article 'Ethnosyntax and the philosophy of grammar', to refer to a proposed new field of enquiry into phenomena to be found at the intersection of grammar, semantics, and culture.

I would like to thank Nick Enfield and Anna Wierzbicka for helpful comments on earlier versions of the chapter as a whole, Katya Margolis and Michael Dunn for advice on Russian, and Alan Rumsey for discusssion of the practices approaches in anthropology. I also benefitted from comments received from participants in the Ethnosyntax Workshop held at the Australian Linguistic Institute, Queensland University, July 1998.

[1] The NSM approach will not be described in any detail in this chapter. For a basic outline, see Wierzbicka (this volume), and for a more detailed introductory treatment Goddard (1998).

Wierzbicka argued that the introduction of a standardized semantic metalanguage (the natural semantic metalanguage) promised to bring new rigour into an area of study anticipated by von Humboldt, Bally, de Courtenay, Boas, Sapir, and Whorf, among others; to wit, the study of 'the philosophies built into the grammar of different languages'. In a later work, Wierzbicka (1988) characterized her view of ethnosyntax as follows:

> The grammatical constructions of any natural language encode certain meanings. These meanings can be 'deciphered' and stated in precise and yet intuitively comprehensible semantic formulae. To the extent to which the semantic metalanguage in which such formulae are worded is language independent and 'culture-free', the meanings encoded in the grammar of different languages can be compared and the differences between them can be shown explicitly. In particular, proceeding in this way we can reveal areas of special elaboration, areas that a given language seems to be particularly 'interested in' and which it seems to regard as particularly important.   (Wierzbicka 1988: 12)

In my view, the term 'ethnosyntax' should ideally be reserved for phenomena of this specific kind, i.e. for morphosyntactic constructions which encode a specifiable culture-related semantic content, but since many contributions to this volume employ the term in a broader way, I distinguish between ethnosyntax in the narrow sense (as just described) and ethnosyntax in the broad sense, which is inclusive of a wide range of disparate connections between grammar and culture. If we employ the additional term 'ethnopragmatics' to designate the study of culture-specific norms, rules, and models of usage, one can say that ethnosyntax in the broad sense overlaps with ethnopragmatics. Three examples will clarify these points.

First, Clancy (1986) has proposed that the verb-final structure of Japanese, with negation appearing as a verbal suffix, is particularly well suited to the Japanese cultural preference for indirectness and its dispreference for overt displays of personal opinion:[2]

> [S]peakers may negate a sentence at the last moment, depending on the addressee's expression (Doi 1974). They may also nominalise and negate entire sentences upon their completion to make assertions less direct; when this is done with negative predicates, multiple embedded negations are created.

In other words, Japanese speakers can skilfully exploit the opportunities which the structure of the language offers them for ambiguity and indirection. This is not ethnosyntax in the narrow sense because the particular grammatical structures do not encode any inherent semantic content which suggest indirection, deliberate inexplicitness, etc.

---

[2] To give the flavour of this style of usage, Clancy cites the following (somewhat exaggerated) example:

'It isn't that we can't do it this way', one Japanese will say.

'Of course,' replies his companion, 'we couldn't deny that it would be impossible to say that it couldn't be done.'

'But unless we can say that it can't be done', his friend adds, 'it would be impossible not to admit that we couldn't avoid doing it' (Loveday 1982; attributed to Frank Gibney).

Second, Duranti (1990) demonstrates that Samoan orators in a *fono* (roughly, 'dispute meeting') exploit the alternative case frames available to them either to highlight or to suppress attributions of agency. An ergatively marked subject is overtly and unequivocally represented as an agent, while source or genitive marking for the implied agent allows a more attenuated attribution of responsibility. In the highly charged context of the *fono*:

> [t]he power struggle between different parties in the *fono* . . . is reconstituted through the choice of specific case markings that reorient or frame the degree of agency by certain human participants. . . . The linguistic code seen as a process rather than as a structure is one of the 'technologies' through which power and social structure can be sustained and re-negotiated. (Duranti 1990: 657, 661)

Duranti's point that his account concerns the linguistic code 'as a process rather than as a structure' is important. What he is talking about is linguistic praxis, oratorical strategies (cf. Rumsey, this volume). The orators exploit the grammatical possibilities of Samoan for their own purposes, and the way in which this is achieved makes a fascinating microstudy in ethnopragmatics in which grammar plays a crucial role. Duranti shows that use of the ergative case during a *fono* can carry a social implication: it 'points an accusatory finger at someone by foregrounding or making public his or her inappropriate or blameful doings' (Duranti 1990: 662). However, such an implication is precisely that—an implication. There is no reason to believe that ergative case in Samoan has any inherent semantic content indicative of inappropriate or blameful action. The same ergative case is used outside the *fono* context in all sorts of mundane utterances to mark the subject as a semantic agent without any 'political' or 'sensitive' implications. Even within a *fono*, ergative case is routinely used when describing the praiseworthy actions of God. So again, this is not ethnosyntax in the narrow sense.

Third, consider Heidegger's celebrated thesis that the early Greek philosophers' preoccupation with abstract 'essences' was fostered and sustained by the existence in Ancient Greek of a productive process for deriving abstract nouns from adjectives and verbs. Moser (1997) bolsters Heidegger's claim by a comparative study of Ancient Chinese philosophical texts, during a period in which Chinese philosophy was 'proto-scientific' in orientation, in a spirit close to contemporaneous Greek texts. Ancient Chinese is said to have been an almost perfect example of an isolating language (much more than modern Chinese), which lacked any linguistic marking of abstract nouns. Moser concludes that:

> there is a case to be made that the Greek theoretical framework for abstraction was prompted and facilitated by the structure of the Greek language itself, while for philosophers working in Chinese there would have been no impetus to explore this area at all. Indeed, Aristotle routinely pointed out and analysed semantic distinctions conveniently marked in Greek that are difficult to pinpoint and express unambiguously in ancient Chinese. (Moser 1997: 320)

This proposed correlation between grammar and the direction of philosophical thought is controversial. But supposing for the sake of argument that it is true, are we seeing ethnosyntax? Not in the narrow sense, because once again it is not being claimed that the relevant linguistic structures literally encode any particular 'ethnophilosophy'.

These and other proposals about ethnosyntax in the broad sense are important and deserve to be taken seriously. In subsequent sections I will try to map out some terminological and conceptual coordinates which can help us to discuss them in an orderly fashion, without getting them mixed up with ethnosyntax in the narrow sense. It is time, however, to look at a canonical example of ethnosyntax in the narrow sense, and for this purpose we can turn to some of Anna Wierzbicka's (1992, 1997) work on Russian. Other well-worked examples of ethnosyntax in Wierzbicka's work are her treatments of the Japanese adversative passive (1988), Italian syntactic reduplication and English 'whimperatives' (1991), and English causatives (1998, this volume).

Wierzbicka (1992, 1997) argues that the semantic theme of 'fatalism' manifests itself not only in the lexicon and phraseology of Russian, but also in its morpho-syntax. At the lexical level, the highly salient concept of *sud'ba* (roughly 'fate', 'destiny') designates a characteristically Russian way of looking at human life—as an incomprehensible experience which is at the mercy, in the words of one authority, 'of some overwhelming necessity to which we must submit' (cf. Wierzbicka 1992: 71–2). *Sud'ba* is used very widely, in very different registers, from colloquial speech to scholarly discourse to literary works. Corpus counts show that it is far more common in Russian than words such as *fate* and *destiny* are in English, being involved in numerous common collocations, set phrases, and proverbs. According to Wierzbicka (1997), *sud'ba* deserves to be identified as a 'key word' of Russian culture, i.e. as a word which designates a focal concept around which an entire cultural domain is organized.

For our purposes, the important thing is that meanings related to the *sud'ba* concept can be found encoded in a whole raft of Russian 'impersonal dative-cum-infinitive' constructions. The following treatment is based on Wierzbicka (1992: 108–16, 413–28), adapted in the light of subsequent work and additional information from Katya Margolis (personal communication). One fairly common construction is illustrated in (1*a*)–(1*c*). The construction has the form:

Negation + existential ('there isn't')—Person X:dative—Noun Y:genitive.

where, roughly speaking, the noun in the dative indicates someone (X) who could potentially benefit from 'having' the noun in the genitive (Y)—but who cannot have it.

(1) *a. Ne budet   tebe   nikakogo morožennogo.*
    NEG be:FUT3SG 2SG:DAT NEG:GEN ice-cream:GEN
    'There'll be no ice-cream for you (because you haven't picked up your toys).'

    b. Ne budet   tebe   pasporta.
    NEG be:FUT3SG 2SG:DAT passport:GEN
    'There'll be no passport for you.'
    c. No znaju,   miru   net prošĉenija.
    but know:1SG world:DAT NEG forgiveness:GEN
    'I know there can be no forgiveness for the world.' (from a poem by Zinaida
    Gippius)

The semantic burden of the construction is to unequivocally rule out any possibility of X being able to obtain the beneficial and desired outcome; and at the same
time to attribute this situation to the fact that someone in a superior position to
X does not want it to happen. The identity of the implied powerful 'someone' is
not stated explicitly. In some contexts, as in (1*a*), it is obvious and quite specific
but it can also be rather vague; in (1*b*) the allusion is presumably to some faceless
authorities, and in (1*c*) the allusion is presumably to God. Schematically, the construction can be explicated as follows:

(2)   Negation + existential ('there isn't') – Person X:dative – Noun Y:genitive =
       it would be good for X if X could have Y
       X wants to have Y
       I know: X cannot have Y
         because someone above X doesn't want it to happen

A second, even more fatalistic, construction is not so common in everyday
speech, but is highly characteristic of Russian folk literature. It has the canonical
form:

Negation – Infinitive verb – Person X:dative

Illustrated in (3*a*)–(3*c*) below, this construction refers to outcomes which are
desirable but which can never eventuate because they are not fated to do so. Notice
that the Russian sentences below do not contain any word corresponding to the
word 'never' which appears in the glosses. Example (3*a*), for instance, has the
form 'not to-see for-you those presents'. According to Galkina-Fedoruk (1958:
214): 'this is the most often used, the most beloved form of expression in Russian
folk speech; these negative-impersonal sentences occur very frequently in *byliny*
(folk epic), in folksong, in proverbs and sayings.'

(3) *a. Ne vidat' tebe   ètix   podarkov.*
    NEG see:INF 2SG:DAT this:3PLGEN present:3PLGEN
    'You'll never see those presents.'
   b. Ne guljat' emu   na vole.
    NEG walk:INF 3SG:DAT in will:PREP
    'He can never walk in freedom.'
   c. Ne raskryt' tebe   svoi   oĉen'ki   jasnye,
    NEG open:INF 2SG:DAT REFL:POSS:3PL eye:DIM:3PL clear:3PL

Ne vzmaxnut' tebe da ručen'ki belye,
NEG wave:INF 2SG:DAT EMPH arm:DIM:3PL white:3PL
Ox, da ne toptat' tebe dorožki torenye . . .
EMPH EMPH NEG tread:INF 2SG:DAT road:DIM:3PL boarded:3PL
'You'll never open those bright little eyes, Those little white hands will
never wave, Oh, and you will never set foot on boarded paths.' (from the
folk genre of lamentation *plac*, lit. a 'weep')

The meaning of this construction can be explicated as in (4). The first part of
the explication proclaims the impossibility of X's carrying out the desired act. The
second part implies that the reason for this situation is somehow elusive and mys-
terious: if one wanted to state a reason, the best one could do would be to attribute
it to the wishes of some power which is 'above' humanity—in effect, an allusion
to *sud'ba* 'fate'.

(4)   Negation – Infinitive Verb – Person X:dative =
        person X wants to do something (Verb)
        I know: X cannot do it
        if someone wanted to say why X cannot do it, this person could say:
            it is like someone above people doesn't want this to happen

A third construction is not so literally fatalistic, but certainly depicts a situation
in which something happens to a person inexplicably, and, in a sense, irresistibly.
The construction combines a dative human subject with a mental verb in the third
person singular neuter reflexive form.

Person X:dative – Mental verb:3SG(neut)Refl.

It implies that for some unknown reason the mental event simply 'happens' inside
us. For example: I may know that I am leaving soon, and yet I may still say *ne
veritsja*, roughly, 'I just can't believe it' (i.e. that I am leaving). The most important
Russian expression of this sort is probably the ubiquitous *xočetsja* lit. 'it wants
itself to me' (and the negated version *ne xočetsja*), which suggests a spontaneous
and involuntary desire. In some ways the construction is parallel to English constructions like *It occurred to me . . .* or *It seemed to me . . .*, but whereas this pattern
has a limited scope in English, in Russian it is both fully productive and extremely
common. Some further examples are given in (5a)–(5b).

(5) *a. Emu xotelos' slyšat' zvuk ee golosa.*
        3SG:DAT want:3SG:REFL hear:INF sound 3SG:POSS voice:GEN
        'He (felt he) wanted to hear the sound of her voice.'
    b. Segodnja mne vspomnilas' Praga—sady.
        today 1SG:DAT remember:3SG:REFL Prague garden:3PL
        'Today I was reminded of Prague—of its gardens.'

(6) and (7) show semantic explications, using examples with negative and positive polarity, respectively:

(6)   *Mne ne xočetsja/veritsja* (lit. it doesn't want/believe itself to me)=
       something happens inside me
       because of this, I cannot want/believe this
       I don't know why

(7)   *Mne xočetsja* (lit. it wants itself to me)=
       something happens inside me
       because of this, I cannot not want this
       I don't know why

We have sampled only three of a large family of Russian grammatical constructions formed with infinitive verbs and with dative (or null) subjects, constructions which refer to things that happen to people against their will or irrespective of their will—to things which are more or less inexplicable but at the same time irresistible. One could also mention the extremely common use in colloquial Russian of impersonal modal predicates with dative-subjects, such as *neobxodimo* 'it is indispensable', *nel'zja* 'one may not', *nado* 'it is necessary', *nužno* 'it is necessary/ required', *sleduet* 'one ought to', and *dolžno* 'one has to'; and the sundry infinitive and reflexive constructions conveying meanings related to helplessness, obligation, and necessity.

All these examples illustrate the defining property of ethnosyntax in the narrow sense—namely, the existence of a specifiable culture-related semantic content which is literally built into the morphosyntactic structures of the language. It is noteworthy that in this Russian example, as in other well-studied examples of ethnosyntax, we find the same or similar semantic content recurring in a whole set of different grammatical constructions.

3.2. ETHNOPRAGMATICS AND ETHNOSYNTAX

Let us now turn to mapping out some of the other ways in which grammar and culture can be correlated, i.e. to ethnosyntax in the broad sense (which overlaps with ethnopragmatics). One phenomenon which meets this description occurs when particular 'ordinary' grammatical constructions happen to be favoured or disfavoured in usage on account of prevailing culture-specific norms. For example, the imperative construction is much more frequent in Polish than in English. According to Wierzbicka (1991), in Polish culture it is considered good to directly and spontaneously express one's feelings, one's opinions, and also one's wishes. There is no cultural norm which inhibits these general cultural principles being applied in the case of one person wanting another person to do something, so naturally people quite freely use the imperative construction, whose core meaning is 'I want you to do this'. In Anglo culture, on the other hand, the value placed on free expression is moderated by another, partly competing cultural principle, which can be labelled the principle of 'personal autonomy'. Roughly speaking, this calls upon people to respect the right of others to make their own decisions about what they will and will not do. Since using a bare on-record imperative could impinge on personal autonomy, the imperative construction is relatively less frequent in English (which has instead evolved an elaborate set of alternative 'whimperative' constructions—see below).

As a second example, one could take the frequency of direct questions in Anglo culture as compared with many Australian Aboriginal cultures. In Anglo culture many kinds of information are regarded as freely available and in the public domain. It is normal for people to conduct conversations based on question–answer pairings, and, indeed, asking questions is regarded favourably in many social situations, as 'showing an interest' in the other person. Questions are prominent in socialization routines with very young children. In many Australian Aboriginal cultures, in contrast, much information is regarded as 'owned' by particular individuals (Eades 1982). Except for orientation questions, Aboriginal people normally do not use direct questioning to enquire about other people's actions or opinions. Information-seeking is conducted using a 'prompting' strategy and volunteering personal information with a view to eliciting in exchange the information one is seeking.

These examples concern culture-specific pragmatic constraints on constructions with rather general semantics, as opposed to constructions which are semantically specialized in culture-specific ways. It is important to point out, however, that culture-specific pragmatic norms tend to spawn semantically specialized constructions—constructions which are tailor-made to meet the communicative priorities of the culture. An obvious example is the brace of 'whimperative' constructions in English, such as *Will you . . . ?*, *Would you . . . ?*, *Could you . . . ?* and so on. The message that 'I want you to do something' is embedded into a more complex configuration which acknowledges the addressee's autonomy by inviting them to say whether or not they will comply (Wierzbicka 1991); in form, at least, the addressee is presented with the option of refusing.

The idea that grammatical elaboration (grammaticalization) can be driven by pragmatic inferencing is well known. Many scholars now agree that the routinization of particular patterns of usage can 'harden' ('fossilize', 'sediment', 'freeze', etc.) into language-specific morphosyntactic constructions; cf. Traugott (1988); Traugott and König (1991); Heine, Claudi, and Hünnemeyer (1991); Hopper and Traugott (1993: 75–7). Contributors to this volume (Burridge, Enfield, Simpson) emphasize that such patterns of usage and the pragmatic inferencing which underlies them may be culture-specific; cf. Wilkins (1991), Evans and Wilkins (2000: 580–5). This is not an idea which is specific to the NSM theory. On the other hand, it is true to say that the NSM theory has a distinctive approach—the 'cultural scripts' approach—to the question of how culture-specific pragmatic norms should be described. I will now describe and illustrate this approach, arguing that it provides methodological advantages over conventional methods and that it facilitates an integrated view of culture-specific pragmatics and semantics, including grammatical semantics.

Studies of communicative style usually assume that in any particular speech community there are certain 'shared understandings' (variously termed 'norms of interpretation', 'rules of speaking', 'discourse strategies', etc.) about how it is appropriate to speak in particular, culturally construed, situations. How can such norms be stated in a clear, testable, and non-ethnocentric fashion? Conventional labels such as 'directness', 'formality', 'involvement', 'politeness', etc. are useful up to a point but are somewhat vague and shifting in their meanings, in the sense that they are used with different meanings by different authors (cf. Wierzbicka 1991; Irvine 1979; Besnier 1994). Furthermore, such terms bring with them an element of ethnocentrism, because the relevant concepts are not usually found in the cultures being described and cannot be translated easily into the languages involved. The solution to these problems, according to NSM researchers, is to formulate hypotheses about culture-specific norms of communication using the metalanguage of universal semantic primes (Wierzbicka 1996*b*, 1996*c*; Goddard and Wierzbicka 1997; Goddard 1997). Wierzbicka proposes the term 'cultural script' to refer to a cultural norm formulated in this way. Because cultural scripts are phrased in simple and translatable terms, they can achieve a high degree of precision and detail while at the same time minimizing the danger of 'terminological ethnocentrism'.

To see what cultural scripts look like, we can briefly consider some examples. As a starting point, we can accept (in line with a wide range of sociological, historical, and culture analytical literature) that among the primary ideals of Anglo culture one may include 'individual freedom' and 'personal autonomy'. Arguably, terms like these stand for a whole complex of interrelated cultural scripts, but one of the most general can perhaps be stated as follows (cf. Wierzbicka 1991; Goddard and Wierzbicka 1997). This script is supposed to represent a component of the dominant cultural ideology in predominantly English-speaking countries like Australia, the United States, and Great Britain.

(8)   Anglo-American 'individual freedom' script:
        people think:
            everyone can do what he or she wants to do
            if it is not bad for other people

In line with this general ideal, there are a range of more specific scripts related to communicative practices. It was suggested above, for example, that speakers of mainstream English are inhibited from using the bare imperative due to the social value placed on individual freedom and personal autonomy. Using cultural scripts, this idea can be spelt out as follows.

(9)   Anglo-American script blocking 'imperative directives':
        if I want someone to do something,
        I can't say to this person something like this:
            'I want you to do this; because of this, you have to do it'

Instead of a bald *Do this!*, Anglo values encourage people to use more elaborate 'interrogative directives' (i.e. whimperatives) such as *Could you do this?*, *Would you mind doing this?*, and the like. Although these constructions clearly convey the message 'I want you to do this', they also acknowledge the addressee's autonomy by embedding this potentially confronting message into a question form, with the effect of inviting the addressee to say whether or not he or she will comply. This strategy can be captured in the following script:

(10)   Anglo-American script for 'interrogative directives':
        if I want to say to someone something like this:
            'I want you to do this'
        it is good to say something like this at the same time:
            'I don't know if you will do it'

These proposed scripts deserve a great deal more discussion and justification, which it is not possible or necessary to provide here. Their purpose here is, first, to illustrate what cultural scripts written in semantic primes look like; second, to illustrate the idea that cultural scripts can constrain the use of ordinary 'general purpose' constructions such as the imperative construction; and third, to illustrate that they may even channel speakers toward particular characteristic modes of expression, which are often catered for by semantically specialized (i.e. 'narrowly' ethnosyntactic) grammatical constructions.

Before going further, it may be worth briefly clarifying a couple of theoretical points. One is that despite possible connotations of the word 'script', cultural scripts are not binding on individuals. They are not supposed to be rules of behaviour but normative rules of interpretation and evaluation. They certainly have the potential to guide behaviour, but it is open to individuals in concrete situations whether to follow (or appear to follow) culturally endorsed principles, and if so, to what extent; or whether to defy, manipulate, or subvert them, play creatively with them, etc. Whether or not cultural scripts are being followed in behavioural terms, however, the claim is that they constitute a kind of shared interpretative background. It also has to be stressed that a few simple examples cannot give an accurate impression of the complex interrelationships between and among the large number of scripts operative in any culture, including various forms of intertextuality, e.g. some being more general than others, some taking priority over others, some competing with others. Equally, it is clear that many scripts must be tailored to particular types of interlocutors, settings, and discourse genres.

Another point concerns the significance of the fact that cultural scripts are phrased in semantic primes. Does this mean 'reducing' pragmatics to semantics? The short answer to this question, which has been the cause of some misunderstanding in the literature, is that it does not. It is indeed a hallmark of the NSM approach that it uses a common framework (i.e. the metalanguage of semantic primes) for representing conceptual content regardless of whether we are dealing with meanings encoded in words, morphosyntax, or intonation patterns, on the one hand, or with 'shared understandings' in the speech community, on the other. But using a common representational framework does not mean dissolving all differences between semantics and pragmatics. The primary difference between the two domains remains as it ever was: namely, whether the conceptual content is or is not directly encoded into linguistic structure.

If we use the same metalanguage to depict meaning wherever we find it, however, it becomes easier to see how the 'semanticization' of pragmatic implicature works as a process of language change. Suppose we agree to distinguish between 'sentence meaning' and 'utterance meaning', on the understanding that utterance meaning takes in not only the meaning which is linguistically encoded but also any additional meaning which the speaker intends the hearer to infer in the context of utterance. Since cultural scripts represent shared interpretative assumptions, they will play a big part in determining and constraining the kind of inferences which speakers can reliably expect their interlocutors to draw in particular circumstances (in addition to any general principles of inference). In everyday social interaction interlocutors deal with utterance meanings: that is, they more or less effortlessly integrate lexico-grammatical meanings with pragmatic implications guided by cultural scripts and other shared interpretative background (cf. Wilkins and Hill 1995; Enfield 2000*b*). Now suppose that the configuration of lexico-grammar and cultural scripts at a particular time leads speakers and hearers to routinely employ certain culture-specific usage patterns in order to produce certain culture-specific inferences (so as to arrive at utterance meanings of a desired kind). Most contributors to this volume agree (see especially Burridge, Enfield, Simpson) that if this goes on for some time in a regular and reliable fashion the pragmatic inferences can easily be reinterpreted, diachronically, as part of grammatically encoded semantics. Talmy Givón (e.g. 1979) has long contended that 'Today's syntax is yesterday's pragmatics.' To extend this insight to the realm of ethnosyntax requires us merely to acknowledge that pragmatics has a substantial culture-specific component. Hence: 'Today's ethnosyntax is yesterday's ethnopragmatics.'[3]

In sum, the main points I have been arguing for in this section are: (i) that some grammar–culture connections which qualify as ethnosyntax in the broad sense are equally well seen as ethnopragmatic in nature, (ii) that to come to grips with ethnopragmatics, we need a principled, testable, and intelligible method for formulating culture-specific pragmatic rules, (iii) that the cultural scripts approach furnishes such a method, (iv) that with the aid of the cultural scripts approach, we can identify cases where ordinary non-specialized constructions are favoured or disfavoured on account of culture-specific pragmatic rules, i.e. ethnosyntax in the broad sense but not in the narrow sense, (v) that we can also identify cases where culture-specific pragmatic rules have motivated the proliferation of semantically specialized grammatical constructions, i.e. ethnosyntax in the narrow sense.

[3] Thanks to Randy LaPolla for this adaptation of Givón's aphorism.

3.3. EXPLORING OTHER VARIETIES OF GRAMMAR–CULTURE CONNECTION

This section sets out some further conceptual and terminological distinctions which I hope can facilitate an orderly discussion of ethnosyntax in the broad sense. This involves coming to grips with different semiotic functions (sign-functions) according to which an utterance or expression can be meaningful. The main thing to be recognized is that the kind of meaning which can be faithfully captured or modelled by means of verbal explications is only one of several ways in which an utterance or expression can be said to be 'meaningful'. Adapting Peircean terminology, one could use the designation 'symbolic meaning' but this term does not seem very suitable in linguistic contexts and I will use the term 'semantic meaning' instead.[4] Crucially, the semantic meaning of an expression is not dependent either on the form of the expression or on any particular utterance of the expression. That is, semantic meaning is not 'form-bound' nor is it 'context-bound' (i.e. dependent on the real-world coordinates of a particular utterance). It is precisely these two properties which enable semantic meaning to be captured in paraphrases, since any paraphrase necessarily has a different form from that of the original expression and is detached from the real-world context of any original utterance. Semantic meaning is to be distinguished from 'iconic meaning', on the one hand, and 'indexical meaning', on the other. Iconic meaning is dependent upon the form of an expression. Indexical meaning is dependent upon the context of an utterance.[5]

By definition, iconic and indexical meanings cannot be literally modelled—paraphrased—in semantic terms. To invoke one of Wittgenstein's (1922: 79 [4.1212]) famous distinctions, they 'show' but they do not 'say'.[6] This might seem to lead to an impasse. How can we talk about meanings which are iconic or indexical in nature, if, as Sweeney's Law is supposed to go: 'you gotta use words to talk'? But the impasse is more apparent than real. Although iconic and indexical meanings cannot be literally modelled in semantic paraphrases, this does not prevent us from describing them 'from the outside', as it were, provided it is recognized

---

[4] Another reason I prefer to avoid the term 'symbolic meaning' is that in cognitive linguistics the word 'symbolic' is often used without regard to distinctions between semantic (symbolic), indexical, and iconic meaning. Langacker (1987), for example, uses 'symbolic' roughly as I would use 'semiotic', i.e. as a cover term for any kind of 'meaningful' phenomenon.

[5] The terms 'iconic' and 'indexical' are often more narrowly defined—as requiring similarity or spatio-temporal contiguity, respectively, between an expression and its referent or Object. This interpretation can be sourced to Roman Jakobson's reformulations of Peirce (1931), but despite this venerable pedigree, in my view it is more fruitful (as well as more faithful to Peirce) to adopt broader characterizations. Note that form-dependence includes, but is not limited to, similarity; and that context-dependence includes, but is not limited to, spatio-temporal contiguity.

[6] There is nothing new in the idea that there are kinds of 'meaning' which are in principle unparaphrasable. To mention only one other precursor, Susanne Langer (1951) draws a fundamental distinction between 'discursive' (digital, language-like) and 'presentational' (analogue, picture-like) symbolism.

that any such descriptions (which are necessarily couched in semantic terms) are fundamentally different in nature from the original iconic and indexical meanings. The distinction between paraphrase and description is crucial here. (Since from the point of view of semantic representation, the main divide runs between semantic meaning, on the one hand, and iconic and indexical meanings, on the other, I will often lump the latter together as 'iconic-indexical' meaning.)

Normally, semantic meaning and iconic-indexical meaning occur intertwined in multiple ways. This can be explored using a concrete example. A certain person once said—notoriously—in a television interview: *Life wasn't meant to be easy.* Though this sentence might seem to express a rather straightforward semantic meaning, one would quickly find, upon setting about to explicate it, that such an impression is misleading and that to explicate the full semantic meaning requires an extended paraphrase containing many separate clauses in the natural semantic metalanguage. As instructive as it may be, however, this semantic explication cannot capture any stylistic qualities which depend on the form of the original, e.g. the choice of words, their sequence, their compact quality. Equally, it cannot capture the effect the utterance had on account of the fact that it came from Malcolm Fraser, the then Prime Minister of Australia, at a particular moment in Australian history—in the middle of a severe economic recession. These are iconic and indexical meaning-effects. Nothing prevents us from describing these effects but when we do so we cannot, as it were, 'reproduce' the effects themselves. On the other hand, when we state the semantic explication we are indeed reproducing the semantic meaning.

Another layer of iconic-indexical meaning was conveyed by the sound of Malcolm Fraser's voice; specifically, from the interaction between his 'social accent' (the so-called Cultivated accent of Australian English[7]) and the content of his dictum. Here was someone whose voice identified him as belonging to the privileged classes counselling the public to accept the hardships of recession as good for their souls. The result, in many quarters, was outrage and indignation. (This example also illustrates the point that iconic-indexical effects may depend on local knowledge, i.e. on the identities and context of the listeners, as well as the speaker.)

We may seem to have strayed from the question of grammar–culture connections, and in a sense that is true; but I believe the digression will turn out to have been useful when we turn to yet another kind of iconic-indexical meaning which can be found in Malcolm Fraser's utterance *Life wasn't meant to be easy*, namely, that of the complementizer *to*. What is this *to* doing here, when in many languages comparable constructions occur without any complementizer (or other formal mark of the subordinate status of the complement)? Though the matter is too complex

---

[7] For those not familiar with Australian English: regional accents are not well-developed in Australia, but at least three distinctive social accents can be identified—Broad, General, and Cultivated. Most speakers use the so-called General accent. The Broad accent is associated with rural origins, and the Cultivated accent, which tends towards a British RP style of pronunciation, is associated with people of the highly educated upper class with traditionalist values.

to be discussed adequately here, one class of English predicates which take complementizing-*to* is 'volitional' verbs and other complex verbs, including certain speech-act verbs, whose meanings contain the complement-taking semantic prime *want*.[8] The verb *mean* is one of these complex verbs, along with *intend*, *hope*, *try*, and many others (*X meant to do it*, *intended to do it*, *hoped to do it*, *tried to do it*, etc.). I would like to claim that verbs like *mean*, *intend*, *hope*, and *try*, so to speak, 'inherit' *to*-complementation from the implied predicate *want*. In a sense then, the presence of *to* in *Life wasn't meant to be easy* indexes an aspect of the semantic-grammatical structure of the sentence, i.e. the underlying presence of the semantic component *want*.

At the level of individual morphemes and formatives, a good deal of grammatical morphology has a language-internal 'structure-indexing' meaning of this kind, rather than expressing semantic meaning. As expected of a phenomenon which conveys non-semantic meaning, we can describe how structure-indexing works but such descriptions are not paraphrases. Misunderstanding on this score is a major source of confusion in discussion of grammatical semantics.

Let us look at another example of structure-indexing morphology, again in the realm of complementation. In English, complements of the semantically primitive verbs *know*, *think*, and *say* can all be introduced by the complementizer *that* (*know that*, *think that*, *say that*). As one might expect, complex verbs of knowing, thinking, and saying behave likewise, e.g. *realize that*, *decide that*, *declare that*. Why? One possible explanation is that although these three semantic primes do not share any semantic component (because they are primes, i.e. indivisible), they do have important non-compositional affiliations. Specifically, they can all take a propositional (i.e. sentence-like) complement, and there is a kind of commutability between these complements: if one can *think that X*, then one can also *say that X*, and (potentially) *know that X*. The fact that the same complementizer, i.e. *that*, occurs with all three primes is an iconic-indexical marker of a shared syntactic property.

There are many kinds of structure-indexing morphology which are more subtle and elusive than these simple examples suggest, and which cannot be directly tied to non-compositional affiliations between semantic primes. Consider the dative case in European languages. In classical grammar, this case was so termed because it was used to mark the recipient of an act of 'giving' (Ancient Greek *ptōsis dotikē* 'the giving case'), but dative case has a multiplicity of other functions differing somewhat from language to language. For example, in both Greek and Latin it marks the complement of various intransitive verbs such as 'help', 'trust', and 'be angry with', but in Greek it is also used to indicate instruments and locations, which are covered by ablative case in Latin (Blake 1994: 144–5). As we saw in Section 3.1, in Russian the dative is found in a wide range of impersonal construc-

[8] Another type of complementizing *to* is associated with predicates of *thinking* in combination with a 'future orientation', e.g. *expect to*, *threaten to*, *certain to*. Verbs of inception, such as *begin* and *start*, form a third class. For discussion of these and other complexities, see Jespersen (1964: 329–48); Wierzbicka (1988: ch. 1); Haspelmath (1989); Dixon (1991: 207–66).

tions. Traditional grammar offered the generalization that the core function of a dative case is to designate an entity as 'indirectly affected', as opposed to accusative case which designates an entity as 'directly affected'. Jakobson (1971) developed this idea further in his celebrated analysis of the Russian case system. He interpreted the difference between dative and accusative in terms of the presence or absence of the feature 'marginality', a contrast which also opposes the instrumental to the nominative. Dative and accusative, on the other hand, share the feature 'directionality', which the instrumental and nominative lack.

Proposals like these are typical of attempts to make inappropriate semantic generalizations about iconic-indexical meaning.[9] The generalization necessarily takes a highly abstract form, which cannot plausibly be regarded as forming part of an individual speaker's intended meaning, and which is not sufficient to predict or account for the actual range of usage or function. Viewed as statements of semantic meaning, such formulations are highly unsatisfactory: difficult or impossible to verify, psychologically implausible, open to the charge of arbitrariness, and so on (cf. Kempson 1977: 18–20, 86–96; Allan 1986: 265–70; Wierzbicka 1980: ch. 1). Rather than reject such formulations altogether, however, I suggest we can interpret—or reinterpret—them as attempts to describe the iconic-indexical meaning of dative case. Seen in this light, their 'semantic insufficiency', the fact they cannot be substituted in place of the original expression, etc., makes good sense.

For present purposes we may have gone far enough. My main goals have been to establish that semantic meaning must be distinguished from iconic-indexical meaning, and to acknowledge that any language is abuzz with multiple interrelating levels of iconic-indexical meaning in parallel with the enormous complexity of semantic meaning. Where does this leave us so far as ethnosyntax is concerned? For one thing, we can see more clearly why ethnosyntax in the broad sense is such a complex and difficult topic. Connections between grammar and culture can be found not only within lexico-grammar and within ethnopragmatics, but the connections within each of these domains can also involve different kinds of sign-function which call for different analytical and descriptive methods. In my view, although we have a proven analytical method for investigating semantic meaning in grammar, i.e. the natural semantic metalanguage, methods for investigating iconic-indexical meaning in grammar are still rather underdeveloped.

The fact that the NSM method is primarily attuned to semantic meaning does not mean, however, that it has nothing to offer the study of iconic-indexical meaning. In the first place, it furnishes us with a test—the only reliable test—to distinguish between the two kinds of meaning. A meaning is semantic in character if and only if it can be faithfully captured in a substitutable paraphrase; otherwise, it is iconic-indexical. If we are not mindful of this distinction, all sorts of pernicious

---

[9] As was shown in s. 3.1 in relation to Russian, it is possible to attribute more concrete, specific meanings to particular dative case constructions; but these are precisely constructional meanings, i.e. meanings expressed by the combination of dative case and other lexico-grammatical features. What is not possible, at the semantic level, is to generalize across all uses of the dative case.

confusions arise.[10] I believe that the NSM method can also make a contribution to developing clearer and more precise descriptions of iconic-indexical meanings. Granted, such meanings are in a sense ineffable in that they can never be completely and faithfully captured in verbal formulations. In this field there is a real place for diagrams and other kinds of visual representation, as in much cognitive linguistics work. But even so, there will always be some need for verbal description, and in this respect the obscure and abstract terminology characteristic of works about indexicality and metapragmatics, e.g. in Michael Silverstein's (1976, 1977) often cited articles, is a real hindrance to getting on with the job. As Wittgenstein (1922: 27) famously remarked: 'what can be said at all must be said clearly, and whereof we cannot speak thereof one must be silent.' When speaking about iconic-indexical meanings, it is as important as ever that we attempt to do so clearly. Maximum clarity—whether in paraphrase or description—can be achieved by framing what we have to say in terms of universal semantic primes.

3.4. THE ROLE OF SEMANTICS IN A SEMIOTIC CONCEPTION OF CULTURE

In this section I want to expand the scope of the discussion further to ask: How does language fit into culture? Like Enfield (2000*a*, 2000*b*, this volume), I believe that any culture is a semiotic system which presupposes a language as a semiotic subsystem. Human cultures are 'saturated' with language. Because language and culture are both semiotic systems (one intermeshed with, and 'enabling', the other) there are many parallels in their formal and functional properties. It is therefore true to say that 'culture is like language' in many respects (and to say this does not mean reducing culture to language). Neither notion can be properly characterized without reference to meaning, and since meaning can arise and manifest itself in various ways—semantic, iconic, indexical—we can expect to find parallel types of meaning phenomena in language and in culture.

What accounts, then, for the current 'anti-linguistic turn' in anthropology (cf. Ortner 1984)? In my view, the problem can be traced back to inadequacies in the structuralist approach to language which dominated linguistics for most of last century. In its heyday, linguistic structuralism enjoyed enormous prestige and anthropologists consciously looked to it for models; Lévi-Strauss's (1963) culture theory

---

[10] As a case in point one can note a number of common fallacies regarding so-called 'shifters' such as *I, you, this, here, now*, etc. Though it is correct to say that using any of these terms creates an indexical meaning (i.e. a meaning dependent on the real-world context of use), it is not true that they are 'pure' indexicals. On the contrary, shifters all have semantic meanings which remain constant across different contexts of use. A second fallacy is that *I* and *you* mean 'the speaker' and 'the addressee', respectively, or, in a more sophisticated formulation, that their meanings are 'socially constituted in the act of speaking'; for counter-arguments, see Sørensen (1963: 96); Wierzbicka (1976). A third fallacy is that linguistic forms which express 'social meanings', e.g. French *tu* vs. *vous*, are exclusively indexical in nature. Wierzbicka (1992: 319–24) shows that it is possible to find a substitutable semantic invariant for *vous* which 'spells out' a language-specific package of interpersonal assumptions and attitudes.

was modelled on Jakobson's distinctive feature phonology[11] and American 'ethno-science' developed hand in hand with componential analysis (cf. D'Andrade 1995). But as a model for anthropology, linguistic stucturalism was fatally flawed, as anthropologists now recognize. Structuralist models of culture (including structur-alist incarnations of cognitive anthropology) are now widely—and in my view right-ly—criticized for their abstractness, excessive regimentation, and mechanism.

None of this means, however, that the basic idea that 'culture is like language' is invalid, for the validity of this idea cannot be evaluated independently of the conception of language which is assumed. The linguistic framework advocated in this chapter, for example, differs starkly from structuralist approaches. It rejects abstract symmetrical formulas in favour of intelligible but complex, text-like expli-cations which often incorporate prototypical scenarios and cultural knowledge. It recognizes that in normal discourse 'literal' meanings are always modulated by pragmatic factors which, it is claimed, can be largely accommodated within a theory of cultural scripts and models. Nothing in the approach denies the exist-ence or importance of manifold iconic-indexical meaning-effects which resonate throughout language and language use. In short, current anthropological critiques of the 'culture is like language' position do not apply to the NSM conception of language—nor, for that matter, to the conception of language held in other streams of cognitive linguistics.

NSM researchers favour a semiotic conception of culture which has much in common with that which Clifford Geertz (1975, 1979) enunciated some thirty years ago: 'a historically transmitted pattern of meanings . . . expressed in sym-bolic forms' (1979: 89). But though he wrote brilliantly about cultural meanings in Bali, Morocco, and Java, Geertz lacked a principled method of semantic analysis. The terms in which the conceptual structure of cultural interpretation can be for-mulated are, he wrote, 'if not wholly nonexistent, very nearly so', with the result that ethnography is not susceptible to 'explicit canons of appraisal' and remains 'essentially contestable' (1975: 24, 29). In view of this admission of non-verifi-ability, it is not surprising that Geertz's semiotic anthropology has since joined structuralism as, in D'Andrade's (1995: 249) words, an 'abandoned agenda'. With other contributors to this volume, I believe that the semiotic conception of culture deserves to be revived, but with two significant augmentations.[12] The first is the addition of a powerful descriptive tool, namely, the natural semantic metalan-guage, for spelling out conceptual meanings both in the lexico-grammar and in culture-specific norms. The second is that we articulate the semiotic possibilities

---

[11] Duranti (1997: 33–4) labels Lévi-Strauss's structuralism as 'the semiotic approach', and summar-izes the French thinker's view as 'all cultures are sign systems'. However, Lévi-Strauss's concept of the sign is extremely limited both because of his fixation on binary opposition and because of his failure to adequately recognize indexicality as a sign-function. These weaknesses are broadly shared by what one may call the Saussurean tradition of semiology (as opposed to the much richer Peircean tradition).

[12] It is also necessary to give up on Geertz's antipathy to cognitive representations, cf. Sperber (1984, 1996); Shore (1996); Enfield (2000b, this volume).

in more detail, making it clear that both language and culture embrace iconic-indexical sign-functions as well as semantic ones.

Once the latter point is recognized, it becomes possible to reconcile a number of competing perspectives on culture. In support of this, I will outline how I see the 'practices approach' (Bourdieu 1977; Hanks 1996) fitting within a semiotic concept of culture. In its extreme form, some of the main propositions of the practices approach can be stated as follows. Language as a social process ('communicative practice') is only one set of practices among many, and the idea that it has any special place in constituting or enabling culture is merely a reflection of Western 'linguistic ideology'. In some cultures, it is claimed, language plays a relatively minor role in constituting and mediating social life. Along with this 'decentring' of language goes a critique of individualist, cognitive approaches to cultural knowledge. Understanding is not, it is claimed, purely or even primarily 'mental' in nature. Rather, practical, physical activities such as body postures, work routines, tool use, and sundry other everyday practices instil 'embodied understandings' of a culture. In this, the practices approach flows together with another influential current of ideas in psychology and cognitive linguistics, namely the so-called 'embodiment' or 'enactionist' paradigm (Johnson 1987; Varela, Thompson, and Rosch 1991).

The seminal text of the practices approach is usually identified as *Outline of a Theory of Practice* (1977) by the French social theorist Pierre Bourdieu. The book's main target is the excessively intellectualist tendency in anthropology, which depicts native people as continually following abstract rules. Let us sample some of Bourdieu's points in regard to the Kabyle people of southern Algeria, where he has done fieldwork. The Kabyle have a marked sexual division of labour, the men tilling the soil and raising cattle and the women cooking and weaving. In classic Lévi-Strauss style, Bourdieu (pp. 90–1) aligns the gender opposition with a set of homologous oppositions in Kabyle house design, which is partitioned into two parts: a dry, high-ceilinged, light-filled room for humans and a damp, low, dark room for their domestic animals (cows, oxen, donkeys, and mules). The oppositions Bourdieu mentions include: fire–water, cooked–raw, high–low, light–shade, day–night, fertilizing–able to be fertilized, and *nif–hurma* [male honour–female honour]. The *novum* of Bourdieu's treatment is his argument (building on the ideas of Marcel Mauss; cf. Strathern 1996) that the Kabyle child growing up in such a house internalizes these oppositions, not in the first instance as concepts, but as bodily orientations and dispositions: 'the "book" from which children learn their vision of the world is read with the body, in and through the movements and displacements which make the space within which they are enacted as much as they are made by it' (Bourdieu 1977: 90). For the Kabyle child, everything is conveyed by 'the hidden persuasion of an implicit pedagogy' (p. 94).[13]

---

[13] Note that Bourdieu refers repeatedly to the role of proverbs, routines, and cultural key words such as *nif* 'male honour' as part of the 'implicit pedagogy', although most commentators downplay this aspect of his description.

Nothing in this is incompatible with a broad-ranging semiotic view of culture. Bourdieu is right to highlight the role of bodily engagement with the built environment (and with tools etc.) as a mode of cultural reproduction. But buildings and tools are semiotic forms, even if their 'meanings' are iconic-indexical in nature. It is true that living in particular culture-specific spaces, working daily with particular culture-specific tools, and so on, exerts a powerful acculturating influence on a person. Bourdieu's picture of physical and verbal practices overlapping and reinforcing one another, reproducing an implicit cultural ideology, is quite consistent with a semiotic view of culture: iconic-indexical meaning operating in parallel with semantic meaning. There is no reason why a practices approach cannot be combined with a conceptual approach if both are situated within a broader semiotic perspective.

Notwithstanding the importance of non-linguistic practices in the cultural semiotic, however, I would still like to insist that language has a privileged place both in culture itself and in the study of culture; first, because language is a precondition for other aspects of culture, including non-linguistic cultural practices and early socialization into culture;[14] and second, because language is inescapably the primary infrastructure for the scientific description of other sign systems. Even diagrams and other visual representations, which can be valuable in simulating certain iconic-indexical effects, cannot work fully until they have been explained in verbal terms (for discussion, see Goddard to appear). It is the semantic capacity of language which is responsible for its 'meta-semiotic' capacity.

All this brings us back to semantics. To study language and culture one must have a plausible, verifiable, and accurate metalanguage, and one which is not biased in favour of any particular language and culture. In my view, the promise of the NSM framework to provide such a metalanguage is of fundamental methodological importance to language and culture studies—not only for the study of the semantic aspects of language, but also for the description of pragmatic, indexical, and non-linguistic aspects of culture at large.

---

[14] At birth the human brain weighs a mere 25% of its eventual adult weight. It continues to grow at fetal rates for the first two years of life, then matures at a slower rate till about the sixth year of life (Shore 1996). This curious state of affairs (unique among primates) apparently represents an evolutionary solution to the problem posed by the relatively large size of the mature brain and limitations on the size of the birth canal. In a sense, human beings are born prematurely. As Shore observes, the implications for the nature of mind are profound. Fully three-quarters of the human brain develops outside the womb, in direct relationship with an external environment which is saturated with human interaction, saturated with culture and with language. '[A]n important part of the evolutionary heritage of the sapient hominid is a nervous system that has evolved under the sway of *a* culture (in general) and which develops in each individual under the sway of *a* culture (in particular)' (Shore 1996: 4). This was brilliantly anticipated by Geertz: '*the human brain is thoroughly dependent upon cultural resources for its very operation*; and those resources are, consequently, not adjuncts to, but constituents of, mental activity' (1975: 76; emphasis in original).

REFERENCES

ALLAN, KEITH. 1986. *Linguistic Meaning*. London: Routledge & Kegan Paul.

BESNIER, NIKO. 1994. 'Involvement in linguistic practice: an ethnographic appraisal'. *Journal of Pragmatics*, 22: 279–99.

BLAKE, BARRY. 1994. *Case*. Cambridge: Cambridge University Press.

BOURDIEU, PIERRE. 1977. *Outline of a Theory of Practice*, trans. by Richard Nice. Cambridge: Cambridge University Press.

CLANCY, PATRICIA. 1986. 'The acquisition of communicative style in Japanese'. In Bambi B. Schieffelin and Elinor Ochs (eds.), *Language Socialization across Cultures*. Cambridge: Cambridge University Press, 213–50.

D'ANDRADE, ROY. 1995. *The Development of Cognitive Anthropology*. Cambridge: Cambridge University Press.

DIXON, R. M. W. 1991. *A New Approach to English Grammar, on Semantic Principles*. Oxford: Clarendon Press.

DOI, TAKEO. 1974. 'Some psychological themes in Japanese human relationships'. In J. C. Condon and M. Saito (eds.), *Intercultural Encounters with Japan: Communication—Contact and Conflict*. Tokyo: Simul, 17–26.

DURANTI, ALESSANDRO. 1990. 'Politics and grammar: agency in Samoan political discourse'. *American Ethnologist*, 17.4: 646–66.

——1997. *Linguistic Anthropology*. Cambridge: Cambridge University Press.

EADES, DIANA. 1982. 'You gotta know how to talk . . .: information seeking in South-East Queensland Aboriginal society'. *Australian Journal of Linguistics*, 2.1: 61–82.

ENFIELD, N. J. 2000a. 'On linguocentrism'. In Martin Pütz and Marjolijn Verspoor (eds.), *Explorations in Linguistic Relativity*. Amsterdam: John Benjamins, 125–57.

——2000b. 'The theory of cultural logic: how individuals combine social intelligence with semiotics to create and maintain cultural meaning'. *Cultural Dynamics*, 12.1: 35–64.

EVANS, NICHOLAS, and WILKINS, DAVID P. 2000. 'In the mind's ear: the semantic extensions of perception verbs in Australian languages'. *Language*, 76.3: 546–92.

FOLEY, WILLIAM A. 1997. *Anthropological Linguistics*. Oxford: Blackwell.

GALKINA-FEDORUK, E. 1958. *Bezličnye predloženija v sovremennom russkom jazyke*. Moscow: Moscow University Press.

GEERTZ, CLIFFORD. 1975. *The Interpretation of Cultures*. London: Hutchinson.

——1979. *Meaning and Order in Moroccan Society: Three Essays in Cultural Analysis*. Cambridge: Cambridge University Press.

GIVÓN, TALMY. 1979. *On Understanding Grammar*. New York: Academic Press.

GODDARD, CLIFF. 1997. 'Cultural values and cultural scripts in Malay (Bahasa Melayu)'. *Journal of Pragmatics*, 27.2: 183–201.

——1998. *Semantic Analysis: A Practical Introduction*. Oxford: Oxford University Press.

——In press. 'Whorf meets Wierzbicka: variation and universals in language and thinking'. *Language Sciences*. (Earlier version delivered at the 5th International Cognitive Linguistics Conference, Amsterdam, 19 July 1997.)

——To appear. 'Verbal explication and the place of NSM semantics in cognitive linguistics'. In June Luchjenbroers (ed.), *Cognitive Linguistics: Investigations across Languages, Fields, and Philosophical Boundaries*.

——and WIERZBICKA, ANNA (eds.). 1994. *Semantic and Lexical Universals: Theory and Empirical Findings*. Amsterdam: John Benjamins.

GODDARD, CLIFF, and WIERZBICKA, ANNA. 1997. 'Discourse and culture'. In Teun A. van Dijk (ed.), *Discourse as Social Process*. London: Sage Publications, 231–57.
——— ———(eds.). In press. *Meaning and Universal Grammar: Theory and Empirical Findings*. Amsterdam: John Benjamins.
GRICE, H. Paul 1975. 'Logic and conversation'. In Peter Cole and Jerry L. Morgan (eds.), *Speech Acts*. New York: Academic Press, 41–58.
HANKS, WILLIAM F. 1996. *Language and Communicative Practices*. Boulder, Colo.: Westview Press.
HASPELMATH, MARTIN. 1989. 'From purposive to infinitive: a universal path of grammaticalization'. *Folia Linguistica Historica*, 10: 287–310.
HEINE, BERND, CLAUDI, ULRIKE, and HÜNNEMEYER, FRIEDERIEKE. 1991. *Grammaticalization: A Conceptual Framework*. Chicago: Chicago University Press.
HOPPER, PAUL J., and TRAUGOTT, ELIZABETH CLOSS. 1993. *Grammaticalization*. Cambridge: Cambridge University Press.
IRVINE, JUDITH T. 1979. 'Formality and informality in communicative events'. *American Anthropologist*, 81.4: 773–90.
JAKOBSON, ROMAN. 1971. *Selected Writings*, ii: *Word and Language*. The Hague: Mouton.
JESPERSEN, OTTO. 1964. *Essentials of English Grammar*. Tuscaloosa: University of Alabama Press.
JOHNSON, MARK. 1987. *The Body in the Mind*. Chicago: Chicago University Press.
KEMPSON, RUTH. 1977. *Semantic Theory*. Cambridge: Cambridge University Press.
LANGACKER, RONALD W. 1987. *Foundations of Cognitive Grammar*, vol i. Stanford, Calif.: Stanford University Press.
LANGER, SUSANNE K. 1951. *Philosophy in a New Key*. Cambridge, Mass.: Harvard University Press (first pub. 1942).
LÉVI-STRAUSS, CLAUDE. 1963. *Structural Anthropology*. New York: Basic Books.
LOVEDAY, L. J. 1982. 'Communicative interference: a framework for contrastively analysing L2 communicative competence exemplified with the linguistic behaviour of Japanese performing in English'. *International Review of Applied Linguistics*, 20.1: 1–16.
MOSER, DAVID. 1997. 'Differences in abstract theories in Greek and Chinese philosophy: evidence of language effects'. Paper delivered at 5th International Cognitive Linguistics Conference, 14–19 July 1997. Vrije Universiteit, Amsterdam.
ORTNER, SHERRY B. 1984. 'Theory in anthropology since the sixties'. *Comparative Studies in Society and History*, 26: 126–66.
PEIRCE, CHARLES SANDERS. 1931. 'Speculative Grammar'. In Charles Hartshorne and Paul Weiss (eds.), *The Collected Papers of Charles Sanders Peirce*. Cambridge, Mass.: Belknap Press of Harvard University Press, 129–269.
SHORE, BRADD. 1996. *Culture in Mind: Cognition, Culture and the Problem of Meaning*. Oxford: Oxford University Press.
SILVERSTEIN, MICHAEL. 1976. 'Shifters, linguistic categories, and cultural description'. In Keith H. Basso and Henry A. Selby (eds.), *Meaning in Anthropology*. Albuquerque: University of New Mexico Press, 11–55.
———1977. 'Cultural prerequisites to grammatical analysis'. In M. Saville-Troike (ed.), *Linguistics and Anthropology*. Washington, DC: Georgetown University Press, 139–51.
SØRENSEN, HOLGER STEEN. 1963. *The Meaning of Proper Names*. Copenhagen: Gad.
SPERBER, DAN. 1984. 'Anthropology and psychology: towards an epidemiology of representations'. *Man*, 20: 73–89.

——*Explaining Culture: A Naturalistic Approach.* Oxford: Blackwell.

STRATHERN, ANDREW J. 1996. *Body Thoughts.* Ann Arbor: University of Michigan Press.

TRAUGOTT, ELIZABETH CLOSS. 1988. 'Pragmatic strengthening and grammaticalization'. In Shelley Axmaker, Annie Jaisser, and Helen Singmaster (eds.), *Proceedings of the Fourteenth Annual Meeting of the Berkeley Linguistics Society,* 406–16.

——and KÖNIG, EKKEHARD. 1991. 'The semantics–pragmatics of grammaticalization revisited'. In Elizabeth C. Traugott and Bernd Heine (eds.), *Approaches to Grammaticalization,* vol. i. Amsterdam: John Benjamins, 189–218.

VARELA, F., THOMPSON, E., and ROSCH, E. 1991. *The Embodied Mind: Cognitive Science and Human Experience.* Cambridge, Mass.: MIT Press.

WIERZBICKA, ANNA. 1976. 'In defense of YOU and ME'. In Wolfgang Girke and Helmut Jachnow (eds.), *Theoretische Linguistik in Osteuropa.* Tübingen: Max Niemeyer Verlag, 1–21.

——1979. 'Ethno-syntax and the philosophy of grammar'. *Studies in Language,* 3.3: 313–83.

——1980. *Lingua Mentalis: The Semantics of Natural Language.* Sydney: Academic.

——1988. *The Semantics of Grammar.* Amsterdam: John Benjamins.

——1991. *Cross-Cultural Pragmatics: The Semantics of Human Interaction.* Berlin: Mouton de Gruyter.

——1992. *Semantics, Culture and Cognition.* Oxford: Oxford University Press.

——1996*a*. *Semantics: Primes and Universals.* Oxford: Oxford University Press.

——1996*b*. 'Contrastive sociolinguistics and the theory of "cultural scripts": Chinese vs. English'. In Marlis Hellinger and Ulrich Ammon (eds.), *Contrastive Sociolinguistics.* Berlin: Mouton de Gruyter, 313–44.

——1996*c*. 'Japanese cultural scripts: Cultural psychology and "cultural grammar"'. *Ethos,* 24.3: 527–55.

——1997. *Understanding Cultures through their Key Words: English, Russian, Polish, German, Japanese.* New York: Oxford University Press.

——1998. 'The semantics of English causative constructions in a universal-typological perspective'. In Michael Tomasello (ed.), *The New Psychology of Language: Cognitive and Functional Approaches to Language Structure.* Hillsdale, NJ: Lawrence Erlbaum, 113–53.

WILKINS, DAVID P. 1991. 'The semantics, pragmatics and diachronic development of "associated motion" in Mparntwe Arrernte'. *Buffalo Working Papers in Linguistics,* 207–57.

——and HILL, DEBORAH. 1995. 'When "go" means "come": questioning the basicness of basic motion verbs'. *Cognitive Linguistics,* 6.2/3: 209–59.

WITTGENSTEIN, LUDWIG. 1922. *Tractatus Logico-Philosophicus,* trans. by C. K. Ogden. London: Routledge (first pub. in German 1921).

4

Culture, Cognition, and the Grammar
of 'Give' Clauses

JOHN NEWMAN

4.1. INTRODUCTION

Investigations into ethnosyntax may take different forms. The most obvious one, perhaps, would be to select linguistic examples from a wide variety of morpho-syntactic phenomena (argument structure, tense, possession, demonstratives, etc.) and argue for the relevance of cultural or social factors in motivating the phenomena. In this chapter, however, I follow a different approach. I choose one specific domain, namely 'give' clauses, and consider a variety of linguistic facts about such clauses across languages and the extent to which one can successfully motivate aspects of this structure by appeal to broad cultural and social factors. I report therefore not just on the facts which lend support to the idea of ethnosyntax, but also on some facts about 'give' clauses which appear independent of any cultural or social factors. While this study has as its focus 'give' clauses, the approach could be extended to any number of phenomena.

'Give' clauses are a particularly interesting subject of study because of the relative complexity of the events they encode (cf. the full discussion of the semantics of 'give' events in Newman 1996: 33–60). A key fact about the giving-event is that it typically refers to events involving three participants: the giver, the thing transferred, and the recipient. A moment's reflection on the interactions between these entities will reveal how varied and complex these interactions are. Among other things, there is an interaction between a giver and a recipient; an interaction between the giver and the thing; an interaction between the recipient and the thing; a change of possession; physical movement of a thing; causation. The diversity and complexity in the syntax and semantics of 'give' clauses cross-linguistically are reflections of the internal complexity of the giving-event itself. In what follows, I explore the extent to which the structure of 'give' clauses may be motivated by cultural and cognitive factors. The linguistic data that underlie this research have been drawn from various languages as part of an ongoing research project explor-

I would like to express my appreciation to Nick Enfield for comments on an earlier draft of this chapter.

ing the syntax and semantics of 'basic' verbs. The chapters of Newman (1998) have also been a source of relevant data for the present study.

As background to the present discussion, it is appropriate to clarify the nature of the relationship between language, culture, and cognition which is here assumed. My approach to linguistic analysis has been very much shaped and guided by the Cognitive Linguistics movement in general (as exemplified by Lakoff 1987) and by the ideas of Cognitive Grammar (as exemplified by Langacker 1987, 1990, 1991) in particular. As both these labels suggest, particular interest and emphasis are given to aspects of human cognition in these approaches. Linguistic analyses of clause structure, for example, will typically involve some reference to cognitive notions such as mental imagery, figure–ground perspectives, alternative ways of conceptualizing scenes, etc. With such an emphasis on cognition, which is thought of as located in an individual, one might wonder how 'culture' can be accommodated when culture is thought of more as a feature of a group rather than an individual. I follow Langacker (1994) in my thinking about this issue and the relationship between language, culture, and cognition in general. Cognition is seen as a necessary prerequisite for any meaningful linguistic or cultural reality. Human language and culture can only exist at all because of the human minds that bring them into existence. Thus, language and culture are seen as facets of cognition rather than being totally independent of it. Furthermore, language and culture are seen as overlapping, rather than being independent of each other. The lexicon is an obvious part of language where one can see a reflection of culture, but there are other, more grammatical aspects of a language which can also reflect cultural norms and expectations. The centrality of culture is explicitly acknowledged by Langacker (1994: 31): 'Cognitive linguistic theories recognize cultural knowledge as the foundation not just of lexicon, but central facets of grammar as well.' While this idea may appear rather unusual, even idiosyncratic, in the context of some contemporary linguistic theorizing, it is a very familiar position in the context of more anthropologically or socially oriented research (Duranti 1997: 23–50; Foley 1997: 3–40), succinctly summed up in the formulation 'one should think of language *in* culture and not just of language *and* culture' (Duranti 1997: 336, following Hoijer 1953). This is a viewpoint which pervades the present volume.

For the purposes of the present discussion, I distinguish the following three categories of 'give' phenomena and I will discuss each in turn:

(1) *a*. Aspects of 'give' clause structure which are determined by broad cognitive principles and have substantial cross-linguistic and cross-cultural validity.
  b. Aspects of 'give' clause structure which reflect an orientation or perspective with significance in the larger culture and are culture- and language-specific.
  c. Aspects of 'give' clause structure which have a special significance within a particular language system, but (apparently) do not reflect larger cultural, non-linguistic values.

While making these distinctions, I do not claim that it is always a straightforward matter to assign aspects of clause structure to one or the other of these categories. The (*b*) category, whereby linguistic and cultural facts are argued to be interrelated, raises many issues concerning the nature and degree of the influence of culture on language (assuming, that is, that one can successfully separate language and culture, cf. Enfield 2000: 141–4): an influence from historically prior time versus influence which is demonstrable in a synchronic way; multiple influences giving rise to a single linguistic result; a single cultural phenomenon with multiple linguistic correlates, etc. One must acknowledge, too, a certain 'linguocentric' disposition in much cognitive and cultural enquiry, i.e. a tendency to approach and understand issues in terms of language as opposed to non-linguistic systems (cf. Enfield 2000: 150 n. 2). This may be a natural, even unavoidable, tendency but it can result in overstating the significance of a cultural or social concept just because the concept has a direct linguistic exponent. Another problem is the directionality of influence where one has determined a language–cognition or language–culture parallelism. Is it a matter of the language determining the non-linguistic phenomenon or vice versa? This is by no means easy to answer in all cases, though in the present discussion I deal with relatively specific linguistic structures which seem more likely to be the result of broader non-linguistic phenomena rather than the other way around.

4.2. CLAUSE STRUCTURE DETERMINED BY BROAD COGNITIVE PRINCIPLES

One may begin with the question of possible universal features in the encoding of giving-events. I would take such universal features to reflect cognitive or biological predispositions of humans. The focus here is on linguistic universals which reflect cognitive predispositions and in Sections 4.2.1 and 4.2.2 below I discuss some possible candidates.

4.2.1. *'Give' as a verbal category*

One might suggest, for example, that each language will have some basic verb which expresses a concept with a meaning like that described above for the giving-event. In other words, languages might be expected to have a verbal word (roughly, if not precisely) translatable as 'give'. Admittedly, the verbal word for 'give' in some languages may carry nuances which are absent in the case of English *give*. One thinks, for example, of the many verbs translatable as 'give' in Cora, as discussed by Casad (1998), reflecting the many different components of the 'give' event which may be highlighted by a speaker. Despite differences in the semantic nuances attaching to 'give' verbs, as well as some syntactic and morphological differences between 'give' constructions in languages, one does normally find some verbal word with the sense of 'give' in clauses depicting giving-events.

The existence of a 'give' verb is not universal, however, since there are languages where a verbal stem meaning 'give' appears to be lacking. Instead, affixes which normally attach to verb stems such as tense, aspect, mood, verb agreement, etc. appear merely as a string of affixes without any verb root in the word. Amele, a Papuan language spoken near Madang in Papua New Guinea and described in Roberts (1987), is a case in point. Examples of the Amele encoding of giving-events are shown in (2).

(2) *a. Naus Dege ho ut-en.*
    Naus Dege pig 3SG.IO-3SG.SUBJ.PAST
    'Naus gave Dege the pig.' (Roberts 1987: 34)
  b. Ija dana leis sab al-ig-a.
    I   man two food 3DU.IO-1SG.SUBJ-PAST
    'I gave the two men food.' (Roberts 1987: 316)

Compare these sentences with a normal three-place predicate like *ihac* 'show' in (3). PRED in (3) refers to a predicate marker *i*, which occurs between a verb stem and a following oblique-marking or indirect object-marking affix. In (3) it appears after the verb stem *ihac* 'show' and before the indirect object.

(3) *Jo   eu ihac-i-ad-ig-en.*
    house that show-PRED-2PL.IO-1SG.SUBJ-FUT
    'I will show that house to you (plural).' (Roberts 1987: 69)

Since the indirect object affixes appear in a position after the verb stem, I analyse the verbs in (2) as beginning with a 'give' stem, realized as a zero morph, followed by the indirect object affixes. This is, in fact, the analysis implicit in Roberts (1987) where 'give' is translated as the zero morph in the dictionary section of the grammar.

The decomposition of 'give' forms can be more fully appreciated in Tables 4.1 and 4.2, adapted from Roberts (1998). Table 4.1 compares the indirect object suffixes used with an indirect object marking verb *siwitoc* 'to share' with the corresponding parts of the 'give' forms, the relevant parts being shown in bold. The *-ec/-oc* in these forms is the infinitival marker. It can be seen that the affixes are identical, for the most part. Roberts (1998: 5) notes that there is some variation in Amele verbs between *-it* and *-ut* affixes for the 3SG, and we do indeed see such variation in Table 4.1. Note also that a PRED *-i* vowel may occur after the verb stem in the case of 'share'. One could analyse all the 'share' forms as having this *-i* suffix after the stem. The suffixes *-it*, *-ih*, *-ig*, when they follow this underlying *-i*, trigger a reduction of the two *i* vowels to one. Table 4.2 illustrates direct object marking in the case of the verb *helec* 'to throw', compared with the forms of 'give'. *Helec* can take direct object and/or indirect object affixes, but the forms shown here contain the direct object affixes. Here one sees a perfect match of affixes in the two columns. As mentioned above, the PRED vowel only appears between a stem and indirect object or oblique affixes, hence the absence in Table 4.2 of the PRED *-i* vowel after the stem *helec*, in contrast to Table 4.1.

TABLE 4.1. Indirect object suffixes in Amele 'share' and 'give'

IO suffix	*siwitoc* 'to share'	zero stem 'to give'
1SG	siw-**it**-ec	**it**-ec
	'to share with me'	'to give to me'
2SG	siw-**ih**-ec	**ih**-ec
	'to share with you.SG'	'to give to you.SG'
3SG	siw-**it**-oc	**ut**-ec
	'to share with him/her'	'to give to him/her'
1PL	siw-**ig**-ec	**ig**-ec
	'to share with us'	'to give to us'
2PL	siw-i-**ad**-ec	**ad**-ec
	'to share with you.PL'	'to give to you.PL'
3PL	siw-i-**ad**-ec	**ad**-ec
	'to share with them'	'to give to them'

TABLE 4.2. Direct object suffixes in Amele 'throw' and 'give'

DO suffix	*helec* 'to throw'	zero stem 'to give to him/her'
1SG	hel-**t**-ec	ut-**t**-ec
	'to throw me'	'to give me to him/her'
2SG	hel-**h**-ec	ut-**h**-ec
	'to throw you.SG'	'to give you.SG to him/her'
3SG	hel-**ud**-ec	ut-**ud**-ec
	'to throw him/her/it'	'to give him/her/it to him/her'
1PL	hel-**g**-ec	ut-**g**-ec
	'to throw us'	'to give us to him/her'
2PL	hel-**ad**-ec	ut-**ad**-ec
	'to throw you.PL'	'to give you.PL to him/her'
3PL	hel-**ad**-ec	ut-**ad**-ec
	'to throw them'	'to give them to him/her'

An important difference between the shape of 'give' words and other verbs in Amele is the difference in relative ordering of the direct object and indirect object prefixes when both are present. With verbs like *helec* 'to throw', the order is DO–IO, whereas in the case of 'give' the order is IO–DO. This is illustrated in (4).

(4) *a. hel-**ad**-**ih**-ec*
      throw-3PL.DO-2SG.IO-infinitive
      'to throw them to you.SG'
    *b. **ut**-**ad**-ec*
      3SG.IO-3PL.DO-infinitive
      'to give them to him/her'

This difference in the order of the IO and DO morphemes shows that the 'give' forms can not simply be described as 'stem-less' variants of three-place predicate verbal forms. Considerations such as this, and some other facts, lead Roberts (1998) to suggest that the 'give' forms should not be analysed as simply containing a zero morph stem. Rather, it is argued, the erstwhile IO morpheme now functions as a new 'give' stem. Under this analysis, *ut* in (4*b*) would be treated as a stem with the meaning 'to give to him/her' and there is only one object suffix, the DO suffix *-ad*. The DO suffix now follows the stem *ut* and is in accordance with the general rules of morpheme ordering in Amele verbs. This may prove the most expedient way to analyse the data from the point of view of satisfying morpheme order constraints, but it does have some uncomfortable consequences. As Roberts (1998) points out, it means there are 343 infinitival forms for 'give' in Amele, taking into account all the possible inflectional categories! So, it is not obvious just what the ideal analysis of these data would be. Nevertheless, it remains true that in many cases, such as (2) above, the words translatable as 'give' appear on the surface to lack a 'give' verb stem. The Amele facts therefore cast some doubt on any universal claim about the presence of a 'give' verb in all languages. Such a claim must be qualified to allow for zero morphs to function as 'give' stem.[1] While there may be alternative ways to analyse these zero morphs, the alternative analyses involve considerable increase in complexity of allomorphy.

It is interesting to reflect on these unusual facts. The realization of a 'give' stem/root as a zero morph (at least on some level of analysis) reflects, I maintain, the basicness of the giving act in our everyday experiential reality. The 'give' clauses in these languages mark overtly, through the presence of an NP and/or through verb marking, the entities involved in the act: the giver, the thing transferred, and the recipient. These key participants appear as core NPs or are indicated by the verb affixes. The act of giving is a very salient and obvious feature of our lives, a basic act occurring between humans, and this obviousness and basicness are relevant to understanding why a verb stem 'give' is not used in these languages. One does expect the giving-idea to correspond to a verbal morpheme in languages and this is so in the overwhelming majority of languages. Exceptions to this, as in Amele, exist because of a quite separate tendency, namely, that experiential basicness corresponds to a more basic kind of linguistic form.[2]

4.2.2. *Figure–ground asymmetries*

Another type of universal which one might seek out is a cognitive predisposition to a particular figure–ground structure which we impose on the giving-event. The terms 'figure' and 'ground' have slightly different meanings depending upon the

---

[1] Interestingly, a similar situation holds in the Amerindian language Koasati (Louisiana). Kimball (1991: 102) notes that the verb 'give' in Koasati is defective in not having any root.

[2] The experiential basicness of the giving-event is distinct from the internal complexity of the event. The two properties of giving—experiential basicness and internal complexity—have different consequences for linguistic encoding. Cf. Newman (1996: 33–4).

context (visual or auditory, dynamic versus static scenes, etc.). In a very general, schematic sense, 'figure' is understood as referring to some part of a scene which 'stands out' compared with some other part(s), which we may call the 'ground'. In Cognitive Grammar, clause structure is also construed as involving a figure–ground organization, with the subject of a clause understood as a particular type of relational figure (cf. Langacker 1991: 312, 319). Thus, in describing possible grammatical subjects of 'give'-type clauses, one is also describing possible figure–ground perspectives.

We may note that all three entities involved in a transferral event may function as the subject (='figure' in the Cognitive Grammar sense). Even within English, we find these three possibilities with transferral events, as in (5).

(5) *a. The teacher {gave, distributed, donated} the books to the students.*
    b. The student {accepted, received} the book award from the dean.
    c. This house has changed hands numerous times.

Despite the grammatical possibilities illustrated in (5), there would appear to be a cognitive preference for the perspective associated with verbs such as *give, distribute, donate*, etc. which have the giver as the subject in the active voice. A relevant piece of research suggesting this is the work of Sridhar (1988: 25, 57–60) who investigated linguistic encodings, cross-linguistically, of subjects' perceptions of miscellaneous scenes. The relevant scenes for our purposes involved a variety of actions, such as a man rolling a ball on a table, a man putting a ball on a plate, a woman rolling a ball to a man, a man giving a ball back to a woman, etc. (Although giving was included in the actions portrayed in the scenes used for Sridhar's study, the author does not give specific results on the descriptions of this action.) In an elaborate and original experiment, these action scenes were shown to 300 under-graduate students from ten different language–culture communities around the world and the students were asked to describe each scene in a simple sentence. A significant result (one of many) of this study concerned the number of students who described the scene with a construction in which the source of the action occurs as the grammatical subject of its clause. In all, 280 of the students (= 93.3 per cent) described the scene in this way. In other words, in describing actions, people tend to take the perspective of the source of the action. In the giving-type of event, the giver is the source of the action and, on the basis of Sridhar's findings, a 'give' verb with the giver as the subject would be the most cognitively natural way

TABLE 4.3. Subject/object asymmetries in English 'give' clauses

a. giver$_{SUBJ}$ and thing$_{OBJ}$	c. *thing$_{SUBJ}$ and giver$_{OBJ}$
I gave the book to Lee.	—
b. giver$_{SUBJ}$ and recipient$_{OBJ}$	d. *recipient$_{SUBJ}$ and giver$_{OBJ}$
I presented the student (with) a book	—

of describing the scene. This does not exclude the possibility of alternative ways of describing a transferral scene, as in (5*b*) and (5*c*), but these would appear to be less preferred ways, all else being equal.

Consistent with Sridhar's findings, we have subject–object possibilities with 'give'-type verbs in English where the giver is the subject, as shown in (*a*) and (*b*) of Table 4.3. But we do not have the subject–object possibilities shown as (*c*) and (*d*). An example for (*c*) in Table 4.3 would have to be something like *The book bniked the dean to me*, meaning 'the dean gave, awarded, presented the book to me'. There are no verbs like that in English or any other language as far as I am aware. Soldiers can abandon one leader and desert to another, but this would not be an act of giving, since the transference is not initiated and willed by the ex-leader. (*d*) would be an example like *The student bniked the teacher* (*with, of,* etc.) *a book*, meaning 'The teacher gave the student a book.' Again, this does not exist in English or in other languages, as far as I am aware with the meaning intended. My focus here, I should emphasize, is on the giving, not the receiving or taking of a thing. In particular, I am not dealing here with 'receive' or 'take' verbs which can, in fact, appear in the (*d*) type structure. Thus, *The student*$_{SUBJ}$ *received/took the teacher*$_{OBJ}$ (*with, of,* etc.) *a book* is possible in some languages, either as a basic double object construction, or as an applicative construction. In Zulu, for example, 'take' verbs can appear in a double object construction like this, with the taker as the subject, the person from whom something is taken as the primary object, and the thing taken as the secondary object (cf. Taylor 1998: 75, 82–7).

The possibility and impossibility of these patterns can therefore be motivated by broad cognitive considerations. In the giving-event, we construe the giver as the source of the action and the giver tends to be encoded in the preferred way we encode sources of actions generally, namely, as the subject of a clause (in the active voice).

4.3. CLAUSE STRUCTURE DETERMINED BY LARGER CULTURAL FORCES

We turn now to a consideration of linguistic phenomena relating to 'give' clauses which appear to reflect pervasive cultural facts. These are the phenomena which one would be most inclined to describe as 'ethnosyntactic'. One turns naturally to a consideration of relatively major cultural themes as motivating factors behind language (cf. Enfield 2000: 150; Burridge, this volume). Ideally, one would like to follow the example of studies such as those of Wierzbicka (1992)—for instance, her detailed motivation of a variety of Russian syntactic constructions by appeal to deep and recurring themes of Russian culture and 'the Russian national psyche' (Wierzbicka 1992: 395–441). She establishes not only a convergence of a number of distinct, yet interrelated, themes, but also their manifestation across the language in a variety of syntactic construction types. This approach requires considerable insight into both language and culture, something which is not so easily attained when one is working cross-linguistically with languages and cultures known only, or mainly, through the published literature. Nevertheless, the literature relating to 'give' and acts of giving does contain some relevant discussion.

Dixon's (1973: 206–7, 210) discussion of meanings of the various 'give'-type verbs in the Australian language Dyirbal compared with English is one example of this kind of phenomenon. In Dyirbal, there are 'give'-type verbs which are differentiated in terms of position and movement, and kinship obligation, but not in terms of commercial significance. For example, *wugan* involves giving where there is no significant movement by the participants. It would be used for handing an object to someone nearby. *Bilan* is used when there is significant movement, such as when the giver walks some distance to pass over the object. *Yuṟan* is used when the giving occurs through something else, such as passing an object through a window. *Gibin* means 'to provide food for relatives'. In English, on the other hand, there are specialized commercially oriented 'give'-type verbs involving money and contracts, like *donate, present, award, pay, lend, sell, rent*, etc.[3] These linguistic differences are quite reasonably seen as reflecting the different role of giving in the two societies. Japanese and Chipewyan provide additional and more fully discussed examples of a broad cultural influence on the language of giving, as summarized in the following sections.

4.3.1. *Japanese 'give' verbs*

The encoding of the giving-event in Japanese requires lexical choices for the verb which reflect something of the social order of Japanese society. In both popular and scholarly accounts of Japanese society, it is acknowledged that there is a pervasive behavioural pattern which one could loosely call 'respectfulness'. Every society has norms governing the etiquette to be observed in human interactions but Japanese society appears to have elaborated and refined its norms in a more striking way than most societies. One essential component of interactional behaviour is the relative status of the participants. The importance of social ranking in Japanese society has been discussed extensively, but it has been particularly well described in works such as Nakane (1970, 1972) who articulated the concept of 'verticality' as a larger organizing principle in social structure. This is an all-pervasive and profound aspect of Japanese society, according to Nakane, which underlies numerous patterns of social structure and personal behaviour. It refers to structures which emphasize the ranking of an individual or institution as higher or lower than other individuals/institutions, as opposed to emphasizing relationships between individuals/institutions as being on the same level. The principle of verticality

---

[3] These verbs show differences in argument structure (*donate money to a hospital*, **donate a hospital money*, **donate a hospital with money*; *present an award to someone*, **present someone an award*, *present someone with an award*, etc.). I do not attempt to motivate these differences in terms of any cultural factors.

emphasizes higher versus lower rank and this can manifest itself in many diverse ways (see Nakane 1970: 25–40 for discussion and examples). Quotes such as the following show its importance for Nakane:

It is because of this rigidity and stability that are produced by ranking that the latter functions as the principal controlling factor of social relations in Japan. The basic orientation of the social order permeates every aspect of society, far beyond the limits of the institutionalised group. This ranking order, in effect, regulates Japanese life. (Nakane 1970: 29–30)

Since ranking order appears so regularly in such essential aspects of daily life, the Japanese cannot help but be made extremely conscious of it. In fact, this consciousness is so strong that official rank is easily extended into private life. (Nakane 1970: 33)

One should note that Nakane's analysis is much more subtle than these isolated quotes might suggest—there are exceptions and there are other competing principles which play a part.[4] While Nakane presents a rather academic analysis of this phenomenon, observations about the importance of social rank are by no means restricted to academic discussion. It features as an aspect of Japanese society in many of the more popular discussions, as in the discussion of 'the tao of status' in March (1996: 103–10). It is, in other words, a relatively obvious emphasis in Japanese society.

The act of giving clearly involves human interaction in so far as it involves both a giver and a recipient in its situational frame and, as such, is subject to the same kinds of considerations which apply in human interactions in the society at large. In particular, in constructing a Japanese GIVE clause, establishing the relative status of the human participants is a necessary prerequisite to making an appropriate choice of verb. The reader is referred to Loveday (1986: 57–78) and Aoyagi (1995) for a full discussion of how relative status as well as other factors are relevant to the expression of GIVE in Japanese. Figs. 4.1–4.3, adapted from Loveday (1986), summarize the basic set of choices for GIVE verbs, without attempting to express all the complexity in the actual use of this system. It can be seen that it is also relevant to clarify whether the speaker of the GIVE utterance is the giver, recipient, or neither (or, more correctly, whether the speaker identifies himself/herself as belonging to the same sociocultural group as giver or recipient, as discussed by Loveday).

---

[4] Quite a different appraisal of the Japanese situation may be found in Mizutani (1981: 121–6) who acknowledges the reality of 'higher' versus 'lower' ranking in Japanese life, but accords it less significance than Nakane. Thus: 'we can say that Japanese culture and the Japanese way of thinking is not fundamentally based on higher and lower relations; Japan is not a vertical society characterized by primarily vertical relationships. Rather the pull and responsiveness toward lateral relations is the fundamental dynamic in Japan' (Mizutani 1981: 139). It is not my purpose to resolve the difference in Nakane's and Mizutani's perspectives. It is sufficient to note that both authors acknowledge ranking, or the vertical principle, as a significant fact of Japanese society. The ranking implicit in the use of the different 'give' verbs manifests the vertical principle, whether or not one takes it to be the most fundamental principle of Japanese societal organization.

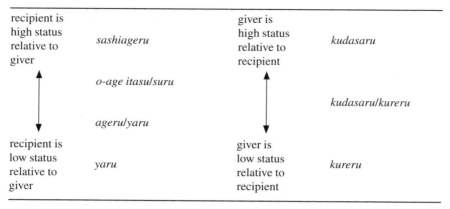

FIG. 4.1. Japanese 'give' verbs used
when speaker identifies with the giver

FIG. 4.2. Japanese 'give' verbs used when
speaker identifies with the recipient

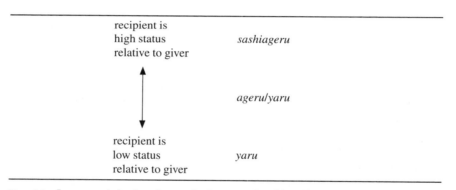

FIG. 4.3. Japanese 'give' verbs used when speaker identifies with neither giver
nor recipient

The verbs in Fig. 4.1 are the appropriate ones to be used when the speaker
identifies with the giver, as in *My daughter gave the university lecturer a camera*,
where *my daughter* is the participant with whom I identify. Fig. 4.2 verbs are used
when the speaker identifies with the recipient, as in *The university lecturer gave
my daughter a camera*. Fig. 4.3 verbs are used when the speaker identifies with
neither of the participants, as in *The student gave the university lecturer a camera*.
There is some overlap between the verbs in Fig. 4.1 and 4.3, which is to say that
the 'default' set of verbs, used when there is no speaker identification with the
participants in the act of giving, is based on the set used when the speaker identi-

fies with the giver.⁵ The concepts of 'identification with giver' and 'identification with recipient' in this context are by no means simple, and various discourse and pragmatic factors may influence a decision to adopt one of the three perspectives. My main interest here, however, lies in the choice between the verbs within each of the three sets, where the appropriate choice depends on the relative status of the giver and recipient, as perceived by the speaker. So, for example, among the verbs in Fig. 4.1, *sashiageru* is the appropriate one in translating a sentence such as *I gave the teacher a book* (the teacher being of higher status than the giver), but only *yaru* may be used in translating *I gave the dog a bone* (the dog being of lower status than the giver). The pair of sentences in (6) illustrates some of these points. In (6*a*), the speaker identifies with, indeed *is* the subject referent, and so the appropriate verb set is that in Fig. 4.1. Since the recipient has high status compared with the giver, *sashiageru* is appropriate. In (6*b*), on the other hand, the speaker identifies with the recipient, so one must choose amongst the set of verbs in Fig. 4.2. Again, since the teacher has higher status than I have, the appropriate verb to use is *kudasaru*.

(6) *a. Watashi wa   sensei ni   hon o   sashiage-mashita.*
     I   TOPIC teacher DAT book ACC give-PAST
     'I gave the teacher a book.'
   b. Sensei ga   watashi ni   hon o   kudasai-mashita.
      teacher NOM me   DAT book ACC give-PAST
      'The teacher gave me a book.'

In Japanese, then, the directionality encoded in the verbs is based on a concept of social verticality, where the speaker must take into account the relative positions of giver and recipient along a vertical social scale. It is significant that the first syllable of *ageru* (which also appears in *sashiageru*), used as the middle-range verb when the speaker gives to others, is written with the Kanji character 上 'up'. The first syllable of *kudasaru*, on the other hand, used as the middle-range verb when others give to the speaker, is written with 下 'down'. While these verbs are native Japanese words and not derived from Chinese, the choice of these particular Kanji characters in these instances may be seen as reflecting a consciousness about a vertical orientation in the society. Hence, giving to others is, through the graphical association, construed as giving upwards while receiving from others is construed as giving downwards to the speaker.

⁵ Another way of describing this state of affairs is to say that the forms in Fig. 4.2 are used with the speaker (or first person) as recipient, while the forms in Figs. 4.1 and 4.3 are used with someone other than the speaker (i.e. second or third person) as recipient. See Greenberg (1993: 12) for some discussion of 'give' verbs distinguished by the person of the recipient in Japanese, Dravidian, and Nile Nubian languages.

4.3.2. *Chipewyan classifier verbs*

Chipewyan (Canada, Athapaskan) provides particularly interesting data relating to 'give'-type words. Part of the interest lies in the classificatory system. This system subcategorizes things handled in the giving-event and expresses this subcategorization through the 'give' verb stem. The 'give' verb stems are further interesting in the way in which they express the manner of interacting with the thing handled. Both these features of 'give' verbs have been argued to have connections with facts and behaviours outside the linguistic system.

The verbal word in Chipewyan is a relatively complex string of morphemes, as illustrated in (7). MOM refers to 'momentaneous aspect'.

(7)   *begháyéniłtį* <
      be-ghá-yé-n(e)-i-ł-tį
      3SG.OBL-to-3SG.OBJ-MOM-1SG.SUBJ-VOICE-PERF.**handle animate object**
      'I have given her to him.' (Rice 1998: 102, from Li 1946: 419.)

It is the final morpheme —the verb stem—which is of interest here. It is glossed as 'handle animate object' in the perfective aspect. Note that the 'animate object' sense is not represented by a separate affix, independently of the verb stem. Rather, the idea of animate object as the thing being handled is part of the meaning of the verb stem. The example illustrates, then, the use of a 'classifier verb stem' whereby the meaning of the verb stem incorporates a classification of the thing handled. The classification imposed on the thing being handled with such verbs is shown in Table 4.4.

TABLE 4.4. Object types distinguished by 'give'- and 'take'-like verbs

AO	animate objects: a baby, a person, a fish, a dog
RO	round or hard/compact objects: a ball, a radio, a coin, a penknife, one berry, one shoe, a ring
SO	stick-like object/empty container: a pen, scissors, a table, a chair, a key, a canoe, a car
FO	flat or flexible objects: a blanket, an article of clothing, a leaf, a pillow, a dollar bill
CC	object in closed container/bundled objects: a single large container (i.e. a box) and contents, a sack of flour, a pack of cigarettes, berries in a jar, a motionless train (in station)
PO	plural objects: a plurality of any of the above categories; rope, eyeglasses, keys, antlers, firewood
OC	object in open container: a pail of water, a plate of berries, tea in a cup, any food on a platter
MM	mushy matter: porridge, butter, mud
GO	granular object/object in heap: an amorphous mass of, e.g. hay, grain, sugar, gravel
UO	unspecified or generic object (for immediate consumption)

Source: Rice 1998.

The system of classifier verb stems briefly summarized above is relevant to a great many verbal predicates, including locational predicates 'sit', 'lie', etc. However, it is particularly striking as a feature of verbs referring to the handling of objects involving meanings such as: 'give', 'hand', 'take', 'put', 'handle', 'lower', 'pick up', 'bring', 'carry', 'misplace', etc. (examples of the 'controlled' sense, explained below); 'toss', 'throw', 'throw out/dispose of', 'hang up', 'set down', 'drop', 'lose', 'push over' (examples of the 'uncontrolled' sense, explained below). The classifier system is observed most extensively in the verbs of handling. Note that a number of the distinctions which the classifier system imposes on handled objects relates to properties associated with handling: granular versus mushy, closed versus open container. Basso (1968), in a study of the related Western Apache language, reports speakers explaining classifications relating to rigidity or flexibility in terms of handleability properties (as cited in Denny 1979: 107). Thus: 'The Apache consider an object to be rigid . . . if, when *held* at its edge or end, it does not bend' (Denny 1979: 107, my italics).

Denny argues for a possible connection between the classifier system of Athapaskan languages like Chipewyan and the environmental setting of the speakers. He describes Athapaskan languages (and Cree and Ojibwa amongst the Algonquian languages) as having a 'proximal' type of classification system. 'Proximal' here refers to a classification based on close contact with objects, especially through handling of objects. The speakers with the proximal system of classification traditionally live in forests of Canada. This is contrasted with a 'distal' type of classification, found in Toba (Guaykuran family) and Eskimo. In these languages, the classification system is based on distinctions such as 'in view' versus 'out of view', 'here' versus 'there', 'vertical' versus 'horizontal', 'out there' versus 'down there' versus 'in there', etc. Denny suggests that the latter system has a natural motivation in a context where interaction at a distance is central to their lifestyle. According to Denny (1979: 104), Eskimos and Tobas hunt in 'open' environments (treeless arctic coasts in the former, prairies of Argentinian Chaco in the latter).

The classification system evident in Table 4.4 accounts for only some of the complexity found with verb stems in Chipewyan. The verb stems relevant to transferral events reflect another pervasive distinction in Chipewyan relating to a 'controlled' versus 'uncontrolled' type of event. These terms are chosen to approximately indicate the semantics involved in the distinction. As explained by Rice (1998: 104): 'These notions are difficult to translate, but the gist of the difference is between careful, controlled, deliberate, respectful, polite, humble, reserved, gentle, or concerned behaviour and actions marked by rough or quick movement, or by a lack of care, reservation, or control.' A 'controlled' variant of a transferral verb stem will give rise to meanings translatable as 'give', 'hand to', 'take from', whereas an 'uncontrolled' variant of the verb stem might translate as 'give unwillingly', 'throw at', 'dump on', etc. 'Controlled' and 'uncontrolled' variants of the relevant transfer verbs are shown in Table 4.5. Note, for example, that the classi-

TABLE 4.5. Some Chipewyan classificatory verb stem forms

Category of thing handled etc.	'Controlled' transfer, 'give/hand/take'		'Uncontrolled' transfer, 'throw at/dump on' etc.	
	impf	perf	impf	perf
AO	-tį́	-tį	-ní	-na
RO	-ʔáih	-ʔą	-shuɬ	-shel
SO	-tį́	-tį	-xéɬ	-xes
FO	-chuth	-chúdh	-ʔar	-ʔar
CC	-ɬtį́	-ɬtą	-xel	-xes
OC	-ká	-ką	-niɬ	-nel
MM	-ɬé	-ɬe	—	—
GO	-dzai	-dzáy	-tsir	-tsir
PO	-le	-la	-deɬ	-del
UO	-chu	-chu	-chu	-chu

Source: Rice 1998.

fier verb stem used in example (7) above, -*ti*, belongs to the 'controlled' variants of 'handle animate object'. A further aspectual distinction of perfective versus imperfective is also manifested in each of the 'controlled' and 'uncontrolled' variants, and these aspectual variants are also shown.

The 'controlled' versus 'uncontrolled' distinction is claimed to have a larger cultural relevance. The 'controlled' type of event may be considered as one manifestation of a highly valued cultural attribute of Athapaskan communities, referred to in the Bearlake Athapaskan culture as *séodįt'é*. Rushforth and Chisholm (1991: 25–35, 146–8) discuss this phenomenon primarily with respect to Bearlake Athapaskan, but they see it as a feature of all the Athapaskan cultures, including Chipewyan (cf. also Rice 1989: 784). It refers to behaviour characterized by the terms mentioned above in connection with 'controlled' events (humble, reserved, gentle, etc.). In fact, Rushforth and Chisholm (1991: 25) see *séodit'é* as an all-encompassing, fundamental ideal of behaviour which motivates a number of other Athapaskan values and norms:

The relationship [of *séodįt'é* to the other beliefs, values, and norms] is based on the idea that pursuit and achievement of the *séodįt'é* ideal requires an individual to exhibit industriousness, generosity, personal autonomy, and restraint in his or her behaviour. To act otherwise (to display laziness, stinginess, bossiness, or unreasoned emotional outbursts) is to demonstrate a marked lack of control in and of one's life.   (Rushforth and Chisholm 1991: 34–5)

The existence of a 'controlled' versus 'uncontrolled' distinction in the verb system, particularly in the system of verbs describing transferral events, appears to reflect a pervasive and profound distinction in the culture at large.

4.4. CLAUSE STRUCTURE WHICH IS NOT OBVIOUSLY DETERMINED BY NON-LINGUISTIC FACTORS

4.4.1. *Maori directional morphemes*

As an example of a language-wide phenomenon *without* obvious correlates in larger cultural patterns, consider the Maori directional morphemes *mai* 'hither (to speaker)' and *atu* 'thither (away from speaker)'. These have become integrated with a 'give' verb stem *hō* (written as *ho* with a short vowel in Bauer 1993: 471), resulting in the two verbs *hōmai* 'give to speaker' and *hōatu* 'give away from speaker'. *Hō* is not an independently occurring free morpheme anymore. Thus we find contrasts as in (8a) and (8b).

(8) *a. Kua hōmai ia   i   te   pukapuka ki ahau.*
     T/A give   he/she OBJ ART book   to me
     'She/he gave the book to me.'
   b. Kua hōatu au i   te   pukapuka ki a   ia.
     T/A give   I   OBJ ART book   to ART him/her
     'I gave the book to him/her.'

The *mai/atu* contrast observable in (8) is pervasive in Maori grammar. Apart from their occurrence as part of the 'give' words, they occur frequently as adverb-like particles, along with *iho* 'downwards' and *ake* 'upwards'. Biggs (1969: 67), for example, says of these directional particles: 'It is a striking feature of Maori that most actions are given a directional aspect by the use of one of these particles'. The use of the particles *mai* and *atu* is much more general than the glosses 'hither' and 'thither' would suggest (cf. Bauer 1993: 470–6). For one thing, there need not be any physical movement involved, as in (9a) and (9b). Here, the particles help to make a contrast between the directionality of smiling, where it is an abstract kind of motion of the smile 'going out' to another person.

(9) *a. I   kata mai   a   Mere ki ahau.*
     T/A smile hither PERS Mary to me
     'Mary smiled at me.' (Bauer 1993: 474, the original 'laugh' gloss for *kata*
      has been replaced by 'smile')
   b. I   kata atu   ahau ki a   Mere.
     T/A smile away I   to PERS Mary
     'I smiled at Mary.' (Bauer 1993: 475)

The *hōmai* form is also appropriate where the recipient is a group with which the speaker identifies closely, and not just the speaker. So, for example, Foster (1991: pp. vi, ix) has *hōmai* in sentences describing God's gift of languages to various races and the giving of the Maori language to the Maori people. Although the giving is not directly to the speaker, the speaker identifies with the recipient (the Maori people, the various races) rather than with God, hence the 'hither (to speaker)' form is appropriate.

The use of *mai* and *atu* (and other particles) at the discourse level is also note-worthy. Hohepa (1981: 44–6) analyses some early Maori texts, showing how these particles can reflect position, movement, etc. of the participants in the story with respect to the narrator, rather than just with respect to each other. In some cases, according to Hohepa, *mai* and *atu* in narrative discourse can only be properly understood by imagining the narrator as positioned between participants and observing actions around himself or herself. Bauer (1993: 472–4) discusses also a very particular and frequent discourse structure involving *mai* and *atu*, whereby the particles signal the to-and-fro flow of dialogue, as illustrated in (10).

(10)   *Ka pātai atu   ia . . . Ka kī mai   rātou . . .*
       T/A ask   away he   T/A say hither they
       Ka mea atu   ia ki a   rātou . . .
       T/A say away he to PERS them
       Ka kata mai   ōna   tuākana ki a   ia.
       T/A laugh hither his.PL brothers to PERS him
       'He asked . . . They replied . . . He said to them . . . His brothers laughed
       at him.' (Bauer 1993: 472)

Foster (1987: 77) illustrates a similar alternation of the particles with the example in (11). Here, a call 'goes out' (*atu*) from the speaker's group to another group of people; the further elaboration of the other group as being the ones who are sitting in some place makes use of the *mai* particle, as though it is now the turn of that group to reply in our direction.

(11)   *Ka karanga atu   tāua   ki ngā tāngata e   noho mai   rā.*
       T/A call   away 2DU.INCL to the.PL people T/A sit   hither DIST
       'We shall call out to the people sitting over there.' (Foster 1987: 77)

In Maori, then, we have a very pervasive feature of clausal organization: the imposition of a *mai* versus *atu* orientation on events. Not only is it pervasive, it is also a very obvious contrast linguistically, with distinct words *mai* and *atu* in the language. And yet there is no particular reason to think it functions as an organizing principle of the society or culture at large, as we find in the case of Japanese 'give' verbs. One could mention the fact that the ceremonial alternating style of speech-making on a marae (Maori meeting house) is indeed referred to as *tū mai tū atu* in some parts of New Zealand (cf. Salmond 1975: 153–5). Literally, this phrase means 'stand hither stand thither', referring presumably to the opposing positioning of the parties doing the speaking as they face each other. This speech-making is a very significant and central aspect of marae life and so the use of *mai* and *atu* to describe this activity is noteworthy. Other non-verbal aspects of marae ceremonial protocol might be relevant here, too, such as the manner of formal welcomes to visitors on the marae. Such welcomes are characterized by the dramatic and stylized ways in which the two parties approach each other. It is an activity where participants and observers are all likely to become highly conscious of a cautious movement of person(s) towards others. Observations such as these are no more than faintly suggestive of some cultural or societal relevance of the *mai–atu* contrast. Certainly there is no unique feature of the New Zealand topography which would motivate this particular contrast, along the lines of what one can suggest in the case of the Athapaskan classifier system.

4.4.2. *The Human Interaction perspective in Nahuatl and Zulu*

Languages may differ as to whether the primary syntactic object of 'give'-type verbs is the recipient (*The principal presented Lee with an award*) or the thing transferred (*The principal presented the award to Lee*). These alternatives may be thought of as encoding different cognitive perspectives of the giving act (cf. Newman 1996: 62–8). Tuggy's (1998: 36–9) terms, Human Interaction and Object Manipulation, nicely capture the difference in perspective: the Human Interaction perspective correlates with the recipient as the primary object, while the Object Manipulation perspective correlates with the thing as the primary object. English, as seen above in Table 4.3, allows both these perspectives. In some languages, the act of giving is strongly associated with just one of these perspectives. Nahuatl and Zulu are examples of such languages.

In connection with Nahuatl, Tuggy (1998) emphasizes that there is a strong preference throughout Nahuatl for verbs of transfer to impose the Human Interaction perspective and this applies to the verb *maka* 'give to'. With this verb, the thing given may appear as a secondary, incorporated object, e.g. *ni-k-tlakual-maka* (I-him-food-give) 'I feed/sustain him' (Tuggy 1998: 44–6). When the noun appears as an incorporated object, it appears in its bare form, lacking the absolutive suffix which would normally occur on the noun. Tuggy emphasizes that it is the recipient morpheme, *k* in this example, which must be analysed as the primary object. Where there is only one pronominal object with *maka*, for example, that (primary) object is construed as a recipient, not the thing given. Thus, *ti-nēch-maka* (you-me-give) can only mean 'you give me it/something'; it can not mean 'you give me to someone' (Tuggy 1998: 45).

It is not just with the basic 'give' verb that this cognitive perspective appears. The existence of causative and applicative constructions in Nahuatl is relevant to understanding why many transferral meanings, apart from 'give', appear as Human Interaction rather than Object Manipulation in Nahuatl. Both of these constructions have the basic structure of Human Interaction. A causative suffix -*tia*, when attached to a verb stem, gives rise to meanings like 'cause someone to do (the verb stem)', with the 'someone' here functioning as the primary object of the causative. So, for example, the causative of *mati* 'to know' is *mach-tia* 'to teach'. Its primary object would be the person taught and the thing known would function as a secondary object. The applicative suffix -*lia*, on the other hand, when attached to a verb stem, creates meanings 'to do (the verb stem) to/for/in spite of someone'. Again, the 'someone' in this meaning appears as the primary object of the applicative verb. Although the causative and applicative formations are based mainly, and extensively, on verb stems, they may also appear with non-verbal stems, including nominals, adjectives, and postpositions. (There are also other suffixes which participate in these constructions.) Whatever the grammatical category of the stem in these constructions, the result is an event construed as Human Interaction with a human functioning as the primary object.

Zulu, as discussed by Taylor (1998), is similar to Nahuatl in its extensive encoding of the Human Interaction perspective. The verb *nika* 'give' occurs in a double object construction, with the recipient as the primary object, as shown in (12). In these examples, SC refers to 'subject concord' and the numerals refer to the concord classes or person/number agreement.

(12)   *Umama u-nika   amantombazana imali.*
        1mother 1SC-give 6girls   9money
        'Mother gives the girls money.'

Like Nahuatl, there are also applicative and causative constructions which create structures of the Human Interaction type. An applicative suffix *-el(a)* and a causative suffix *-is(a)*, when attached to verb stems, help to create meanings like those described above for Nahuatl. (13)–(14) illustrate these suffixes.

(13) *a. Ngi-theng-e   iphepha.*
        1SG:SC-buy-PAST 5paper
        'I bought a newspaper.'
    b. Ngi-theng-el-e   ubaba iphepha.
        1SG:SC-buy-APPL-PAST 1father 5paper
        'I bought father a newspaper.'/'I bought a newspaper for father.'

(14) *a. Umfana wa-phuza   amanzi.*
        1boy   1SC:PAST-drink 6water
        'The boy drank water.'
    b. Isalukazi sa-phuz-isa   umfana amanzi.
        7old   woman 7SC:PAST-drink-CAUS 1boy   6water
        'The old woman made the boy drink water.'/'The old woman gave the boy water to drink.'

Taylor shows how facts of word order, passivization, and (to some extent optional) object concord all support the analysis of the human recipient, beneficiary, or causee in these constructions as the primary object.

In both Nahuatl and Zulu, then, Human Interaction is a pervasive perspective in the encoding of events. 'Give' verbs in these languages build upon this perspective and in this they reflect a general tendency in each of these languages. However, there is no reason to think there is any social or cultural basis to this linguistic patterning. It is a perspective on the giving-event which appears to have only linguistic ramifications. There is no apparent reason whatsoever to think that Nahuatl and Zulu speakers, for example, are more prone to view humans as affected entities than are speakers of languages which do not have this same tendency towards the Human Interaction perspective on giving-events. Nor are there any obvious grounds for thinking that Nahuatl and Zulu speakers are more conscious of, or sensitive to, human interactions than are speakers of other languages.

A relevant cultural or social patterning, like that which can be established for the Japanese and Chipewyan above, seems to be lacking in the case of the linguistic facts mentioned in this section.

4.5. CONCLUSION

Language has evolved within the context of larger cultural and social behaviours, constrained and guided by principles of human perception, articulation, and cognition—this is the 'situated' view of language and linguistic structure (cf. Langacker 1994: 28). It is only natural, therefore, to enquire into ways in which the grammatical structures of languages support and reflect these other structures. The present volume testifies to the viability of this avenue of enquiry and to the interesting results it can yield. However, it is also important not to overestimate the extent to which culture and grammatical structures can be directly connected.

The procedure I have followed here is not to seek only the positive evidence in support of ethnosyntax as a viable and revealing field of linguistics. Nor is it to seek out only the negative evidence which would count against the hypothesis of ethnosyntax. Rather, my approach has been to investigate one type of event and its expression cross-linguistically. In the course of this investigation, some positive evidence for language–cognition and language–culture connections has indeed been found. But there are also aspects of the organization of 'give' clauses which do not obviously support such connections. The Maori facts about the directional particles and the Zulu and Nahuatl facts about the Human Interaction archetype of giving, as discussed in Section 4.4, illustrate significant, pervasive grammatical devices which have no obvious correlates outside the linguistic systems they are part of. Perhaps, in the future, sophisticated tests of the speakers of these languages might reveal deeper language–culture correlations than can be observed superficially. One thinks, in this connection, of the kinds of tests carried out by Lucy, Levinson, and others (Lucy 1992*a*, 1992*b*; Levinson 1992; Pederson *et al.* 1998), albeit tests which in some cases are argued as supporting the influence of language structure on thought rather than the other way around.[6] But until such time, we must accept that not all parts of grammar have convincing language–cognition and language–culture connections. By focusing on one type of event—giving—and its various realizations across languages, we are able to approach the question of ethnosyntax in a cross-linguistically interesting way. Proceeding in

---

[6] Note the cautionary warning that Pederson *et al.* (1998: 565 n. 9) issue with respect to extending their methodology to investigating connections between grammatical distinctions and cognition. They comment that typologically distinct languages pose serious difficulties for extending the methodology in this way.

94 *John Newman*

this way, we may hope to better understand the actual extent of linguistic and extra-linguistic connections.

REFERENCES

AOYAGI, MUNEKAZU H. 1995. 'Japanese categories during social interaction'. In John R. Taylor and Robert E. MacLaury (eds.), *Language and the Cognitive Construal of the World*. Trends in Linguistics 82. Berlin: Mouton de Gruyter, 331–63.

BASSO, K. H. 1968. 'The Western Apache classificatory verb system: a formal analysis'. *Southwestern Journal of Anthropology*, 24: 252–66.

BAUER, WINIFRED. 1993. *Maori*. London: Routledge.

BIGGS, BRUCE. 1969. *Let's Learn Maori: A Guide to the Study of the Maori Language*. Wellington: Reed Education.

CASAD, EUGENE H. 1998. 'Lots of ways to GIVE in Cora'. In Newman 1998: 135–74.

DENNY, J. PETER. 1979. 'The "extendedness" variable in classifier semantics: Universal features and cultural variation'. In Madeleine Mathiot (ed.), *Ethnolinguistics: Boas, Sapir and Whorf Revisited*. Contributions to the Sociology of Language 27. The Hague: Mouton, 97–119.

DIXON, R. M. W. 1973. 'The semantics of giving'. In Maurice Gross, Morris Halle, and Marcel-Paul Schützenberger (eds.), *The Formal Analysis of Natural Languages*. The Hague: Mouton, 205–23.

DURANTI, ALESSANDRO. 1997. *Linguistic Anthropology*. Cambridge Textbooks in Linguistics. Cambridge: Cambridge University Press

ENFIELD, N. J. 2000. 'On linguocentrism'. In Martin Pütz and Marjolijn H. Verspoor (eds.), *Explorations in Linguistic Relativity*. Current Issues in Linguistic Theory 199. Amsterdam and Philadelphia: John Benjamins, 125–57.

FOLEY, WILLIAM A. 1997. *Anthropological Linguistics: An Introduction*. Oxford: Blackwell.

FOSTER, JOHN. 1987. *He Whakamaarama: A New Course in Maori*. Auckland: Heinemann Reed.

——1991. *He tuhituhi Maori*. Auckland: Reed Books.

GREENBERG, JOSEPH H. 1993. 'The second person is rightly so called'. In Mushira Eid and Gregory Iverson (eds.), *Principles and Prediction: The Analysis of Natural Language. Papers in Honor of Gerald Sanders*. Current Issues in Linguistic Theory 98. Amsterdam: John Benjamins, 9–23.

HOHEPA, PATRICK W. 1981. 'A look at Maori narrative structure'. In Jim Hollyman and Andrew Pawley (eds.), *Studies in Pacific Languages and Cultures: In Honour of Bruce Biggs*. Auckland: Linguistic Society of New Zealand, 35–46.

HOIJER, HARRY. 1953. 'The relation of language to culture'. In Alfred L. Kroeber (ed.), *Anthropology Today*. Chicago: Chicago University Press, 554–73.

KIMBALL, GEOFFREY D. 1991. *Koasati Grammar*. Studies in the Anthropology of North American Indians. Lincoln: University of Nebraska Press.

LAKOFF, GEORGE. 1987. *Women, Fire, and Dangerous Things: What Categories Reveal about the Mind*. Chicago: University of Chicago Press.

LANGACKER, RONALD W. 1987. *Foundations of Cognitive Grammar*, i: *Theoretical Prerequisites*. Stanford, Calif.: Stanford University Press.

——1990. *Concept, Image, and Symbol: The Cognitive Basis of Grammar*. Cognitive

Linguistics Research 1. Berlin: Mouton de Gruyter.

——1991. *Foundations of Cognitive Grammar*, ii: *Descriptive Applications*. Stanford, Calif.: Stanford University Press.

——1994. 'Culture, cognition and grammar'. In Martin Pütz (ed.), *Language Contact and Language Conflict*. Amsterdam: John Benjamins, 25–53.

LEVINSON, STEPHEN C. 1992. *Language and Cognition: The Cognitive Consequences of Spatial Description in Guugu Yimithirr*. Working Paper 13. Nijmegen: Cognitive Anthropology Research Group, Max Planck Institute for Psycholinguistics.

LI, FANG KUE. 1946. 'Chipewyan'. In Cornelius Osgood (ed.), *Linguistic Structures of Native America*. New York: Viking Fund Publications 6, 398–429 (first pub. 1928).

LOVEDAY, LEO. 1986. *Explorations in Japanese Linguistics*. Pragmatics and Beyond VII:1. Amsterdam: John Benjamins.

LUCY, JOHN. 1992a. *Grammatical Categories and Cognition: A Case Study of the Linguistic Relativity Hypothesis*. Cambridge: Cambridge University Press.

——1992b. *Language Diversity and Thought: A Reformulation of the Linguistic Relativity Hypothesis*. Cambridge: Cambridge University Press.

MARCH, ROBERT M. 1996. *Reading the Japanese Mind: The Realities behind their Thoughts and Actions*. Tokyo: Kodansha International.

MIZUTANI, OSAMU. 1981. *Japanese: The Spoken Language in Japanese Life*, trans. Janet Ashby. Tokyo: Japan Times (originally published as *Nihongo-no Seitai*, Tokyo: Sotakusha Inc., 1979).

NAKANE, CHIE. 1970. *Japanese Society*. London: Weidenfeld & Nicolson.

——1972. *Human Relations in Japan*. Summary translation of *Tateshakai no Ningen Kankei* [Personal Relations in a Vertical Society]. Tokyo: Ministry of Foreign Affairs.

NEWMAN, JOHN. 1996. *Give: A Cognitive Linguistic Study*. Cognitive Linguistics Research 7. Berlin: Mouton de Gruyter.

——(ed.) 1998. *The Linguistics of Giving*. Typological Studies in Language 36. Amsterdam: John Benjamins.

PEDERSON, ERIC, DANZIGER, EVE, WILKINS, DAVID, LEVINSON, STEPHEN, KITA, SOTARO, and SENFT, GUNTER. 1998. 'Semantic typology and spatial conceptualization'. *Language*, 74: 557–89.

RICE, KEREN. 1989. *A Grammar of Slave*. Berlin: Mouton.

RICE, SALLY. 1998. 'Giving and taking in Chipewyan: the semantics of THING-marking classificatory verbs'. In Newman 1998: 97–134.

ROBERTS, JOHN. 1987. *Amele*. Beckenham: Croom Helm.

——1998. 'Amele GIVE'. In Newman 1998: 1–33.

RUSHFORTH, SCOTT, and CHISHOLM, JAMES S. 1991. *Cultural Persistence: Continuity in Meaning and Moral Responsibility among the Bearlake Athapaskans*. Tucson: University of Arizona Press.

SALMOND, ANNE. 1975. *Hui: A Study of Maori Ceremonial Greetings*. Wellington: A. H. & A. W. Reed.

SRIDHAR, S. N. 1988. *Cognition and Sentence Production: A Cross-Linguistic Study*. Springer Series in Language and Communication 22. New York: Springer-Verlag.

TAYLOR, JOHN R. 1998. 'Double object constructions in Zulu'. In Newman 1998: 67–95.

TUGGY, DAVID. 1998. 'Giving in Nawatl'. In Newman 1998: 35–65.

WIERZBICKA, ANNA. 1992. *Semantics, Culture, and Cognition: Universal Human Concepts in Culture-Specific Configurations*. New York: Oxford University Press.

PART II

Culture, Semantics, and Grammar

5

Masculine and Feminine in the Northern Iroquoian Languages

WALLACE CHAFE

The Iroquoian languages constitute one of the major language families of eastern North America (see Lounsbury 1978 for a general orientation). There are two major branches: a group of fairly closely related languages that make up the Northern Iroquoian branch, and a single Southern Iroquoian language, Cherokee. The northern languages still spoken include Mohawk, Oneida, Onondaga, Cayuga, Seneca, and Tuscarora. There were a number of others at the time of first European contact, but we know little about most of them except for Huron, which was unusually well documented by missionaries and others (e.g. Fraser 1920; Barbeau 1960; Lagarde 1980). In the Northern Iroquoian languages there is a striking correlation between certain patterns of verb morphology and certain culture patterns that are believed to have been current during the period when the morphology developed as it did. The morphological patterns are clear enough, and their cultural correlates can be reconstructed with reasonable certainty from later historical records, as well as from practices that have persisted until more recent times and are to some extent still observable.

5.1. MORPHOSYNTACTIC PATTERNS

All the Iroquoian languages, including Cherokee, have polysynthetic verbs with many features in common, but one of the ways the Northern Iroquoian languages differ from Cherokee is in their larger inventory of pronominal prefixes—elements within the verb that express the person, number, case, and (in the northern languages but not in Cherokee) the gender of core participants in events and states. The increase in the number of these prefixes in Northern Iroquoian is attributable to the elaboration of third person marking. Whereas Cherokee makes no distinction of third person gender, the northern languages use different prefixes for masculine, feminine, and neuter referents. These three genders are not at all of equal status, however, and it is the conspicuously different treatment of masculine and feminine that will be of interest here.[1] Speculations on the historical development

---

[1] Neuter might be better glossed as 'non-human', since it covers both animals and inanimate entities. It is overtly marked only when an event or state has no core participant that is human.

of these gender markings were offered in Chafe (1977, 1999) and Cysouw (MS).

I will focus here on the pronominal prefix system that is shared, with minor differences, by Mohawk, Oneida, Onondaga, and Seneca. For independent reasons I will not elaborate on the systems of Tuscarora and Cayuga, both of which show deviations that are not relevant here (Chafe 1977). Within Northern Iroquoian the deepest split is between Tuscarora and the other languages. The latter are often grouped together under the term Lake Iroquoian because of their geographical proximity to the Great Lakes. Although Cayuga today resembles Seneca very closely, there are anomalies in its pronominal prefix system that suggest an earlier divergence and later recontact, as explored in Chafe and Foster (1981).

In addition to their pronominal prefixes, the polysynthetic verbs of these languages include inflectional elements that orient events and states in terms of aspect, space, epistemology, and other properties. It is interesting to contrast the cultural relevance of the pronominal prefixes, as discussed below, with the more questionable relevance of the three so-called modal prefixes that are obligatory with verbs in the ubiquitous perfective aspect. These modal prefixes encode three degrees of certainty with which a speaker evaluates an event or state, ranging from a 'factual' prefix reconstructable as *waʔ-, through a 'predictive' prefix reconstructable as *ę-, to a 'hypothetical' prefix reconstructable as *ara-.[2] The obligatoriness and ubiquitousness of these prefixes might suggest that Northern Iroquoian speakers must pay more attention to epistemological evaluations than is necessary when speaking English, and that may in fact be true. It is impossible to speak a Northern Iroquoian language without taking these and other epistemological considerations into account. With no evidence of associated non-linguistic culture patterns, however, it would be circular to conclude that Northern Iroquoian culture is (or was) in some sense more epistemologically oriented than some others, whatever that might mean.[3]

With the pronominal prefixes, however, and particularly with their marking of gender, the situation is quite different. These prefixes are even more obligatory than the markers of epistemology; no verb can appear without one. And because gender entails a categorization of human beings, cultural correlates are more likely to be at hand. We can look first at the intransitive agent and patient prefixes in these languages (prefixes that express only a single core participant), as set forth in Fig. 5.1.

The agent and patient 'non-specific' prefixes have a function similar to that of French *on* or German *man*, translatable as 'one' or 'they' or 'people (in general)'.

---

[2] Here and in what follows I will use prototypical reconstructed forms as abbreviations for sets of alternations that differ somewhat from one language to the next.

[3] Virtually all Northern Iroquoian speakers today use English more often than an Iroquoian language, and as a result the modal prefixes now have a tendency to be associated with English tense. The factual prefix, which more often than not accompanies a past event, tends to be reinterpreted as a past tense marker, and the predictive as future tense. Before the overwhelming influence of English, however, it would appear that these prefixes functioned basically to mark epistemology, with tense at best an inference.

	Agents:			Patients:	
	Singular	Dual	Plural	Singular	Non-singular
Non-specific	*ye-*			*yako-*	
Masculine	*hra-*	*hni-*	*hrati-*	*hro-*	*hroti-*
Feminine	*ye-*	*kni-*	*wati-*	*yako-*	*yoti-*
Neuter	*ka-*			*yo-*	

FIG. 5.1. Third person prefixes in Lake Iroquoian minus Cayuga and Huron

Number is irrelevant to them, but it can be seen that they are homonymous with the feminine singular prefixes, a fact to which we will return. Fig. 5.1 also shows that the agent prefixes distinguish three numbers (including dual), whereas the patient prefixes distinguish only singular and non-singular. Of greater interest here is the fact that, for both agents and patients, there are three genders in the singular but only two in the dual and plural, where feminine and neuter fall together and there is only a masculine versus non-masculine distinction. This differentiation of masculine from everything else, including women, animals, and inanimate objects, is our first example of an imbalance in the expression of gender. Another example, not visible in Fig. 5.1, is the fact that in speaking of groups of people (with dual and plural agents or non-singular patients), the masculine form is used if any member of the group is male. For example, given a group of plural agents, the prefix *hrati-* is used both for an all-male group and for a mixed group of males and females, whereas *wati-* is used only if the group is entirely female (or non-human).

In Mohawk, Oneida, and Onondaga, but not in Seneca, the feminine singular situation is more complex than shown in Fig. 5.1. A feminine singular referent in those languages may be expressed either with the form shown in Fig. 5.1 (identical with the non-specific prefix) or, alternatively, with the neuter form *ka-*. Thus, in those three languages the coalescence of feminine and neuter extends in part to the singular also, although one has a choice between the neuter and the non-specific form. This choice is determined by a set of factors that were described for Oneida by Abbott (1984), and that apply in a similar fashion in Mohawk and Onondaga. Essentially, the feminine *ye-* prefix 'is used to convey the impression that the female referred to is small, graceful, dainty, or petite', and the neuter *ka-* prefix 'is used to convey the impression the female is large, awkward, or aggressive' (Abbott 1984: 127). Abbott quotes Karin Michelson (1982) as suggesting that in Canadian Oneida the neuter prefix sometimes conveys 'an indifferent or detached attitude, sometimes a lack of respect, and sometimes an acknowledgment that the referent has authority or power over the speaker' (quoted in Abbott 1984: 128). The basis of the choice between these two prefixes is complex and may vary even from one speaker to another, but these quotes give at least some idea of its nature.

In terms of historical development, one can reconstruct a Proto-Iroquoian system in which there was a third person category with no gender distinction, to which Proto-Northern-Iroquoian added a marker of masculine singular. The result was a stage at which all third persons other than masculine singular were still marked with a single form, *ka- for agents and *yo- for patients. Coexisting with these specific forms were the non-specific markers *ye- and *yako-. That is, in fact, approximately the system that survived in Huron as long as that language was spoken.

In the other Lake languages, however, perhaps motivated by the already established marking of masculine referents, there arose a practice of marking feminine referents with the non-specific forms *ye- and *yako-. These forms were now ambiguous between their earlier non-specific function and their new use as markers of feminine. In both Seneca and Cayuga they sooner or later completely replaced the earlier *ka- and *yo-, becoming the only markers of feminine, as in Fig. 5.1.[4] In Mohawk, Oneida, and Onondaga, however, both usages survived, with the options described above.

In summary, so far as the intransitive prefixes are concerned, there was first a stage without gender marking (combining masculine, feminine, and neuter in an all-purpose third person), then a stage with an opposition of masculine to everything else (combining feminine and neuter), and then either a system combining feminine and non-specific or a system with both options (feminine-non-specific alternating with feminine-neuter). It would be misleading, however, to assert that women are currently referred to as 'it' or 'one' or both, even though homonymy suggests that to be the case. The *ka-/*yo- and *ye-/*yako- prefixes are now perceived as ambiguous, the first meaning sometimes 'it' and sometimes 'she', and the second meaning sometimes 'one' and sometimes 'she'. It can be said that the meaning 'feminine' does now exist in these languages, although there is no unique form with which to express it. Masculine acquired such a unique form at an early stage.

So far we have looked only at the intransitive prefixes. The distinctiveness of the masculine category is even more apparent in the transitive prefixes, which combine agents with patients. When, for example, either first or second person referents are combined with third person ('I saw him', 'he saw you', etc.), it is only when the third person is masculine singular that all possible first and second person distinctions are made. Fig. 5.2 lists for reconstructed Lake Iroquoian the prefixes that pair a first or second person agent with a third person patient. In the first column are the prefixes in which that patient is masculine singular, in the second column are

---

[4] The same was true in Tuscarora, either as an independent convergence or, more tantalizingly, because Tuscarora may have shared a brief common history with Cayuga, which later influenced Seneca through diffusion (Chafe and Foster 1981). In other words, the use of *ye- and *yako- for feminine may have arisen in a short-lived Tuscarora-Cayuga branch of Northern Iroquoian, later spreading from Cayuga to Seneca and ultimately to Onondaga, Oneida, and Mohawk, where it now coexists with the *ka- and *yo- alternative.

Third person patient:

Agent:		Masculine singular	Anything else
	First singular	*he-	*khe-
	Exclusive dual	*shakni-	*yakhi-
	Exclusive plural	*shakwa-	
	Inclusive dual	*shetni-	*yethi-
	Inclusive plural	*shetwa-	
	Second singular	*hehs-	*she-
	Second dual	*shesni-	*yetshi-
	Second plural	*sheswa-	

FIG. 5.2. First and second person agents with third person patients

those in which that patient is any human third person other than masculine singular: either feminine singular or any variety of non-singular. For example, the prefix *he- in the upper left corner means 'I (did something to) him', whereas *khe- means 'I (did something to) her or them (without regard to gender)'. It can be seen, too, that the 'anything else' category erases the dual vs. plural distinction that is made when the patient is masculine singular.

Conversely, Fig. 5.3 shows the Lake Iroquoian combinations of third person agents with first and second person patients. (The axes have been rotated in order to highlight the comparison.) Here somewhat more attention is given to feminine singular. When the first or second person patient is singular, there is a special feminine singular agent form (though it is derived from the non-specific agent form),

Third person agent:

Patient:		Masculine singular	Feminine singular	Non-singular
	First singular	*hak-	*yǫk-	*hǫk-
	First dual	*shǫkni-	*yǫkhi-	
	First plural	*shǫkwa-		
	Second singular	*hya-	*yesa-	*hǫsa-
	Second dual	*shesni-	*yetshi-	
	Second plural	*sheswa-		

FIG. 5.3. Third person agents with first and second person patients

but when the first or second person patient is dual or plural there is still only a masculine singular versus 'anything else' distinction for third person agents. Furthermore, it is only with masculine singular agents that the first and second person patients distinguish dual and plural number.

5.2. CULTURAL PATTERNS

The Lake Iroquoian languages show a total inventory of approximately seventy pronominal prefixes, among which, as we have seen, the masculine category stands out, and particularly masculine singular. I want now to suggest that the development of such a system may not be unrelated to non-linguistic culture patterns that were in place when the development occurred. We have no historical records from that time, a thousand or more years ago. Extensive written documentation of Northern Iroquoian culture began to accumulate in the seventeenth century, when French missionaries became active in eastern Canada. There are especially rich descriptions by Jesuit missionaries of Huron culture, available now in documents referred to as the Jesuit Relations (Thwaites 1896–1901). From these documents and others it would appear that the basic structure of Huron society was little different from that of the Mohawk, Oneida, Onondaga, Cayuga, and Seneca (the original Five Nations of the Iroquois), as recorded later.

Bruce Trigger, in his monumental work on the history and ethnography of the Huron (Trigger 1976), remarks that

the most basic distinction in Huron society was that made between the sexes . . . Almost every task was considered to be either exclusively men's work or exclusively women's work, and every Huron was expected to be familiar with all or most of the tasks appropriate to his or her sex. For the most part, men engaged in tasks that required considerable physical strength, or which took them away from home for long periods. Women performed tasks of a more routine nature that kept them in, or close to, their villages.   (Trigger 1976: 34)

Elsewhere Trigger says:

In addition to hunting and fishing, clearing land, building houses, and manufacturing tools, the major activities that men engaged in were trading, waging war, and government. These activities frequently brought men into contact with Huron from other villages and with foreigners. Particularly as a result of their trading activities, Huron men were more aware of cultural differences than Huron women were, and were accustomed to tolerating such differences. While women were the guardians of family life and its traditions, men were charged with the responsibility for safety and order, which involved maintaining their village's links with the outside world.   (Trigger 1976: 45)

Of special importance were council meetings, attended only by men, where

decisions were made that influenced many aspects of village life . . . The council arranged public feasts, dances, and lacrosse matches, and decided for whom special curing rites requiring village participation would be performed. The council also undertook to see that no one was in need and coordinated communal projects, such as constructing palisades and relocating the village. All legal disputes arising between members of the different clan segments that lived in the village were adjudicated by the council. (Trigger 1976: 56–7)

Elisabeth Tooker remarks in her ethnography of the Huron, based on the Jesuit Relations and other sources,

The 'old men' in a village decided all matters within the village and their advice was tantamount to an order . . . One 50-year-old Huron man, after he had been told that he could not go to the seminary, emphasized this attitude in his reply to the Jesuits. He told them: 'It seems to me that you are not right to prefer children to grown men. Young people are not listened to in our country; if they should relate wonders, they would not be believed. But men speak; they have solid understanding, and what they say is believed. Hence, I shall make a better report of your doctrine, when I return to my country, than will the children that you seek.' (Tooker 1964: 42)

Elsewhere Tooker says:

Despite the extensive characterization of Iroquois society as being a matriarchy, women had, usually, no voice in council meetings. They exercised their influence behind the scenes, not directly by speaking or attending council meetings. Even today women do not speak in the Longhouse. (Tooker 1964: 48)

The most influential women in traditional Iroquois society were the clan matrons, or clan mothers. William Fenton writes of 'their role in conferring titles, and their power to censure their appointees and to remove them from office', but adds that 'each matron had a warrior who acted as her intermediary with the council, and he might serve as "speaker for the women"' (Fenton 1998: 198–200).

On the Cattaraugus Seneca Reservation in New York I recorded an account by Roy Jimerson of a seventeenth-century rivalry between the Seneca and their neighbours the Kahkwa, in the course of which the Kahkwa were defeated and absorbed into the Seneca population. Much of this account was centred on an athletic contest, a test of male prowess, that was viewed by an entire Seneca town. Of particular interest was the way the audience was distributed. Mr Jimerson's account can be translated as follows: 'They formed a circle; in front stood the chiefs and the warriors. And behind them stood the mothers. And different still were the children.' In other words it was the men who had the front-row seats, with the women behind them, and the children elsewhere.

All this is to suggest that sex roles were distributed in Iroquois society in such a way that men were conspicuous, often even flamboyant, and invested with decision-making powers, whereas women stayed in the background, a position from which they nevertheless exerted considerable influence on what men did. Women were neither unimportant nor undervalued. On the contrary, they were responsible for keeping life going, both from day to day and from generation to generation. The importance of women in Iroquoian culture has been emphasized by the anthropologist Cara Richards, who went so far as to exclaim, 'If you must be born a woman, try to be an Onondaga.' She noted a continuation of female roles from the past into the present:

Historically, the relatively high status of Iroquois women is well documented. Descent was traditionally traced through the women, land belongs to the women, and chiefs are appointed by the women—who theoretically can depose them at will. This means that female children are important to a family, the opinions of women carry weight, and women have some legal and political power. Even after four hundred years of contact with the male-oriented European culture and its American descendant, Iroquois women still maintain their high status and may even have improved it somewhat.   (Richards 1974: 401)

Nevertheless, traditionally at least, it was the males who stood out as highly visible figures against this essential female background. It would seem that the pronominal prefix system that developed in these languages, with its special marking and greater differentiation of masculine gender and its association of women with undifferentiated people in general (the extension of the non-specific prefix to express feminine gender), correlates remarkably well with these distinct roles in Northern Iroquoian society.

How valid, then, would it be to hypothesize a causal relation between the culture pattern and the morphology? How justified would we be in hypothesizing that the Northern Iroquoian pronominal prefix system developed as it did, with its skewing in favour of masculine gender, *because of* the conspicuous nature of men in Iroquois society of the time? In favour of this hypothesis is the striking nature of the correlation. Without question men played a more overt, more conspicuous role than women, and without question the masculine singular category plays a more conspicuous role in the prefix system. Simply to ignore this correlation would be to forfeit a desire to understand why language and culture are the way they are. Furthermore, it is more plausible that the linguistic pattern should have arisen because of the culture pattern than vice versa. A scenario in which the high visibility of men arose through complex interactions of both genetic and cultural forces, independently of language (but perhaps later reinforced by language), is not hard to imagine, as opposed to a scenario in which the linguistic pattern arose first for no apparent reason and then became responsible for men behaving as they did. There was nothing internal to the language that would have motivated such a development.

Against this hypothesis, on the other hand, is the fact that many other societies in North America and elsewhere share similar traits of male visibility, and yet have not developed analogous morphological traits in their languages. Many examples could be cited. As just one illustration especially familiar to me, the Caddo language (e.g. Chafe 1976, in press), although it was spoken earlier in a society that showed similar properties of male conspicuousness in warfare, hunting, and government, and although it too exhibited polysynthetic verbs with pronominal prefixes of similar function, makes no gender distinctions in those prefixes. Certainly one cannot predict that a language spoken in a society characterized by high male visibility will develop a morphology with a skewing toward masculine gender. But language change and culture change are always like this. Once a linguistic change has taken place, one may be able to locate its motivation in non-linguistic circumstances without having to postulate that similar circumstances will everywhere be responsible for the same kind of change. It is thus preferable to speak of the culture pattern as *motivating* the linguistic pattern, not *causing* it, if causation is understood to imply predictability.

I have described a linguistic development that took place a thousand or more years ago. It is the essence of grammaticalization that it separates form and function over time, form remaining relatively constant (aside from phonological attrition) while function changes or even disappears. At a later stage the form may survive as only a relic of its original motivation. An analogous development took place in the history of Iroquoian cultural practices. The earlier warfare pattern ceased to exist with the American war of independence from Britain, during which Iroquoian territory was devastated by colonial forces. With warfare no longer possible, possibilities for hunting became more and more restricted as the Iroquoian land base shrank to a few small reservations. The conspicuous role of men in government remained, however, although in more recent times women have emerged from their background position to assume increasingly overt political power.

The preservation of form with changing function has been particularly well illustrated in the case of the Mohawk. Forty years ago the anthropologist Morris Freilich suggested a continuity between the earlier role of Mohawk men and contemporary cultural practices (Freilich 1958; see also the popular description in Mitchell 1959). Freilich described Mohawk society as it existed prior to extensive white contact in the following terms:

A matrilineal society composed of matrilocally extended families with women supplying the community with essential foods, having fixed residence, and taking care of home and family . . . The men lived in a world of men . . . To a great extent men were their own masters; no one could order them to do anything (except in retribution for criminal offenses). The men chose whether they would join a war party, and could leave it any time they so desired, suffering only the loss of public esteem. The great prestige of the warrior status made for frequent war parties. Colloquially speaking the warrior returned to the tune of 'Home the Conquering Hero Comes', and to hear it again and again, he necessarily had to keep leaving for war.   (Freilich 1958: 475)

When the ancient hunting and warfare pattern could no longer be maintained, Mohawk men turned to alternative occupations that also took them far from home and offered a significant element of danger: the fur trade, timber rafting, river boating, dock work, and participation in circuses. But fortuitously in 1886, as a result of the construction of a St Lawrence River bridge that abutted on the Caughnawaga Reserve, Mohawk men took up structural high steel work with enthusiasm and in ever-increasing numbers, and many have continued in that employment to the present. It is work that also involves long periods away from home and returning periodically as conquering heroes (now with considerable sums of money rather than captives or game), working in an all-male group with a minimum of hierarchical authority, and 'having chances to display daring and courage and thereby gain personal prestige both from the whole community and from the group one fought or worked with' (Freilich 1958: 478). These traits show a fascinating retention of an abstract culture pattern whose function is now quite different, a change from providing meat and wreaking vengeance on one's enemies to building the frameworks of enormous bridges and buildings.

Thus, among the Mohawk at least, the conspicuousness of masculine gender in the language is still associated with a highly visible cultural role for males. It is hardly likely that the language was responsible for the maintenance of that role, but it is interesting to note that the correlation still exists. The significance of this case should not, however, be exaggerated. Aside from the fact that there are many Mohawk men who are not involved in high steel work, this example of cultural retention characterizes the Mohawk more than other Northern Iroquoian groups. To a large extent the masculine gender bias has been retained as little more than a relic of its earlier functional origin. The present state of the ambiguous feminine marking is illustrated in an experience reported by Marianne Mithun, who conducts workshops for Mohawk language teachers. When Mithun pointed out to the teachers the uses of the *ye- and *ka- prefixes as described above (the first derived from a meaning like 'one' and the second from a meaning like 'it'), the teachers were shocked to realize consciously for the first time that they spoke as they did. One even made a motion that they resolve to stop using the *ka- prefix in that way, but the usage was so ingrained and automatic that only a few minutes later one of the teachers was heard to be employing it in reference to another.

5.3. SUMMARY

In summary, I described a morphological pattern in which there is an obvious bias toward masculine gender paired with ambiguity and lack of distinctiveness in the expression of feminine gender. I then described an ancient culture pattern in which males had a conspicuous, flamboyant, constantly changing, and individualized role that contrasted with the stable, undifferentiated, background role of women. I discussed the plausibility of hypothesizing a motivational relation between the culture pattern and the morphology. Turning then to the present situation, I mentioned the fact that in one case there has been retention of an earlier cultural form with a new function, so that to some extent the morphology still reflects something of cultural relevance. Finally, I mentioned that this correspondence between morphology and culture is no longer present elsewhere in Northern Iroquoian culture, and especially that the morphological backgrounding of feminine gender hardly reflects the role of women in Iroquoian society today. It survives as a relic of an earlier function, albeit a relic that is still unconsciously present whenever the language is used.

REFERENCES

ABBOTT, CLIFFORD. 1984. 'Two feminine genders in Oneida'. *Anthropological Linguistics*, 26: 125–37.

BARBEAU, MARIUS. 1960. 'Huron-Wyandot traditional narratives in translations and native texts'. *National Museum of Canada, Bulletin 165, Anthropological Series 47*. Ottawa: Queen's Printer and Controller of Stationery.

CHAFE, WALLACE. 1976. *The Caddoan, Iroquoian, and Siouan Languages*. The Hague: Mouton.

——1977. 'The evolution of third person verb agreement in the Iroquoian languages'. In Li 1977: 493–524.

——1999. 'Florescence as a force in grammaticalization'. In Gildea 1999: 39–64.

——In press. 'Caddo'. In Hardy and Scancarelli in press.

——and FOSTER, MICHAEL K. 1981. 'Prehistoric divergences and recontacts between Cayuga, Seneca, and the other Northern Iroquoian languages'. *International Journal of American Linguistics*, 47: 121–42.

CYSOUW, MICHAEL. MS. 'A history of Iroquoian gender marking'.

FENTON, WILLIAM N. 1998. *The Great Law and the Longhouse: A Political History of the Iroquois Confederacy*. Norman: University of Oklahoma Press.

FRASER, ALEXANDER. 1920. *Huron Manuscripts from Rev. Pierre Potier's Collections*. 15th Report of the Bureau of Archives for the Province of Ontario. Toronto: Clarkson W. James.

FREILICH, MORRIS. 1958. 'Cultural persistence among the modern Iroquois'. *Anthropos*, 53: 473–83.

GILDEA, S. (ed.). 1999. *Reconstructing Grammar: Comparative Linguistics and Grammaticalization*. Amsterdam: John Benjamins.

HARDY, HEATHER, and SCANCARELLI, JANINE (eds.). In press. *The Native Languages of the Southeastern United States*. Lincoln: The University of Nebraska Press.

LAGARDE, PIERRETTE L. 1980. *Le verbe huron: Étude morphologique d'après une description grammaticale de la seconde moitié du XVIIème siècle*. Paris: Éditions l'Harmattan.

LI, CHARLES N. (ed.). 1977. *Mechanisms of Syntactic Change*. Austin: University of Texas Press.

LOUNSBURY, FLOYD G. 1978. 'Iroquoian languages'. In Trigger 1978: 334–43.

MATTHIASSON, CAROLYN J. (ed.). 1974. *Many Sisters: Women in Cross-Cultural Perspective*. New York: Free Press.

MICHELSON, KARIN. 1982. 'Two feminine pronominal prefixes in Oneida'. Paper read before the Association for the Anthropological Study of Play, London, Ontario.

MITCHELL, JOSEPH. 1959. 'The Mohawks in high steel'. In Wilson 1959: 3–36.

RICHARDS, CARA B. 1974. 'Onondaga women: among the liberated'. In Matthiasson 1974, 401–19.

THWAITES, REUBEN G. 1896–1901. *The Jesuit Relations and Allied Documents*. 73 vols. Cleveland: Burrows Brothers Company.

TOOKER, ELISABETH. 1964. *An Ethnography of the Huron Indians, 1615–1649*. Bureau of American Ethnology Bulletin 190. (Repr. Syracuse, NY: Syracuse University Press, 1991.)

TRIGGER, BRUCE. 1976. *The Children of Aataentsic: A History of the Huron People to 1660*. Kingston: McGill-Queen's University Press.

——(ed.). 1978. *Handbook of North American Indians*, xv: *Northeast*. Washington: Smithsonian Institution.

WILSON, EDMUND. 1959. *Apologies to the Iroquois*. New York: Farrar, Straus, & Giroux. (Repr. Syracuse, NY: Syracuse University Press, 1992.)

6

Using *He* and *She* for Inanimate Referents in English: Questions of Grammar and World View

ANDREW PAWLEY

6.1. INTRODUCTION

I am going to tell a cautionary tale about making connections between grammatical patterns and ways of thinking. Although it is cautionary its implications are by no means entirely negative.

In a typically bold essay on 'Ethno-syntax and the philosophy of grammar', Anna Wierzbicka (1979) suggested that the syntactic structures of a language codify certain language-specific meanings and so, by their very nature, incorporate a certain view of the world. Others have made somewhat similar claims. In his book *The Linguistic Structure of Reality*, George Grace (1987) observed that the constructions of a language are a set of resources for saying things about the world. Each construction type, together with the lexicon, provides a schema, a means for making quick verbal sketches of events and situations, sketches that are necessarily highly selective in the elements they pick out and highly conventionalized in the ways they interpret the relations between these elements. If languages A and B differ in some of their constructions and lexical categories they cannot say exactly the same range of things; they will not be fully intertranslatable. To the extent that this is so, the speakers of A and B will by definition construct different linguistic realities.

It is difficult to quarrel with these proposals. However, the same arguments can be applied to different grammatical and lexical choices within a language. A language will offer its speakers a choice of ways for talking about a situation (more accurately, for construing or interpreting it). Each alternative can be said to

I am indebted to Lea Brown and Anna Wierzbicka for reading and commenting on an earlier version of this chapter and to Frances Syder for taping and transcribing T54. Peter Siemund kindly provided a copy of his unpublished comparative study of gender assignment in several varieties of English and allowed me to draw on some of his findings, and Anna Wierzbicka kindly provided a copy of an unpublished paper and allowed me to cite from it. I am grateful to the New Zealand Council for Educational Research for funding research assistance in gathering conversation data between 1972 and 1976.

embody a certain world view. Thus, we do not need to compare different languages to find contrasting world views. We can look for them in the different constructions of a single language. The problem, perhaps, lies in how far we want to press the association between conventional ways of talking and the more fundamental and pervasive ways of thinking and feeling.

Pronoun use is often cited, with good reason, as a domain in languages where grammatical usage can be highly sensitive to cultural attitudes and mores. The well-known paper by Brown and Gilman (1960) on the social uses of second person pronoun shifts in European languages is only one of many studies along these lines. Here I discuss some little-recognized but widespread patterns of pronoun shifts in English and consider the semantic and cognitive bases of these.

In some varieties of English *he* or *she* (or their case variants) are used extensively to refer to entities that are inanimate in the grammarian's sense: something that is not a living animal or human.[1] I will refer to this practice as *(grammatical) animation, or as animating (inanimate) referents*. The selection of a particular pronoun, *he, she,* or *it*, to refer to a particular referent or class of referents will be termed *gender assignment* and the choice of *he* or *she* will be called *animate gender assignment*. Two studies of grammatical animation in varieties spoken in Australia and in two regions of the United States will be compared with particular attention to the questions: What are the functions of animation? Do gender assignments to inanimate entities follow consistent semantic principles? How long have these patterns of pronoun use been widespread in English? Can we infer from speakers' uses of animation and of particular gender assignments anything about cultural norms or speakers' purposes, values, attitudes or emotions? For instance, is there a semantic or cultural basis for the fact that vehicles are consistently feminine and trees consistently masculine for male speakers of both regional varieties? And why are knives and carpets sometimes masculine and sometimes feminine?

The two studies yield similar conclusions in some points. In some important conclusions, however, the authors diverge sharply, particularly with respect to (*a*) the semantic basis of gender assignment and (*b*) the degree to which this can be associated with cultural values or with personal attitudes and feelings. I will argue that many of the data in the American study can be reinterpreted to fit the semantic principles exhibited by the Tasmanian data. However, there remains some material that cannot be reconciled with the Tasmanian data, chiefly some patterns of usage by American women.

Let me begin with the Tasmanian study.

---

[1] The Australian and American patterns of gender assignment considered in this chapter appear to differ in important ways from that described for 'Wessex English' (centred in Somerset, Dorset, and Devon) by Rogers (1979) and Paddock (1991) and from the closely related Newfoundland system (Paddock 1991). Siemund (2001) compares these systems. Grammatical animation is, of course, not unknown in certain varieties of formal written and spoken English. Ships and nations are commonly animated, for example. But animation is fairly highly restricted in its scope in formal English.

6.2. GENDER ASSIGNMENT IN TASMANIAN VERNACULAR ENGLISH

6.2.1. *Tasmanian Vernacular English as a style*

In the early 1970s Frances Syder and I began collecting a corpus of taped English conversational speech for the purpose of investigating the social and linguistic organization of conversation. Part of the data was collected in Tasmania, the southernmost state in Australia, where recordings mainly involved our own relatives. Animation, as exemplified by the following two excerpts, is a prominent feature in the speech of many Tasmanians. In all examples, instances of animated pronouns (and sometimes coreferential nouns) are marked in boldface. Editorial comments are in square brackets.

In (1) the speaker is Rex, a retired farmer and café owner aged about 70. He recalls to his nephew Ken how when they were small boys on the farm Ken and his cousin Mark (Rex's son) once tried to uproot a massive turnip.

(1)   Rex: I was ploughing there and I'd 'ad some turnips in . . .
          and there was a *big* **turnip** there,
          'e was like *that*, y' know, nearly as big as a kerosene tin,
          and you two fellas was down there tryin' to get **it** out . . .
          you'd . . . twisted **'im**, and pulled the thing,
       Ken: an' we couldn't get **'im**
       Rex: Couldn't get **'im**/
       Yous ha/you had **'im** loose and you didn't realize
          . . . y' had **'im** broke off at the/
       Ken: root.
       Rex: At the root . . . But **'e** was a big turnip.
          Yous 'd worked on **it**!

There are eight pronouns that clearly refer to the turnip. Seven are masculine, one is neuter. The *it* in the last clause possibly refers more generally to the task of pulling the turnip out. In extract (2), from an anecdote about one of the wood-chopping competitions that are a regular feature of Tasmanian fairs, the main topic is an axe. The speaker is Harvey, a farmer and businessman in his late fifties. Six feminine pronouns for inanimate referents occur here. The first evidently refers to the block of wood the chopper is cutting, the next five to the axe which he damages in the process.

(2)   Old Kit . . .'e 'ad the only **chopping axe** John Behan had,
          Nobody 'ad two them days y' know, in the bad old days,
          and John 'ad a pretty good **axe** . . .
          . . . they got Kit entered in this Chop, y' know . . .
          'e was off say three or five or whatever.

When they said 'Five!' 'e's no sooner [unclear] than 'e hit **'er** [the block],
y' know,
and 'e chopped two or three six-inch nails clean off . . .
'e dug himself in too low, y' see,
and 'e fetches **'er** [the axe]
and 'e looks at **'er**, y' see,
. . . and 'e holds **'er** round to John,
and 'e's got a great big gap clean through the face of **'er**,
and 'e said 'Cripes!' Hahaha!
when 'e turned—when 'e showed **it** to John.

It is useful to distinguish between *animation* and *personification*. We can say a speaker has *personified* an inanimate referent when he explicitly attributes to it not only animate gender but various qualities that we think of as human, e.g. intentions, motives, emotions, features of character or personality. (Of course, animals, especially mammals, also have many of these qualities so the term 'personification' itself betrays our anthropocentric view of the world.) In the following extracts from written sources, the authors are clearly personifying the inanimate referent.

(3)   At the first glance I saw that **she** was a high-class **vessel**, a harmonious creature in the lines of **her** fine body, in the proportioned tallness of **her** spars. Whatever **her** age and history, **she** had preserved the stamp of **her** origin . . . **she** looked like a creature of high breed—an Arab steed among a string of cart-horses. (Joseph Conrad, letter, cited in Sherry 1988: 49)

(4)   What strikes you about the **Old Course** when you see **her** for the first time is that **she**'s far more interesting than on television. Sure, **she** can be tamed if the weather's calm. Curtis Strange shot 62 here in the 1988 Dunhill Cup. There are still plenty of hazards to entrap the golfer who treats **the old lady** with anything but the utmost respect, however. Throw in the variable North Sea winds that so often buffet the course, and **she** can become a right **bitch**. ('On St Andrews Golf Course', *Australian*, 17 July 1995)

Most mature speakers of Tasmanian English command a range of speech styles (are polylectal). Animation is one of a cluster of features that define a style that has elsewhere been called Tasmanian Vernacular English (TVE) (Pawley 1995*a*, 1995*b*). This is for many Tasmanians the most informal and relaxed style, the basilect. The full range of characteristics distinguishing TVE from other varieties of English need not concern us here, but it should be noted that TVE is marked by frequent use of a number of non-standard usages, such as *h*-dropping, *-in'* instead of *-ing* (as in *doin'*), *was* or *'s* for *were* with plural subjects (as *they 's late*), *them* for *those*, *rum 'un* for an amusing or eccentric person, and the use in narratives of the construction *old X* to refer a known character named X.

TVE shows another departure in pronoun use from formal Standard English which will also be included in the discussion. Animals of unknown sex are typically assigned an animate pronoun in TVE. That pronoun is always masculine.

In Tasmanian English, as elsewhere, the use of non-standard values of linguistic variables typically marks informality and intimacy. The more informal and intimate the situation the higher the incidence of non-standard features. The highest frequency of animation is found among male speakers. When men in the countryside or working-class men in the cities meet informally to converse and tell stories, constant use of a wide range of TVE features is *de rigueur*. Women TVE speakers use animation too, but tend to do so more sparingly.

Tasmania is the only region of Australia for which gender assignment has been analysed in a sizeable body of tape-recorded speech. However, I also have quite extensive notes from casual observations of speech and from written sources in other regions of Australia and in New Zealand. These materials indicate that the TVE conventions for gender assignment summarized below in (6) are followed by some speakers in all regions of these two countries.

TVE can be regarded as a conservative variety of spoken English in certain respects. Comparative evidence suggests that it preserves features that were extremely widespread in the speech of working-class city and rural Australians in the nineteenth and early twentieth centuries. While these features still persist in pockets all around Australia, and especially in country areas, they have lost ground in recent generations in the cities and towns. No doubt because of the relative isolation of Tasmania these features persist more strongly there than in many other regions of Australia.

6.2.2. *Who uses animation and when?*

Whether or not a TVE speaker chooses to 'animate' an entity in a particular instance depends on a number of factors. The entity must be referential (specific or definite). Other factors include its importance in the discourse (as a main topic, background element, etc.), its sequential position in the discourse, and its inherent salience. These semantic and pragmatic considerations interact with speakers' wider purposes.

Any referent that becomes a focus of interest may be animated. But not all referents that are important in the discourse are equally likely to be animated. The inherent salience of the referent seems to be an important variable in the case of plants and animals. When referring to animals of unknown sex, animation is more frequent when the referent is a large animal (e.g. mammal, reptile, bird, fish), where it is almost categorical, and least frequent with very small animals such as insects. With plants, animation is most often used with trees and less often with small plants. Mass nouns as well as count nouns may be animated.

Once a speaker has chosen in the first instance to refer to a particular referent by an animate or inanimate pronoun, he or she is likely to keep to that choice in immediately following references within the same discourse unit (narrative, instruction, joke, etc.). However, the demands of role play or characterization or situation sometimes call for style shifts. Radical shifts between TVE and more formal styles can occur when speakers act out roles. In the following passage the speaker (Chas, a farmer, whom we will meet again) has been speaking pure TVE but adopts a relatively formal style when quoting himself talking to a lawyer.

(5)   Chas: 'But if you wanto collect the bill,' I said,
          'you go ahead and co*llect* it,' I said.
          'But *I* won't be *pay*ing it.'

The use of *it* instead of an animate pronoun is only one of several elements which give (5) its formal tone. Note also the use of more formal spoken English versus informal alternants in Chas's pronunciation (e.g. *wanto* instead of *wanna*, and *paying* instead of *payin'*).

6.2.3. *An account of animate gender assignment in TVE*

The most systematic data for TVE come from tape-recorded conversations in which eight men and four women are represented. A larger sample of speakers and a wider range of discourse contexts will doubtless yield some refinements to these conclusions. In particular, female paradigmatic speakers of TVE are under-represented in our corpus.

Tables 6.1–6.6 (see below), showing frequencies of particular kinds of gender assignment, represent Transcript 54, the record of a single ninety-minute tape-recorded conversation.[2] This was a continuous session of relaxed conversation and story-telling between two men and two women. Most of the talking is done by the two men, Charles and Harvey, who are paradigmatic speakers of basilectal TVE.

6.2.3.1. Rules for animate gender assignment in animated style

Analysis of the TVE data reveals certain consistent semantic correlates of animate gender assignment to non-human referents.

- A distinction must be made in the first place between referents that have *fixed animate gender* (i.e. which must be masculine or must be feminine) and things that have *variable animate gender* (which can be either masculine or feminine).
- The class of inanimate things whose animate gender is variable consists roughly of portable goods, such as implements, toys, clothing, furniture, machines other than vehicles (e.g. watches, clocks, radios, computers, refrigerators), carpets, pieces of wood, stones, wire, and items of food. Within this class there are principled semantic bases for the selection of an animate gender.[3]
- All other inanimates have fixed gender. Plants are always masculine. Excluding portable goods, almost everything else is feminine. Elements of the natural

[2] Other complete transcripts are not to hand at the time of writing.
[3] Of course, all types of concrete referent can be represented by models which are portable—people, houses, the world—but it is necessary to distinguish between authentic types and models or toys.

inanimate environment—such as land, sea, mountains, rivers, roads, storms, floods, lightning, rain, sun and moon, night and day, soil, grass, farms and gold-mines—are *she*. So are non-portable goods, such as houses, fences, boats and other vehicles, and body-parts (with one exception). And so too are abstract ref-erents, such as events and situations, life, jobs, cities, countries and units of time, and utterances. Thus it is reasonable to say that in TVE the unmarked gender for inanimates is feminine.

• Animals of unknown sex are masculine.

It is important to emphasize that there are two different systems of animate gender assignment at work in TVE (aside from that of Standard English, which is always available for stylistic contrast). The semantic principles operating in fixed gender assignment are quite different from those operating in variable gender assign-ment.

The following is an attempt to reduce animation and gender assignment in our TVE data to a few simple rules.

(6) **Rules for gender assignment to non-human referents in TVE**
     A. Choose between animated style and more formal styles, according to social context and purpose.
     B. If animated style is chosen assign animate gender to all referents that are salient in the discourse, according to the following conventions:
        a. When referring to portable goods (other than vehicles) use *he* to express an attitude of detachment (objectivity, indifference) towards the referent, otherwise use *she*.
        b. Other referents can have only one gender:
           (i)   For plants and animals use *he*.
           (ii) For the male genitals use *he*.
           (iii) For everything else use *she*.

These rules say little about the semantic bases of gender assignment and the ques-tion of whether we are dealing with natural semantic classes in all cases. The semantic bases of fixed gender assignment will be discussed in Section 6.2.4. The bases of variable gender assignment with portable goods are more problematic and will be discussed in Section 6.2.5.

6.2.4. *Referents with fixed gender*

6.2.4.1. Things that are always masculine

6.2.4.1.1. Trees and other plants   Besides trees, which figure prominently, the TVE corpus includes occasional references to various other plants: vines, turnips, carrots, potatoes, and flowers. Living plants are always masculine when there is animation. In Transcript 54 there are sixteen clear references to trees using a third person singular pronoun. All are masculine.

The speaker in (7) is Mark, a forester in his mid-fifties. When (7) was recorded he was walking around his 40-acre patch of bushland with his cousin Ken, visiting from another state, commenting on the plants as they ambled along. In Mark's speech, trees and shrubs, living or dead, upright or fallen, are consistently *he*—19 out of 19 in this extract. The sole reference to a creeper in (7) is also *he*:

(7)   Max: There's a **tree** up here died for no apparent reason.
           'e was healthy—'n there 'e is, dead!
           . . . I felled 'im [another dead tree]—'e was dangerous,
           That one there, **he**'s a **stringybark**.
           [points] 'e's a **blackwood**.
           That one there, 'e's a **wild cherry**.
           'as little cherries on 'im and they're good to eat too, them cherries.
           [points] an' 'e's a **peppermint**.
           See the leaves, they're different.
           . . . That **stringybark** [points], 'e's got a left-handed twist [in the grain of the wood and the bark].
           They reckon 'e'll still split if 'e's got a left-handed twist,
           but that'd be testin' 'em.
           See, 'e don't start twistin' till 'e gets above that limb, does 'e?
           Hard as a bull's forehead, that bloody wood is.
           . . . . The **snottygobble** [parasitic creeper] 's into this one,
           but 'e's not goin' to kill 'im.
           . . . See **that log** lying there
           Got a load of wood in 'im, 'asn't 'e?

In the next extract one speaker, Trevor, recalls a dispute over tree-felling rights on a patch of leased bushland.

(8)   Trev: . . . but Frazer and we had a bloody row over some wood . . .
           We was up there cuttin' and Frazer come on to us you see, . . .
           'oh well', 'e said, 'I suppose you can 'ave *im* [a tree]
           but we already 'ad 'im, all bar a few pieces, cut up and loaded,
           and Frazer said 'I suppose you can have 'im,' he said
           'Yeah, but don't touch that one over there'.
           But we'd been passing 'im with the axe
           and 'e was only a bit of—bloody—papery—shell.
           'e wasn't/
      Dave: 'e wasn't worth it.
      Trev: No. That's why we left 'im.
           We'd had 'im.
      Dave: You left 'im for Frazer, wi-with pleasure.
      Trev: Yes.
      Dave: Not enough of 'im.

Trev: No! **'e** was/
Dave: Too rotten.
Trev: Yeah. **'e** was dry enough but **'e** was only about an inch or an inch and a half thick . . .

In (9) Ken has called on his Uncle Bill who has just started a small vegetable patch next to the lawn in front of his house.

(9)   Ken: What's that growing in the lawn there? Are you cultivating that?
        Bill: That's a carrot! I've been waterin' **'im**, lookin'after **'im**.

In *The Gardening Program* (on ABC television) two expert gardeners, both middle-aged men, are inspecting a small shrubby flowering plant.

(10)   A. **He**'s been cut, by the look of it.
        B. Yes.

6.2.4.1.2. Timber, parts of trees, and basic timber products   Data for TVE on (natural) parts of trees are limited to branches, boles (trunks), stumps, logs (of fallen trees), bark, and roots. Generally these take the masculine pronoun when viewed as parts of a tree.

(11)   Mark: See that branch up there. **He**'s what they call a widder-maker [i.e. 'widow-maker'; a large dead branch capable of killing a bushman if it falls].

However, there is one instance of a tree root referred to as *her* when viewed as an extension of the ground, which appears in example (17), below.
    What might be called basic timber products, such as cut logs, slabs, posts, planks, and palings, belong to the portable goods category and may be either masculine or feminine (see s. 6.2.5). These are usually masculine in our data. In example (13) (from a video made by the Australian Parks Services), a bushman from near Canberra, Bill Boyd, is talking to another man about how timber was cut to make slab houses. Note the shift from *him* to *her* when the speaker moves from the cutting of a post to the removal of a tool (wedge).

(13)   What we'll be looking for is **a tree** with a straight barrel on **'im**
        You can tell after you've hit **'im** if **'e**'s sound.
        Mostly the slab you cut in the bush, you loaded **'im** on to your transport and took **'im** home to work on **'im** at the homestead itself . . .
        The first post you've got to make fairly even, make **'im** 10 inches or 8 inches wide. You lay **'im** flat and you square **'im** half way down, you square **'im** fairly even, then you turn **'im** over . . . .
        Mostly you can leave **'er** [the wedge] up on the [timber].

6.2.4.1.3. Animals of unknown sex   In TVE any creature of unknown sex, e.g. a wallaby, crow, rabbit, snake, fish, or mosquito, when animated, is always *he*.

TABLE 6.1. Gender assignment for animals of unknown sex in T54

	He	She	It
Harv	10	0	0
Chas	24	0	0
Total	34	0	0

TABLE 6.2. Gender assignment for animals of known sex in T54

	Animate	Neuter
Harv	9	0
Chas	10	0
Total	19	0

Tables 6.1 and 6.2 show that in Transcript 54 all pronominal references to animals were made using animate pronouns.

In extract (14) Harvey is telling his interlocutors about men poaching a sheep or two on the way home from a trapping or hunting expedition during the depression years.

(14)   Harv: But what they used to like to do about the day before they came
              back, was to get **one of Von Breddow's sheep** y' see,
              as close to home as they could there,
              and they'd kill **'im** and hang **'im** up in the—in the scrub you see.
         Chas: Yes.
         Harv: . . . sometimes they'd hang **'im** up tonight y' see,
              and go to pick **'im** up tomorrow night,
              'e'd be gone.
              Some of the other fellas seen **'im**.

In (15) Mark and Ken are talking about a wild goat that Mark shot.

(15)   Ken: You didn't eat **'im**?
         Mark: Well, **'e** wasn't no teenager.
         Ken: **'E**'d 'a been pretty tough.

6.2.4.2. Things that are always feminine

6.2.4.2.1. Vehicles   Vehicles show a very high frequency of animation. The animate pronoun is invariably feminine. Examples (16)–(17) are about a truck and a bulldozer, respectively.

TABLE 6.3. Gender assignment for vehicles in T54

	He	She	It
Harv	0	13	2
Chas	0	8	0
Total	0	21	2

(16)   Chas: Alec 'ad this old **D30 International**
              and they're cartin' wood [recording stops momentarily]
              and by *jees* **she** went *down*, **this truck**!
              I'm not sure they didn't unload the wood and *still* couldn't get **'er** out.

(17)   Harv: But when 'e first bought **the bulldozer**
            'e told me he took **'er** out in the bush
            and he'd be taking **'er** up all them big stringy gums . . .
            and the old bulldozer's got one claw up on this 'ere,
            on **a green root** y' see,
            and **she**'s just skidding on **'er**.
         Chas: Yes.
         Harv: See. Well, 'e don't know what to do about it, Alec,
            'e just opened up and left **'er** there.
         Just swears at **'er**.

Wheelbarrows are, I suppose, somewhat marginal members of the vehicle family.
In (18) the speaker is Mark and the pronoun is first neuter and then feminine. It
may be significant that the speaker animates the barrow once he begins to describe
its role in a particular event.

(18)   Mark: Ol' Colin had this **wheelbarra**.
            They reckon **it** could carry three-quarters of a ton o' wood.
            Well, 'e loaded **'er** up and carried the wood down to the store,
            and she [the owner of the wood] gave 'im a plate of scones for it.
            Not a lot was it?

6.2.4.2.2. Elements of the inanimate landscape   Elements of the natural inanimate landscape—land, mountains, rivers, minerals, wind, rain, lightning, etc. are
always feminine when animated. References to this semantic domain are scarce in
our tape-recorded TVE corpus but figure in many casual observations.

(19)   [of the wind]   **She**'s a bit keen today. Should've brung me fur coat.
(20)   [of a storm]   **She** made a mess of that crop.

The following two passages are from two of Sarah Campion's novels, *Bonanza*
and *Mo Burdekin*, which depict the conversations of Australian miners a century
ago. Campion's settings are in the Australian mainland, not in Tasmania. In the
following passages the speakers are talking about drilling for artesian water (21),
and about a reef of gold (22) and gold mines (23).

(21)   'Garn, y'old crow, stop croaking and look at the **water**. Howzit goin',
            mates?'
            . . . '**She**'s come at last, blast **her** pretty eyes. Gawd, we wos long enough
            gittin' downta **it**. But **she**'s comin' up nice, now, . . .' (Campion 1942:
            206–7)

(22)   The atmosphere of the saloon, thick, stale, rich and forbidden, tickled his
            delighted nostrils, talk fell thick on his delighted ears. 'D' yer reckon the
            lode'll live that far?' 'O' course, why, between such walls as **she**'s got that

reef 'll live to kingdom come—cor in the last foot o' the underlie that reef opens out ter nigh on thirteen feet. Put yer cash in **O'Brady's Beauty**, cocky, an' yer'll never live to regret it!' (Campion 1941: 169)

(23) 'They've started stoping wi' four men on No. 2 winze, west o' the shaft, in two foot o' stone. **She** ain't eggsackly bonzer, but **she**'s good enough. Stopes between 3 and 4 winzes'll 'ave ter lie till sich time as they gits mullock room at No. 3.' 'Wot, you talkin' o' **the Bull Frog** [gold mine] that's let on tribute? Cor, **she** ain't no blunny good, **she**'s a bad 'un **she** is, a fair cow.' (Campion 1942: 246)

There is one story in the TVE corpus that refers to hay. Two of the four pronouns referring to hay are feminine, two are neuter.

(24) Chas: . . . they had this bloody piebald horse,
    and I was leadin',
    pullin' **this hay** up with one o' them—what they call a grabstacker . . .
    and Tim . . . he might 've been building the stack, I think, Tim,
    prob'ly with loose hay.
     . . . They'd sweep **'er** in,
Harv: They'd sweep, yes mm.
Chas: Sweep **'er** in,
    and then they . . . they had a pole up in the air,
    and they was pulling **it** [the hay] over a block, y' see
     . . . That's how they got **it** up on top of the stack, this hay . . .

6.2.4.2.3. Buildings and other non-portable manufactured objects   Non-portable man-made elements in the landscape, e.g. houses, roads, dams, and bridges, are invariably feminine when animated.

(25) [Real estate agent, showing off a hillside **house**]
    She's certainly got a view, this one.

(26) [Driver commenting on a **road** on his farm]
    Yeah, **she**'s a rough old track. Must put the grader on **'er** one o' these days.

6.2.4.2.4. Body-parts and bodily conditions   All body-parts are feminine except for the male genitals. Bodily conditions, such as cold, aches and pains, and diseases, are also feminine.

(27) [Middle-aged man in reply to an enquiry about a **knee**]
    She's a lot better than **she** was, I can tell you that.

(28) [Man of 30 or so, speaking of a **wisdom tooth**]
    She was no use to me anyway, so I 'ad **her** out.

6.2.4.2.5. Abstract referents   For abstract entities, such as an event or situation, emotion, utterance, principle, time, law, task, or occupation, the neuter pronoun is much more frequent in TVE, but when an abstract entity is animated the pronoun is invariably feminine. In (29) the speaker is talking about a tense situation developing as a result of men stealing game from snares.

TABLE 6.4. Gender marking for abstract referents in T54

	He	She	It
Situations	0	3	12
Time/day/era	0	1	4
Conditions of weather or terrain	0	0	2
Utterances	0	0	4
Specific actions and states	0	0	4
Total	0	4	26

(29)   Chas: I bet **she** was on out there,
        when they was snarin', them fellows
        and **it** had got so bad that—they—
        nobody could go near another bloke's snares, could they?
        Or they'd get shot.

In the next example, a real estate agent refers first to his employment and second to a delicate situation relating to his job:

(30)   When **she**'s your livelihood **she**'s a bit awkward.

There are two cases where a man's job takes an animate pronoun. In both cases the pronoun is feminine. The first is in (30) above. In (31) the first speaker, Nigel, is a young man who had been working at two jobs for several years.

(31)   Nigel: I've given up me **morning job**.
        Ken: Have you?
        Nigel: Yeah, I gave **'er** away. I'm a new man.

The Australian tennis player Patrick Rafter, when asked whether his retirement would be short term or permanent, answered as follows:

(32)   Rafter: **She**'ll be clean, mate, don't worry about that!

6.2.4.3. What is there to explain about fixed gender assignment?

In cases where gender assignment is rigid a grammarian may feel that, having established the correlation between grammatical markers and semantic categories, his or her job is done. On the other hand, one who is curious about the relation between grammar, semantics, and cultural values and practices will crave an

explanation of this state of affairs. Why are certain inanimate categories, when animated, always *he* and why are others always *she*? And why are certain categories
variable?

For example, both plants and animals of unknown sex are assigned the same
gender, masculine. The unifying factor, perhaps, is that they are living things.
However, in languages of the world it is rare to find a grammatical category 'living
things' that includes plants as well as animals, so while this explanation is plausible it is not altogether convincing. Anna Wierzbicka (personal communication)
has suggested that living things are masculine because in English traditionally the
unmarked gender for humans is masculine. But this still leaves us with the question why so much of the world—elements of landscape and weather, body-parts,
houses, vehicles, and so on—should be feminine.

Many Australian English speakers will readily offer rationalizations for certain
categories; for example, men will tell you that vehicles and weather, like women,
are temperamental, changeable, and so on. I have always felt that such accounts are
bits of folk semantics. They may well reveal something about people's gender stereotypes and sense of humour, but as explanations of linguistic usages they should
be taken with the same large pinch of salt that folk etymologies usually require.
Whatever the ultimate origins of rigid feminine gender assignment to inanimates,
it may be that this is now simply a stylistic convention associated with certain
semantic categories in TVE and other varieties of English. However, we will return
to this question below.

6.2.5. *Things that may be either masculine or feminine*

6.2.5.1. Two hypotheses about the semantics of variable gender assignment

Things that show variable animate gender demand a dynamic semantic or pragmatic explanation (just as the decision to animate does). In TVE things that may
be either masculine or feminine are typically items of portable property—goods
which can be carried (as opposed to vehicles, which carry people or goods). The
circumstances that determine gender choice for members of this broad class are not
completely clear. The variation cannot be due to an inherent property of the object
itself. It must therefore reflect some external factor, such as the speaker's attitude,
or a relationship between the referent and some other entity in the discourse.

When I first tried to account for variable gender choice in TVE usage (see (6)
above and associated discussion) I suggested that a crucial factor seems to be the
presence or absence of '(emotional) attachment' (or 'involvement'). The hypothesis is that the speaker will use *she* if he or she, or other participants in the discourse, have some personal interest in or emotional involvement with the referent,
but will otherwise use *he*. That is to say, the choice of *he* indicates an attitude of
detachment, objectivity, or distance. Thus, an axe, knife, coat, chair, or table that is
the speaker's or addressee's personal possession, or if it is admired or is the focus

of anger or sadness, or if it is otherwise of interest, will be *she*. But if one sells these goods for a living, and is speaking of them as objects for sale, display, or delivery, he or she may refer to one of them as *he*. Using the masculine pronoun is appropriate, for example, when a salesman is talking about the carpets or refrigerators that he is selling or when a plumber is buying or fitting pipes.

Wierzbicka (n.d.) justifiably finds my appeal to 'attachment' unsatisfactory because this notion is too elastic and vague. She suggests that what underlies the choice of *she* with portable goods (and certain other entities) is the idea of being able to be manipulate the referent, being able to do something to or with it. The brutal truth is that animation is a male invention and ultimately the assignment of feminine gender to certain objects is driven by a sexual simile. Men use *she* for objects that they feel they can do things to, as they can to a woman. By contrast, they use a masculine pronoun when their feelings towards the object are more objective or detached, as they typically are towards other men. This may not be a very edifying or elevated motive for assigning feminine gender, Wierzbicka says, but that is life.

Wierzbicka also proposes to include vehicles under the rubric of things that are manipulated. It is true that vehicles are always feminine in TVE, she says, but otherwise they have nothing in common with other entities that are obligatorily feminine, such as features of the inanimate environment. Thus, Wierzbicka proposes that in example (18) above, Mark's shift from *it* to *her*, when referring to the wheelbarrow, corresponds to a shift from describing the capacity of the barrow to an act of manipulating the barrow. The strong preference for assigning feminine gender to tools, and to food and drink, is attributed to the same factor: like vehicles, these are things that we manipulate or do things to.

Wierzbicka's hypothesis deserves to be taken seriously. The difficulty is to find ways where this proposal and my own might be falsified. Ideally, we need a corpus which contains many instances of variable gender assignment, allowing statistically significant correlations of particular choices with particular discourse contexts. Unfortunately, we do not have this. We must make do with sifting among the more limited data that are available. So let us press on with this task.

6.2.5.1.1. Tools and other implements   Not all portable goods are treated exactly alike in TVE. The feminine association is stronger with some kinds of

TABLE 6.5. Gender marking for tools in T54

	He	She	It
Axe	0	4	1
Cross-saw	0	0	2
Grab-stacker	0	0	2
Totals	0	4	5

goods than others. Tools and machines—axes, knives, saws, hammers, radios, TVs, and vacuum cleaners, for instance—are more likely to be feminine than, say, a pen or a cup, or a screw or nail. The range of tools represented in T54 is small and does not give a clear indication of the statistical pattern for this class.

In (33) Mark and Ken are putting screws on a trailer. Mark is the speaker, Ken is using the screwdriver.

(33)   Mark: Bloody oath! You're gettin' **'im** tight!
         Tighten **'im**.—OK, 'e's tight.
         [a bit later] Give it to **'er** [i.e. apply full force to the screw]

Why is the screw first *him* and then *her* in (33)? If the detachment hypothesis is right the screw should take the same pronoun throughout this conversation, presumably the masculine one. Wierzbicka (n.d.) suggests that Mark shifts to feminine pronoun in (33) in the last line because he is exhorting Ken to apply full force to the screw.

The next two examples concern a timber gun and a wheel, respectively. Both items are the speaker's personal property.

(34)   That timber gun, **she** splits the log open.
(35)   **She**'s got one stud missing on **it**.

Why the shift from *she* to *it* in (35)? The sentence appears to be a blend of two constructions: *She's got one stud missing* and *There's one stud missing on it*, with the result that the wheel is given two pronominal references, first, as subject of the sentence and second in a locative phrase. The locative phrase 'on it' appears to be an afterthought. One can speculate that a noun in the more topical subject position is more likely to be animated than a noun in a locative phrase.

(36)   [One man talking to another about a **computer**, over morning tea]
         You'll be doing this the old fashioned way, Bill. The modern way is to take
         your computer and set **'er** up in the village.

(37)   [Ad on Australian TV station, farmer talking about an **electric fence**]
         Try nature's test, piece of grass on the fence. Feel a tingle? **She**'s workin'!

In the next two examples men are talking about objects of their work, as salesmen or tradesmen, and use the masculine pronoun.

(38)   [Electrician, from Canberra, trying different **switches** on a switch board]
         Let's try **him**. No, well it must be **this fella**.

(39)   [Melbourne auctioneer, talking about a **floor polisher**]
         Lot 4 A once again **electric floor polisher**
         Nice one
         They never break down
         away you go for a floor polisher

quick 20 bucks for **'im**
10 dollars quick 10 dollars
5 dollars, 5 dollars for the floor polisher
2 and a half dollars who wants **'im**
first up can 'ave **'im** floor polisher 2 and a half
ooh not very impressive crowd today Laurie and Christmas is coming up
too
nobody want **'im** 2 and a half bucks quick
I'll put **'im** with lot 5 Laurie. Can't say we don't try.
(Harris 1992)

6.2.5.1.2. Furniture, carpets   Pieces of furniture are sometimes *he* sometimes *she*, perhaps according to whether they are personal property or objects for sale.

(40)   [Woman to her son, who is moving a small **table** in her house]
          Put **'er** down there.

(41)   [Salesman is showing **carpets** to two customers. He made roughly fifty
          pronominal references to carpets during the sales conversation; all were
          masculine.]
          That **fella** he's a poly [polyester blend], **he**'s two fifty.
          He's a blend, **that bloke**.
          I've had **'im** for a while, it'd be nice to turn **'im** over.
          I'll give **'im** to you for four hundred.

Wierzbicka (n.d.) comments that (41) shows that the salesman is thinking about the carpet in an even-handed objective way (as a professional doing his job should), not like the way a man feels about a woman, but like the way he feels about other men. One might say the same of the auctioneer in (39).

6.2.5.1.3. Implements used in games   Implements used in games are almost invariably *she* in our Australian English data, when animated. For example the ball and the stumps used in cricket are *she*, as is the pitch on which the game is played. It is worth noting that the first published Laws of Cricket, issued in London in 1744, consistently used *she* for the ball (Parker 1949).

(42)   [TV cricket commentator, Channel 9, 12 December 1992. The reference
          is to one of the **stumps** as a batsman is bowled out.]
          Look at that middle stump! Back **she** goes! . . . And the West Indies are
          one for 60.

(43)   [Same commentator, as the **ball** is snicked by the batsman and flies to a
          slip fielder, who juggles the ball]
          He nearly dropped **'er**. That was a near thing!

(44)   [**Soccer ball** has been kicked into a macrocarpa tree. Player, shaking the branch]
        She's stuck. Come down, you bitch!

The ball and stumps are central participants in these situations. They are certainly things that are the undergoers of vigorous action. On the other hand, the players and spectators are not emotionally neutral about them, as the dramatic intonation and choice of words in these utterances shows. The 'attachment' hypothesis predicts that there will be circumstances under which speakers feel indifferent or detached towards these implements and will assign them a masculine pronoun.

6.2.5.1.4. Food and drink   When animated, items of food and drink are nearly always feminine in Transcript 54 (although they are occasionally masculine, as in (48), below). In (45) Harvey and Chas combine in an amusing anecdote about how a certain hardy timber miller reacted when a dog ran off with the leg of mutton that was to be for the millers' lunch.

TABLE 6.6. Gender-assignment for food and drink in T54

	He	She	It
Food	0	8	6
Drink	0	8	3
Totals	0	16	9

(45)   Harv: . . . what was there when the dog took the i-, the the **leg of mutton** under the house? . . .
        Bill's just coming in, I s'pose when the dog,
        when 'e sees 'im come out with **'er**.
        Chas: . . . Bill went in to carve the meat up
        and out come the bloody dog.
        Harv: With the meat!
        Chas: . . . No, 'e said '**She**'ll be blamed well all right.'
        . . . bit of blamed good meat.
        He brushed it [the dirt?]-
        a bit of blamed dirt on **it** won't 'urt you
        and brushed it off.
        Harv: And took **'er** in and put **'er** on the plate!
        Chas: Yeah. Carved **'er** up, yeah.

(46)   [Man cooking in a pizza shop refers to a **pizza** that has not been collected]
        She's been there for a while.

(47)   [Woman refers to a **pot of potatoes** on the stove]
        She's nearly cooked.

(48)   [Men at a picnic lunch]
        A: Can I have that **sandwich**?
        B: No you can't, **he**'s mine.

6.2.5.2. Summary

The preceding brief survey is inconclusive about the precise bases of variable animate gender assignment in TVE. The evidence is sufficient to show that neither the 'thing that one is attached to' hypothesis nor the 'thing that one manipulates' hypothesis is entirely sufficient to explain all cases. For example, there are cases when the manipulated referent is *he*, instead of *she*. Wierzbicka appeals to 'detachment' to explain these cases, as for instance a salesman or tradesman seeking to convey professional objectivity. This is a very reasonable proposal but is difficult to evaluate without a large body of examples. And there are many cases when a piece of personal property or other goods are referred to as *she*, even though not in the context of an action where they are manipulated. Of course one can say that the speaker thinks of them as things that *can* be manipulated. But here the argument is in danger of becoming circular, or at least leaving the realm of testable claims, unless we can find independent linguistic or behavioural evidence to support it.

6.3. GENDER ASSIGNMENT IN TWO REGIONS OF THE USA

6.3.1. *'Intimate' vs. 'normative' patterns of pronoun use in LA and Buffalo*

I turn now to the second study (Mathiot 1978), a pioneering study of gender assignment in spoken English in two parts of the USA. A special virtue of this paper is that it includes the data on which Mathiot's analysis is based.[4]

Over a period of three and a half years in the 1960s Madeleine Mathiot took notes on gender assignment in Los Angeles County, recording uses of *he* and *she* for inanimate referents, and cases where a mature human was referred to as *it*, in informal face-to-face talk. Subsequently, Mathiot and her assistant Marjorie Roberts observed pronoun use in Buffalo in the state of New York, over a period of some six years. In addition to their observations of conversational uses they constructed a questionnaire to ask people about their own and their acquaintances' use of masculine and feminine pronouns for inanimates. The questionnaire did not produce reliable judgements regarding people's own speech practices and was abandoned in favour of relying on observations of spontaneous speech. However, questioning informants about their reasons for gender assignment did produce interesting data on attitudes and rationalizations.

---

[4] Professor Mathiot kindly sent me a copy of her paper in the late 1980s after hearing about the Tasmanian study.

Mathiot's analysis of the cultural significance of gender assignment proceeds on two levels of abstraction: semantic and cognitive. In semantic analysis the question is: What is the relation between linguistic form and referent? In cognitive analysis it is: What do the results of the semantic analysis reveal about that aspect of reality referred to by means of the grammatical category under study? Semantic analysis is based on 'inferences drawn directly from the data', while cognitive analysis is based on 'inferences drawn from the results of the semantic analysis' (Mathiot 1978: 1–2).

Mathiot refers to non-standard uses of pronouns as 'the intimate pattern', in contrast to the 'normative pattern' prescribed by the grammar books and other authorities. In the normative pattern, *he* and *she* always mean 'human' while *it* means either 'not human' or of 'ambiguous human status'. In the opposition between *he* and *she*, *he* is the unmarked term and *she* is marked. Thus, while *she* always means 'female', *he* means either 'male' or 'unspecified as to sex'. Mathiot mentions the case of babies who are regarded as lovable but as lacking the faculty of reason, so are not fully human and are referred to as *it*. This faculty she takes to be the critical semantic feature defining humans. (Besides babies, fetuses, ghosts, corpses, and aliens can be *it* in the normative pattern.)

The intimate pattern is said to have three semantic elements: *personification* (or *upgrading* of a non-human referent), *denial of human status* (or *downgrading* of a human referent) and *sex role reversal* (calling a man *she*, or a woman *he*). Gender assignments in the intimate style were used to draw inferences about the patterns of covert meaning signalled by the use of pronouns.

The striking characteristic of the use of 'he', 'she' and 'it' in the intimate pattern is the speaker's disregard for the attributes that serve as the defining criteria in the normative pattern: (1) *human status* and (2) *biological sex*, and (3) the *permanence of status* of entities. . . .

It is proposed that through the disregard of the rules of the normative pattern the speaker *unconsciously* expresses an alternative cultural conception of the nature of entities, more specifically of humanness, maleness and femaleness. The meanings conveyed through the intimate pattern are therefore all covert meanings.   (Mathiot 1978: 7; emphasis in original)

Mathiot thinks that any non-human entity can be upgraded ('animated', in my terms). Downgrading is much more restricted in its application. It is typically used to show contempt for an adult person (someone who does not behave like a civilized human being). Mathiot also uses 'downgrading' to refer to cases where the speaker shifts to *it* for an inanimate entity that earlier in the discourse has been upgraded to *he* or *she*.

Mathiot and Roberts found that the intimate pattern of pronoun use occurred only in informal contexts. When employees were dealing with a customer or their boss, for instance, they kept to the normative pattern.

Mathiot thinks of the intimate pattern as having been originated by men, though imitated by women, and regards the values it expresses as primarily male ones.

Thus, male views of women and of their own sex are expressed in the choice of pronoun for inanimates. Men think of women typically as beautiful, as objects to be won or treasured, as rewards or sources of pride and sensual pleasure or as decorative creatures untouched by human needs—all images that evoke appreciation. But they also think of women as incompetent, in that they are seen as emotional, weak, unintelligent, and as a challenge to manhood—images that evoke contempt, irritation, or frustration. Objects that evoke these feelings are likely to be referred to as *she*. By contrast, men typically think of themselves as brave, strong, good-natured, and competent but as ugly. Thus objects that evoke feelings of respect, self-esteem, or self-deprecation are likely to be called *he*.

Women's pattern of gender assignment differs in some respects from that of men. These differences are taken to imply different cultural values, e.g. they indicate that women think of men as infantile and of themselves as mature.

The commentaries introducing examples in Sections 6.3.2 and 6.3.3 summarize Mathiot's interpretations of cognitive bases of gender assignment by male and female speakers.

6.3.2. *Patterns of upgrading typical of men*

6.3.2.1. Typically male uses of *he*

In the following examples the use of *he* is said to express male speakers' conceptions of men as brave or good-natured.

(49)   [Homeowner describing a **rabbit** he has been fighting with]
        There **he** was, just as bold as brass walking through my garden. I could
        have killed **him**.

(50)   [During the Vietnam War the **Viet Cong** were heard being referred to as
        he.]

In the following examples *he* and *she* are interpreted as expressing men's associations of emotional competence with males:

(51)   [Radio announcer referring to the spacecraft **Mariner IV**]
        We told **him** to open **his** camera and **he** did.

(52)   [Reporter describing how a **watchdog** did his duty]
        If not for this the prowler would have gone unnoticed. The dog is the hero
        of the neighbourhood since **he** saved the day.

6.3.2.2. Male uses of *she*

In (53)–(58) *she* expresses the speakers' conception of women as a challenge to men.

(53)   [Workman trying to fix a **key** that keeps getting stuck]
        . . . That's why **she** is so hard to turn.

(54)   [Two movers having trouble getting a big **refrigerator** through a door-way]
         Now push **her** in!

(55)   [Workman fixing a **metal strip** along a window]
         I'll just bend **her** out, just a little more.

(56)   [Same man, adjusting **nylon strings** holding a flower pot]
         Just cut **her** right here!

(57)   [Young skier talking about a **slope**]
         You ski down **her**.

(58)   [Teenage boy advising another surfer about catching a **wave**]
         You catch **her** at **her** height.

In the next two examples **she** refers to a prized possession.

(59)   [Man talking about a **car**]
         Her points are gone and **her** battery needs water. Other than that, **she**'s in good shape.

(60)   [Man talking about a **bike** he has owned for years]
         She has just about had it.

In examples (61)–(64) men use *she* to express the speaker's conception of the entity as important or valuable.

(61)   [Workman unloading **crates**]
         Hey, watch what you're doing with **her**. Treat **her** nice.

(62)   [**Car** salesman]
         It's the cleanest on the lot. **She**'ll sell for twelve hundred dollars.

(63)   [**Chairlift ticket**]
         Don't lose **her**!

(64)   [New **TV set**]
         Let's see how **she** goes!

In (65)–(67) it is suggested that men use *she* to show emotional incompetence.

(65)   [Reporter being televised sitting on a boat]
         The **river** is rising fast. **She**'s expected to crest at noon.

(66)   [Young man talking about the **wind**]
         She's blowing hard. It almost blew over the tree.

(67)   [Farmer]
         The **storm** wrecked my whole farm. **She** spared nothing.

6.3.3. *Upgrading patterns specific to women*

Certain uses by women of *he* for inanimates reveal their view of men as typically helpless, infantile, or cute, or as exasperating or annoying.

In (68)–(75) the use of *he* is attributed to the (female) speaker's conception of the entity referred to as small and/or helpless:

(68)   [**Cactus**, whose owner calls all her plants *he*, even big ones]
        He's so little but **he**'s cute.

(69)   [**Fern**]
        If you are going to throw **him** out, don't. I would like to keep **him**.

(70)   [**Wasp**]
        Don't hurt **him**!

(71)   [**Chair**]
        He has lost his leg, so don't sit on **him** unless you like the floor.

(72)   [**Car**]
        The Little Fellow is not feeling well. We took **him** to the garage but it didn't help **him** much. We'll have to get rid of **him** soon.

(73)   [**Bird**] Look at that crazy bird. **He**'s going to break his wings beating them against the window like that!

(74)   [Waitress talking about a **doughnut** with a lit candle in the middle]
        Oh! Isn't **he** cute! I don't want to eat **him**!

(75)   [Office worker talking about a **paper clip**]
        Oh! **He**'s a cute one. Look how little **he** is. I don't know what you can use him for but **he** is cute.

In the following examples the use of *he* expresses a woman's annoyance or exasperation at the entity referred to (it is suggested that the switch to *it* indicates an increase in negative feelings towards the entity).

(76)   [**Bedspread**, speaker is a clerk in a department store]
        This one has been around long enough! I say, get rid of **it**! **He** is A season. Get rid of **it**!

(77)   [**Towel**, clerk in department store]
        Do you realize how many times I have picked **him** up? He keeps slipping off the shelf. Next time this happens I'm going to leave **it** on the floor. See how **he** likes it.

(78)   [**Typewriter**]
        What the hell is the matter with this thing? **It** just won't work for me. **He** usually isn't like this.

(79)   **[Bicycle]**
        I was going to give **him** a name. But after two blowouts, what can I call
        it?

(80)   [Clerk in department store, about a **rug**]
        He has been such a trouble. Nobody likes **him** . . .

In the final example, the masculine pronoun is said to connote inconsequentiality.

(81) [Neighbour, having received an apology for late return of a small **vase**]
        Oh! Don't make anything of **him**.

6.4. A REANALYSIS OF THE AMERICAN DATA

These two studies of gender assignment in informal varieties of English spoken in
Australia and the USA were carried out independently using somewhat different
methods. The authors' conclusions show some common ground but diverge quite
sharply in certain respects. However, I believe the differences are much less than
appears in the two analyses. In this section I propose a reanalysis of parts of the
American data.

6.4.1. *Points of agreement*

Let me begin with the points of agreement. My reading of the Tasmanian data
accords with Mathiot's view of the American data on several points:

   (*a*) The 'animated' (or 'upgraded') uses of pronouns marks intimacy and infor-
          mality.
   (*b*) The nonstandard uses of pronouns are most strongly maintained by men,
          with women's use of them less frequent and probably imitative.
   (*c*) Some inanimate referents can be referred either as *he* and *she*.
   (*d*) The choice of animate pronoun in such cases conveys some sort of affective
          information.

I also accept Mathiot's interpretation of 'downgrading' a human referent (where
someone uses *it* for another person, other than a child) as a device for belittling
someone.

6.4.2. *Points of disagreement*

A crucial point of disagreement concerns the scope of variable animate gender
assignment, where a given inanimate referent can be either *he* or *she*. Mathiot
assumes that, for her American speakers, any inanimate entity can take either a
masculine or feminine pronoun. By contrast, I regard variable gender in TVE as
applying only to a class that can be approximately defined as 'portable goods'.

Naturally, this difference has a marked effect on the way one approaches the semantic and pragmatic analysis of gender assignment. Whereas fixed gender assignment can be described in terms of inherent semantic properties inherent to a class, variable animate gender demands a different kind of analysis. It is thus not surprising that Mathiot takes her analysis of all instances of gender assignment to a more abstract, 'cognitive' level, looking for correlations with gender stereotypes, a step which was not seriously attempted in my study of the Australian material.

Examination of the examples cited by Mathiot of upgrading in men's speech suggests that she has considerably overestimated the scope of variable gender, especially among her male informants. Nearly all the eighty examples spoken by American men are entirely in accord with the rules for Tasmanian Vernacular English.

Plants and animals of unknown sex are masculine, and all other things excluding portable goods are feminine. Portable goods vary between masculine and feminine, as one would expect from the Tasmanian rules, but in the American male sample are predominantly feminine. The patterns evident in the women's speech agree up to a point with those for the men. Animals of unknown sex are masculine for women, and plants are generally so (ten masculine against four feminine pronouns).

TABLE 6.7. Distribution of referents in animated usage in Mathiot (1978)

	He	She
Animals of unknown sex		
Men	4	0
Women	5	1
Trees and plants		
Men	6	0 or 1[5]
Women	10	4
Tools and implements		
Men	1	9
Women	9	3
Other artefacts of house and garden		
Men	1	3
Women	17	2
Vehicles		
Men	0	41
Women	15	5
Environment		
Men	0	0
Women	0	7

[5] The one example of a man using a feminine pronoun for a plant is questionable because the reference could also be to the general situation.

The tabulation of frequencies (Table 6.7) is drawn from Siemund (2001). In his tables Siemund does not use a portable goods category but instead recognizes categories of 'tools and implements' and 'artefacts of house and garden'. These striking agreements across geographically distant varieties of English cannot be coincidental. It is extremely unlikely that the resemblances between Tasmanian and north-east USA English have spread by diffusion, or that they have developed independently. The most reasonable explanation is that they represent shared inheritance of a pattern that existed in Britain at a fairly early stage in the colonization of North America, say in the eighteenth century. I have argued elsewhere that a pattern similar to TVE goes back to at least the sixteenth century in England (Pawley 1995*a*).

It may be that Mathiot's interest in the cultural resonances of gender assignment led her to overlook these more mundane linguistic regularities. Interpreting people's motives for grammatical choices is a tricky business. The argument can easily become circular. Why does someone use a feminine pronoun for referent X in a certain instance? Because X is seen as having certain feminine characteristics. How do we know the speaker regards X as having feminine characteristics? Because the speaker uses a feminine pronoun for it. It is hard to see how one's speculations might be falsified in such cases, without independent evidence of a sort that we seldom find. Often the affective meaning attributed to the pronouns seems merely to be the affective meaning given by the whole sentence, or by the adjective, and cannot be safely attributed to the pronoun itself.

If American men, like Tasmanians, use fixed gender assignment for most semantic domains, does this undermine Mathiot's main enterprise, which is to seek explanations for gender assignment in terms of cultural values? I think not. Wierzbicka has made a vigorous case for extending the enterprise to the Tasmanian data. But, to repeat, it is a tricky business. Here, and in Section 6.2.4.1, I have pointed to some methodological issues in pursuing this goal.

Mathiot's data show some striking differences between men's and women's usages, differences which cannot be reconciled with the Tasmanian data. For the American women vehicles are three times more often *he* than *she*. What is going on here? Taking a leaf out of Mathiot's book, one might suggest that women regard their cars as sex symbols, reversing the gender assignment they know men apply to cars. For tools and domestic equipment the American women also strongly favour *he*. Combining these two categories gives a total of twenty-six masculine pronouns as against five feminine for women, compared with two and twelve for men, almost a complete reversal of ratio. I am dubious of the reasons proposed by Mathiot to explain particular choices, because similar reasons were proposed to explain male gender assignments to plants, animals, and cars, where no such reasons are necessary. But I cannot offer an alternative cognitive or cultural explanation for the male–female differences in the American data. Making sense of gender assignment in varieties of English remains a challenge.

In terms of cognitive and/or cultural patterns, one thing that makes gender assignment in English of particular interest is that speakers who command both formal standard English and non-standard varieties such as TVE must, presumably, shift between two different ways of viewing the world. There is no difference in principle between polylectal and bilingual speakers. Whether these linguistic shifts correspond to cognitive shifts of a fundamental nature is another question.

6.5. AFTERTHOUGHT: A WHORFIAN EXPLANATION OF A BLIND SPOT

The pervasiveness of grammatical animation in informal English speech has not been widely noticed by English grammarians until recently. Why not? One can offer a sort of Whorfian explanation.

The normative tradition influences one's perceptions of languages, what one notices and remembers. Mathiot found this with her informants. Many said they used only the normative pattern of gender assignment even though this was palpably false. She concludes that people are remarkably unaware of the intimate pattern (or else remarkably aware of the normative pattern). It happens that the conventions for grammatical animation, like certain other stylistic features, are largely below the level of consciousness, and introspective judgements about the frequency and conventions of animation are unreliable.

My own experience with many Australians and New Zealanders (though not with paradigmatic speakers of TVE) is similar. In particular I have been surprised by the lack of awareness by some Australian and New Zealand linguists of a pattern of usage that can be heard all around them. The most reasonable conclusion is that these linguists' perceptions of English usage patterns are strongly influenced by their knowledge of normative patterns. The persistence of this blind spot has been aided by the rarity of careful studies of natural spoken discourse until fairly recent times.

REFERENCES

BROWN, ROGER, and GILMAN, ALBERT. 1960. 'The pronouns of power and solidarity.' In Thomas E. Sebeok (ed.), *Style in Language*. Cambridge, Mass.: MIT Press, 253–76.
CAMPION, SARAH. 1941. *Mo Burdekin*. London: Peter Davies.
——1942. *Bonanza*. London: Peter Davies.
GRACE, GEORGE. 1987. *The Linguistic Construction of Reality*. New York: Croom Helm.
HARRIS, ELIZABETH. 1992. 'Auction this day'. Ph.D. thesis, Department of Linguistics, La Trobe University.
MATHIOT, MADELEINE, assisted by MARJORIE ROBERTS. 1978. 'Sex roles as revealed through referential gender in American English'. In M. Mathiot (ed.), *Boas, Sapir and Whorf Revisited*. The Hague: Mouton, 1–47.

PADDOCK, HAROLD. 1991. 'The actuation problem for gender change in Wessex versus Newfoundland.' In P. Trudgill and J. Chambers (eds.), *Dialects of English: Studies in Grammatical Variation*. London: Longman, 29–47.

PARKER, ERIC. 1949. *The History of Cricket*. London: Seeley Service & Co.

PAWLEY, ANDREW. 1995*a*. 'Gender assignment in Tasmanian English'. Typescript. Department of Linguistics, Research School of Pacific and Asian Studies, Australian National University.

——1995*b*. 'Some characteristics of Tasmanian Vernacular English'. Typescript. Paper read to Australian Linguistic Society Conference, Canberra, September 1995.

ROGERS, NORMAN. 1979. *Wessex Dialect*. Bradford-on-Avon: Moonraker Press.

SHERRY, NORMAN. 1988. *Conrad*. New York: Thames & Hudson.

SIEMUND, PETER. 2001. 'Pronominal gender in English: a study of English varieties from a cross-linguistic perspective'. Freie Universität Berlin, Fachbereich Philosophie und Geisteswissenschaften, Institut für Englische Philologie.

WIERZBICKA, ANNA. 1979. 'Ethnosyntax and the philosophy of grammar'. *Studies in Language*, 3.3: 313–83.

——n.d. 'Sexism in grammar: the semantics of gender in Australian English'. Printout. School of Language Studies, Faculty of Arts, Australian National University.

7

A Study in Unified Diversity: English and Mixtec Locatives

RONALD W. LANGACKER

Among the fascinations of natural language is its amenability to being character-ized by two apparently contradictory statements: (i) that all languages are basic-ally alike; and (ii) that languages may be fundamentally different from one another and can vary without essential limit. Linguistic theorists face the challenge of accommodating the observations and insights that support these opposing pos-itions. Ideally, an overall account of language structure should specify both the nature of its universality and the extent of its diversity, as well as the source of each. One facet of this problem constitutes the focus of the present volume: how much of the structural diversity of languages can be attributed to the differing cultural preoccupations of their speakers? I will not attempt to answer that question directly. Instead, I will caution against overestimating the extent of cross-linguistic varia-tion, even in cases where grammatical differences are initially rather striking.

This cautionary stance does not indicate any negative attitude toward the basic hypothesis of ethnosyntax. I believe in fact that culture has myriad manifestations in grammar (Langacker 1994). I feel, moreover, that the patterns favoured in a language are reasonably viewed as constituting a culturally appropriate 'cogni-tive style'. At the same time, linguistic (as well as cultural) diversity can be seen as developing from a shared array of resources reflecting universal aspects of the human body, mind, and experience. These shared resources define a vast field of structural possibilities, which are nonetheless quite limited relative to those con-ceivable for arbitrary creatures in arbitrary worlds. Since we take these limits for granted, language structures can seem profoundly different despite their common basis. I suggest that linguistic diversity stems primarily from how that basis is exploited: the specific options chosen, their combinatory potential, and the extent to which comparable structures are conventionally utilized.

I will approach these matters from the standpoint of *cognitive grammar* (Lan-gacker 1987*a*, 1990*a*, 1991, 1999*b*). The vision of a basic unity underlying the impressively rich diversity of structures encountered both within a language and

An earlier version of this chapter appeared as Langacker 1999*a*. I would like to thank the editors of the journal *RASK* for their kind permission to reproduce this revised version.

cross-linguistically is fundamental to this theory. It claims, for example, that lexicon, morphology, and syntax form a continuum fully describable as assemblies of *symbolic structures* (i.e. symbolic pairings between *semantic* and *phonological* structures). It thereby achieves a unified account of phenomena traditionally but problematically assigned to distinct 'components' of the grammar, while at the same time recognizing and accommodating the continuous parameters of variation that render symbolic assemblies so diverse.[1] Cognitive grammar adopts a similar perspective with respect to cross-language comparison. On the one hand it emphasizes the semantic and grammatical uniqueness of every language. Formal differences are taken as symptomatic of semantic differences. Moreover, every language evolves vast inventories of constructions each of which embodies a particular way of construing certain kinds of situations. This effusion of symbolic resources is nonetheless seen as manifesting a common human potential deriving from biological endowment, bodily experience, and basic cognitive abilities. A limited array of descriptive constructs have been proposed that are central to the characterization of lexico-grammatical structure in all its diversity.

This chapter focuses on unity-in-diversity in the domain of locative expressions. It discusses why languages vary so greatly in how they code such a fundamental aspect of human experience. Examined in particular are two languages—English and Mixtec—whose representations of spatial relationships are strikingly different. A comparison of their descriptions in cognitive grammar will serve to elucidate the specific nature of both their divergence and their commonality. Briefly considered as well is the frequent path of grammaticization whereby nouns evolve into adpositions.

7.1. GENERAL OBSERVATIONS

One does not go very far out on a limb in asserting that every language has ways of expressing spatial location and paths of spatial motion. Nor is there much risk in suggesting that such notions are in some sense basic, as witnessed by the propensity of locative expressions to grammaticize (note the infinitival *to*) and to serve as the basis for metaphorical extension to other domains of experience (e.g. *go out on a limb*). This seems only natural. We are, after all, spatial creatures who must occupy and navigate a spatial world. We are also creatures whose primary sense—vision—is specially suited for the detection and representation of spatial relationships.

Because they are fundamental and utterly ubiquitous, spatial relations are easily taken for granted. Scholars tend to think of them as being readily describable and well understood. Also, since spatial experience is quite similar for all people in many basic respects, there is a tendency to assume that its linguistic expression

---

[1] Among these factors are size, novelty, regularity, productivity, specificity, and the kinds of meanings expressed. There is no reason whatever to believe that natural distinctions made with respect to one parameter will invariably delimit the same set of elements as those made with respect to any other.

is roughly comparable from language to language. Such factors are hard to measure, and it is not unlikely that these attitudes have some basis. The actual investigation of locative systems has nonetheless brought unanticipated findings and raised
theoretical issues that are far from resolution. To take just one example, the work
of Herskovits (1985, 1986, 1988) and especially Vandeloise (e.g. 1985*a*, 1985*b*,
1988, 1991, 1994) raises the question of the extent to which spatial prepositions
are actually spatial in nature. They show that normal prepositional usage is replete
with examples which seemingly vitiate any straightforward geometric characterization. We say, for instance, that a pear is *in* a bowl even when it rests on a mound
of fruit which raises every part of it above the uppermost part of the bowl and thus
places it wholly outside the bowl's convex closure. Vandeloise argues that prepositional meaning is more fundamentally a matter of *function* than of spatial configuration. The functions *container* and *contents* allow one to describe the distribution
of *in* more coherently and revealingly than does spatial inclusion.

In recent years, empirical investigation has turned up considerably more variety in the linguistic coding of spatial relations than theorists might have contem-
plated a priori. For instance, not every language instantiates the familiar pattern
of describing the location of objects mainly in relative terms, i.e. just in relation
to other objects. An attested alternative, exemplified by the Australian language
Guugu Yimithirr (Haviland 1992; Levinson 1992), is to rely primarily on fixed
directions: 'There are languages that encode very few "prepositional" notions, do
not use left and right in an extended spatial sense, and indeed require the conception of spatial relations in a fundamentally non relative manner . . . In Guugu Yimithirr . . . nearly all spatial descriptions involve essential reference to something
like our cardinal directions . . . To describe someone as standing in front of the
tree, one says something equivalent (as appropriate) to "George is just North of the
tree" . . . , or to tell someone where you left your tobacco "I left it on the Southern
edge of the Western table in your house", or to ask someone to turn off the camping
gas stove "turn the knob West" and so on' (Levinson 1992: 2–3).

Let us briefly note just a few other departures from the Standard Average European style of expressing locative relationships. Cora (a Uto-Aztecan language of
Mexico) is striking for the sheer density of locative expressions. It is usual for a
clause to harbour at least one and commonly several locative elements in the form of
adverbial particles, adpositional constructions, and verb-prefix combinations. Also
striking is the central role the system accords to topographical features (e.g. 'off to
the side in the face of the slope at a medium distance'), which it projects metaphorically to other domains, including the human body (Casad 1982, 1984; Casad and
Langacker 1985). Another Mexican language, Zapotec (Oto-Manguean), is noteworthy for the highly regular way in which a complete set of seven body-part terms
is applied to other kinds of entities (MacLaury 1989). A comparable pattern of
extension is one factor in the Mixtec locatives discussed below.

Even these few examples should make it clear that languages vary quite substantially in the kinds of information conveyed by locative expressions as well as their

conventional ways of construing and portraying objectively similar situations.[2] Of course, extensive commonalities can also be noted. English too makes use of cardinal directions, topographical features, and the metaphorical extension of body-part terms. The contrast with the languages cited is thus not absolute but more a matter of emphasis or centrality, as measured by such factors as frequency, specificity, systematicity, and degree of grammaticization. Pending a comprehensive cross-linguistic survey, it seems reasonable to expect a certain number of basic spatial notions (e.g. *contact, separation, inclusion, proximity, line, surface, source-path-goal*) to figure prominently in the locative systems of all languages. I also suspect one would find many interesting parallelisms by comparing in detail the verb-prefix systems of Russian (as analysed in Janda 1986, 1988) and of Cora (Casad 1982, 1993). A primary function of each system is to specify the location or configuration of the verbal process in *image schematic* terms (cf. Johnson 1987; Lakoff 1987).

The cross-language similarities of locative systems should therefore not be underestimated, and later sections will emphasize certain abstract commonalities in the systems of English and Mixtec. The point remains, however, that every language develops a unique and extremely rich inventory of conventional symbolic resources for expressing relations in space and (by extension) in other domains. Whatever their specific nature, the universal constraints and conceptual primitives underlying locative systems allow extraordinary diversity with respect to their combination into higher-order structures as well as the conventionally determined ways of applying such structures to particular kinds of situations in space and myriad other realms of experience.

Although we have focused thus far on diversity in the content of locative expressions, languages also show substantial variation in regard to its formal manifestation. Noteworthy here is the exploration by Talmy (1975, 1991) of language-specific patterns in the 'conceptual conflation' of events, i.e. the packaging of distinguishable event components into single lexemes. In the case of spatial motion, Talmy documents alternative ways of packaging conceptual components pertaining to the manner of motion, its path, and properties of the mover ('figure') as well as the entity with respect to which it moves ('ground'). He observes, for example, that Atsugewi (a Hokan language of northern California) has a series of verb roots that conflate the idea of motion or location with properties of the figure, e.g. *qput* 'for dirtlike material to move/be-located'. It further has a series of verb suffixes that specify both a path and properties of the ground, as in *-ict̓* 'into a liquid'. The two combine productively to form verb stems compactly encoding what has to be expressed in English via lengthy periphrasis: *qputict̓* 'for dirtlike material to move into a liquid'.

Hence there is nothing inevitable about the English-type pattern of coding paths and locations by means of prepositional phrases. Some languages have very few

---

[2] For further discussion of the range of variation in locative systems, see Bloom *et al.* 1996 and Talmy 2000: ch. 2.

preposition-like elements and rely on other devices for conveying comparable information. Palauan, for example, evidently has just one (Georgopoulos 1985: 43). Another language with very few prepositions is Chalcatongo Mixtec (an Oto-Manguean language spoken in Mexico), as described in Brugman (1983) and Brugman and Macaulay (1986). A comparison of the English and Mixtec systems will be our main concern in what follows.

7.2. THE MIXTEC SYSTEM

From the Anglocentric perspective, the variety of Mixtec described by Brugman and Macaulay is noteworthy for the essential absence of elements clearly identifiable as adpositions. Whereas English generally uses a prepositional phrase to specify a spatial path or location, the Mixtec equivalent instead contains a noun-noun compound, the first component of which is a body-part term:

(1)   *nindečé i̧i̧   saà šini žúnu*
        flew   one bird head tree
        'A bird flew over the tree.'

Of the three elements found in the language that might be considered prepositional, two derive historically from body-part terms, while the third is non-locative (benefactive) and possibly analysable. Brugman thus suspects that there are no 'primary prepositions' in the language.

The lexemes that function as the first member of these path- or location-specifying compounds are *šíni* 'head', *ha₹à* 'foot/leg', *siki* 'back [animal]', *ini* 'stomach', *nda₹a* 'hand/arm', *žata* 'back [human]', *čìì* 'belly', and *nuù* 'face'. They are the basic terms for the body-parts in question and are recognized as such even in locative uses. Both these lexemes and the compounds they form show the behaviour we expect of nouns, e.g. they can be possessed and act as clausal subjects:

(2)   *šini-rí   ₹ú₹ù*
        head-my hurt
        'My head hurts.'

(3)   *nda₹a žúnu tá₹nu*
        hand tree break
        'The tree's branch is breaking.'

Brugman discusses their categorial status in some detail and concludes that they are best analysed as nouns even in locational expressions. She does however allow that in these uses the body-part terms are less than fully noun-like, having undergone to varying degrees a process of abstraction and grammaticization.

Example (3) illustrates the extension of terms for the body to designate the analogous parts of other kinds of entities. While this type of metaphor is quite frequent in English (*the foot of my bed*, *the shoulder of the road*, *the face of the slope*, etc.), in Mixtec it has to be described as highly pervasive if not systematic. The body-part nouns in question can even be applied to facets of other body-parts. Thus in (4), *nuù* 'face' refers to the palm of an open hand, and in (5), *ini* 'stomach' designates the interior of a closed fist.

(4) *hítuu nuù ndàʔa-ri*
    lie   face hand-my
    'It [chalk] is lying on my hand.'

(5) *hítuu ini   ndàʔa-ri*
    lie   stomach hand-my
    'It [chalk] is lying in my hand.'

Despite their interest, we will not dwell on the specifics of these extensions (Brugman discusses them at some length). Our concern is rather to understand how these constructions work in principle.

More is involved than just metaphor. Compare (1) with (6):

(6) *súʔunu-ro   hísndée šini žúnu wąą*
    clothes-your be:on head tree that
    'Your clothes are on that tree.'

In (6), the 'head' of the tree is straightforwardly identified with its upper part. The clothes are directly in contact with that part. By contrast, sentence (1) carries no implication that the bird touched any part of the tree. It merely indicates that some or all of the bird's flight occurs in a region of space *contiguous* to the top of the tree (hence the translation with 'over'). Likewise in (7) and (8):

(7) *ndukoo haʔa žúnu*
    sit   foot tree
    'He is sitting at the foot of the tree.'

(8) *rùʔù nindii-ri nùù maría*
    I   stand-I face Maria
    'I am standing in front of Maria.'

Sentence (7) does not entail that the subject is touching the trunk or roots of the tree, nor would (8) normally be interpreted to mean that I am standing on Maria's face. Once again, they merely indicate that the subject occupies a region contiguous to the part named by the body-part term, whether this is used in its basic sense or is understood metaphorically.

Examples like (1), (7), and (8) are clearly instances of *metonymy*. Mixtec has a regular and productive pattern of semantic extension whereby terms that refer to parts of the body (or their metaphorical analogue) are instead used to designate regions in space *associated* with the parts in question. In a systematic fashion, each term can thus receive any of four basic interpretations. First, it may simply designate a part of the body, as in (2). Alternatively, as seen in (8), it may be construed metonymically as designating the region in space contiguous to the body-part. A third option, exemplified in (3) and (6), is metaphorical transfer from the body to the corresponding part of some other kind of entity. Finally, metaphor and metonymy can both be involved, as in (1) and (7). Here the term winds up designating the region in space contiguous to the metaphoric analogue of a body-part.[3]

Grasping these metaphoric and metonymic patterns constitutes a first level of understanding of the Mixtec locative system. A second level is attained by considering the noun-noun compounds in relation to the locational verbs they co-occur with. This was done by Brugman and Macaulay (1986), who give them the approximate glosses 'be located', 'be standing', 'be sitting', 'be lying', 'be in', 'be on', and 'be in (hidden from view)'. One evident reason why the Mixtec system strikes us as 'exotic' is the different strategy it employs for the lexical packaging of conceptual components ('conceptual conflation' in Talmy's terms): some of the *relational* content that English conveys by means of prepositions is apparently subsumed by the verb stem. Its complement can thus be nominal (a noun-noun compound) instead of relational (like a prepositional phrase). As it stands, however, this description is little more than impressionistic. It remains to achieve a more explicit characterization spelled out in precise technical detail. A main concern in what follows will be to approximate this third level of understanding.

7.3. SOME ENGLISH LOCATIVE CONSTRUCTIONS

A brief examination of English locatives will serve to lay the groundwork for comparison, as well as to introduce some basic notions of cognitive grammar. The theory claims that grammar forms a continuum with lexicon, and that its characterization reduces to assemblies of *symbolic* structures (each residing in the association between a *semantic* and a *phonological* structure—its two *poles*). The reduction of grammar to symbolic assemblies requires a conceptualist semantics that recognizes our ability to structure and portray the same conceived situation in alternative ways. This capacity to impose alternative *construals* on the same conceptual 'content' is pertinent to the description of every semantic structure, and thus every symbolic structure. Inherent in selecting a particular lexico-grammatical element or construction is the implicit decision to construe things in a certain way. Since grammatical elements are usually quite schematic in terms of their content, their primary semantic contribution lies in the construal they impose (cf. Talmy 1988b).

---

[3] The metaphorical and metonymic patterns are highly systematic and fully productive (see the discussion in MacLaury 1989 for the related language Zapotec). For this reason I will simply use the body-part gloss (e.g. 'head') for any of the four interpretations. This does not however imply that speakers learn only the body-part sense of each expression. In the *usage-based* perspective of cognitive grammar (Langacker 2000), it is naturally assumed that particular metaphoric and metonymic extensions (even as applied to particular kinds of objects) are also learned and acquire the status of conventional units, depending on frequency of occurrence.

Let me cite just a few examples of construal (for detailed discussion, see Langacker 1987*a*, 1988, 1990*a*, 1995). We have, first, the ability to conceive and portray a situation at different levels of specificity and detail. For instance, *hammer*, *tool*, and *thing* are successively more *schematic*. We also have the ability to conceive of one structure against the 'background' of another, as in metaphor, where the source domain provides the background for construing the target domain. A third dimension of construal is 'perspective', including 'vantage point' and a variety of other factors. In addition, various kinds of 'prominence' have to be recognized and distinguished. Two of these—*profiling* and *trajector/landmark alignment*—are pivotal in the characterization of grammatical structure.

Within its conceptual *base* (the content it evokes), an expression always selects some substructure as its *profile*, defined as the entity it designates (its referent within the conceptualization). The word *lid*, for instance, evokes as its base the schematized conception of a container and its cover, choosing the latter for its profile. An expression can profile either a *thing* or a *relationship*, in accordance with abstract definitions of these terms (Langacker 1987*a*, 1987*c*). For expressions that profile relationships, an additional kind of prominence comes into play: the degree of salience accorded the relational participants. It is usual for one participant to stand out as the entity a relational expression is concerned with locating, characterizing, or assessing in some fashion. This is called the *trajector*. Often the profiled relationship makes salient reference to a second participant, called a *landmark*. The verb *see*, for example, profiles a perceptual relationship in which the status of trajector and landmark is respectively conferred on the perceiver and the entity perceived. Trajector and landmark status can be thought of metaphorically as primary and secondary spotlights of 'focal prominence' that can be directed at various entities within a scene.

The nature of an expression's profile determines its grammatical category. Abbreviatory notations for some basic classes are given in Fig. 7.1, where heavy lines indicate profiling. A circle represents a thing, and a line connecting two entities stands for a relationship. A relation is either *simple* or *complex*, depending on whether it reduces to a single configuration or has to be characterized as a series

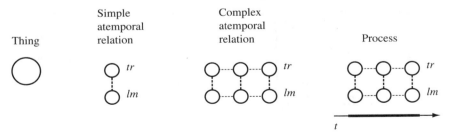

FIG. 7.1

of configurations. A *process* is a complex relation whose evolution through time (*t*) is rendered salient. The labels *tr* and *lm* identify a profiled relation's trajector and landmark. Although these focused participants are shown as things, it is also possible for another relation to function in either capacity. The dotted *correspondence* lines indicate that the component *states* of a complex relation all have the same trajector and the same landmark.

A noun profiles a thing, as do pronouns, determiners, and complex nominal expressions. Expressions with a process for their profile include verbs, finite clauses, and the clausal equivalent of determiners (in the case of English, tense and the modals—see Langacker 1985, 1990*b*, 1991). Various kinds of non-processual relations (said to be *atemporal* because their evolution through time is backgrounded) are designated by such classes as adjectives, adverbs, infinitives, and participles. Of prime concern here are prepositions and prepositional phrases, which profile atemporal relations having a thing as their landmark. The profiled relation is simple for prepositional expressions that specify a location, and complex when they describe a path (which can be analysed as a series of locational specifications).

Consider the preposition *on*, sketched on the lower left in Fig. 7.2. In its basic sense, *on* designates a simple (i.e. single-configuration) relation of contact and support, canonically along the vertical axis. This relation is indicated by the double-headed arrow. Its trajector and landmark are both things, and each is characterized only schematically (so far as the preposition itself is concerned). Grammatical

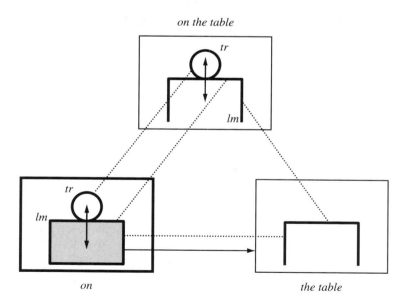

FIG. 7.2

constructions serve to combine the preposition with other elements which specify these focal participants in finer detail. Fig. 7.2 represents the prepositional-phrase construction, in which a noun phrase specifies the preposition's landmark. In the terminology of cognitive grammar, the two *component structures*—*on* and *the table*—are *integrated* to form the *composite structure*, namely *on the table*.[4] Phonologically, their integration involves adjacency in the speech stream and a particular temporal ordering. It is only semantic integration that concerns us here.

A construction is an assembly of symbolic structures linked by correspondences. As shown in Fig. 7.2 by the horizontal dotted line, the pivotal correspondence in a prepositional-phrase construction equates the schematic landmark of the preposition with the profile of the noun phrase. Because it is generally more specific, the noun phrase is said to *elaborate* the preposition's landmark. The horizontal arrow calls attention to this elaborative relationship, and shading signals the landmark's status as an *elaboration site*. To the extent that an expression is compositional,[5] we can think of the composite structure as being derived by superimposing corresponding elements and merging their specifications. Moreover, the composite structure usually profiles the same entity as one of its component structures; in the present example, the prepositional phrase *on the table* designates the same locative relationship as the preposition *on* (and describes it in finer detail). The component whose profile is inherited at the composite structure level is called the *profile determinant* and enclosed with a heavy-line box. A *head* is the profile determinant at a given level of organization, and a *complement* is a component structure that elaborates a salient substructure of the head. The head in a prepositional phrase is thus the preposition, and the object noun phrase (which elaborates its landmark) is a complement.[6]

A construction's composite structure can simultaneously function as a component structure in a higher-order construction. For instance, Fig. 7.3 shows the integration of *be* with *on the table* to form the complex clausal predicate *be on the table*. In most of its uses, *be* takes a complement which profiles an atemporal relation. A finite clause profiles a process, a relationship that is temporal in the sense that its evolution through time is foregrounded. Thus, in deriving a clausal head, *be* serves to temporalize an atemporal relation, deriving a composite structure of the form *be+X* that designates a process.

Like the other auxiliary verbs of English, *be* profiles a highly schematic process (Langacker 1991: 5.3.4). Its meaning includes the notion of a process—a profiled relationship saliently followed in its evolution through time—but gives no detail about the specific nature of that relationship. More precisely, *be* profiles a

---

[4] Here and elsewhere, the semantic contribution of articles will be ignored to avoid irrelevant complications.

[5] Cognitive grammar posits only *partial* compositionality (Langacker 1987*a*: ch. 12).

[6] In a *modifier* construction, a salient substructure of the modifier is instead elaborated by the head.

be on the table

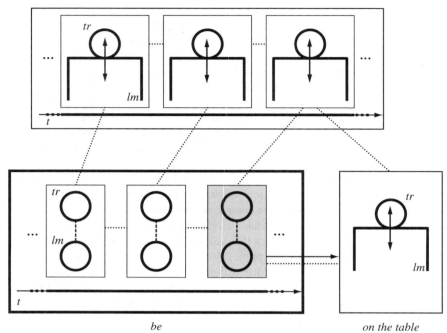

be   *on the table*

FIG. 7.3

schematic *imperfective* process, in which the profiled relation is construed as being constant through time without inherent bounding.[7] In the diagram, the dotted correspondence lines internal to *be* indicate that the component states (enclosed in boxes) are identical, and the absence of bounding is represented by ellipses. The integration of *be* and *on the table* is simply a matter of equating the relation profiled by *on the table* with the one that *be* portrays as continuing unchanged through time.[8] *Be* is the head in this construction and thus determines the processual nature of the composite expression, whereas the prepositional phrase provides the essential content and specifies what particular relation is being followed in its temporal continuation. *On the table* is a complement because it elaborates a salient substructure of the head. To derive a full finite clause, the composite expression *be on the*

---

[7] It thus embodies the abstract semantic commonality of imperfective verbs (*resemble, believe, have, know, like, exist,* etc.) and shares their basic aspectual properties.

[8] The diagram shows *on the table* as elaborating a particular component state of *be*, but the choice is arbitrary, since these states are all identical.

table is combined with other elements at higher levels of grammatical organization: a specification of tense/modality, and a noun phrase that elaborates its schematic trajector and is thus identified as the clausal subject.

7.4. SOME THEORETICAL ISSUES

A Mixtec sentence like (1), repeated here for convenience, contains two nominal elements: a subject (*įį saà*) and another nominal analysed as a noun-noun compound (*šini žúnu*).

(1) *nindečé įį saà šini žúnu*
     flew   one bird head tree
     'A bird flew over the tree.'

One question that arises is why such sentences should be intransitive.[9] They consist of a verb and two non-oblique noun phrases—the subject and another complement. Why is this second complement not a direct object? The answer requires a theoretical account of transitivity that goes beyond equating it with the mere occurrence of two direct complements in a single clause.

From a cognitive linguistic perspective, transitivity does not reside in any particular structural configuration, but is rather a conceptual property arising from the global semantics of a clause and even its contextual interpretation (Rice 1987; see also Hopper and Thompson 1980). Prototypically, it is force-dynamic (Talmy 1988*a*), involving the *energetic interaction* between an *agent* and a *patient*. From this prototype, it extends to encompass numerous other kinds of relationships, all of which nonetheless conform to the schematic characterization of an *interaction* between *participants*.

There is good linguistic evidence for a basic conceptual distinction between *participants* on the one hand and *settings/locations* on the other (Langacker 1986, 1987*b*, 1993). We think of the world as being populated by discrete objects of limited size—participants—that move around within global, relatively stable spatial settings. If the term *setting* is understood as referring to the global surroundings, a *location* is any 'fragment' of the setting, such as the position of a single participant. Canonically, participants merely *occupy* a setting or a location, whereas they *interact* with one another. Even when it remains covert, the distinction between participants and settings/locations proves to have extensive grammatical significance. In particular, since transitivity centres on the notion of energetic interaction, a clause can only be transitive to the extent that its subject and object are construed as

---

[9] Brugman and Macaulay (1986) describe the verbs as being 'formally intransitive'. While they do not cite the morphological basis for this characterization, it is surely valid. I know of specific morphological indications of intransitivity (e.g. absence of an object-marking prefix on the verb) for comparable expressions in other languages.

participants rather than settings or locations. It is therefore possible that a clause which appears to be transitive in terms of its overt form is actually non-transitive because its subject or object receives a locational construal.[10]

To take just one example, the verb *contain* construes its subject as a location:

(9)   *This manuscript contains many errors.*

On the basis of its form (with non-oblique noun phrases in pre- and postverbal position) a sentence like (9) ought to be transitive. However, by the usual test of passivizability, it is not:

(10)   **Many errors are contained by this manuscript.*

It is non-transitive because its subject is locational, whereas transitivity hinges on participant interaction.

Another theoretical issue is how a sentence like (1) can express a locative relationship between two entities when there is no relational element (like a preposition) that connects them by taking them both as arguments. This problem is only apparent, stemming from an impoverished view of linguistic semantics and grammatical composition. From the standpoint of cognitive grammar, linguistic meanings are elaborate conceptualizations any facet of which may participate in the correspondences defining grammatical constructions. A relationship inherent in a component conception can thus be exploited in grammatical and semantic composition even if it is not singled out as the profile of any constitutive element. In the next section we will see how this works in the case of the Mixtec data.

7.5. MIXTEC LOCATIVE CONSTRUCTIONS

The Mixtec locatives are readily described in cognitive grammar. We can best see this by working through a specific example (repeated from above) step by step:

(7)   *ndukoo haʔa žúnu*
         sit   foot tree
         'He is sitting at the foot of the tree.'

Let us start with the noun-noun compound. Its head is the first noun, *haʔa*, which in its basic sense designates a part of the body. In (7), however, it assumes a meaning derived from the basic sense by regular patterns of metaphor and metonymy, as shown in Fig. 7.4. Via metaphor (FOOT → FOOT′) it comes to designate an

---

[10] In cognitive grammar, subjects and objects are schematically characterized as nominal expressions that respectively elaborate the trajector and the landmark of the process profiled at the clausal level of organization. A trajector and landmark are in turn characterized as the elements accorded primary and secondary focal prominence in a profiled relationship. In the case of a process, the most agent-like and patient-like participants usually manage to attract this prominence. It can however be conferred on other elements, even settings and locations, resulting in marked constructions suitable for special discourse purposes.

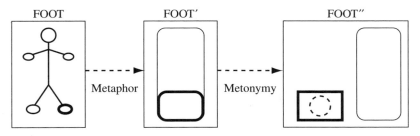

FIG. 7.4

entity which resembles the human foot in being the lower portion of an object with significant vertical extension. Via metonymy (FOOT′ → FOOT″), it comes to designate instead the region in space contiguous to that part of the object.[11] Observe the notational convention of using a rectangle (rather than a closed curve) for the profiled region, to indicate its construal as a location. Whereas a body-part or the analogous part of an object is susceptible to being construed as either a location or a participant, a spatial region *per se* is presumably locational under normal circumstances. Observe as well the inclusion of a dashed-line circle in the profiled region. The very notion of a location evokes to some degree the conception of an entity which occupies that location. The dashed-line circle represents this actual or potential occupant.

While the compound *ha?a žúnu* can designate either the bottom part of a tree or the contiguous spatial region, in expressions like (7) it assumes the latter value. Its assembly thus involves the semantic integration of FOOT″ and TREE, as diagrammed in Fig. 7.5. The construction is quite straightforward. It hinges on a correspondence between the profile of TREE and the unprofiled, vertically extended object evoked by FOOT″. Since the latter makes only schematic reference to this object, TREE serves to elaborate its specifications. FOOT″ is also the construction's head, because the composite structure inherits its profile: the compound as a whole does not designate the tree itself, but rather a spatial region at its base.

In this construction, the two component structures are nouns. Each profiles a kind of thing: a spatial region, and a physical object.[12] There is no explicit relational element which links them by taking them both as arguments. Yet the construction is easily described, using the same basic constructs the theory deploys

---

[11] Since these compounds represent the normal way of labelling parts of objects and expressing locative relationships in the language, FOOT′ and FOOT″ are undoubtedly established senses of *ha?a*, alongside FOOT. We are dealing, then, with *polysemy*: the structures in Fig. 7.4 are part of a network comprising the related conventional meanings of the lexeme. The details of how these notions apply to various kinds of objects presumably involve a mixture of conventionality and creativity.

[12] The term thing is used in its abstract technical sense, which does however approximate one conventional value of the lexeme in everyday English. Note the following: *A region in space may not be everything, but at least it's something, it's not nothing.*

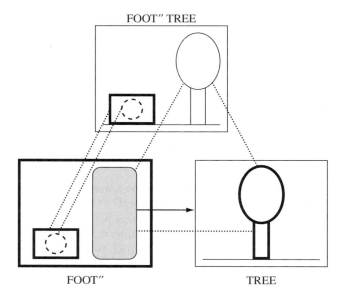

FIG. 7.5

for the description of virtually every construction—notions such as profiling, pro-file determinance, correspondence, and elaboration. Important here are two fun-damental aspects of cognitive semantics, namely the profile/base distinction and conceptual overlap. The first makes it clear how a nominal expression is capable of serving an essentially relational function. Even though *haʔa* profiles a thing, it evokes a relationship as a central feature of the conceptual base with respect to which the profile is characterized. Whether it designates a body-part, the analo-gous part of some other object, or an associated region in space, the profiled entity is conceived and identified through the relation it bears to another, unprofiled thing having significant vertical extension. This relationship is inherited as part of the composite structure's meaning—it does not have to be profiled by an element at any level to be included in the composite semantic value. The second factor, con-ceptual overlap, is reflected in the correspondence between the unprofiled thing evoked by *haʔa* and the profile of *žúnu* 'tree'. TREE elaborates a schematic entity inherent in FOOT″, so there is no need for any other morphological element to establish a connection between them. The requisite link is given by these elements themselves and the correspondence imposed by the construction.

   The last step we need to consider is the integration of *ndukoo* 'sit' with the compound *haʔa žúnu* (foot tree) 'foot of the tree'. As shown in Fig. 7.6, one of the two component structures is the composite structure from Fig. 7.5, which pro-files a region in space. The other component structure, SIT, designates a (presumably imperfective) process in which a certain relationship continues through time unchanged. Such a relation has two facets: postural and locational. The postural specifications of SIT involve both body configuration (crouched, as opposed to fully extended) and force-dynamics (the rump as the primary locus of support). In Fig. 7.6, they are represented abstractly by the vertical double-headed arrow internal to the trajector. With respect to location, SIT specifies a particular orientation (alignment of the trunk more or less along the vertical axis), as well as the absence of motion, and thus makes salient the conception of the trajector being in a certain place. Its location, depicted as a rectangle, may well be a focused element with landmark status.

Hence SIT saliently evokes a schematic location, while FOOT″ profiles a location characterized with greater specificity. Their integration is just a matter of equating these two locations, as well as their occupants (the trajector of SIT, and the potential occupant of the foot-of-the-tree region). Because SIT is the head in this construction, the composite structure profiles a process in which the trajector, for an indefinite span of time, maintains a certain posture in a fixed location beneath a tree. If the sentence had an overt subject, it would elaborate this schematic trajector.

SIT FOOT″ TREE

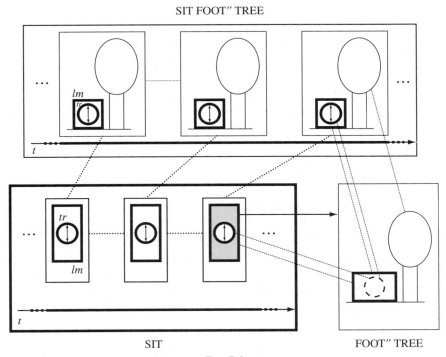

SIT   FOOT″ TREE

FIG. 7.6

Once again, the absence of an overt linking element is unproblematic. The conception of a locative relationship does not have to be introduced by a separate relational element (such as a preposition), being inherent in the meaning of each component structure: it is one facet of SIT's relational profile, and is present (though unprofiled) in the case of FOOT″ TREE. Hence the verbal semantics itself contributes the notion of the trajector being in a certain location, which the nominal compound—through conceptual overlap—renders specific. The compound is a complement because it elaborates a salient substructure of the verbal head. It is not however a direct object, for its referent is a location rather than a participant.

From the glosses supplied by Brugman and Macaulay (1986), namely 'be located', 'be standing', 'be sitting', 'be lying', 'be in', 'be on', and 'be in (hidden from view)', we can reasonably suppose that the Mixtec verbs of location all profile the extension through time of a locative relationship, which they specify in different ways to a limited degree. The most schematic, 'be located', is still more specific than English *be* (Fig. 7.3), since the profiled relation is specifically locational, whereas *be* is used with any kind of atemporal relation (including adjectives, participles, infinitives, and predicate nominatives).[13] Of course, locational compounds are not restricted to sentences containing just these verbs. They occur, for example, with verbs of motion:

(1)   *nindečé įį   saà šini žúnu*
        flew   one bird head tree
        'A bird flew over the tree.'

A verb such as 'fly' incorporates the conception of the mover following a spatial path, whereby it successively occupies a series of locations. Its integration with the locative compound requires only that one or more of these locations be put in correspondence with the location the compound designates.

These compounds occur with other kinds of verbs as well:

(11)   *nikąžáa ini   ndúča*
        drowned stomach water
        'Someone drowned in the water.'

(12)   *sáʔa-rí ndučaʔá nuù molcajete*
        make-I salsa   face mortar
        'I'm going to make salsa in the mortar.'

The notion of spatial location is not particularly salient with these verbs, but neither is it entirely absent—physical events and their participants are always located in some place. While integration depends on conceptual overlap, there is no absolute requirement that the corresponding entities have to be prominent. These con-

[13] Since *be* regularly occurs in construction with a locational complement, it presumably has a conventionally established variant in which a locative relation in particular is extended through time. This specialized variant may be quite comparable to the most schematic locational verb of Mixtec.

structions are thus analogous to Fig. 7.6, involving a correspondence between the location evoked by the verb and the one profiled by the compound, except that the former is relatively non-salient within the verbal semantics.[14]

7.6. FROM NOUNS TO ADPOSITIONS

It is common for body-part expressions to evolve historically into adpositions. Vestiges of this path of grammaticization are seen, for example, in prepositional locutions such as *beside*, *ahead of*, and *in back of*. In the simplest case, the source construction may be quite analogous to the Mixtec compounds, so that the change is simply N N > P N (e.g. HEAD N > OVER N).

Suppose, then, that the body-part nouns of Mixtec should continue along their path of grammaticization and eventually evolve into true prepositions (i.e. relational expressions with argument structure). This would not necessarily entail any change in the overt form of the compounds or the sentences containing them. It would however involve a change in meaning (e.g. HEAD > OVER) and a concomitant change in grammatical class (N > P). In the terminology of cognitive grammar, the element shifts from one that profiles a thing to one that profiles an atemporal relation. The specific nature of this change holds a certain amount of theoretical interest, as independently motivated constructs of the theory allow it to be described with some precision.[15]

One construct we have not yet discussed is the notion *search domain*, first proposed by Hawkins (1984). A search domain is defined as the region to which a locative element confines its trajector, i.e. the set of trajector positions that would satisfy its specifications. The grounds for positing this construct start with the basic observation that a locative expression usually does not pin down the trajector's location with full precision, but merely places it within a certain region. That region is not the expression's landmark (e.g. the entity designated by a prepositional object), but rather some area characterized with reference to it. By way of example, the search domains of *above* and *beside* are very roughly indicated (by shading) in Fig. 7.7.

Reference to this construct is essential for the explicit description of numerous constructions in different languages (Langacker 1993). To take just one example, we need it to describe sentences like (13), which are fully acceptable for many speakers of English:

(13)   *Under the bed is all dusty.*

A prepositional phrase like *under the bed* normally profiles a locative relationship. However, the property of being dusty can hardly be ascribed to a spatial rela-

---

[14] By definition, this makes the compound less of a complement and more adjunct-like. Recall that a complement is a component structure which elaborates a salient substructure of the head (salience being a matter of degree).

[15] This characterization slightly elaborates the one presented by Rubba (1994), who documents several synchronically observable stages in the evolution of nouns to prepositions in modern Aramaic.

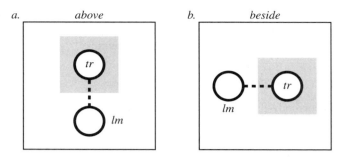

FIG. 7.7

tion *per se*. I therefore analyse the prepositional phrase in (13) as undergoing a semantic extension, wherein the profile shifts from the relationship to an associated entity whose characterization as dusty is non-anomalous, namely a region in space.[16] Because they profile regions (which are things), the phrases in question are actually nouns (as defined in cognitive grammar) and can therefore function as subjects. For us the essential point is that the region each phrase designates is the search domain implicit in its basic relational meaning. The semantic extension serves to reify this latent region and render it salient as the profiled entity.

This pattern of extension is sketched in Fig. 7.8. From a prepositional phrase, it derives a nominal expression that names a location characterized with reference to a thing (specified by the prepositional object). Because the resulting noun is locational, it invites the conception of the profiled region being occupied by some other entity, as indicated by the dashed-line circle.[17]

The grammaticization of a body-part noun into a preposition is essentially the inverse of this extension. The first step in this process, the initial extension shown in Fig. 7.9, is the same kind of metonymy shown previously in Fig. 7.4 (FOOT′ > FOOT″): a noun that profiles a body-part (or a body-part analogue) is instead construed as designating a contiguous region in space. The noun is thus locational, which suggests the possibility of something occupying the profiled region. Observe that a locational noun's semantic characterization incorporates several entities that qualify as things by the technical definition: (i) the profiled region; (ii) its potential occupant; and (iii) the reference object with respect to which the profiled region (and hence its occupant) is situated.[18]

---

[16] A shift in profile constitutes metonymy, a type of semantic extension that is not just common but ubiquitous. These examples involve a productive metonymic pattern that applies to complex novel expressions. Such patterns are independently attested and are readily described in cognitive grammar.

[17] Figs. 7.8 and 7.9 are intended as generalized representations. While these diagrams necessarily show elements in specific positions with respect to one another, they should not be interpreted as referring to any particular spatial relationship or body-part analogue.

[18] To simplify matters, I leave aside the possibility of the region's potential occupant, and ultimately the preposition's trajector, being not a thing but another relationship. The choice determines whether prepositions and prepositional phrases function adjectivally or adverbially.

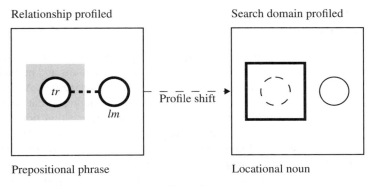

Fig. 7.8

Note further that a preposition, even though it profiles a relationship, also invokes three entities that count as things: (i) its search domain; (ii) its trajector; and (iii) its landmark. Thus a locational noun and a preposition incorporate comparable elements arranged in a comparable configuration. In each case element (i) is a spatial region, whereas elements (ii) and (iii) are object-like participants. In each case element (ii) occupies region (i). Moreover, region (i) is in each case characterized with reference to element (iii). A locational noun and a preposition may therefore subsume the same conceptual content. The change from nominal to prepositional status, the second extension shown in Fig. 7.9, may simply be a matter of adjusting the relative prominence of certain elements (an aspect of construal). In particular, the profile shifts from the spatial region to the spatial relationship. Region (i) undergoes a diminution in prominence but remains as the preposition's search domain, implicit and non-salient. Conversely, elements (ii) and (iii) rise in prominence to become the focal participants in the profiled relationship (its trajector and landmark).

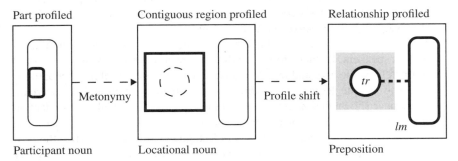

Fig. 7. 9

7.7. CONCLUSION

The grammaticization of locational nouns into adpositions brings us back to the original theme of diversity-out-of-unity. On the one hand, nouns and prepositions represent distinct classes with very different grammatical properties. At the same time, however, their relationship via grammaticization suggests that locational nouns, at least, must be quite similar to adpositions, a suggestion borne out by the proposed analysis. We have seen, in fact, that their conceptual content may be quite comparable—what distinguishes them is the construal imposed on that content, specifically in regard to the prominence accorded various entities. The rather striking instance of grammatical diversity we set out to examine proves, in the last analysis, to be relatively superficial. The description proposed does not contradict the possible claim of underlying conceptual unity.

I would like to point out, in conclusion, that the same inventory of basic phenomena and descriptive constructs have been invoked for the characterization of both English and Mixtec locative constructions. For instance, both languages make liberal use of body-part metaphors and metonymy based on spatial contiguity. Both languages have verbs of motion, posture, and location, characterized at different levels of schematicity. Each has constructions for describing spatial paths and locations, and each affords some basis for positing a conceptual distinction between settings/locations and participants. Moreover, the same fundamental constructs of cognitive grammar prove sufficient for the description of locative constructions in the two languages: profiling, trajector/landmark alignment, correspondence, elaboration, profile determinance, etc.

Despite this extensive commonality, there is ample room for linguistic diversity. The same conceptual content is susceptible to being construed, symbolized, and lexically packaged in alternative ways. Languages vary in the kinds of notions they select for explicit coding, as well as in how commonly and systematically they employ particular devices. A limited set of basic constructs allows an open-ended variety of symbolic assemblies to be formed, including (as we have seen) alternative compositional means of arriving at the same composite conception. Hence their largely common basis does not prevent languages from developing rich and richly divergent inventories of symbolic resources.

The symbolic resources of a language are central and vital to the cultural heritage of its speakers. It stands to reason that the specific form they assume should be intimately connected, and tend to resonate, with their cultural preoccupations. Needless to say, the degree and the direction of influence are difficult to ascertain. I hope to have shown that an assessment of these matters is critically dependent on linguistic analysis, and thus on the framework adopted for that purpose, since these determine the apparent nature and extent of language differences, hence the possible scope of ethnosyntax. I further hope to have shown that such differences may be less profound and less extensive than they might seem to be on first examination. If correct, this by no means invalidates the ethnosyntax hypothesis. It may however contribute to an accurate, empirically defensible formulation of it.

REFERENCES

BLOOM, PAUL, *et al.* (eds.) 1996. *Language and Space.* Cambridge, Mass.: MIT Press.

BRUGMAN, CLAUDIA. 1983. 'The use of body-part terms as locatives in Chalcatongo Mixtec'. *Survey of California and Other Indian Languages*, 4: 235–90.

——and MACAULAY, MONICA. 1986. 'Interacting semantic systems: Mixtec expressions of location'. *Proceedings of the Annual Meeting of the Berkeley Linguistics Society*, 12: 315–27.

CASAD, EUGENE H. 1982. 'Cora locationals and structured imagery'. Ph.D. dissertation, San Diego, University of California.

——1984. 'Cora'. In Ronald W. Langacker (ed.), *Studies in Uto-Aztecan Grammar*, iv: *Southern Uto-Aztecan Grammatical Sketches.* SIL Publications in Linguistics 56. Dallas: Summer Institute of Linguistics and University of Texas at Arlington, 151–459.

——1993. '"Locations", "paths" and the Cora verb'. In Richard A. Geiger and Brygida Rudzka-Ostyn (eds.), *Conceptualizations and Mental Processing in Language.* Cognitive Linguistics Research 3. Berlin: Mouton de Gruyter, 593–645.

——and LANGACKER, RONALD W. 1985. '"Inside" and "outside" in Cora grammar'. *International Journal of American Linguistics*, 51: 247–81.

GEORGOPOULOS, CAROL. 1985. 'The syntax of variable binding in Palauan'. Ph.D. dissertation, San Diego, University of California.

HAVILAND, JOHN B. 1992. *Anchoring, Iconicity, and Orientation in Guugu Yimidhirr Pointing Gestures.* Max Planck Institute for Psycholinguistics, Cognitive Anthropology Research Group. Report No. 8.

HAWKINS, BRUCE W. 1984. 'The semantics of English spatial prepositions'. Ph.D. dissertation, San Diego, University of California.

HERSKOVITS, ANNETTE H. 1985. 'Semantics and pragmatics of locative expressions'. *Cognitive Science*, 9: 341–78.

——1986. *Language and Spatial Cognition: An Interdisciplinary Study of the Prepositions in English.* Cambridge: Cambridge University Press.

——1988. 'Spatial expressions and the plasticity of meaning'. In Rudzka-Ostyn 1988: 271–97.

HOPPER, PAUL J., and THOMPSON, SANDRA A. 1980. 'Transitivity in grammar and discourse'. *Language*, 56: 251–99.

JANDA, LAURA A. 1986. *A Semantic Analysis of the Russian Verbal Prefixes za-, pere-, do-, and ot-.* Slavistische Beiträge 192. Munich: Verlag Otto Sagner.

——1988. 'The mapping of elements of cognitive space onto grammatical relations: an example from Russian verbal prefixation'. In Rudzka-Ostyn 1988: 327–43.

JOHNSON, MARK. 1987. *The Body in the Mind: The Bodily Basis of Meaning, Imagination, and Reason.* Chicago: University of Chicago Press.

LAKOFF, GEORGE. 1987. *Women, Fire, and Dangerous Things: What Categories Reveal About the Mind.* Chicago: University of Chicago Press.

LANGACKER, RONALD W. 1985. 'Observations and speculations on subjectivity'. In John Haiman (ed.), *Iconicity in Syntax.* Typological Studies in Language 6. Amsterdam: John Benjamins, 109–50.

LANGACKER, RONALD W. 1986. 'Settings, participants, and grammatical relations'. *Proceedings of the Annual Meeting of the Pacific Linguistics Conference*, 2: 1–31.

——1987*a*. *Foundations of Cognitive Grammar*, i: *Theoretical Prerequisites*. Stanford, Calif.: Stanford University Press.

——1987*b*. 'Grammatical ramifications of the setting/participant distinction'. *Proceedings of the Annual Meeting of the Berkeley Linguistics Society*, 13: 383–94.

——1987*c*. 'Nouns and verbs'. *Language*, 63: 53–94.

——1988. 'A view of linguistic semantics'. In Rudzka-Ostyn 1988: 49–90.

——1990*a*. *Concept, Image, and Symbol: The Cognitive Basis of Grammar*. Cognitive Linguistics Research 1. Berlin: Mouton de Gruyter.

——1990*b*. 'Subjectification'. *Cognitive Linguistics*, 1: 5–38.

——1991. *Foundations of Cognitive Grammar*, ii: *Descriptive Application*. Stanford, Calif.: Stanford University Press.

——1993. 'Grammatical traces of some "invisible" semantic constructs'. *Language Sciences*, 15: 323–55.

——1994. 'Culture, cognition, and grammar'. In Martin Pütz (ed.), *Language Contact and Language Conflict*. Philadelphia and Amsterdam: John Benjamins, 25–53.

——1995. 'Viewing in cognition and grammar'. In Philip W. Davis (ed.), *Alternative Linguistics: Descriptive and Theoretical Modes*. Current Issues in Linguistic Theory 102. Amsterdam: John Benjamins, 153–212.

——1999*a*. 'A study in unified diversity: English and Mixtec locatives'. *RASK* 9/10: 215–56. [=Jacob L. Mey and Andrzej Bogusławski (eds.), *'E Pluribus Una': The One in the Many* (For Anna Wierzbicka), Odense: Odense University Press.]

——1999*b*. *Grammar and Conceptualization*. Cognitive Linguistics Research 14. Berlin: Mouton de Gruyter.

——2000, 'A dynamic usage-based model'. In Michael Barlow and Suzanne Kemmer (eds.), *Usage-Based Models of Language*. Stanford, Calif.: CSLI Publications, 1–63.

LEVINSON, STEPHEN C. 1992. *Language and Cognition: The Cognitive Consequences of Spatial Description in Guugu Yimithirr*. Max Planck Institute for Psycholinguistics, Cognitive Anthropology Research Group. Report No. 13.

MACLAURY, ROBERT E. 1989. 'Zapotec body-part locatives: prototypes and metaphoric extensions'. *International Journal of American Linguistics*, 55: 119–54.

RICE, SALLY. 1987. 'Towards a Cognitive Model of Transitivity'. Ph.D. dissertation, San Diego, University of California.

RUBBA, JO. 1994. 'Grammaticization as semantic change: a case study of preposition development'. In William Pagliuca (ed.), *Perspectives on Grammaticalization*. Current Issues in Linguistic Theory 109. Amsterdam: John Benjamins, 81–101.

RUDZKA-OSTYN, BRYGIDA (ed.). 1988. *Topics in Cognitive Linguistics*. Current Issues in Linguistic Theory 50. Amsterdam: John Benjamins.

TALMY, LEONARD. 1975. 'Semantics and syntax of motion'. In John Kimball (ed.), *Syntax and Semantics*, iv. New York: Academic Press, 181–238.

——1988*a*. 'Force dynamics in language and cognition'. *Cognitive Science*, 12: 49–100.

——1988*b*. 'The relation of grammar to cognition'. In Rudzka-Ostyn 1988: 165–205.

——1991. 'Path to realization: a typology of event conflation'. *Proceedings of the Annual Meeting of the Berkeley Linguistics Society*, 17: 480–519.

——2000. *Toward a Cognitive Semantics*, ii: *Typology and Process in Concept Structuring*. Cambridge, Mass.: MIT Press.

VANDELOISE, CLAUDE. 1985*a*. 'Au-delà des descriptions géométriques et logiques de l'espace: une description fonctionnelle'. *Lingvisticae Investigationes*, 9: 109–29.

——1985*b*. 'Les Prépositions *sur/sous* et la relation porteur/porté'. *Leuvense Bijdragen*, 74: 457–81.

——1988. 'Length, width, and potential passing'. In Rudzka-Ostyn 1988: 403–27.

——1991. *Spatial Prepositions: A Case Study from French*. Chicago: University of Chicago Press.

——1994. 'Methodology and analyses of the preposition *in*'. *Cognitive Linguistics*, 5: 157–84.

8

English Causative Constructions in an Ethnosyntactic Perspective: Focusing on *Let*

ANNA WIERZBICKA

8.1. ETHNOSYNTAX: LINKS BETWEEN CULTURE AND GRAMMAR

While it is generally agreed that, metaphorically speaking, words are carriers of meaning, it is less widely recognized that grammatical categories of a language, too, encode meaning. But in fact this is what grammar is all about: certain meanings are so important to communities of speakers that they become not just lexicalized (linked with individual words) but grammaticalized, that is, embodied in the language's structural patterns.

Some meanings are of such central importance in the human conceptualization of the world that we find them grammatically embodied in most, if not all, languages of the world. This holds, for example, for the following prototypical cognitive scenario:

> person X did something to thing Y
> because of this something happened to Y at the same time
> after this Y was not like it was before

For example, if person X breaks (or opens) thing Y, X does something to Y, because of this something happens to Y at the same time, and after this Y is broken (or open), unlike before. The question of *how* 'transitivity', which is based on this prototypical cognitive scenario, gets grammatically encoded in different languages of the world has been extensively discussed in the literature (cf. e.g. Hopper and Thompson 1980; Moravcsik 1978; Givón 1984; Comrie 1981; Tsunoda 1981; Wierzbicka 1981, 1988, 1996*a*) and cannot be discussed here. What matters here is the cognitive salience of the prototypical 'transitive' scenario, reflected in the role this scenario plays in grammar (for further discussion, see Wierzbicka 1998*b*).

I am very grateful to colleagues who read the first draft of this chapter and gave me valuable comments and suggestions, and in particular, to Nick Enfield and Cliff Goddard. I would also like to acknowledge the importance of comments on the German data which I have received from Gabi Schmidt, Arie Verhagen, and, most particularly, Uwe Durst. For her comments on the Russian data, and for drawing my attention to Vera Podlesskaya's article on 'give', thanks are due to Sasha Aikhenvald.

Another meaning which is grammaticalized very widely in languages of the world is that linked with the category of the 'imperative'. The meaning in question, or at least its core, can be formulated as follows: 'I want you to do something.' The grammatical categories which encode this meaning often have various language-specific extensions, covering, for example, additional meanings such as 'I want something good to happen to you' or 'I want something bad to happen to you' (cf. Wierzbicka 1996*a*); but the semantic prototype on the basis of which 'imperatives' are identified, cross-linguistically, undoubtedly includes the core element 'I want you to do something.'

Grammatical categories like 'imperative' or 'transitivity', defined with reference to cognitive scenarios such as those given above, can be said to belong to 'universal grammar'. In addition to such widely recurring categories, however, every language has grammatical categories which are more or less language-specific. The meanings encoded in such categories are likely to have special cultural significance in the society associated with a given language.

For example, the grammatical distinction between feminine and masculine genders, which plays a significant role in the grammar of very many languages, clearly reflects a semantic distinction with a universal significance; on the other hand, the category of an 'edible gender', which we find, for example, in some Australian Aboriginal languages, is not similarly widespread in languages of the world, and may well reflect existential preoccupations of nomadic tribes for whom the distinctions between edible and non-edible plants and creatures require more attention, on a daily basis, than they do in the life of many other societies. The fact that in the languages of some coastal tribes there are also grammatical distinctions between 'land creatures', 'fish', 'dangerous sea creatures', and 'big edible sea creatures' (cf. e.g. Goddard 1998, with reference to Nicholas Evans's work on Kayardild) highlights this point even more spectacularly.

What applies to material life applies also to social, mental, and spiritual life as well. Sapir (1949: 27) said, famously, that 'Languages differ widely in the nature of their vocabularies. Distinctions which seem inevitable to us may be utterly ignored in languages which reflect an entirely different type of culture, while these in turn insist on distinctions which are all but unintelligible to us.' I would add to this that languages differ widely in the nature (or 'content') of their grammars. Grammatical distinctions which may seem inevitable to us—such as, for example, those between 'past', 'present', and 'future', or between 'singular' and 'plural', or between 'definiteness' and 'indefiniteness'—may be utterly ignored in languages which reflect entirely different types of culture, while these in turn may insist on grammatical distinctions which may seem quite unnecessary or even unintelligible to us—such as, for example, those between different types of 'evidentials' (cf. e.g. Chafe and Nichols 1986; Wierzbicka 1996*a*: ch. 15), or those between 'alternating' and 'parallel' generations in Australian languages (cf. Wierzbicka 1992: ch. 10 and the references cited there).

Clearly, the reason why a notion like 'an alternating generation' is encoded in the grammar of some Australian languages—but not, for example, in the grammar of English or Russian—is that this notion plays a role in the Australian societies in question (where, for example, the generations of one's grandparents or grandchildren are expected to be treated differently from those of one's parents, great-grandparents, or great-grandchildren).

Although it has of course to be treated cautiously and prudently, the principle of 'cultural elaboration' applies to grammar as much as it applies to the lexicon. It is clearly not an accident that, for example, the Hanunóo language of the Philippines has dozens of words for different kinds of rice (cf. Conklin 1957), and to anyone who knows anything about Russian culture, it is clearly not an accident that Russian has several different everyday words for different kinds of 'friends' rather than one basic everyday word like the English *friend* (see Wierzbicka 1997: ch. 2). Similarly, it is clearly not an accident that Russian has an extremely rich and elaborate system of expressive derivation applicable to proper names (names of persons), whereas in languages like English the corresponding system of expressive derivation is extremely limited (cf. e.g. *John* and *Johnny* in English, vs. *Ivan* and *Vanja, Vanečka, Vanjuša, Vanjuška, Vanjušečka*, and so on in Russian; for discussion, see Wierzbicka 1992: ch. 7; cf. also Friedrich 1966); or that Russian grammar has a rich system of grammatical constructions involving the notion of 'the unknown' or of the 'out-of-controlness' of events in human lives (cf. Wierzbicka 1992: ch. 2).

In this chapter, I will focus on one area of 'cultural elaboration' in grammar, namely, on the elaboration of causal relations in modern English.

In the area of causation, divergences between different languages are very considerable, and very intriguing. At one extreme, there appear to be languages with hardly any causative constructions at all, apart from basic purposive constructions and *because*-clauses. Evans (1986) has argued that the Australian Aboriginal language Kayardild may be a case in point. At the other extreme, there are languages such as English, with a wide range of causative constructions, especially in the area of human interaction. Between these two poles, there is a wide range of variation—both in the amount of attention given to causal relations and in the kind of qualitative distinctions drawn by different languages. The observation that among the European languages English shows the greatest differentiation in the area of causation—more so than French, Italian, or Russian—is entirely in line with Bally's (1920) semantic typology of European languages, advanced in his pioneering early study *Impressionisme et grammaire*. Bally contrasted two 'psychological tendencies' manifested in the syntax of different languages: an 'impressionistic' one, focusing on phenomena as they present themselves to human beings, and an analytical one, focusing on the presumed relations between causes and effects. He argued that the 'impressionistic', phenomenological orientation is more in evidence in Russian than it is in German, more in German than it is in French, and more in French than it is in English. Conversely, the analytical, causal orientation is more in evidence in English than it is in French, more in French than in German, and more in German than in Russian.

In earlier work (Wierzbicka 1980, 1988, 1992) I sought to complement Bally's observations by noting that Russian syntax pays more attention to accidental, 'inexplicable' causation and to the interplay between human life and the forces of nature than does English syntax (with German, Italian, and French occupying intermediate positions in this regard); and I have argued that the high degree of attention which the English language gives to causal relations focuses in particular on kinds and shades of human interaction: it is particularly concerned with the interplay between causation and volition.

As I noted in my *Semantics of Grammar*, English has an extremely wide range of causative constructions. This wealth is concealed, to some extent, by the use of the same key words such as *make*, *have*, or *let* in many different constructions, all of which may appear to be examples of a single '*make* construction', '*have* construction', or '*let* construction'. In fact, there are reasons to distinguish, on both semantic and structural grounds, more than a dozen different '*make* constructions' in English (for evidence and argumentation see Wierzbicka 1998*a*), and probably more than a dozen different '*have* constructions' (cf. Wierzbicka 1988). As this chapter seeks to demonstrate, English has also a wide range of different '*let* constructions'. To give just a few preliminary examples of the wealth of causative constructions found in English (for further discussion, see Chappell 1978; Wierzbicka 1988) let me mention the following twelve:

X made Y V_{INT}-INF	(e.g. X made Y wash the dishes)
X made Y $V_{non\text{-}INT}$-INF	(e.g. X made Y cry)
X made Y ADJ	(e.g. X made Y furious)
X had Y V_{INT}-INF	(e.g. X had Y wash the dishes)
X had X's Z V_{INT}-ed	(e.g. X had her boots mended)
X had Y V_{INT}-ing	(e.g. X had Y staying with her)
X got Y to V_{INT}-INF	(e.g. X got Y to wash the dishes)
X got Y ADJ	(e.g. X got Y furious)
X got herself V_{INT}-ed	(e.g. X got herself kicked out)
X V_{INT}-ed Y into doing Z	(e.g. X talked/tricked Y into resigning)
X V_{asp}-ed Y V-ing	(e.g. X kept Y waiting)

As mentioned earlier, grammatical elaboration of conceptual domains often goes hand in hand with lexical elaboration. Kinship in Australian languages is one case in point (cf. e.g. Hale 1966; Dench 1982, 1987; Heath, Merlan, and Rumsey 1982). Causal interaction in English is, I think, another. For example, if one compares English and Russian speech-acts, one will discover that the English lexicon pays more attention to different strategies of human causation—just as English grammar pays more attention to this area than Russian grammar. Other semantic areas are more elaborated in Russian than in English (cf. e.g. Wierzbicka 1992; 1997).

8.2. CAUSATION AND PATTERNS OF SOCIAL INTERACTION

In trying to understand the extraordinary wealth of causative constructions found in modern English (not only in comparison with other European languages but also from a universal perspective) we should ask, I think, for its cultural roots. Why is it that so much attention is focused in English on the precise nature of causal relations between various actions and various events? I would like to put forward two interpretative hypotheses in this regard.

First, as democracy developed in a large-scale modern society—first of all, in America (cf. Tocqueville 1953)—a new style of human relations evolved, to accommodate the need for both an increased scale of interpersonal interactions and a new footing on which these interactions were to be conducted (cf. Stearns and Stearns 1986). The new managerial type of society, too, needed an increased scale of interpersonal causations: for the society to function smoothly and efficiently, lots of people had to be, roughly speaking, told what they were to do. This had to happen, however, in the context of a democracy, where people might be willing to take 'directions' or to follow 'instructions' but not to obey 'orders' or 'commands'.

But to talk of a shift from 'orders' to 'directions' and 'instructions' is a simplification. In fact, a whole range of new concepts has developed and become socially salient, concepts to do with different kinds of interpersonal causation. For example, there are significant differences between 'telling' someone to type up some letters, 'ordering' someone to do so, 'directing' them to do so, and 'having some letters typed up'. In modern Anglo society, as it developed first of all in America, the idea of 'having some things done' has become increasingly important; it is an idea of a set-up which does not involve one person bending the will of another person, but which depends on having structures within which many people are willing to do—within certain spheres of life, such as office work or interaction at a service station—things that someone else wants them to do, while at the same time preserving their personal autonomy and full control over other areas of their personal life.

The cultural emphasis on personal autonomy, characteristic of the modern Anglo society and reflected in a variety of ways in modern English (cf. e.g. Wierzbicka 1991, 1996*b*), is no doubt closely related to the expansion of causative constructions in modern English, as is also the emphasis on the need for voluntary cooperation among equals (cf. Fukuyama 1995). In a large-scale society, where service encounters have come to occupy a vital role in everyday life and where people are acutely aware of their right to, and need for, personal autonomy, the nuances of causation assume an extraordinary importance.

For example, if I am working in a service profession (say, as a waitress, or a taxi driver) my livelihood depends on my being willing to do what other people want me to do (and to do it because they say they want me to do it); but the relationship with my customers has to be negotiated in such a way that I do not abrogate my personal autonomy in the process. I am willing to 'serve' my customers but I am not willing to treat them as my superiors. If I am working in an institution such as a university or in public administration, I may well have 'bosses', 'superiors', or 'heads of department', whose will I may have to bow to, on an everyday basis; but again, if I am a modern Anglo person I will not want to abrogate my personal autonomy because of this, and I will only agree to follow my bosses' will in the context of assumptions which ensure the recognition of both my autonomy and my essential 'equality' with the bosses. Even in the realm of family interaction, it has become crucial in the modern Anglo world that parental authority has to be exercised, and indeed conceived of, in ways that are consistent with the children's right to, and need for, personal autonomy.

All these modern ideas and expectations needed new ways of speaking and, I suggest, they found their expression in the plethora of causative constructions so characteristic of modern (nineteenth- and twentieth-century) English. It is of course true that democracy reaches wide outside the Anglo world, and that so does the ethos of equality, of the rights of the individual, and of personal autonomy. It is not true, however, that the cultural emphasis on personal autonomy is equally characteristic of the German-speaking world, or the Spanish-speaking world, or the Russian-speaking world as it is of mainstream Anglo culture (cf. e.g. Wierzbicka 1998c).

There are considerable and partly grammaticalized differences in ways of speaking separating English from German, Spanish, Italian, and most other European languages, above all, differences involving the use of the imperative. The extraordinary growth of various 'whimperatives' in modern English (Wierzbicka 1991; cf. also Matsumoto 1988; Goddard, this volume) linked with the growing avoidance of the straight imperative, is an unparalleled phenomenon, with obvious cultural significance. In fact, the growth of conventional expressions such as 'would you do X', 'will you do X', 'could you do X', 'would you mind doing X', and so on—all aimed at avoiding the impression that one is trying to impose one's will on somebody else—seems to have proceeded in parallel with the growth of causative constructions and the emergence of new varieties of *make* constructions, *have* constructions and *let* constructions in modern English. (For further discussion, cf. Wierzbicka 1998a.)

It goes without saying that in any attempts to correlate features of grammar with features of culture and society great care must be exercised, to avoid subjectivism and arbitrariness (cf. Hymes 1962). But while it may be easier and 'safer' to compare, say, ethnobiological classifications encoded in the lexicon than different systems of 'ethnocausology' encoded in grammar, the latter task is at least as important and as rewarding as the former.

8.3. 'NSM' (NATURAL SEMANTIC METALANGUAGE) AS A TOOL FOR STUDYING ETHNOSYNTAX

The approach to linguistic description illustrated in this chapter (the so-called 'NSM' approach) is based on two fundamental assumptions: that every language has an irreducible core in terms of which the speakers can understand all complex thoughts and utterances, and that the irreducible cores of all natural languages match, so that we can speak, effectively, of the irreducible core of all languages, reflecting the irreducible core of human thought.

As Leibniz eloquently argued three centuries ago, not everything can be explained: at some point, all explanations must come to an end, for a *regressus ad infinitum* explains nothing. Some things must be self-explanatory (intuitively clear), or we could never understand anything. The power of any explanation depends therefore on the intuitive clarity of the indefinable conceptual primes which constitute its ultimate foundation.

A natural language is a powerful system in which very complex and diverse meanings can be formulated and conveyed to other people. In the NSM theory of language it is assumed that the intelligibility of all such meanings depends on the existence of a basic set of conceptual primes which do not require any explanations for they are intuitively clear to us (and presumably, innate); and which can be found through in-depth analysis of any natural language.

Cross-linguistic empirical work undertaken within the NSM framework suggests that there are some sixty universal conceptual primes. Using their English exponents, we can present them in Table 8.1 (cf. Wierzbicka 1996*a*; Goddard 1998, Goddard and Wierzbicka 1994).

The first hypothesis, then, is that in all languages lexical exponents for each of the sixty or so conceptual primes can be found. The second, concomitant, hypothesis is that in all languages conceptual primes can enter into the same combinations. For example, it can be expected not only that in any language lexical exponents can be found for the basic notions PEOPLE, THING, THIS, TWO, ALL, BIG, BAD, DO, SEE, MOVE, HAPPEN, and CAN, but also that in any language these ele-

TABLE 8.1. Universal semantic primes

Substantives	I, YOU, SOMEONE, SOMETHING, PEOPLE, BODY
Determiners	THIS, THE SAME, OTHER
Quantifiers	ONE, TWO, SOME, MANY/MUCH, ALL
Attributes	GOOD, BAD, BIG, SMALL
Mental predicates	THINK, KNOW, WANT, FEEL, SEE, HEAR
Speech	SAY, WORD, TRUE
Actions, events, movements	DO, HAPPEN, MOVE
Existence and possession	THERE IS, HAVE
Life and death	LIVE, DIE
Logical concepts	NOT, MAYBE, CAN, BECAUSE, IF
Time	WHEN, NOW, AFTER, BEFORE, A LONG TIME, A SHORT TIME, FOR SOME TIME; MOMENT
Space	WHERE, HERE, ABOVE, BELOW, FAR, NEAR; SIDE, INSIDE; TOUCH (CONTACT)
Intensifier, augmentor	VERY, MORE
Taxonomy, partonomy	KIND OF, PART OF
Similarity	LIKE

ments can be put together to create meaningful combinations such as the following ones:

ALL PEOPLE DO THIS
I SEE TWO THINGS
IF YOU DO THIS, SOMETHING BAD CAN HAPPEN TO YOU

Of course the word order and the morphosyntactic 'trappings' may differ from language to language, but the hypothesis is that the elements, their combinations, and their meaning will be the same. (Cf. Goddard and Wierzbicka in press.) This means that just as we can have a rudimentary universal lexicon of indefinable concepts we can also have a rudimentary universal grammar of such concepts, and if we have a mini-lexicon and a mini-grammar then we can have a mini-language—a mini-language which is carved out of natural languages and which can be used for the description and comparison of languages, both in their lexicon and in their grammar: a 'natural semantic metalanguage' (NSM).

Since this metalanguage is carved out of natural language (any natural language), the semantic explications constructed in it are intuitively meaningful and have psychological reality. Consequently, unlike semantic formulas based on various artificial formalisms, NSM formulas are open to verification (they can be tested against native speakers' intuitions).

8.4. THE MEANING OF CAUSATIVES IN A CROSS-LINGUISTIC PERSPECTIVE

The literature on the syntax of causative constructions in different languages is huge; the literature on their semantics is relatively modest. But the use of such constructions is largely determined by their meaning. Since little is known about their meaning, a language learner looking for some guidelines to the actual use of such constructions can seldom find any statements anywhere that are clear, precise, and reliable. But it is not just the language learner who would be disappointed by the literature on causatives. The area of causation has an enormous inherent interest from the point of view of the 'philosophy of grammar' and the psychology of language: after all, the causative constructions a language has show how the speakers of this language draw distinctions between different kinds of causal relations, how they perceive and interpret causal links between events and human actions. And yet our knowledge and understanding of 'ethnocausology' is incomparably far behind that of ethnozoology, ethnobotany, or ethnogeology (cf. e.g. Brown 1984; Berlin 1992).

Of course the folk-interpretations of causal links are less accessible to direct observation than those of more tangible, concrete phenomena, but they are not inaccessible to empirical study. The syntax of a language provides a wealth of evidence in this regard—if we can find ways of analysing this evidence in an illuminating and non-arbitrary way.

I believe that here as elsewhere—and perhaps even more in this case than in many other cases—the key to such analysis lies in the choice of a suitable semantic metalanguage. In the existing literature on causatives, the semantics of different constructions is usually discussed in terms of ready-made labels such as 'direct vs. indirect causation', 'contactive vs. distant causation', 'strong coercion vs. weak coercion', 'authority vs. absence of authority', 'factitive vs. permissive causation', or 'manipulative vs. directive causation' (cf., for example, Comrie 1974, 1985; Talmy 1976; Givón 1975; Kachru 1976; Ruwet 1976; Shibatani 1973, 1976*a*; Xolodovič 1969; Song 1996). But labels of this kind are often more misleading than helpful and they do not have much explanatory or predictive power, for the meaning of the constructions to which they are applied differs from language to language.

Generally speaking, the common use of ready-made labels such as 'direct/ indirect causation', 'contactive/distant causation', or 'strongly coercive/weakly coercive causatives' is based on the mistaken (in my view) assumption that there are certain types of causation which can first be described a priori, and then identified in individual languages. But detailed semantic analysis shows that the actual causative constructions are usually quite unique in the meaning they encapsulate. What is called 'direct causation' or 'strongly coercive causation' in one language is usually different from what is called 'direct causation' or 'strongly coercive causation' in another. This is not to say that there are no recurring motives, no cross-linguistic similarities in the area of causation. Far from it. The point is that usually causative constructions encapsulate a unique combination of components. The individual components—such as, for example, 'Y wanted this to happen' or 'Y didn't want this to happen'—frequently recur in the world's languages (cf. Harkins 1995). But the configurations of such components tend to be unique, and cannot be adequately captured in global labels such as 'indirect', 'manipulative', 'distant', and the like.

From the point of view advocated here, finding out the configuration of universal concepts encoded in a given causative construction is not seen as a final touch which can be added to the presentation of the results once the main analysis has already been completed. Rather, finding out (by trial and error) what this hidden configuration of universal concepts is, is the essence of the analysis. Assigning to a construction a label such as 'coercion', 'authority', or 'contact' does not bring us any closer to the understanding of its meaning, it only creates an illusion that progress has been made.

For example, in English, 'interpersonal causation' can be described by means of several different causative constructions:

(1) *a.* Mary made John return the money.
    b. Mary had John return the money.
    c. Mary got John to return the money.
    d. Mary forced John to return the money.

    e. Mary talked John into returning the money.
    f. Mary let John return the money.

Each of the sentences above means something different, and no labels such as 'direct', 'indirect', 'strong', 'weak', 'coercive', 'manipulative', 'contactive', or 'permissive' can clarify the nature of these differences (as they could not clarify the differences between any of these constructions and causative constructions in other languages). On the other hand, the use of universal semantic primes allows us to identify intelligible and testable semantic components. For example, we can say that the construction 'Mary made John do Z' (e.g. return the money) implies that John had to return the money (i.e. couldn't not do it), whereas 'Mary had John return the money' does not imply that (for detailed discussion and justification see Wierzbicka 1998*a*). We can also say that the construction 'Mary let John return the money' implies that John wanted to do it, whereas neither the 'make' construction nor the 'have' construction implies that.

    In what follows, I will examine fairly extensively a whole family of English causative constructions based on the verb *let*. (For comparison of this family of constructions with other English causative constructions see Wierzbicka 1998*a*.) First, however, I show how the 'NSM' method of analysis allows us to clarify the meaning of causative constructions in a language other than English: German.

8.5. THE GERMAN *LASSEN* CONSTRUCTIONS

German has a number of causative constructions based on the auxiliary verb *lassen*. In this section, I will only consider the use of *lassen* in combination with a human causee and a verb of intentional action (V_{INT}), according to the schematic formula:

$$NP^1_{Human} \; lie\beta \; NP^2_{Human} \; V_{INT}$$

As we will see later, the presence of a noun phrase referring to the causee is in fact optional, as it is in the case of the English *have* construction (if passive is used):

(2)   Mary had her hair done (thesis retyped)

In different contexts, the *lassen* construction is best translated into English with different constructions, based on the verbs *make, have, get, cause,* or *let,* but as this very fact shows, it cannot be semantically equated with any one of these constructions, e.g.:

(3)   *Ich habe mir   Bleistift und neues Papier geben lassen.* (Speer 1975: 19)
        I   have to-me pencil and new   paper to give let/have
        'I have asked for a pencil and new paper.'

The verb *lassen* does not mean 'ask for', but how else can one render in English the meaning of the phrase *geben lassen* when it refers (as in this case) to a request from a prisoner to the prison authorities? Clearly, the prisoner can neither 'make' the guards give him new writing paper nor 'have' them give it to him. He could perhaps 'get' them to do it, but by translating *lassen* as *get* we would significantly distort the meaning of the original sentence, for 'getting someone to do something' implies something like overcoming some actual or potential unwillingness on the part of the causee, and there is no trace of this in the German sentence.

In this example, then, and also in the following one, the best translation might be one relying on speech-act verbs such as *ask for* or *request* rather than on any general causatives:

(4)   *Vom Doktor eine Schlaftablette geben lassen.* (Speer 1975: 44)
         from doctor one sleeping.tablet to give let/have/make/get
         '[to ask] the doctor for a sleeping tablet (and get one)'. [A note in a diary.]

But a translation based on the verb *ask for* or *request* is not accurate either, for it does not convey the idea that the request was effective.

Furthermore, consider the following sentence:

(5)   *Im Anschluß an seinen Monolog drückte Hitler auf den Klingelknopf und
         ließ Bormann kommen.* (Speer 1975: 101)
         'Having completed his monologue Hitler pressed the bell and [thus] sum-
         moned Bormann.'

In this case, the speech-act verbs *ask for* and *request* are clearly inappropriate, and *summon* is much more suitable; but clearly, *summon* brings with it presuppositions which are absent in the earlier two examples.

In the following example, in which the causee is the causer's personal assistant, the English *have* construction seems to fit the context best:

(6)   *Im Jahre 1938 hatte er [Streicher] ihm durch seinen persönlichen Adjutan-
         ten zum Geburtstag demonstrativ einen großen Distelstrauß überreichen
         lassen.* (Speer 1975: 173)
         'In 1938, Streicher [a Gauleiter of Nuremberg] had his personal assistant
         deliver to him [Leibel, mayor of Nuremberg] on his birthday, demonstra-
         tively, a large bunch of thistles.'

As we have seen, the range of the *lassen* causative is so broad that it can accommodate requests from a prisoner to the prison authorities, instructions from a district chief to his assistant, and orders from a dictator to his underlings. There is no causative verb or construction in English which would fit a range of relations as broad as this. Yet the meaning of the *lassen* causative (with an agentive verb) can be accurately portrayed in universal semantic primitives. As a first approximation, we could propose the following formula, which would be compatible with all the examples considered so far:[1]

---

[1] This is in fact an explication which I proposed for the *lassen* construction in an earlier work (Wierzbicka 1998a). It was based on an insufficiently broad range of examples.

Person X ließ (let/made/had/asked etc.) person Y to do Z=
(*a*) X wanted Y to do Z
(*b*) because X wanted Y to do this X did something
(*c*) because X did this Y knew that X wanted Y to do Z
(*d*) because Y knew this Y did Z

This formula is so clear and precise that it can be easily tested against further examples. When it is so tested, however, it emerges that it is not always applicable, and that it needs to be revised. Consider, for example, the following sentence:

(7) *Ich ließ die Studenten eher nach Hause gehen, weil ich krank war.*
     A. I let the students go home earlier because I was sick.
     B. I 'had' the students go home earlier because I was sick
     (i.e. I sent the students home earlier because I was sick).

As the above glosses indicate, from an English speaker's point of view, the sentence above has two distinct interpretations, which can be roughly identified by means of the causatives 'let' and 'have'. On the A interpretation ('let'), it is assumed that the students wanted to go home earlier and that the teacher yielded to the students' wishes. On the B interpretation, however, it is assumed that the teacher wanted the students to go home earlier, and that she simply acted on her own 'want' (without considering the students' wishes at all).

If we interpreted the German sentence through the prism of the English language, we would have to say that it is ambiguous and we would have to assign to it two alternative interpretations. From a German point of view, however, the sentence is not ambiguous; and the question whether the students wanted to go home or not simply does not arise. What matters is that the students' earlier departure would have happened because of something that the teacher did; and also, that the teacher was aware of this causal link between her own action and the students' action. More precisely, this can be represented as follows:

(*a*) X (the teacher) did (said) something (W)
(*b*) because X did this, Y (the students) did Z (went home early)
(*c*) X knew that if X did this, Y would do Z

Alternatively, it could be suggested that the phrasing of the last component (*c*) should be negative: 'X knew that if X didn't do this, Y wouldn't do Z'; and in the case of a teacher dismissing the children both phrasings would seem to be equally applicable. In other cases, however—for example, in the following sentence—the positive phrasing makes more sense:

(8) *Sie [die Gestapo] warfen Beschimpfungen und Bedrohungen dazwischen*
     . . ., sie ließen die Bilder der früheren Vorsteher und Rabbiner von den
     Wänden entfernen. (Klemperer 1996: ii. 213)
     Amidst insults and threats, they [the Gestapo] 'had' (*ließen*) the photographs of earlier [Jewish] leaders and rabbis removed from the walls.

A positive interpretation would clearly make sense: 'The Gestapo knew that if they ordered the photographs to be removed, the photographs *would* be removed because of this (by the unnamed and no doubt unwilling causees).' A negative interpretation, however, would make less sense here: 'the Gestapo knew that if they didn't order the photographs to be removed they would not be removed.' The idea of the photographs not being removed does not enter anybody's mind, and there is no reason to suppose that the Gestapo consider the 'non-removal of the photographs' at all. This is in contrast to a *let* construction, which would indeed imply this:

(9)   The Gestapo let the Jewish officials remove the photographs.

The *let* sentence implies not only that the Jewish officials *wanted* to remove the photographs but also that the Gestapo knew that they (the officials) would *not* remove the photographs if the Gestapo did something (such as saying: 'we don't want you to do it').

Another example:

(10)   *Der Rottenführer . . . läßt uns um halb fünf gehen, erleichtert was er kann.*
        (Klemperer 1996: ii. 27)
        'The overseer lets us go home (or: sends us home) at half past four, makes
        things easier for us whenever he can.'

In this example, the workers are Jews doing forced labour, and the overseer is a humane German who is trying to lighten their burden. Yet the sentence does not mean the same as the English sentence '[he] lets us go home at half past four'. The use of *let* in the English sentence would entail that the workers *want* to go home early, and so the sentence could not be used if the workers were sent home early against their wishes. The German sentence, however, could be used in this latter case, too (unlikely as it might seem without supportive context). Thus, the *lassen* construction establishes a causal link between one person's (or group's) action and the action of someone else, without referring explicitly to the causee's wants:

(*a*) X (the overseer) does (says) something (W)
(*b*) because of this Y (we) do Z (go home early)
(*c*) X knows that if X does (says) W, Y will do Z

The German sentence is *not* ambiguous between a 'let' and a 'send' interpretation but simply focuses on the causal relation between the action of the overseer and that of the workers (plus the overseer's awareness of the consequences of his action); the rest is clear from the context, not from the semantics of *lassen*.

The irrelevance of the causee's wishes is often reflected in the fact that, as mentioned earlier, the causee is not identified in the sentence at all. This happens, in particular, in reflexive sentences, in which the causee does something to the causer, as in the following example:

(11)   *Er erzählte, sein Vater, Landwirt, habe sich 1873 taufen lassen.* (Klemperer 1996: ii. 104)

   (*a*) 'He told [us] that his father, a landowner, had himself baptized in 1873.'

   (*b*) 'He told [us] that his father, a landowner, let [someone] baptize him in 1873.'

A natural English translation of this sentence would be (*a*) rather than (*b*), but if a sentence like (*b*) were to be translated into German it would be the *lassen* construction which would have to be used (unless one used the lexical verb *erlauben* 'to allow'):

(12)   He told us that his father let them baptize him in 1873.
      'Er erzählte, sein Vater habe sich 1873 taufen lassen.'

But the German gloss in (12) loses the implication that someone was eager to do the baptizing. Thus, here as elsewhere, the meaning of the sentence with the *lassen* construction can be explicated without any reference to the causee's wishes:

Er erzählte, sein Vater habe sich 1873 taufen lassen.
(*a*)   X (his father) did (said) something (W)
(*b*)   because of this someone else (Y) did Z (baptized X)
(*c*)   X knew that if X did (said) this (W) Y would do Z

An explicit reference to the causee can also be omitted in non-reflexive *lassen* sentences, e.g. in the following one:

(13)   *Ich ließ   ihn nur grüßen.* (Klemperer 1996: ii. 339)
      I   let/had him only greet.INF
      'I only sent him greetings'

In this case, the causee, who is the person conveying the speaker's greetings to somebody else, is not mentioned, and his willingness or unwillingness to pass on the greetings is not considered at all:

(*a*)   X(I) did (said) something (W)
(*b*)   because of this someone else (Y) did something (Z)
(*c*)   X knew that if X did (said) this (W), Y would do Z

An example with a clearly unwilling causee is provided by the following sentences:

(14)   *Zugleich . . . hat er sich . . . von mir 200M Vorschuß zahlen lassen. Wie lange halte ich diesen Kampf aus?*
      'At the same time, he had me pay him 200 Marks as an advance. For how long can I endure this struggle?'

Consider also the following example:

(15)   *Kätchen hat mir . . . eine Szene gemacht, weil ich in ihrer Abwesenheit
        ihren Bruder in ihrem Zimmer warten ließ.* (Klemperer 1996, ii. 183)
        'Kate got furious with me because I "let"/"had" her brother wait in her
        room.'

The speaker may have either *told* Kate's brother to wait in her room, or *let* him wait
there: we do not know whose idea it was, and we do not know whether the brother
wanted to wait there or not; but the *lassen* construction is applicable regardless.

  (*a*)   X (I) did (said) something (W)
  (*b*)   because of this Y (Kate's brother) did Z (waited in her room)
  (*c*)   X knew that if I did (said) this (W) Y would do Z

This last example is all the more instructive in that without context, the collocation *warten lassen* 'to let/make [someone] wait' lends itself most naturally to an
interpretation implying an unwilling causee, as in the following example:

(16)   *Sie ließ mich schon oft warten, bediente die später gekommenen zuerst
        oder plauderte endlos mit einem Kunden vor mir.* (Klemperer 1996: ii.
        562)
        'She [the woman at the counter] had often made me wait, she first served
        the customers who came later, or chatted endlessly with the one before
        me.'

It is quite clear that the speaker waits because of what the woman at the counter
does, and that the woman at the counter is aware of the causal links between her
actions and the hero's waiting. In this case, it is also quite clear that the hero is
waiting unwillingly, but as the preceding example shows, the phrase *warten lassen*
can also be applicable to a situation in which the causee wants to wait (e.g. to wait
for someone in a particular room).

   It could be argued perhaps that in all the instances of *lassen* discussed here the
causer *wants* the action to happen (whereas the causee may be either willing or
unwilling), and that, accordingly, one further component should be added to the
explication: 'X wanted Y to do Z.' It does not seem, however, that such a component could always be justified. It is true that the *lassen* construction presents the
causer as fully responsible for the event (the causer knows that if he or she did
something, something else would happen because of this), but the causer can also
'allow' the action unwillingly. For example, the speaker who let Kate's brother
wait for her in her room may have done so unwillingly, and if so then the component 'X wanted Y to do Z' would not be appropriate here.

   We must conclude, then, that the semantic invariant of the *lassen* construction
(with a human causee and a verb of action) includes only the three components
postulated here: (*a*) X did (said) something (W), (*b*) because of this Y did something (Z), (*c*) X knew that if X (said) W, Y would do Z, and does not include any
references to either the causee's or the causer's wanting.

Given the fact that the German *lassen* causative is often translated into English by means of the *have* causative it is interesting to consider the relations between the two. Often, the meaning of these two constructions may seem to be identical, for example:

(17) *a. Ich habe mir die Haare schneiden lassen.*
    b. I have had my hair cut.

But the invariants of the two constructions are different: roughly speaking, (*b*) implies, first, that the causer has some objective other than compliance from the causee, second, that the causer speaks to the causee, and third, that the causer assumes that the causee is willing to take directions from the causer. Thus, the *have* construction requires, in principle, transitive verbs, because it is the *object* of the causee's action which matters for the causer (as in (*c*) below) rather than the causee's action as such (as in (*d*) below):

(17) *c.* He had his secretary retype all the letters.
    d. *He had his secretary wait/come/go.

By contrast—as we have seen—*lassen* can well combine with intransitive verbs such as *warten* 'wait', *kommen* 'come', or *gehen* 'go'.

    The assumption of the causee's willingness to comply would explain why one could not use the *have* construction in a sentence where the causee is forced by the causer to do something. For example, the sentence:

(18)   The Gestapo had the Jewish officials remove from the walls the photo-graphs of the earlier community leaders.

would imply that the officials were willing to do so, which of course the German *lassen* sentence does not imply. (For further discussion of the English *have* construction, cf. Wierzbicka 1998*a*.)

8.6. THE ENGLISH *LET* CONSTRUCTIONS

8.6.1. *Introduction*

The auxiliary verb *let* plays an extremely important role in the field of English causatives. A whole family of different constructions (or, if one prefers, subconstructions) are based on it. All these subconstructions appear to share a common theme which could be articulated as follows:

X let Y do Z /X let Z happen to Y. =
(*a*)   X knew that if X didn't do something to Y
       Y would do Z (or: Z would happen to Y)
(*b*)   at the same time X knew that if X did something to Y
       Y would not do Z (or: Z would not happen to Y)
(*c*)   X didn't do anything to Y
(*d*)   Y did Z (or: Z happened to Y)

Given the existence of this common theme it may seem unnecessary to list any 'subconstructions' or subtypes of the *let* construction at all, beyond just noting that there are two variants of this construction, one with 'do' and one with 'happen' ('X let Y do Z' or 'X let Z happen to Y'), and also that the 'causee' Y can be either a person (or an animal) or a thing. But a description of this kind would not have full predictive power and thus would be inferior to one which recognizes a whole family of *let* subconstructions, with a common semantic theme but with many differences, too—differences which are not fully predictable from the context or from the lexical meaning of the verb. Consider for example the following sentence types:

(19) *a.* Person X got person Y to do Z. (e.g. John got Mary to fix the car.)
     b. Person X let person Y do Z. (e.g. John let Mary fix the car.)

Is it possible that in either (*a*) or (*b*) person Y had already been doing Z before X had had a chance to do anything to Y? As it turns out, such a situation is possible with a *let* sentence (*c*) but not with a *get* sentence (*d*):

(19) *c.* Person X let person Y sleep (on). (e.g. John let Mary sleep on.)
     d. Person X got person Y to go to sleep (*to sleep on). (e.g. *John got Mary to sleep on.)

To account for such facts we need to posit for the *let* construction—but not for the *get* construction—a subconstruction including the component 'Y was doing something for some time.'

There are also other components which are compatible with (some types of) the *let* construction but not with some other causative constructions, and these, too, need to be listed if our description is to have full predictive power. For mnemonic purposes, we can distinguish the different types of the *let* construction by means of labels such as 'permission', 'non-interruption', 'indifference', 'non-prevention', 'non-intervention', 'negligence', and 'tolerance', but these are not expected to have much predictive power or explanatory value by themselves. What really matters is not labels but semantic explications.

Before I proceed to discuss the individual *let* constructions I want, however, to make some comments on the common theme articulated above, which is different from the common theme behind the German *lassen* constructions. As we have seen in the preceding section, the German *lassen* construction implies that the causer *did* something, whereas the *let* constructions imply, generally speaking, that the causer did *not* do anything. In some situations, a person's behaviour can be interpreted either as a case of 'doing something' or as a case of 'not doing something', and in such situations both *let* and *lassen* can be used, for example:

(20) *a.* Mary let the children watch television.
     b. Mary ließ die Kinder fernsehen.

Sentence (*a*) implies that Mary didn't stop the children from watching the television, whereas (*b*) implies that she allowed, or even instructed, them to do so. When the difference between 'letting' (not stopping) and 'allowing' (giving a nod) is only a matter of interpretation, both *let* and *allow* can be used in English, and *lassen* can be used in German. When, however, the situation can only be construed in terms of 'doing something' rather than 'not doing something', *let* cannot be used at all, whereas *lassen* can. For example, in the sentence in which Hitler 'summoned' Bormann by pressing a bell, *lassen* can be used, but *let* could not.

Generally speaking, then, the common theme of English *let* constructions involves the idea of 'refraining from doing something'; and in the case of human causees, on which this chapter focuses, the notion of 'refraining from doing something to other people'—a notion which I suggest has a great deal of cultural significance. By grammaticalizing this notion in a variety of *let* constructions English grammar suggests, so to speak, that it may be important at times to refrain from doing anything to other people—a suggestion highly consonant with the modern Anglo ethos of 'non-interference', 'non-imposition', and 'negative freedom' (cf. Berlin 1969; Wierzbicka 1997: ch. 3). In the sections which follow I will show how the general theme of 'refraining from doing something to other people' manifests itself in the individual *let* constructions (with a human 'causee').[2]

Often, 'letting someone do what they want to do' involves saying something which amounts to giving them permission to do so; but although I have called the construction in question 'the *let* of permission', the *let* construction differs in this respect from speech-act verbs like *permit*: to *permit* someone to do something one has to say something, whereas to *let* them do what they want to do one does not have to say anything.

In some situations, 'letting someone do something' may seem to imply doing something physically rather than 'not doing something', but if so, then the implication is pragmatic (deduced from the context) rather than semantic. For example, if person X is holding person Y tightly by the wrists and thus preventing Y from going somewhere, Y may beg X, 'Let me go!', expecting that X will do something (take her hands off Y's wrists). The sentence does not *mean*, however, that X should take her hands off Y's wrists but rather that she shouldn't prevent Y from going: taking her hands off Y's wrists is a *situational* requirement, independent of the meaning of the sentence as such. The sentence *Let me go!* is different in this respect from the expression *Let go!*, which does encode in its meaning the idea of doing something (physically, not by speech): taking one's hands (or some other body-parts) off someone or something.

For reasons of space, I will not discuss here *let* constructions with an inanimate causee, such as, for example, 'He let the vegetables rot.' I will note, however, that while these do not share the full theme of 'refraining from doing something to

---

[2] It could be argued that the person who 'lets someone else do something' should not be called a 'causer', nor a person who is 'let to do something' a 'causee'. Since, however, the semantic structure of the constructions under discussion is made clear by means of explications, I retain the label 'causee' for the sake of brevity and convenience.

other people', they, too, reflect an interest in the significance of 'people NOT DOING something (rather than DOING something)'. I will return to this point in the final section of the chapter.

Anticipating the discussion in the final sections of this part (8.6.7–8.6.12) I will also mention another important theme emerging from the examination of different *let* constructions: the theme of 'cooperation', visible in constructions such as 'let's do Z', 'let me know/see/have a look', or 'let me propose/suggest/conclude'. The two themes (roughly, 'non-interference' and 'cooperation') are related, because as we will see later, the main concern of the 'cooperative' *let* constructions is how to 'cooperate' in a 'non-imposing' way, that is, how to 'cooperate' while acknowledging the rights of the addressee as an autonomous and free individual, on an equal footing with the speaker.

8.6.2. Let *of 'permission'*

Example:

(21)   She let him go to the party (once). (Cf. She allowed him to go to the party.)

Grammatical formula:

$$NP^1_{Human} \text{ let } NP^2_{Human} V_{DO.INT} (ADV_{FREQ}) \text{ [*some more; one more time]}$$

In this subconstruction, one person (NP^1_{Human}) 'lets' another person (NP^2_{Human}) do something of the kind that can only be done intentionally ($V_{DO.INT}$). Verbs of 'happening' (such as *fall* or *trip*) are not included, and neither are verbs of 'involuntary action' (such as *moan* or *giggle*). The adverbial of frequency (ADV_{FREQ}) is relevant because it allows us to distinguish between, on the one hand, situations where the causee is already involved in an action and the causer chooses not to interrupt it, and on the other, situations where the action has not started yet and the causer chooses not to prevent it. As we will see later, the interpretation of English *let* sentences is sensitive to this distinction, and I will distinguish the two types as the '*let* of permission' and the '*let* of non-interruption'.

The semantic conditions on the '*let* of permission' are as follows: (*a*) the causer knows that the causee wants to do something and will do it if he or she only can; (*b*) the causer knows that he or she can prevent the causee from doing it (e.g. by saying 'I don't want you to do this' or something to that effect), and that the causee knows it; (*c*) the causer refrains from doing so; (*d*) the causer's non-action is intentional; (*e*) because of the causer's intentional non-action the causee can do what he or she wants to do; (*f*) after this the causee does it. Unlike in the case of the verb *permit* (X permitted Y to do Z), the causer does not have to *say* anything; what matters is that the causer intentionally refrains from saying 'No', and that because of this the causee can (and does) proceed.

Explication

> *Person X let person Y do Z (once).*
>
> (*a*) X knew that Y wanted to do Z
>
> (*b*) X knew that if X didn't say anything about this to Y, Y would do it
>
> (*c*) at the same time X knew that if X said to Y, 'I don't want you to do this,' Y could not do it
>
> (*d*) X didn't say anything like this to Y
>
> (*e*) because X didn't say anything like this to Y, Y could do Z
>
> (*f*) Y did Z

What this explication shows is that, from the speaker's point of view, person X enabled person Y to do what Y wanted to do by refraining from interfering with Y's actions. Let us now compare, in the light of the above discussion, the two superficially similar sentences, one English and one German:

(22) *a.* Mary let John come (go).

   b. Mary ließ John kommen (gehen).

On the face of it, we have here two analogous constructions, and given that dictionaries treat *let* and *lassen* as translation equivalents, the meaning of (*a*) and (*b*) could be expected to be the same. But the use of NSM explications allows us to show that in fact the meaning is not the same, and to identify the differences in a precise and verifiable manner: in (*a*), we know that it was John who wanted to come (or go), and Mary did not do anything to prevent him, whereas in (*b*) we do not know what John wanted, but we do know that Mary did (said) something, knowing that if she did John would come (or go), and that John came (or went) because Mary had done it.

Thus, the English construction (in contrast to the German one) encodes the idea of refraining from doing something to another person—and thus enabling this person to do what they want to do, highlighting in this a major Anglo cultural theme.

To see that the general theme of 'refraining from doing something to other people' is a modern development in English, consider the following examples of *let*-sentences from earlier epochs (from *OED* 1993):

(23) *a.* c.1440 He lete make a proclamacion ðorȝ (for/through?) all his Empire.

   b. 1781 On my arrival I was not let to wait long.

In (*a*), the king clearly does something, so that the proclamation is made through all his empire, rather than refrains from doing anything. In contemporary (twentieth-century) English *let* could not be used in this way. In some (but by no means all) comparable contexts, a *have* causative could be used instead.

In sentence (*b*), *let* is also used to imply action rather than inaction, and so the sentence could not be used in twentieth-century English. The closest contemporary counterpart would be 'I was not made to wait long', but this would introduce the idea that 'I had to wait', absent from the older use of *let*.

Anna Wierzbicka

OED (1993) lists the examples above under the heading 'To cause', which it treats as a separate meaning, alongside a supposed meaning described as 'Not to prevent; to suffer, permit, allow'. This latter (supposed) meaning is illustrated with examples such as the following ones:

(23) *c.* 1548 Kyng gave him fair wordes, and let him depart home.
    d. 1602 Your son Thomas will not let us work at all.

In fact, however, there are no compelling reasons to posit polysemy here: all the examples given (including (*a*), (*b*), (*c*), and (*d*) cited here) lend themselves to a unitary interpretation in terms of the causer 'doing something'—and in fact is rather similar to the use of the causative *lassen* in German, which was discussed in Section 8.5. (On the use of *let* in Middle English and in earlier Modern English, see e.g. Fischer 1992; Visser 1973.)

8.6.3. Let *of 'non-interruption'*

Example:

(24)   She let him sleep (work in peace; play in the mud) [a little longer].

Grammatical formula:

$$NP^1_{Human} \text{ let } NP^2_{Human} V_{DO. DUR} (ADV_{CONT}) \text{ [some more; *one more time]}$$

In this subconstruction, the verb cannot be momentary, that is, has to be 'durative' (DUR), and it has to refer to someone 'doing' something (DO). The assumption is that the causee is already doing something (something that presumably he or she wants to do), and that the causer intentionally refrains from interrupting what the causee is doing. As discussed earlier, the optional slot for an adverbial of continuation highlights this. (Capital letters in the explication are used to draw the reader's attention to the main differences between subconstructions.)

Explication
Person X let person Y do Z for some more time. =
  (*a*) X knew that Y WAS DOING SOMETHING (Z) FOR SOME TIME BECAUSE Y wanted to do it
  (*b*) X knew that if X didn't do anything to Y, Y would do Z FOR SOME MORE TIME
  (*c*) at the same time X knew that if X did something to Y, Y couldn't do it ANY MORE
  (*d*) X didn't do anything to Y
  (*e*) because X didn't do anything to Y, Y could do Z FOR SOME MORE TIME
  (*f*) Y did Z FOR SOME MORE TIME

The differences between the 'let of permission' and the 'let of non-interruption' can be summarized as follows. First, in the former case, the causee is not doing anything yet, and the causer can prevent the action, whereas in the latter, the causee is already doing something, and the causer can only prevent the *continuation* of the action, not the action itself; and second, in the former case the causer can prevent the causee's action primarily by *saying something* to the causee, whereas in the latter case, the causee can prevent the continuation of the action primarily by *doing something to* the causee. The distinction between saying something to a person and 'doing something to a person' lies largely in the eye of the beholder, but 'the eye of the beholder' is precisely what semantic analysis is concerned with. Proto-typically at least, one 'lets someone sleep' by not waking them up, whereas one lets someone 'go to a party' or 'borrow one's car' by not saying to them: 'I don't want you to do it.' As mentioned earlier, the distinction between the '*let* of permission' and the '*let* of non-interruption' is also justified by the fact that there seems to be no '*get* of non-interruption' or '*have* of non-interruption', analogous to the '*let* of non-interruption': one can hardly 'get somebody to continue' doing what he or she is already doing, or to 'have them continue' to do so, as one can 'let someone continue'.

Unlike in the case of 'the *let* of permission', in the present type there is no question of the causer 'saying' anything to the causee. Furthermore, what the causer's inaction is seen as responsible for is not the causee's action, but the *continuation* of the already occurring action.

8.6.4. Let *of 'apparent indifference'*

Example:

(25)   Person X let person Y cry (sulk, stew, fume; ?laugh)

Grammatical formula:

NP^1_{Human} let NP^2_{Human} $V_{DO.\ EXPR.DUR}$ [*some more; *one more time] [*NP^3]

In this type, as in the previous one, the causee is already doing something. This time, however, the assumption is that the causee feels 'something bad', wants someone else to know about these bad feelings, and that the action is expressive of the causee's feelings, and notably 'bad feelings'. The verbs normally used in this type of sentence are those suggestive of 'bad feelings', such as *cry* or *sulk*, but other verbs can sometimes be used too, if they are compatible with the assumption that they may be expressive of 'bad' rather than 'good' feelings. For example, if person X is laughing sarcastically, one *can* say 'she let him laugh'. The sentence 'Let her laugh!' appears to suggest, by itself, that the laugh may be associated with some 'bad feelings' (malice, contempt, hostility, or the like).

Explication

Person X let person Y 'express their bad feelings' =

(a′) Y WAS DOING SOMETHING LIKE PEOPLE DO WHEN THEY FEEL SOMETHING
     BAD
(a)   X knew that Y was doing it because Y wanted to do it
(b)   X knew that if X didn't do something to Y, Y would do Z FOR SOME
     MORE TIME
(c)   at the same time X knew that if X did something to Y, Y wouldn't do
     this ANY MORE
(d)   X didn't do anything to Y
(e)   —
(f)   Y did Z for some more time

Unlike in the case of 'permission' or 'non-interruption', this time there is no assumption that the causee *couldn't* do whatever he or she is doing if the causer did something and this is why in the formula component (e) is empty.

The phrase 'do something to (another person)' used throughout this explication may seem inappropriate, given that in idiomatic English it tends to suggest something 'bad' and intrusive (cf. 'What did you do to her?'). In the language of semantic explications, however, the distinction between 'do' and 'do to' reflects a basic conceptual distinction grammaticalized in most languages in the distinction between 'intransitive' and 'transitive' verbs (cf. Wierzbicka 1998b), and the 'do to' notion which underlies transitivity is not similarly linked with doing something bad or intrusive. (Stroking, kissing, or comforting another person would also be represented in NSM explications as 'doing something *to*' that person.)

8.6.5. Let *of 'non-prevention'*

Examples:

(26)   She let him die.
       She let him fall.

Grammatical formula:

$$NP^1_{Human} \text{ let } NP^2_{Human} \text{ } V_{HAPPEN}$$

The sentence 'she let him die' implies that the causee was sick and in a critical condition and that the causer knew this. In addition, it implies that the causer could expect the causee to die (shortly) and also that the causer could prevent this from happening (by doing something 'to' the causee). For some reason, however, the causer did not do anything, and after this, the expected event happened. There is no further implication, however, that because of the causer's inaction the event 'could happen' (no component (e)); and it is even not clear that the event happened *because* of the causer's inaction. What does seem clear is that the causer knew that he or she could prevent the event in question by doing something but did not do it.

Explication

> *Person X let person Y die (fall)* =
>
> (*a'*) X knew that something (Z) COULD HAPPEN to person Y (at this time)
>
> (*b*) X knew that if X didn't do something to Y, (Z) would happen to Y (at this time)
>
> (*c*) at the same time X knew that if X did something to Y, Z would not happen to Y (at this time)
>
> (*d*) X didn't do anything to Y
>
> (*e*) —
>
> (*f*) Z happened to Y

Is the event that the causer failed to prevent seen as bad? Often it is, but someone can also say, for example, 'Let me die!' on the assumption that death will be a good, liberating event rather than a bad one. The question is whether a sentence such as 'X let Y die' should be seen as ambiguous or rather as indeterminate. Often, a question of this kind can be resolved by pointing to a correlation between evaluation and intention: events seen as 'bad' are often also seen as unintended, whereas events seen as intended are not seen as 'bad'.

In the case of 'letting someone die', however, this test appears to give a negative result: the sentence 'X let Y die' is compatible with an interpretation which sees dying as bad and X's inaction as intentional, as well as with other interpretations. It appears, then, that in this case there are no sufficient grounds for positing ambiguity and that this sentence type should be seen, rather, as indeterminate, and this is how it is presented in the explication.

8.6.6. Let *of 'tolerance'*

Examples:

(27)   Let her be!
       Live and let live!
       Let me finish!
       Let her do as she pleases.

Grammatical formula:

> Let_{IMP} NP^2_{Human} $V_{DO\ or\ BE}$ [*some more; *one more time; *NP^3_{Human}]

The '*let* of tolerance' is normally (or at least typically) used in the imperative: it would be unusual to say, for example,

(28)   ?He let her be.
       ??She let him live.

'Let be' and 'let live' could be regarded as frozen expressions, and verbs other than *be* and *live* can be used in a wider range of forms (not necessarily in the imperative) to produce the '*let* of tolerance' effect, but normally they, too, require some modals or at least some illocutionary verbs implying 'want' or 'can (cannot)', for example:

(29)   You've got to let her make her own mistakes.
         He vowed to let her make her own mistakes.
         ?He let her make her own mistakes.
         *?Yesterday he let her make her own mistakes.

What the '*let* of tolerance' pattern does is to acknowledge a certain ideology, roughly speaking, the ideology of tolerance, and so it is normally not used for purely factual statements. For example, the sentence 'Let me finish!' implies not only a desire not to be interrupted but also a hint of disagreement: 'you may not like or agree with what I am saying but nonetheless you've got to let me finish.'

Similarly, the sentence 'Let her be!' does hint at a possible disapproval of whatever the person referred to is or is not doing. Nonetheless, disapproval or not, this person, too, deserves some tolerance. The phrase 'Let her (him etc.) be!' is different in this respect from the apparently similar in meaning phrase 'Leave her (him etc.) alone!' Both convey, roughly speaking, the message 'Don't do this to her any more; she doesn't want this,' but in addition, the first, in contrast to the second, implies that the addressee should desist even if there *are* some possible grounds for disapproval. For example, if X is tormenting Y out of sheer cruelty and malice, one would say to X, 'Leave her alone!' rather than 'Let her be!' On the other hand, if Y is doing something that the speaker slightly disapproves of but does not want to oppose (acknowledging Y's right to decide for herself whether or not she wants to do it), then 'Let her be!' can be seen as more appropriate.

Explication
     Let her be! (*Let her make her own mistakes!*)=
     (*a*) you know that Y wants to do Z
     (*a'*) MAYBE YOU THINK THAT IF Y DOES Z IT WILL BE BAD
     (*b*) you think that if you don't do anything to Y, Y will do Z
     (*c*) at the same time you think that if you do something to Y, Y will not do Z
     (*d'*) I SAY: IT WILL NOT BE GOOD IF YOU DO SOMETHING TO Y
     (*d*) IT WILL BE GOOD IF YOU DON'T DO ANYTHING TO Y
     (*d''*)YOU KNOW: WHEN A PERSON WANTS TO DO SOMETHING IT IS NOT GOOD IF
            OTHER PEOPLE SAY TO THIS PERSON 'YOU CAN'T DO IT'
     (*e*) —
     (*f*) —

One thing which clearly distinguishes this formula from the others is the component labelled here (a') ('(maybe) you think that if this person (Y) does this (Z) it will be bad'), which can be regarded as a hallmark of tolerance: the ideal embedded in the word *tolerance* requires that we will not try to stop other people from doing what they want to do even if we think that what they want to do is not good (as long as it is not bad for other people).

Another distinguishing feature of the present type, also related to the ideal of tolerance, is a hint of disapproval from the speaker for the addressee, reflected in the component 'it will not be good if you do something to Y (because you think these things)', and also the admonition related to it: 'you know: when a person wants to do something it is not good if other people say to this person "you can't do it".'

All in all, it can be said that the *'let* of tolerance' incorporates in its very meaning an important Anglo cultural script, and thus provides further evidence of the validity of this script in contemporary Anglo culture. (For detailed discussion of 'cultural scripts' see Wierzbicka 1991, 1996*b*, 1998*c*; cf. Goddard, this volume.) In a sense, the whole family of modern *'let* constructions' discussed here provides evidence for Anglo cultural scripts (of 'autonomy', 'non-interference', and so on); but the *'let* of tolerance' construction does so in an especially striking way, since it not only *serves* a particular cultural norm but in fact *articulates* it in its very meaning.

8.6.7. Let *of 'shared information'*

In some cases, a *let* construction can also refer to an intended result due to the causer's action. One case in point is the expression *let* (*someone*) *know*, similar in meaning to *inform*, but also sharing some components with the other *let* types discussed here. Typically, *let know* is used in the imperative, interrogative, or hypothetical rather than indicative mood:

(30)   Let me know (what happened).
        Did you let her know?
        It would be good to let them know.

The *let know* expression, although superficially similar in meaning to *inform*, can perhaps be seen as reflecting the cultural assumption enshrined in modern Anglo culture that it is natural for people to want to know all sorts of things, and that in principle people have the right to have their questions answered (except for so-called 'personal questions', which should not be asked in the first place; cf. Eades 1982). By the same token, telling people something that they want to know can be seen as simply not preventing them from knowing it (i.e. not withholding knowledge).

Looked at from this perspective, the *let know* expression, although implying action, can be seen as a natural extension of the *let* construction of 'inaction'. According to the *Oxford English Dictionary* (1993), *let* in the sense of 'cause' is archaic in English and has only survived in the expression 'let someone know'. It is certainly true that in Middle English *let* could be used in the sense of 'positive causation', as *lassen* can be used in contemporary German (cf. 8.6.2). But this does not prove that the expression 'let me know', as used in contemporary English, is an archaism rather than an innovation.

In Shakespeare's English, *let* could indeed be combined with *know*, but not in the sense in which these words are combined in the modern expression 'let me know', as the following examples (from *OED*) illustrate:

(31)   If your name is Horatio, as I am let to know it is.

Here, 'to let to know' means something close to 'to tell', or, as the *OED* puts it, 'to inform'. In some nineteenth-century examples quoted by the *OED* as examples of the same sense of *let*, *let know* means in fact something closer to 'to give to understand', e.g.:

(32)   There was always some body of Churchmen which disliked them, and took every opportunity of letting them know it. (1883)

But the present-day expression 'let me know' (and its variants, such as 'could you let me know') has a distinct meaning implying cooperation among autonomous individuals, a meaning incompatible with contexts like that in the second (1883) example above. In fact, even sentences with the imperative 'let me know' such as the following one from Shakespeare:

(33)   What is the end of study, let me know.

sound odd to present-day speakers of English, because they do not conform to the present-day meaning of the 'let me know' construction. In the sentence above, 'let me know' implies something like 'tell me'; but in contemporary English 'let me know' does not mean 'tell me', and, in particular, it cannot apply to something that the addressee knows now (as in 'let me know what your name is'). 'Let me know' implies that when you know something in the future, I want you to share this knowledge with me (and not withhold it from me), and that I assume you will do it, not because you will have to do it but because you will be willing to do it, in the spirit of cooperation between autonomous persons.

Explication
  let me know. . . . (cf. 'tell me')
  (*a*)   I want to know something
  (*a'*)   I think you will know it some time after now
  (*b*)   I think you know that if you don't say it to me I will not know it
  (*c*)   at the same time you know that if you say it to me I will know it
  (*d*)   I think you will not say 'I don't want to do it'
  (*d'*)   I know you don't have to do it
  (*d''*) I think you will do it because you will want to do it
  (*e*)   after this I will know it

In further support of this analysis, I would note that it is not true that *let know* is the only 'causative *let* expression' in twentieth-century English, as the *OED* implies: there are other expressions, especially 'imperative' ones, which can be seen as expressing 'causation by action', and these may throw some light on the meaning, and cultural role, of the expression *let know*, as it is used in modern English. Consider, for example, the following sentences:

(34) Let me have a look.
      Let me see it.
      Let me have a copy.

What sentences of this kind do is to convey a directive in an apparently non-imposing way: they sound as if the speaker were only asking the addressee for permission to do something, whereas in fact the addressee is also required to do something himself (herself). A straight imperative or an overt 'I want'-sentence could seem, in a similar situation, an act of forceful self-assertion and imposition:

(35) I want to have a look.
      I want to see it.
      Show it to me.
      Give me a copy.

The *let* construction—rather like a 'whimperative' (cf. Wierzbicka 1991)—allows the speaker to avoid giving such an impression.

It could be said that the *let* construction under consideration is the only one in which the causer is actually required to *do* something. In fact, however, the emphasis is not on 'doing' but on 'knowing': the way the speaker presents the request suggests that its goal is the sharing of information. This is why one would not use the *let* construction asking for food or other material things unrelated to knowledge:

(36) ?Let me have a pencil/an apple/ten dollars.

The expression 'let me have a copy (of your article)' is acceptable because it can be construed as a request for information (I want to read the article). The assumption is that the addressee can be expected to be willing to give the speaker access to some information.

Explication
  Let me have a copy
  (a) I want to have something (Z) because I want to know some things (W)
  (a') I know that you can know these things
  (b) I know that if you don't do something I will not have Z
  (c) at the same time I know that if you do something I can have it
  (d) I think you will not say: 'I don't want to do it'
  (d') I know that you don't have to do it
  (d") I think you will do it because you will want to do it
  (e) after this I will have Z
  (f) because of this I will know W

As this explication suggests, the speaker is not saying (not even implicitly), 'I want you to do it—I think you will do it because of this', which could sound hectoring and imposing. Rather, he or she is saying (implicitly), 'I want to have something because I want to know something'—'I know that if you do something I will have it'—'I think you will not say: I don't want to do it', thus indicating that he or she is counting on the addressee's cooperation, while at the same time politely acknowledging the addressee's right to prevent the speaker from getting access to the desired information.

8.6.8. Let *me do Z for you (offering to perform a service)*

Example:

(37)   Here—let me open the door for you. (Malouf 1985: 19)

Grammatical formula:

Let me $V_{DO.INT}$ for you

English has a common conversational routine, in which the speaker proposes to perform some small service for the addressee and in doing so verbally goes through the motions of asking for the addressee's permission. The speaker is not really asking for permission and is not anticipating any opposition, yet symbolically at least he (she) is giving the addressee a chance to decline the offer and in this way is acknowledging the addressee's autonomy and his (her) right to do things for themselves.

A sentence such as 'let me open the door for you' sounds more 'polite' in English than its counterpart simply declaring the speaker's intention ('I will open the door for you' or 'I want to open the door for you'). The 'let me do X for you' routine does not apply to future situations and future actions but only to present ones and it is normally restricted to doing something that otherwise the addressee would need to do, and would 'have trouble' doing. For example, sentences such as:

(38)   Let me carry it for you.
        Let me write it down for you.

can refer only to the immediate situation, as the infelicity of the following sentences shows:

(39)   ?Let me carry it for you tomorrow.
        ?Let me write it down for you when I find it.

But just sparing the addressee the trouble of doing something by doing it oneself is not enough for the *let*-routine under discussion to be felicitous. For example, it is appropriate for the host to say (40*a*) but not (*b*) to a guest who is about to leave:

(40)   *a.* Let me open the door for you.
        b. ?Let me close the door for you.

If the host does not do anything, the guest will have to first open the door and then close it (from the other side), so it would seem that the host has two ways of sparing the guest a bit of trouble: either by opening the door before the guest leaves or by closing it afterwards. But the 'let me do X for you' routine is only appropriate in the former case.

One reason seems to be that the speaker wants to do something that will be 'good for the addressee', and it is good for the addressee to have the door opened, so that he or she can leave. On the other hand, having the door closed is something that is good for the host, not for the guest—and so the 'let me do X for you' routine is not appropriate.

This is still not the whole story, however, and the missing aspect is highlighted by the common phrase 'Let me help you.' As this phrase suggests, what the speaker is trying to be seen as doing is cooperating with the addressee rather than doing the addressee a favour: the assumption is that the addressee has a goal, and that the speaker wants to be given the green light to assist the addressee in achieving that goal. For example, if the addressee is leaving, I can assist him (or her) by opening the door, but not by closing the door, for having the door closed is not instrumental in the addressee's overall goal of leaving, whereas having the door open is. This leads us to the following explication:

Explication
  Let me do Z for you =
  (*a*)   I SAY: I WANT TO DO SOMETHING GOOD (Z) FOR YOU NOW
  (*a′*)   I KNOW THAT YOU WANT TO DO SOMETHING NOW
  (*a″*)   BECAUSE I KNOW THIS I THINK IT WILL BE GOOD FOR YOU IF I DO Z NOW
  (*b*)   I want you to know: if you don't say that you don't want me to do it
              I will do it
  (*c*)   at the same time I know: if you say that you don't want me to do it
              I can't do it
  (*d*)   I think you will not say it
  (*e*)   because you will not say it I will know that I can do it
  (*f*)   I WILL DO IT NOW

8.6.9. *Let's do Z!*

Examples:

(40)   Let's go. Let's do it. Yes, let's.

Grammatical formula:

  Let's $V_{DO.INT.}$

The expression *let's* (contracted from *let us*) differs in meaning, as well as in register, from the somewhat archaic or elevated *let us* (e.g. *Let us remember!*, *Let us pray*). Roughly speaking, *let us* assumes authority and expects compliance; by contrast, *let's* envisages a joint action which is based on consensus and which cannot proceed if any of the prospective participants voices any objections to it, and so it implies an egalitarian rather than authoritarian attitude.

The archaic *Let us do Z!* construction implies that the speaker, who is a member of a group, wants the group to do something, and assumes that if he (she) voices this want, the group as a whole will comply. More precisely:

Explication

Let us pray! (Let us remember!) [archaic; 'guidance'] =
(*a'*) I think it will be good if we do Z
(*a*)   I say: I want us to do it
(*f'*) I think: because I say this it will happen

Presumably, the construction seems dated partly because its meaning is inconsistent with the modern Anglo democratic ethos: normally, it is no longer expected that groups will 'follow the leader' and do some things simply because of what the leader thinks and wants.

On the other hand, the common modern *Let's do Z!* construction reflects a different ethos: an ethos valuing voluntary cooperation of free and equal individuals. The construction *Let's do Z!* shares with the *Let us do Z!* construction two components: 'I want us to do Z' and 'I think it will be good if we do Z.' It adds to it, however, two further, 'addressee-oriented', components: 'I think you will say you want the same' and 'I know: if you say that you don't want the same we can't do it'. It also expresses the speaker's confidence in the addressee's cooperation: 'I think you will not say this'. Thus:

Let's do Z! ['suggestion']
(*a'*) I think it will be good if we do Z now
(*a*)   I say: I want us to do it
(*a''*) I THINK YOU WILL SAY YOU WANT THE SAME
(*b*)   I know: if you say you want the same it will happen
(*c*)   at the same time I know: if you say that you don't want it to happen it can't happen
(*d*)   I think you will not say it
(*e*)   —
(*f*)   —

8.6.10. *Let* of cooperative dialogue

Examples:

(42) *a.* Let me conclude by saying . . .
     b. Let me explain/suggest/assure you . . .
     c. Let me start by saying this . . .

> *d.* Let me propose a toast for . . .
> *e.* Let me ask you . . .
> *f.* *Let me order you . . . (Cf. I order you . . .)
> *g.* ?Let me beg you . . . (Cf. I beg you . . .)

Grammatical formula:

Let me V_{SAY}

The formula '*Let me* Verb' normally includes a verb of speech or a verb which can at least be interpreted as such, as a verb of sequence (e.g. Let me start with . . .; let me now turn to . . .).

The most obvious semantic component of the 'Let me V_{SAY}' construction is, clearly, 'I want to say something'. At the same time, however, the speaker signals his (her) wish to involve the addressee in the speech act and to acknowledge the addressee's (real or imaginary) presence and rights as a participant in the communication process. More precisely, the semantic structure linked with this formula can be spelled out as follows:

Explication
Let me conclude =
> (*a*) I say: I want to say something (Z) now
> (*b*) I want you to know that if you don't say that you don't want it to happen I will say this thing (Z)
> (*c*) I know that if you say that you don't want it to happen I can't do it
> (*d*) I think you will not say it
> (*e*) because I think you will not say it I think I can do it
> (*f*) I will do it now

Again, Shakespearian sentences like

(43)   Let me ask my sister pardon.
        Let me entreat you.

sound odd to a twentieth-century ear, because they do not conform to the cultural logic underlying the present-day array of *let* constructions: 'let me ask you' would be acceptable because it would comply with the principles of non-imposition and cooperation between the speaker and the addressee, but 'let me ask my sister pardon' does not have the same justification and sounds odd.

The sentence 'let me entreat you' does involve interaction between the speaker and the addressee, but it also sounds odd, and not only because *entreat* is now an archaic word. 'Let me beg you' would also sound odd, although 'I beg you' is still quite acceptable, as is also 'let me suggest' or 'let me explain'. Here, the reason for the incongruity lies in the inequality between the speaker and the addressee, implied by the verb *beg*, and the implication of 'equal rights' of the interlocutors, implied by the 'let-me-V_{say}' construction. (Cf. also 'let me ask you' vs. *'let me order you'.)

Both from a formal and a semantic point of view there is a similarity between sentences like 'Let me explain' and those like 'Let me finish' discussed earlier. But in the case of 'Let me finish' there is a real danger that the addressee may try to prevent the speaker from having his or her say. In the case of 'Let me explain', however, there is no such danger, and there is no implicit appeal to people's right to do what they want to do and say what they want to say.

Of course the expression 'Let me Verb' is only a formula, one might even say, an 'empty formula'—a conventional speech routine. But formulas of this kind are seldom really 'empty'. Even if the speaker does not 'mean' what the formula conveys this fact cannot detract from the significance of the ritual re-enacted each time a formula of this kind is used (cf. Ameka 1987, 1994).

The fact that one does not say in English 'let me go now' or 'let me have a cup of tea' to announce one's intention of doing something, whereas one does say 'let me explain' or 'let me propose . . .', requires an explanation. My explanation is that in the case of speech acts the speaker's action affects the addressee, and so the formula 'let me V_{say}' implicitly acknowledges the addressee's rights in the speech situation. This explanation is consistent with the explanation which I have proposed for a wide range of other phenomena, such as, above all, the wealth of 'whimperatives' in contemporary English (cf. Wierzbicka 1985, 1991). It is also consistent with the fact that one can say 'let me suggest' or 'let me ask', but not '*let me order you' or '*let me beg you'; the addressee's rights are acknowledged if the addressee is seen as an equal (and both *order* and *beg* imply inequality).

8.6.11. Let *of cooperative interaction*

Consider the following three sentences:

(44) *a.* Let me talk to him.
       b. Let me get back to you on this.
       c. *Let me apologize to her.

Why is it that sentences (*a*) and (*b*) are fully acceptable whereas sentence (*c*) sounds odd? The reason seems clear: (*a*) and (*b*) can be construed as referring to 'cooperative interaction' between the speaker and the addressee, whereas (*c*) cannot be so construed because it concerns the relationship between the speaker and a third party and has nothing to do with the addressee. In (*a*), the addressee is not mentioned either, but it is easy to construe the talking to a third party as involving some matter of joint concern to the speaker and the addressee. What is relevant in the present construction, then, is, first, that the speaker and the addressee have a shared goal (they both want the same thing to happen), second, that the speaker offers to do something to bring this goal about, third, that the speaker is only going to proceed if the addressee does not object, and fourth, that the speaker assumes that the addressee will not object.

Grammatical formula:

Let me V$_{\text{DO.INT}}$ (*for you)

Explication

Let me get back to you on this. =
(*a'*)   I know that you want something to happen
(*a''*) I know that I want the same thing to happen
(*a*)   because I know this I think it will be good if I do Z
(*a'''*) I say: I want to do something (Z)
(*b*)   I want you to know: if you don't say that you don't want me to do it I will do it
(*c*)   at the same time I know: if you say that you don't want me to do it I can't do it
(*d*)   I think you will not say it
(*e*)   —
(*f*)   —

8.6.12. Let *of cooperative thinking*

The '*Let* of cooperative thinking', which could also be called '*let* of deliberation', can be illustrated with the following examples:

(45) *a.* Let me see . . . (*Let you see . . .)
     b. Let me think . . .

Grammatical formula:

Let me V$_{\text{Think}}$

Since thinking is, above all, an individual rather than social activity, it may seem odd that verbs of thinking occur in the frame 'Let me V' at all: if I want to think, nobody could stop me, and my thinking does not require other people's cooperation. When, however, sentences like 'Let me see . . .' or 'Let me think . . .' are seen against the background of the '*let* of cooperative interaction' and, especially, the '*let* of cooperative dialogue', their function becomes clear: they imply, so to speak, a request for an interruption in our ongoing interaction (so that the speaker can think for a while), and since such an interruption would affect not only the speaker but also the addressee, it does make sense for the speaker to ask for the addressee's 'cooperation'. As in the case of the '*let* of cooperative dialogue', such a request can be regarded as a pseudo-request, simply enacting a certain conventional conversational routine. But, as noted earlier, conventional conversational routines reflect culturally important attitudes and assumptions about social interaction.

Explication

> *Let me see . . .* =
> (*a*) I say: I want to think about it for some time
> (*b*) I want you to know that if you don't say that you don't want me to do it I
>   will do it
> (*c*) I know that if you say that you don't want me to do it I can't do it
> (*d*) I think you will not say it
> (*e*) because I think you will not say it I can do it
> (*f*) I'm doing it now

8.7. A COMPARATIVE GLANCE AT RUSSIAN AND GERMAN

The extraordinary wealth of sentence types based on *let* in modern English points to one of the cultural preoccupations of modern Anglo culture. As Matsumoto (1988: 404) observed, Anglo culture assigns a key role to 'the want of every "competent adult member" that his actions be unimpeded by others' (Matsumoto is quoting here Brown and Levinson 1978: 67), and 'his freedom of action unhindered and his attention unimpeded' (Brown and Levinson 1978: 134). Matsumoto argues that Anglo theorists in general, and Brown and Levinson in particular, have mistakenly attributed to these concerns a universal significance. The story of *let* is linked, I believe, with the story of such cultural preoccupations, reflected in Anglo pragmatic norms (cf. Wierzbicka 1985, 1991) and with the role of concepts like 'freedom', 'tolerance', and 'non-interference' in English discourse (cf. Wierzbicka 1997: ch. 3).

For example, it is surely not an accident that most of the *let* constructions identified here for English have no counterparts in either German or Russian, and that in fact many of the *let* sentences adduced in this chapter cannot be translated idiomatically into either German or Russian.

Thus, the closest Russian counterpart of the English *let* family is the family of causatives based on the verb *dat'*, literally 'to give' (for a detailed study of *dat'* constructions in modern Russian see Podlesskaya to appear). But the range of the *dat'* family in Russian is much more restricted than that of the *let* family in English. Only a few of the types identified here for English could be translated into Russian by means of a *dat'* causative, and those which could—for example the '*let* of non-interruption'—would be by and large limited (except for contrastive uses) to modally qualified predicates, and especially to negative or imperative uses. For example:

(46)   *Ona   ne   dala emu   spat'.*
        she.NOM NEG gave him.DAT sleep.INF
        'She didn't let him sleep.'

(47)   *Daj   emu spat'.*
        give.IMP him sleep.INF
        'Let him sleep.'

(48) ?*Ona   dala   emu   spat'.*
      she.NOM give.3SG.PAST him.DAT sleep.INF
      'She let him sleep.'

Furthermore, one could hardly use a *dat'* construction to translate a sentence of the *'let* of non-prevention' type:

(49) She let him fall.
      ?*Ona dala emu upast'.*

although, again, a negative sentence would sound better:

(50) *Ona ne dala emu upast'.*
      'She didn't let him fall.'

By and large, the same applies to the *'let* of tolerance' type. The exact meaning of a sentence like 'let her be!' cannot be expressed in Russian at all, the closest approximation being *ostav' ee* 'leave her (alone)'. As mentioned earlier, however, 'leave her alone!' does not mean the same as 'let her be!' and does not appeal to a general ideology of tolerance.

Similarly untranslatable is the general slogan 'Live and let live!', although a negative declarative sentence meant as a complaint or criticism is possible:

(51) *Ona mne   žit'   ne   daet.*
      she me.DAT live.INF NEG gives.3SG.PRES
      'She doesn't let me live.'

The *'let* of intentional interpersonal causation' does have a counterpart in Russian but one restricted to agentive verbs like *posmotret'* 'to look' or *poslušat'* 'to listen' and excluding non-agentive verbs like *znat'* 'to know' or *videt'* 'to see':

(52) *Daj   mne   posmotret'/poslušat'.*
      give.IMP me.DAT look.INF/   listen.INF
      'Let me have a look/listen.'

On the other hand, sentences like 'let me know', 'let me see', or 'let me have a copy' cannot be exactly translated into Russian at all (although the sentence *daj mne znat'* does have a restricted use as an idiomatic expression, not equivalent to *let me know*). The closest one could do is to use an imperative: *skaži* 'tell (me)' or *pokaži* 'show (me)' or *daj* 'give (me)'; but of course a straight imperative does not have the same 'tactful' and 'non-imposing' connotations that expressions like 'let me know' or 'let me see' do:

(53) *Daj   mne   videt'.*
      give.IMP.PL me.DAT.PL see.INF
      (Let me see.)

Nor could one use a *dat'* construction to offer to perform a service, as in the English sentence 'let me open the door for you'.

(54)   ?*Daj   mne   otkryt'   tebe   dver'.*
       give.IMP me.DAT open.INF you.DAT door.ACC
       (Let me open the door for you.)

The closest one could do in a similar situation would be to use the verb *razrešit'* 'to allow' (with a 'polite' plural form), thus substituting lexical for grammatical means:

(55)   *Razrešite   mne   otkryt'   vam   dver'.*
       allow.IMP.PL me.DAT open.INF you.DAT.PL door.ACC
       'Allow me to open the door for you.'

Nor could one render in Russian the exact sense, and tone, of English sentences like 'let me explain . . .', 'let me assure you . . .', or 'let me propose a toast for . . .'. In Russian, in corresponding situations one would simply say *ja xoču . . .*, 'I want . . .'.

One generalization which suggests itself very strongly on the basis of a comparison of the English *let* constructions and the Russian *dat'* constructions is that the English constructions reflect the general theme of 'negative freedom' (that is, roughly, non-interference) so characteristic of modern Anglo culture (cf. Berlin 1969; Wierzbicka 1997), whereas the Russian *dat'* constructions do not reflect any such theme. The *let* family implies, roughly speaking, 'not doing something', whereas the *dat'* family (in accordance with the basic lexical meaning of *dat'*) implies 'doing something'. Consider, for example, the following sentence:

(56)   *Maša   dala Petru   počitat' svoj   dnevnik.*
       Mary.NOM gave Peter.DAT read.INF own-ACC diary.ACC

This sentence could be translated, roughly, into English as 'Mary let Peter read her diary', but it could also be translated as 'Mary gave Peter her diary to read'. The English sentence 'Mary let Peter read her diary' suggests that Mary did not stop Peter from reading her diary rather than that she actively encouraged him to do so. But the Russian sentence suggests that Maša *did* something, and in this it is similar to the English sentence 'Mary gave Peter her diary to read' rather than to 'Mary let Peter read her diary'.

Similarly, the Russian sentence:

(57)   *Maša   dala Petru   est'.*
       Mary.NOM gave Peter.DAT eat.INF

is virtually impossible to translate into English, because it implies not only that Mary set some food in front of Peter but also that Peter ate it because of this. Mary did not simply 'let' Peter eat; rather, she 'caused' him to eat, she ensured that he ate, she almost 'made' him eat (although in Russian the implication is that Peter was willing rather than unwilling to do so).

To undertake a survey of the different causative uses of the Russian verb *dat'* (in an NSM framework) would require a separate study, at least as long as the present study of the English *let* causatives, but the preliminary discussion given here should be sufficient to throw into relief—by way of contrast—the focus on 'negative freedom', on 'non-interference', on 'not doing anything', so characteristic of the English *let* causatives.

Of course the preoccupation of modern Anglo culture with 'non-interference', 'negative freedom', and 'personal autonomy' can only explain—at least directly—the wealth of *let* constructions involving both a human causer and a human causee. One can speculate, however, that once the idea of the consequences of inaction (of not doing anything) becomes salient in a language's semantic system it can easily spread from the interpersonal realm to the realm of inanimate causees.

If the speakers' attention is focused on the question of 'letting' (or 'not letting') other people do things, it may also come to be focused on the question of 'letting' (or 'not letting') things happen (to things). There may, however, be other explanations as well, including some addressing, more generally, the extraordinary elaboration of the theme of 'cause' and 'effect' in modern Anglo philosophy, 'pop-philosophy' and 'scientific outlook' (cf. Wierzbicka 1992: ch. 2). I cannot, however, pursue this theme any further in the confines of the present chapter.

Nor can I undertake here a truly comprehensive discussion of the German *lassen* causatives, which also deserve a full-scale study based on the same *tertium comparationis*, that is, on the empirically established set of lexico-grammatical universals. All I can do here is to remind the reader of the wide range of the German *lassen* causatives, glossing over any distinctions based on the wants of the addressee (see s. 8.5); and also mention that German has no equivalents of English *let* causatives and quasi-causatives such as 'let me know', 'let me have a look', 'let me open the door for you', or 'let me explain (suggest, assure you, etc.)'. Instead, one would say, idiomatically, 'Sag mir bescheid' (lit. 'tell me with certainty'), 'Kann ich mal sehen?' (lit. 'could I have a look?'), 'Warten Sie—ich öffne ihnen die Tür' (lit. 'wait ("polite form")—I open the door for you'), 'Ich möchte erklären, daß . . .' (lit. 'I would like to explain that . . .') or 'Ich würde vorschlagen . . .' (lit. 'I would propose . . .'). The general point I wish to make here is that to undertake such comparisons between English and other languages we must first disentangle the complex network of various English constructions and expressions in which *let* is involved, and elucidate their meaning. For this, a rigorous and universally applicable semantic framework is simply indispensable.

The semantic history of *let* constructions in English is a vast and fascinating topic which requires a separate study. But the general trend is fairly clear: it is, on the whole, a shift from positive causation, in a very broad sense (often spanning, effectively, 'action' and 'inaction') to 'negative causation', that is, to 'enabling by not preventing'.

As, for example, Fischer (1992: 29) puts it, *let* was 'the central causative verb' in Middle English, and it had a distinct sense of 'cause, allow', that is, a sense apparently spanning (as the German *lassen* still does) 'positive' and 'negative' causation, but in fact interpretable in *all* cases in terms of 'doing something'. This is clearly not the case in contemporary English, in which *let* refers, by and large, to abstention from action rather than to action. Apparent exceptions such as 'let me know' or 'let me have a look' confirm, in their own way, the cultural logic behind this general trend, since they imply something like cooperation among autonomous individuals and focus on shared knowledge rather than on the action required from the addressee.

8.8. CONCLUSION: CAUSATION AND ETHNOSYNTAX

It is generally recognized that languages differ in the amount—and kind—of attention they give to different aspects of reality through their lexical systems: Arabic has numerous words for sand, Hanunóo for rice, and so on. But the idea that languages differ in the amount—and kind—of attention they give to abstract ideas and relations such as causation, time, or human emotions has seldom been seriously explored. Yet it seems obvious that while cross-linguistic divergences of this latter kind are harder to investigate, their cultural significance can be far greater than that of more visible differences in the area of concrete lexicon.

It goes without saying that to be credible, investigations of this kind must dissociate themselves from any attempts to evaluate languages in terms of their expressive or logical power (in the style of ninteenth- and early twentieth-century theorists such as Lévy-Brühl, cf. e.g. Lévy-Brühl 1923, 1926). But this does not mean that we have to ignore the semantic dimensions of grammar, and their possible cultural underpinnings.

Syntactic typology which deliberately closes its eyes to semantic and cultural dimensions of formal diversity of languages is, ultimately, sterile and unilluminating. The introduction of semantic and cultural dimensions involves certain dangers, but these dangers must be faced. Rather than avoid facing them we should try to sharpen our analytical tools and to develop safeguards of various kinds. I believe that one important safeguard is that of studying the 'areas of semantic elaboration' in the grammar and in the lexicon of a language at the same time. Above all, however, we need a semantic metalanguage for a cross-cultural comparison of meanings, a metalanguage which can be used for describing and comparing all meanings—whether they are encoded in the lexicon or in grammar.

REFERENCES

AMEKA, FELIX. 1987. 'A comparative analysis of linguistic routines in two languages: English and Ewe'. *Journal of Pragmatics*, 11.3: 299–326.
——1994. 'Areal conversational routines and cross-cultural communication in a multilingual society'. In Heiner Pürschel (ed.), *Intercultural Communication: Proceedings of the 17th International LAUD Symposium*, Duisburg 23–7 March 1992. Bern: Peter Lang, 441–59.

BALLY, CHARLES. 1920. 'Impressionisme et grammaire'. In *Mélanges d'histoire littéraire et de philologie offerts à Bernard Bouvier*. Geneva: Société Anonyme des Éditions Sonor, 261–79.

BERLIN, BRENT. 1992. *Ethnobiological Classification: Principles of Categorization of Plants and Animals in Traditional Societies*. Princeton: Princeton University Press.

BERLIN, ISAIAH. 1969. *Four Essays on Liberty*. Oxford: Clarendon Press.

BROWN, CECIL. 1984. *Language and Living Things: Uniformities in Folk Classification and Naming*. New Brunswick, NJ: Rutgers University Press.

BROWN, PENELOPE, and LEVINSON, STEPHEN. 1978. 'Universals in Language Usage: Politeness Phenomena'. In Esther N. Goody (ed.), *Questions and Politeness: Strategies in Social Interaction*. Cambridge: Cambridge University Press, 56–324.

—— ——1987. *Politeness: Some Universals in Language Usage*. Cambridge: Cambridge University Press.

CHAFE, WALLACE, and NICHOLS, JOHANNA (eds.). 1986. *Evidentiality: The Linguistic Encoding of Epistemology*. Norwood, NJ: Ablex.

CHAPPELL, HILARY M. 1978. 'Semantics of some causatives in Chinese and English'. BA honours thesis, Australian National University.

COMRIE, BERNARD. 1974. 'Causatives in universal grammar'. *Transactions of the Philological Society*, 1–32.

——1981. *Language Universals and Linguistic Typology: Syntax and Morphology*. Oxford: Blackwell.

——1985. 'Causative verb formation and other verb-deriving morphology'. In Tim Shopen (ed.), *Language Typology and Syntactic Description*, vol. iii. Cambridge: Cambridge University Press, 309–48.

CONKLIN, HAROLD. 1957. *Hanunóo Agriculture*. Rome: Food and Agriculture Organization of the United Nations.

DENCH, ALAN. 1982. 'Kin terms and pronouns of the Panyjima language of Northwest Australia'. *Anthropological Forum*, 1: 109–20.

——1987. 'Kinship and collective activity in the Ngayarda languages of Western Australia'. *Language in Society*, 16.3: 321–40.

DE TOCQUEVILLE, ALEXIS. 1953. *Democracy in America*, trans. Henry Reeve, ed. Phillips Bradley. New York: Knopf (first pub. 1835–40).

EADES, DIANA. 1982. 'You gotta know how to talk . . .: information seeking in South-East Queensland Aboriginal Society'. *Australian Journal of Linguistics*, 2.1: 61–82.

EVANS, NICHOLAS. 1986. 'The unimportance of CAUSE in Kayardild'. *Language in Aboriginal Australia*, 2: 9–17.

FISCHER, OLGA. 1992. 'Syntactic change and borrowing: the case of the accusative and infinitive construction in English'. In M. Gevitsen and D. Stein (eds.), *Internal and External Factors in Syntactic Change*. Berlin: Mouton de Gruyter, 17–88.

FRIEDRICH, PAUL. 1966. 'Structural implications of Russian pronominal usage'. In William Bright (ed.), *Sociolinguistics*. The Hague: Mouton. 214–53.

FUKUYAMA, FRANCIS. 1995. *Trust*. London: Penguin Books.

GIVÓN, TALMY. 1975. 'Cause and control: on the semantics of interpersonal manipulation'. In John P. Kimball (ed.), *Syntax and Semantics*, vol. iv. New York: Academic Press, 59–89.

——1984. *Syntax: A Functional-Typological Introduction*, vol i. Amsterdam: John Benjamins.

GODDARD, CLIFF (ed.). 1997. 'Studies in the syntax of universal semantic primitives'. *Language Sciences*, 19.3.

——1998. *Semantic Analysis: A Practical Introduction*. Oxford: Oxford University Press.

——and WIERZBICKA, ANNA (eds.). 1994. *Semantic and Lexical Universals: Theory and Empirical Findings*. Amsterdam: John Benjamins.

————In press. *Meaning and Universal Grammar*. Amsterdam: John Benjamins.

HALE, KENNETH. 1966. 'Kinship reflections in syntax: some Australian languages'. *Word*, 22: 318–24.

HARKINS, JEAN. 1995. 'Desire in language and thought: a study in cross-cultural semantics'. Ph.D. thesis, Australian National University, Canberra.

HEATH, JEFFREY, MERLAN, FRANCESCA, and RUMSEY, ALAN (eds.). 1982. *Languages of Kinship in Aboriginal Australia*. Sydney: Sydney University Press.

HOPPER, PAUL, and THOMPSON, SANDRA. 1980. 'Transitivity in grammar and discourse'. *Language*, 56.2: 251–99.

HYMES, DELL. 1962. 'The ethnography of speaking'. In Thomas Gladwin and William C. Sturtevant (eds.), *Anthropology and Human Behaviour*. Washington: Anthropological Society of Washington, 13–53.

KACHRU, YAMUNA. 1976. 'On the semantics of the causative construction in Hindi-Urdu'. In Shibatani 1976*b*: 353–69.

KLEMPERER, VICTOR. 1996. *Ich will Zeugnis ablegen bis zum letzten: Tagebücher 1942–1945*, vol. ii. Berlin: Aufbau Verlag.

LÉVY-BRÜHL, LUCIEN. 1923. *Primitive Mentality*. London: George Allen & Unwin.

——1926. *How Natives Think* [*Les Fonctions mentales dans les sociétés inférieures*], trans. Lilian A. Clare. London: Allen & Unwin. (Repr. New York: Arno Press, 1979.)

MALOUF, DAVID. 1985. *Antipodes: Stories*. London: Chatto & Windus.

MATSUMOTO, Y. 1988. 'Reexamination of the universality of face: politeness phenomena in Japanese'. *Journal of Pragmatics*, 12: 403–26.

MORAVCSIK, EDITH. 1978. 'On the case marking of objects'. In Joseph H. Greenberg (ed.), *Universals of Human Language*, vol. iv. Stanford, Calif.: Stanford University Press, 249–89.

OED. 1993. *The Oxford English Dictionary*. [CDRom.] Oxford: Clarendon Press.

PODLESSKAYA, VERA. To appear. 'Benefactive and other manifestations of the "giving" metaphor in Russian'.

RUWET, NICHOLAS. 1976. *Problems in French Syntax: Transformational Generative Studies*, trans. S. Robins. London: Longman.

SAPIR, EDWARD. 1949. 'Language'. Reprinted in David G. Mandelbaum (ed.), *Selected Writings of Edward Sapir in Language, Culture and Personality*. Berkeley and Los Angeles: University of California Press, 7–32 (first pub. 1933).

SHIBATANI, MASAYOSHI. 1973. 'Semantics of Japanese causativization'. *Foundations of Language*, 9: 327–73.

——1976*a*. 'The grammar of causative constructions: a conspectus'. In Shibatani 1976*b*, 1–10.

——(ed.). 1976*b*. *The Grammar of Causative Constructions*. Syntax and Semantics, 6. New York: Academic Press.

SONG, JAE JUNG. 1996. *Causatives and Causation: A Universal-Typological Perspective*. London: Longman.

SPEER, ALBERT. 1975. *Spandauer Tagebücher*. Frankfurt: Propyläen.

STEARNS, PETER, and STEARNS, CAROL Z. 1986. *Anger: The Struggle for Emotional Control in America's History*. Chicago: University of Chicago Press.

TALMY, LEONARD. 1976. 'Semantic causative types'. In Shibatani 1976*b*: 43–116.

TSUNODA, TASAKU. 1981. 'Split case-marking patterns in verb types and tense/aspect/ mood'. *Linguistics*, 19.5/6: 389–438.

VISSER, F. TH. 1973. *An Historical Syntax of the English Language*. Leiden: E. J. Brill.

WIERZBICKA, ANNA. 1980. *The Case for Surface Case*. Ann Arbor: Karoma.

——1981. 'Case marking and human nature'. *Australian Journal of Linguistics*, 1: 43–80.

——1985. 'Different cultures, different languages, different speech acts: Polish vs. English'. *Journal of Pragmatics*, 9: 145–78.

——1988. *The Semantics of Grammar*. Amsterdam: John Benjamins.

——1991. *Cross-cultural Pragmatics: The Semantics of Human Interaction*. Berlin: Mouton de Gruyter.

——1992. *Semantics, Culture, and Cognition: Universal Human Concepts in Culture-Specific Configurations*. New York: Oxford University Press.

——1996*a*. *Semantics: Primes and Universals*. Oxford: Oxford University Press.

——1996*b*. 'Contrastive sociolinguistics and the theory of "cultural scripts": Chinese vs. English'. In Marlis Hellinger and Ulrich Ammon (eds.), *Contrastive Sociolinguistics*. Berlin: Mouton de Gruyter, 313–44.

——1997. *Understanding Cultures through their Key Words: English, Russian, Polish, German, Japanese*. New York: Oxford University Press.

——1998*a*. 'The semantics of English causative constructions in a universal-typological perspective'. In Michael Tomasello (ed.), *The New Psychology of Language: Cognitive and Functional Approaches to Language Structure*. Hillsdale, NJ: Lawrence Erlbaum, 113–53.

——1998*b*. 'Anchoring linguistic typology in universal human concepts'. *Linguistic Typology*, 2.3: 141–94.

——1998*c*. 'German cultural scripts: public signs as a key to social attitudes and cultural values'. *Discourse and Society*, 9.2: 265–306.

XOLODOVIČ, A. A. (ed.). 1969. *Typologija Kauzativnyx Konstrukcij*. Leningrad: Nauka.

PART III
Culture, Pragmatics, and Grammaticalization

9

Changes within Pennsylvania German Grammar as Enactments of Anabaptist World View

KATE BURRIDGE

9.1. INTRODUCTION

I first became convinced of the need to include cultural information about a speech community in grammatical descriptions when I encountered the exceptional body-part syntax of early Germanic, especially medieval Dutch. Traditionally constructions involving oblique subjects instead of the expected nominative had been dismissed as errors—evidence that speakers at this time were losing grip of case functions and endings. The medical texts I was examining from this period, however, made it clear that, far from being scribal slips, these body-part constructions encoded fine semantic distinctions which had to do with prominence and degree of involvement. Furthermore, these 'errors', together with other construction types, were enacting prevailing medical thinking of that time—a thinking that encompassed beliefs about the body that emphasized specifically its vulnerability to external forces. Illness was generally linked to the supernatural, either demonological influences or the wrath of celestial powers (i.e. disease as retribution for sins and indiscretions).[1] In other words, current medical opinion was there nicely embodied in the syntax. In particular, the absence of an expected nominative subject and the use instead of an oblique case captured the passive role of body and person in processes and states believed to be controlled by outside forces

This chapter has depended on the kindness and generous support of so many members of the Mennonite community in Waterloo County. To all these people, I owe a special debt of gratitude for their continued friendship and their time and patience in answering my constant stream of questions. Many thanks also to the Edna Staebler Research Scheme whose financial support gave me the opportunity of further exploring the question of the effects of culture on Pennsylvania German. I am also extremely grateful to Cliff Goddard, Catherine Travis, Anna Wierzbicka, and especially to Nick Enfield for many helpful discussions and comments.

[1] That people arrived at such fantastic conclusions about the workings of the body and disease etiology is hardly surprising. What is a disease after all? There are symptoms and there are sick patients, but there is usually nothing tangible in the disease itself. It arrives out of the blue and then just as mysteriously transmits itself from person to person, affecting some while leaving others curiously untouched. The mystery would have been that much greater during the Middle Ages. Physicians had little knowledge of physiology and few sophisticated instruments to guide them; recall that at this time it was even illegal to open up a human body.

(see Wierzbicka's portrayal of 'the unknown' in syntax 1979: 369–77; see also Burridge 1995).

This chapter examines two recent developments in Pennsylvania German grammar that go against usual pathways of grammatical change and appear to be driven by the cultural and religious preoccupations of the speakers. For one, Pennsylvania German appears to offer a bona fide example of degrammaticalization, whereby a lexical verb *wotte* 'to wish' has re-evolved out of a grammaticalized modal verb. In addition, it shows the unusual development of a lexical verb *zehle* 'to count' into a marker of future. This future is interesting precisely because it does not appear to fit neatly into any of the grammaticalization schemas identified for the development of future meaning. Both these curious developments I argue are linguistic enactments of Anabaptist principles and values.

The chapter falls into four sections. Section 9.2 provides the necessary historical and religious backdrop. Section 9.3 presents those aspects of Anabaptist 'self-image' that are crucial to the continued survival of the language and that I claim are also shaping its grammatical structure. Section 9.4 examines the two developments just mentioned; namely, the recent degrammaticalization of a modal verb and the grammaticalization of a new future auxiliary. Section 9.5 provides concluding remarks on the role of culture in the making of grammar.

9.2. BACKDROP

The Pennsylvania German speakers examined here are the Old Order Mennonites of Swiss-German origin, in particular those who left Pennsylvania for Canada at the end of the eighteenth and beginning of the nineteenth centuries. While the Old Order started out as a purely religious group, it has now become a distinct cultural-ethnic group and one which contrasts remarkably with mainstream North American culture. Fishman (1982: 33–5) describes the Old Order Amish in Pennsylvania as a rare example of stable societal biculturism (or 'di-ethnia'). This is also an apt description of the Old Order Mennonites in Canada—as in Pennsylvania we see here a stable situation involving two distinct sets of cultural behaviours. Clearly what people believe in will shape their lives and their language—but this, I believe, is especially obvious in Pennsylvania German speech communities where religion, society, and language are so totally entwined. This is after all why the language has been such a 'success story'. After nearly four centuries it is alive and well in North America, holding its own well and truly against English. Yet for a group like the Old Order Mennonites the question of formal language maintenance efforts never arises. There is no chance of them ever actively propagating the language. For these people it is simple—language and faith are one. One cannot continue without the other. Their language, like their buggies, forms an integral part of their 'separate and peculiar' status.

To understand the habitual cultural preoccupations of Canada's 'separate and peculiar people', it is necessary to present something of the religious and historical background of the Mennonites, especially the early persecution experience, which did much to shape the lively speech community we find today. It is also important to realize at the outset that this community represents (1) a religious body (with religion as the spiritual idea existing in the minds of people); (2) a distinct ethnic group (with Swiss and southern German origins reflected still in their unique dress and dialect); (3) a distinct cultural minority (with culture as the 'group personality' of the Pennsylvania Germans and also the public expression of that personality). The Old Order Mennonites are all of these, and language is intimately bound up in all three. As the descriptions by sociologists like Fretz (1989) and Hostetler (1993) (on the Amish) make clear, this religion places extraordinary demands on the everyday living of its people. Every aspect of the Old Order lifestyle is saturated with symbols which express a commitment to qualities like frugality, equality, and humility and, in particular, the subordination of the individual to God's will—for some groups even the use of hooks and eyes in place of the more fashionable buttons symbolizes resistance to vanity and pride. To my mind, it would be remarkable indeed if language were not also somehow affected; if these symbols of subordination were not reflected in some way in the grammatical structuring of this language.

9.2.1. *Who are the Mennonites?*

The Mennonites, together with the Amish and Hutterites, form the three major groups within Anabaptism. The Anabaptist religion originally emerged as a counter church movement during the sixteenth century in Europe, beginning in Switzerland and later spreading to Holland and Germany. The name Anabaptist refers to the practice of rebaptizing individuals already baptized as children. Members of these groups argue that infant baptism is not in keeping with their concept of the Church as a voluntary group of believers and accordingly they rebaptize anyone who wishes to join them—adult baptism therefore is a symbol of their faith.

From the beginning, the Anabaptists advocated rigid separation of Church and State and for themselves total separation from the 'world'. They accepted the Bible as their sole guide of faith and practice—the Bible was their authority, not the Roman Catholic Church and Pope. Inevitably they clashed with the Roman Catholic and Protestant churches of the time. Thousands were imprisoned and burnt at the stake and the strong desire of present-day groups to maintain a separate existence is not surprising in the light of what their ancestors suffered during this period. Many families today own a copy of *The Martyrs' Mirror*. This huge book, first published in Holland in 1660, offers vivid accounts of all the Anabaptist martyrs of the Post-Reformation. Together with forceful reminders in hymns and sermons, it strongly reinforces a desire for isolation.

During the seventeenth century, the Quaker William Penn issued the Anabaptists with an invitation to settle in Pennsylvania. Britain promised that in America they would be given religious freedom and with that many Dutch, German, and

Swiss immigrated during the seventeenth and eighteenth centuries. At the end of the eighteenth and at the beginning of the nineteenth century many resettled in Canada. This was a direct result of the American War of Independence and the anti-German sentiment which followed. Their pacifist principles had already marked them as traitors in the eyes of some of their compatriots, and their situation considerably worsened when the British employed German troops. So they left in their horse-drawn buggies, some ending up near the Canadian border, but most settling in Waterloo County (about 70 km west of Toronto).

The Mennonite Order comprises over 40,000 members but this covers many different subgroups, including large numbers of Russian Mennonites who speak a form of Low German. (For an excellent account of the different Amish-Mennonite congregations in Waterloo County, see Fretz 1989.) In fact, the Swiss-German Mennonites of all the Anabaptist groups in North America have the largest number of separate congregations. Since the 1870s they have been experiencing continued factionalism and the result is a complex pattern of different sub- and splinter groups. The major reason for these schisms is the different degrees to which members will interpret the scriptural quotation 'Stellet euch nicht dieser Welt gleich' [And be not conformed to this world]. The initial split, for instance, came about because certain groups were admitting worldly church practices like Sunday school. They were also more liberal in their attire. The question of nonconformity poses enormous problems and has led to great tension and serious splits within their community. Biblical exactness is an important factor in maintaining their separate status and close sense of community, but paradoxically it is also a reason for the continuing factionalism. To an outsider the situation is complicated and confusing and it is often difficult to tell the sociological and religious differences between the groups. Differences can be subtle, such as a difference in dress styles or buggy technology, or they can involve more serious issues such as education of the young, or the adoption of new farming methods. To simplify matters, the Amish-Mennonite Anabaptists are generally divided into two major groups—the Plain and the Non-Plain People (where *plain* refers to 'unadorned'). This is a gross simplification admittedly, but in terms of the sociolinguistic situation it is a useful distinction to make.

The Plain People (colloquially the 'Horse and Buggy People' or *Fuhrleit* in German) are the most conservative and consist largely of the group of Old Order Mennonites, who are the focus of this chapter. There are some 27,000 Swiss-German Mennonites in Ontario and the Old Order make up approximately 12 per cent of the total population. They are rural and isolated and alone the group comprises half of the total farming population of Ontario. Their separate and simple way of life attracts much attention. People often do not understand the theological reasons behind their refusal to accept modern ways, and assume that they are pursuing eccentric behaviour simply for its own sake. Members of the Old Order have a very distinctive style of dress which has changed little over the centuries. They drive horse-drawn buggies, are opposed to modern conveniences like cars, radios, televisions, telephones, etc., and refuse all forms of government aid and insurance. The Old Order want to keep change to a minimum—'ufhalde de alde Wege' [maintain the old ways]. Nonetheless, some accommodations are now being made by certain subgroups; for example, with respect to electricity and telephones. It seems these groups are more ready to accept both electricity and phones because they are perceived to be less of a threat to community living. Cars, on the other hand, are clearly a greater threat, since they make it possible to travel vast distances, presumably also outside the community, where one would be much more vulnerable to worldly influences. To leave the community would be to leave the 'true' Church. The problem facing the Old Order is that once they start to accommodate to new ways, where is the line to be drawn? Once they start to admit change, the outside culture has a foot in the door and the real fear then is that this contact with the outside will destroy their close sense of community. They have only to look at their more progressive members to see that these fears are well grounded. It is really only the Old Order who have managed to retain this sense of community and remain truly 'abgesandert vun die Welt' [apart from the world] and it is the Old Order who are the key to the survival of Pennsylvania German. For these people language has a deeply religious significance and this will guarantee its survival.

The Non-Plain People make up the vast majority of the Mennonites and they fall into two distinct groups—the Transitionals and the Progressives. The Transitionals number only about 20 per cent and are almost all rural (although this is changing as more seek employment in cities and towns). Most of their members come from the large group of Waterloo-Markham Mennonites. This group still follows many of the same beliefs and behaviour patterns as the Old Order Mennonites, but have accommodated more to modern ways. For example, although they use the same meeting houses as the Old Order Mennonites, their church services are part English and part German. In addition, black cars now replace the horse and buggy. Their dress, like their cars, is plain and without decoration, but not in the same distinctive tradition of the Old Orders (for that reason, they are sometimes referred to as the 'Modern Plain'). Although they are associated with the Progressives under this label Non-Plain, sociologically and linguistically they are actually more closely bound to the Old Orders. The Progressives are largely urban and represent the modern groups. Generally speaking, they are indistinguishable from those who participate in mainstream Canadian life, and of this group, only the old generation are Pennsylvania German-speaking. Table 9.1 provides a summary of these three major groups.

But this is painting a neat picture of what in reality is nowhere near as orderly. Even the Old Order has experienced factionalism and the result is a number of different conservative sub- and splinter groups. Clearly the best way is to view the whole complex situation in terms of a continuum—from the ultra-conservative groups to the most progressive. Along this continuum it is also possible to plot the different speakers according to their language skills—from the most competent to those with a passive knowledge only. Competence in Pennsylvania German

TABLE 9.1. The three major divisions of the Mennonites

The Plain People
Old Order Mennonites—ultra-conservative, rural and isolated, no modern conveniences, regular use of German (family, community, and work), infrequent use of English (with outsiders only).

The Non-Plain People
Transitional Mennonites (or 'Modern Plain')—modern conveniences, rural and urban, regular use of both German and English.
Progressive Mennonites (modern groups)—indistinguishable from mainstream Canadians, regular use of English, some German if necessary.

accords generally with the degree of religious conservatism. It is not of course that religion directly bears on the linguistic abilities of these people, but, as should be clear from the discussion below, it is on account of what their religion entails.

9.3. MENNONITE PRINCIPLES AND THE SURVIVAL OF PENNSYLVANIA GERMAN

The Old Order Mennonites in Canada are diglossic. Pennsylvania German (in this schema the L(ow)-variety) is spoken (rarely written) and is the language of home and community. English (the H(igh)-variety) is read and written and is only spoken when dealing with non-Pennsylvania German-speaking outsiders. English is not learned by the Old Order children until they go to school at the age of 6 years. Most Old Order children attend parochial schools taught and run by their own community. Even though English is compulsory here, these schools are nonetheless important for language maintenance. Only Old Order children attend. This helps to enhance a feeling of group consciousness and means that the children are insulated from any outside influences. School continues until the age of 14 when they return to the farms.

At the same time, these people also have a knowledge of High German. This is not the same as Modern High German today but is (archaic) Luther German—the language of the Luther Bible, but with influence from their own Pennsylvania German dialect. High German is understandably very important to them and is held in high esteem. As the word of God, everyone must be able to read it and children are taught it by family and at school. It is only ever used for religious purposes—sermons are given in the dialect, not in High German, as is sometimes thought to be the case. People do not converse in it, unless to quote from the Bible. Clearly High German is functionally very restricted and in this model is best described as a classical variety.

There is no evidence that the Old Order Mennonites are about to lose their language and the secret of its survival surely lies in its symbolic value. So-called low-prestige language varieties clearly have values for their speakers that are quite different from those associated with the more overtly prestigious varieties. This is why they can sometimes show such surprisingly strong resistance against the more powerful standard dialects. In the case of the Mennonites, however, it is more than just the solidarity status of Pennsylvania German. As I see it, there are three aspects to the Mennonite way of life and religion which contribute most to the continued survival of Pennsylvania German within specifically the Old Order—their separateness, their nonconformity, and, most importantly, their humility. As will become apparent, it is these three aspects of the Mennonite 'self-image' that are also significant in shaping many of the structural patterns of Pennsylvania German. (For a more detailed account of the question of language survival see Burridge 2002.)

9.3.1. *'Be separated from the world': separateness*

Other German-speaking groups, who arrived in various waves during Ontario's history (for example the Roman Catholic and Lutheran communities), have assimilated into mainstream culture and have quickly surrendered their language. These people usually immigrated as individuals, not as organized religions and family groups like the Mennonites and Amish, and this most certainly would have accelerated the assimilation process. The Old Orders, on the other hand, have from the beginning always emphasized rigid separation from the world and through mutual self-help, and through economic, social, and spiritual self-reliance, they have been able to achieve this (cf. Fretz 1989 for details). In the words of Alan Buehler, a former Old Order Mennonite:

Iere Glawe is—los uns net involved waere mit em Government, awer los Government un Kaerich separate sei. Los uns e separate Volk sei, wu uns egene Noot un Schulde bezale, un unser God diene so wie mir des Wad verschteen. Se dien als bede far des Government, as God mecht des fiere, so as sie in Friede un e ruhich Leve fiere mechte. Awer es das Government un Kaerich separate bleive kenne.

[Their belief is—let us not be involved with the Government, but let State and Church be separate. Let us be a separated people, looking after our own needs and obligations, and serving our God in our own way. They always pray for the Government, that God may guide it in such a way that they may continue to live in peace and quiet. But Government and Church must remain separated.   (Buehler 1977: 174; my translation)]

Pennsylvania German has always provided an important barrier to the outside world, allowing not only for insider identification, but most importantly for outsider separation. It is one of their main means of remaining detached and isolated from worldly influences. Its loss would also mean the loss of this separate status and, for this group, would be equivalent to losing their faith.

9.3.2. *'. . . And be a peculiar people': nonconformity*

Some linguists (for example, Huffines 1980) have attributed the successful maintenance of US Pennsylvania German to the fact that any change is itself considered to be sinful by these people. I would argue, however, at least for the Canadian context I am describing, that it is not so much change itself, but rather what change entails. Their doctrine of nonconformity, it is true, means that they keep change to a minimum, but I do not believe that new ways are rejected out of hand simply because they are considered necessarily bad things. For example, even though as farmers the Old Order will have little to do with the modernization of machinery, they are extremely interested and, what is more, well up in the latest techniques and new technologies. These they learn about through reading newspapers and farming magazines. It is my experience that many display considerable interest in what is going on in the rest of the world. They are not opposed to change as such—in fact they are not averse to accommodating changes, if they think it will be of some benefit to the community as a whole. It is just that most modern inno-vations are viewed as unnecessary for a truly Christian discipleship. In order to maintain their old way of life, the conservative Old Order Mennonites realize the importance of keeping their language. Their shared language, their shared dress, their horse and buggy are indispensable—without them their social struc-ture would not continue. Losing these social symbols would be the same as losing essential elements of their faith. As the biblical quote reads: 'But ye are a chosen generation, a royal priesthood, an holy nation, a peculiar people' (1 Peter 2: 9).

9.3.3. *'Love not the world': humility and simplicity*

It seems that there are many, both within and outside the community, who view Pennsylvania German as simply a degenerate form of German. For these people, the language has all the negative connotations often associated with 'dialect' or 'vernacular'. To an outsider like myself, it seems that even the speakers themselves generally hold their language in low esteem and under normal circumstances this would mean almost certain decline and shift to English. But nothing could be fur-ther from the truth. In fact here lies one of the secrets of the language's success at survival. It has to do with the importance which is placed on the need for humility. As Buehler (1977: 98), once more writing on his Old Order heritage, describes:

Se brauche des Wad 'Demuut' viel . . . zu iere duut des Wad mene plaini Gleder. Es Eng-lisch-Deitsch Dictionary saagt des Wad meent 'to be humble and meek'.

[They use the word 'Demuut' a lot . . . to them this word means a plain dress. The English-German dictionary says this word means 'to be humble and meek'.   (Buehler's transla-tion)]

Pennsylvania German, like plain dress, has therefore an important symbolic func-tion within their community. This dialect of German is viewed by the Old Order as a sign of humility and is therefore a good and godly thing. It is not pride—pride is what they abhor most—but, if you like, pride turned on its head. If High German is the word of God, the language of their Scriptures, then the low status of the dialect variety which they speak is seen as an appropriate symbol of their humility. The plainer and the more basic, the better. Its low status has therefore a positive, even sacred, value for the Old Orders.

9.4. MENNONITE PRINCIPLES AND THE MAKING
OF GRAMMAR

If we venture beyond the purely lexical level, then the world view of Pennsylvania German speakers shows up most obviously in the pronominal and nominal address system of the language—quite simply, there are no available styles of naming and addressing to express deference and attribute power or prestige. For one, Pennsylvania German never acquired the *du* (informal)/*Sie* (formal) distinction of the second person pronouns of Standard German. It has only invariant *du* which is used irrespective of age, sex, status, and degree of familiarity of the interlocutors. As Enninger (1985: 255) neatly describes it, 'after all, intra-group interaction is performed in the solidarity network of brethren and sisters which is at the same time a kinship network of close to distant relatives, i.e. *die freindschaft*. A ritual passage from *Vous* to *Tu* is, consequently, nonexistent.' In addition, everyone gives and receives first names only, again regardless of relative familiarity, status, age, and sex. There exist no titles and no honorifics; this is true even for use on public occasions, like a church service or during any of the rites of passage. This practice arises directly from the people's doctrine of humility and simplicity. Interestingly, there are no terms of endearment like *darling* either—couples address each other by their given name or by no name at all. Nicknames are used, but principally for the purpose of identification—first names are overwhelmingly Old Testament, and there is a limited pool of family names.

Mennonite values are also enacted in the significant role of silence: silent prayer, tolerance of long between-turn silences, and also patterns of greetings, leave-takings, pleases and thankyous, where silence is commonplace—for this community, speech does not have the sort of interpersonal function of, say, mainstream North American culture. There are greeting formulas, of course, but silence in place of a verbal greeting is not unusual. Similarly, 'pleases' and 'thankyous' may not be uttered; there is often silence, for example, at the dinner table when food is being passed around (see descriptions by Enninger 1991). The notion of 'phatic communion', in other words, the kind of mandatory speech used to establish social rapport during an encounter, has no value in this integrated community, where people are deeply involved with one another and where there is no social distance. Basically, if you are speaking Pennsylvania German to someone you probably know them personally. Besides, with so many external symbols already available, like clothing for example, an individual's social characteristics and values are always immediately obvious. There is not the same need for language to express information about values and social relationships as there is in the more mainstream culture. Quite simply, such things can be taken for granted in this community.

These different aspects of Pennsylvania German are recognizably symbolic of the Mennonite value system. Like lexical gaps, and lexical richness, they involve examples of linguistic patterns that are linked to culture in a very obvious way, to the extent that they are occasionally talked about by the Old Orders themselves. But what about those structural patterns of the language that are more than skin deep? Below I discuss some recent developments in Pennsylvania German grammar which to my mind are also quite clearly shaped by the Mennonite 'self-image'. Here we are dealing with the working of cultural influence at a much more subtle level.

9.4.1. *Setting the scene: grammaticalization*

Grammaticalization is basically a cover term for what are essentially a number of different historical processes which together work to create grammar. By now the processes are well known. But briefly they are these: morphemes or combinations of morphemes shift from a lexical to a grammatical function, or from a grammatical to an even more grammatical function. This shift to an increased grammatical status—for example full verb to modal auxiliary—is defined by interrelated changes at the semantic, phonological, and grammatical levels. Overall meaning becomes more general and more abstract as the concrete and specific notions associated with the lexical verb gradually erode away and are replaced by notions of modality. As pointed out by Traugott and König (1991) and Sweetser (1988), however, increasing abstractness does not necessarily mean loss of meaning. Grammaticalization can result in significant semantic enrichment when pragmatic inferences are lexicalized. (See also Evans and Wilkins 2000 and Enfield 2002 where this process is explicitly illustrated.) A feature of modal verbs for instance, and one which distinguishes them from other verbs, is their ability to express attitudes and judgements that have been taken up by a speaker. On the level of phonology, the increased grammatical status will inevitably mean less stress and ultimately loss of segmental features; i.e. phonological reduction. This sort of weakening is generally accompanied by an increasing dependence on surrounding material. Forms, previously free-standing, become less free and more bound. Auxiliaries may reduce to clitics and these over time may then become verbal affixes. With grammaticalization also comes diminishing categoriality—items will typically lose the grammatical trimmings of their category, and hybrid forms emerge. Verbs advancing to modal auxiliaries will lose their verbal characteristics such as the ability to take direct objects and finite clause complements; to form imperatives, passives, nominalizations; to inflect for person, number, tense, and so on. With further grammaticalization items will generalize to more and more contexts of use and the end point can be a shift from optional to obligatory status. Finally, original syntactic freedom will typically give way to a fixing of position and the grammaticalized item will no longer be eligible for pragmatic processes involving considerations of topicality, focus, emphasis, and so on.

Characteristic of grammaticalization and its accompanying processes is unidirectionality. Grammatical morphemes do not reacquire lexical semantics. They do not assume a fuller form once they have reduced, nor do they re-evolve the grammatical properties of major categories like nouns and verbs (see discussion in Hopper and Traugott 1993: ch. 5). This is what makes Pennsylvania German *wotte* 'to wish' such a curious case. Its shift from modal to fully-fledged verb has been towards *decreasing* grammatical expression; it has seen an enrichment of semantic substance and a return of precisely those morphosyntactic properties which were lost when *wotte* became a modal verb.[2]

9.4.2. *Pennsylvania German modals*

Pennsylvania German has seven clearly identifiable modal verbs: *misse* 'to have to'; *selle* 'to be supposed to'; *kenne* 'to be able to'; *welle* 'to want to'; *daerfe* 'to be allowed to'; *maage* 'to like to' (rare); and *brauche* 'to need to'. These verbs signal the psychological attitude of speakers towards what is being said; for example, they may express a speaker's doubt or uncertainty about the truth of the action or event. They therefore show a wide and complex range of meanings, dealing with notions like truth, possibility, probability, necessity, contingency, permission, hypothesis, desire and so on. Table 9.2 gives the conjugations of two modals *welle* and *kenne* in full. The other verbs pattern similarly.

TABLE 9.2. Modal verbs

		Singular	Plural
kenne 'to be able to, can'	1.	*Ich kann*	*Mir kenne*
	2.	*Du kannscht*	*Dihr kennet*
	3.	*Er, sie, es kann*	*Sie kenne*
welle 'to want to'	1.	*Ich will*	*Mir welle*
	2.	*Du witt*[a]	*Dihr wellet*
	3.	*Er, sie, es will*	*Sie welle*

[a]*Welle* shows an unusual contracted second person form.

The following list summarizes the properties which distinguish these particular verbs from other verbs and identify them as a semantically coherent and well-structured class in their own right.

---

[2] Other potential counter-examples to unidirectionality involve the lexicalization of grammatical items; e.g. Australian English *a gonna* 'one who is always "going to/gonna" do something'; *the druthers* 'things you would rather do'. Papers in Traugott and Heine (1991), namely, those by Campbell, Greenberg, and Keesing, also point out that directionality can be reversed under certain conditions.

- Expression of modal meaning.
- Occurrence in post-auxiliary ellipsis (e.g. *Er kann nett koche awwer ich kann* 'He can't cook but I can').
- No noun phrase, finite clause or adverbial/prepositional phrase complements.
- Bare infinitive complements.
- Defective finite paradigm (no third person singular inflection).
- Defective non-finite paradigm (no past participle; restricted use of infinitive).
- No passive.
- No imperative form.
- Distinctive subjunctive forms (but see discussion below).

The subjunctive is now formed periphrastically via *duh* 'to do', with the exception of a handful of very common verbs. The separate subjunctive forms of the modal verbs are the survivors of what were originally preterite subjunctives. As the forms in Table 9.3 indicate, they have undergone a number of phonological changes that have had the effect of establishing greater cohesion within the group (for example, the spread of umlaut for the forms of *selle/solle* 'be supposed to' and *welle/wolle* 'will'—the subsequent unrounding of the umlauted front vowels [ö > e] is a general feature of this dialect). The subjunctive forms *sotte* and *wotte* are no longer heard in Waterloo County, but have lost out to *sette* and *wette*. In addition, the phonological substance of these two verbs in particular has eroded considerably, with the original [lt] cluster now reduced to a medial flap [ɾ]. Note also the recent analogical shift of *misste* to *messte* which now identifies this particular verb more strongly with the group through the similarity of the root vowel.

In current Canadian Pennsylvania German, there is good evidence that these original preterite subjunctive verb forms are in the process of splitting off from their corresponding present forms, in ways that are reminiscent of the developing independence of the originally preterite forms *would*, *could*, *should*, and *might* in English. Increasingly these verbs have been subjected to developments which have had the effect of severing the synchronic ties with their present indicative partners

TABLE 9.3. Modal subjunctives

Infinitive	Subjunctive (1st and 3rd person plural)	
(Pennsylvania German)	Pennsylvania German	Standard German
kenne 'can'	*kennte*	*könnten*
brauche 'need'	*breichte*	*bräuchten* (colloquial)
daerfe 'be allowed to'	*daerfte*	*dürften*
maage 'may'	*mechte*	*möchten*
misse 'must'	*misste/messte*	*müßten*
selle/solle 'be supposed to'	*sette*	*sollten*
welle/wolle 'will'	*wette* (originally also *wotte*)	*wollten*

and establishing their own autonomy. They are now best considered as separate lexemes.

9.4.2.1. The story of *wotte*

So far the Pennsylvania German modals appear to present a paradigm case of grammaticalization, as they gradually make their way along the familiar road to auxiliaryhood. The modal *welle* 'will', for example, is already well along the grammaticalization path, further advanced in fact than its Standard German cousin *wollen*, which retains a number of verb-like features; e.g. the ability to passivize and to take sentential complements without subject reference identity between the auxiliary and the main verb. In addition *wette*, the preterite subjunctive form of *welle*, has split off and has established itself as an autonomous modal verb. In fact, it possesses even fewer verb-like properties; e.g. it prefers non-finite verb complements, and cannot be governed by other auxiliaries or occur with markers of non-finiteness. In Ontario Pennsylvania German the verb *welle* has actually now undergone a further split. *Wotte*, originally the rounded vowel variant of the preterite subjunctive, has also recently established itself as an autonomous verb. But in ways which violate the unidirectionality of grammaticalization processes it has re-evolved into a lexical verb expressing 'wishing' and 'desiring'. In an extraordinarily short period of time, it has come to replace the lexical verb *winsche* 'to wish'.

The history of English shows a number of examples of verbs which diverge functionally and split into a modal auxiliary and a new full lexical form; for example, the development of lexemic splits in *can* and *need* in early Modern English (see Warner 1993: 201–3). The differences in both form and meaning between the lexical verb *con*, *cun* 'learn, study' and the old preterite present (pre-)modal *can* eventually became so pronounced that the lexical item was said to have split in two: one form with the lexical function of a full verb and the other with the grammatical function of a modal auxiliary; compare also the related verb forms *couth* 'learned' and *could*. An analogous differentiation is still under way with modal and non-modal uses of *need* (compare: *Morris dancers needn't jump*; *Morris dancers don't need to jump*). These cases show the familiar process of divergence or split, whereby lexical items grammaticalize and split into a grammatical form, with the original form surviving alongside as an autonomous lexical item; i.e. A > A/B (> B); see Hopper and Traugott (1993: 116–20). The case of *wotte* is quite different, however. It is not simply that lexical *wotte* has always been around and is strengthening its position by innovating morphosyntactic properties expected of an ordinary lexical verb (as was the case with *con* for example). In other words, it is not simply continuing the original lexical stage, but is actually making its way back from a more grammaticalized stage. In shifting from a grammatical to a lexical morphosyntax, *wotte* has undone all the morphosyntactic changes which it underwent during its transition to auxiliaryhood. The following features now identify it well and truly as a main verb and distinguish it from the modals *welle* and *wette*:

- it has lost all traces of former modal notions;
- it now forms the subjunctive with auxiliary *duh* 'to do';
- it requires subjects with human referents;
- it can no longer take infinitive complements: e.g. **Ich wott kumme* 'I want to come';
- it no longer requires subject reference identity: e.g. *Ich wott, du kennscht frieher kumme* 'I wish you could come sooner';
- it can now be nominalized: e.g. *Wotte is net goed* 'Wishing isn't good';
- it can appear in the progressive; i.e. as an infinitival substantive governed by *am*, a fused preposition and article (literally, *an* + *em* 'on/at the'); e.g. *Er is juscht am wotte* 'He is just wishing';
- it can form imperatives: e.g. *Wott net fer sell* 'Don't wish for that';
- it has acquired more typical main verb conjugation, innovating a distinct past participle form: e.g. *Er hat gewott* 'He wished';
- it can be governed by other auxiliaries—the new future auxiliaries *zehle* and *geh* (*Er zehlt wotte* 'He will wish'), modal auxiliaries (*Ich muss wotte* 'I must wish'), periphrastic *duh* 'to do', either in the indicative (*Er dut als wotte* 'He is always wishing') or in the subjunctive (*Wenn ich juscht noch een Wunsch hett, daet ich wotte . . .* 'If I had just one more wish, I would wish . . .').

The three-way split *welle–wette–wotte* has had the effect of better integrating *welle* as a modal verb, since some of its more verb-like properties have been transferred to *wotte*. This is in contrast to Standard German *wollen* which is the most verb-like of all the modals, and (as described by Heine 1993: 74–5) falls closer to the lexical end of the grammaticalization continuum from full verb to grammatical marker.

9.4.2.2. How this split has occurred: cultural considerations

The linguistic factors behind this lexical split are the same as those instrumental in bringing about the general split between the preterite subjunctives and their present indicative forms; *wotte* was after all originally a variant pronunciation of the preterite subjunctive *wette*. Briefly, the factors were these. The demise of the tense–mood relationship, in particular the weakening distinctiveness of the subjunctive and the loss of the preterite tense, helped to establish the autonomy of the preterite forms. Their independence was also given a boost by their high frequency and of course their phonological irregularity; e.g. the formal distance between pairs like *welle* and the contracted form *wotte* (originally *wollte*). But while the other preterite subjunctives moved in the expected direction of increased grammaticalization, *wotte* moved off in the opposite direction and shifted from a grammatical to a lexical status. How could this happen? Tracking the progress of *wotte* with respect to its form, distribution, frequency, and meaning components is difficult without historical textual evidence at hand. Nonetheless, I submit the following as a reconstruction of the chain of events that led to the reinterpretation of *wotte* as a lexical verb, showing in particular how cultural factors have been a force behind these changes.

The clue lies in the pragmatic use of the preterite subjunctive to convey reserve or reluctance on the part of the speaker. I suggest that the seeds for this exceptional change were sown in those contexts where *wotte* was used as a cautious and moderate substitute for the indicative in utterances expressing a sense of 'wishing'. Compare the current Standard German use of the past subjunctive in sentences like (1) below. Here the unreality conveyed by the subjunctive can indicate that the speaker is not counting on the wish being fulfilled. Curme appropriately dubs this 'the subjunctive of modest wish' in his 1904 grammar. For example:

(1)   *Ich wollte,*   *ich wäre zu Hause*
        I   wish(pret.subj) I   were at home
        'I wish I were home.' (see Curme 1904: 228 and Durrell 1991: 344)

It is this sort of remote application of the preterite subjunctive (i.e. where it is used with present time reference) which has helped to blur the original tense–mood distinction of the modal verbs and therefore to establish the autonomy of the other original preterite subjunctives like *sette*, *wette*, etc. as separate modals.[3] The conditions are therefore ideal for further grammaticalization of *wotte*. So the puzzle remains— why didn't *wotte* develop along the same lines as *wette* or its English counterpart *would*? Alternatively, why didn't it simply fall by the wayside like *sotte*, the variant form of *sette*? To explain this, it is necessary to go beyond purely linguistic factors, to the shared beliefs and values of this close-knit speech community.

As indicated earlier, the Pennsylvania German speakers are a group of people deeply committed to qualities like frugality, equality, sharing, simplicity, and above all humility (see Fretz 1989). In particular, theirs is a belief system that totally subordinates self-will and self-love to the will of God. 'Wishful thinking' is therefore in direct conflict with their faith. Speakers are quite clearly uncomfortable with a blunt expression of desire or will. It is hardly surprising then that the usual German verb of 'wishing' and 'desiring' *winsche* has all but disappeared from the language. In its place is a verb whose origins lie in a modal, in particular a past subjunctive form of that modal. The use of the past subjunctive has always had a range of different tentative or remote applications in Germanic. Its element of unreality means it can offer a more indirect, a more cautious, a more modest, a more polite, even a more objective mode of expression than the more pedestrian indicative. For example, by using the past subjunctive a speaker can moderate the tone of a request (e.g. English *Would you ring me?*) and temper a blunt expression of will. For a community of speakers uncomfortable with 'wishful thinking', it is hardly surprising that *wotte*, the 'subjunctive of modest wish', has developed as their favourite construction to express desire.

---

[3] Warner 1993:148 ff. and Plank 1984 also describe the opaque use of the subjunctive as an important factor in the developing independence of English preterite forms *would*, *should*, and so on.

Frequency as always is a crucial factor here too. As language change shows time and time again, frequent use inevitably leads to a diminishing of expressiveness. In this case, I suggest that frequency has meant that the subjunctive's element of unreality and its accompanying expressive and emotional force has been lost. (This contrasts with the pragmatic strengthening usually associated with grammaticalization; see conclusion at this end of this chapter.) Stripped of its pragmatic component, *wotte* becomes the blunt expression of desire and is reinterpreted as a lexical verb with a full sense of 'wishing'. This reanalysis is also made possible by the functional and formal decline of the inflected preterite subjunctive in the language.

9.4.2.3. Summary

The history of Pennsylvania German modal verbs offers a paradigm case of grammaticalization; in particular, the transition of main verb to modal auxiliary. The original preterite subjunctive forms of these verbs have now established themselves as separate modal lexemes, now virtually independent of their corresponding indicative 'present tense' forms. Ongoing change would see the rise of other (more abstract) grammatical functions; for example, dynamic modality (desire, ability) typically develops into epistemic modality (probability, possibility), as does deontic modality (obligation) (cf. Heine 1993: 66–9). The split of *welle* and *wotte* therefore comes as a surprise. An originally inflectionally related pair of words has lost its inflectional relation; yet *wotte* (unlike *wette*) does not further grammaticalize, but rather re-evolves a lexical meaning and innovates morphosyntactic properties characteristic of a full verb. This is not the usual instance of split; i.e. where an item dissociates itself from its modal counterpart and simply strengthens its position as a lexical verb. Here I suggest pragmatic factors arising from Mennonite religious principles have diverted the more usual path of development and produced a genuine counter-example to unidirectionality in language change. The context which allowed this development to take place was the frequent use of preterite subjunctive *wotte* in place of the indicative, as a more remote and tentative expression of 'wishing'. The social-ethical value these Mennonites place on the subordination of individual will has given rise to a strong aversion to 'wishful thinking' in the community. Speakers, not surprisingly, have opted for the 'subjunctive of modest wish' to express their appeals and desires. Its subsequent loss of pragmatic force then triggered (in what appears to be a very short period of time) the reanalysis of *wotte* as a fully-fledged lexical verb, totally displacing the inherited verb of 'wishing' *winsche*. Its atypical form already opaque to tense and mood would have encouraged the reanalysis.

It is interesting to note that the verb *welle* 'will' (Standard German *wollen*) has itself an optative source which already in Proto-Germanic had the function of an indicative. As Hermann Paul (1982: 219) described it, 'Seit alters wird der Indikativ Präsens dieses Verbs durch Optativformen gebildet, weil die Wunschform in der Rede vorherrschte' [From antiquity the indicative present of this verb has been formed out of optative forms, because the wishing form prevailed in speech]. Clearly the tempering of expressions of desire is not confined to the Pennsylvania Germans.

9.4.3. *The Pennsylvania German future*

The most comprehensive study on grammaticalization and future is provided by Bybee, Pagliuca, and Perkins (1991). What is striking about their cross-linguistic account (a survey involving seventy-five languages) is the extent to which the same small set of lexical items provide the input for the grammaticalization of future marking and invariably the same paths of change are followed. They identify four of the most common paths based on the following source structures:

(*a*) aspectual forms (marking imperfective or perfective);
(*b*) agent-oriented modalities (expressing desire, obligation, ability);
(*c*) verbs denoting movement towards some goal (for example, 'go'/'come to');
(*d*) temporal adverbs.

Traditional sketch grammars on US Pennsylvania German (e.g. Buffington and Barba 1965) describe the most usual means of marking future as the present tense. Presents which have a future use are included under aspectual forms in (*a*) above. Without an obvious future meaning, they are typically supported, either explicitly or implicitly, by context. For example:

(2) *Ich geh ins   schteddel marriye   frie*
     I   go in-the town   tomorrow early
     'I'm going to town tomorrow morning.'

These grammars also describe a 'become' future from the verb *waerre* (or *warre*) 'to become' (Standard German *werden*). In Canadian Pennsylvania German *waerre* no longer has future as its primary sense (i.e. pure prediction), but rather probability or supposition. Thus a sentence like (3) below is no longer a prediction that something will happen, but that it is likely to be the case.

(3) *Er waert es hawwe*
     he FUT   it has
     'He probably has it.'

The transfer of *waerre* from future to epistemic modality (invoking possibility/probability) is typical of 'old' futures which fall late on the grammaticalization path (cf. Bybee, Pagliuca, and Perkins 1991). This change follows the familiar diachronic-semantic schema which has been identified for grammaticalization changes and which was outlined above; namely, less abstract > more abstract.

My conversational data reveals at least two new futures currently replacing *waerre*. One of these derives from a movement verb; namely, *geh* 'to go' (path (*c*) above). For example:

(4)   *Ich hab geglaubt — es geht iem happene*
       I   have thought — it FUT him happen
       'I thought—it's gonna happen to him!'

But the most usual future auxiliary in Canadian Pennsylvania German is one that does not fit into any of the above four grammaticalization schemas identified earlier. It is a future which derives from the ordinary verb *zehle* meaning 'to count' (Standard German *zählen*). For example, *Ich zehl achtzich Verwandte* 'I count 80 relatives'.

(5)   *Er zehlt e haus baue*
       he FUT a house build
       'He's going to build a house.'

9.4.3.1. Counting on the future: the story of *zehle*

Items which enlist for grammatical service are generally drawn from core vocabulary. They are culture independent, and refer to the most fundamental of human experiences and activities. Accordingly, they typically have quite general meanings, which is why they are used more frequently and in a wide range of contexts. A verb like *zehle* 'to count', which has such specific semantics and accordingly restricted contexts of use, would not obviously qualify as a likely recruit. It neither possesses a highly generalized semantics, nor is it among the most frequently used items. Unfortunately, without the luxury of textual evidence, it is difficult to determine precisely how the shift took place. Nonetheless, much can be gleaned from the synchronic behaviour of an item. There is also the support of cross-linguistic findings about grammaticalization and the principles based upon these findings which linguists like Lehmann (1982) and Hopper (1991) have formulated. It is also revealing to trace developments of verbs with closely related meanings. Take, for example, the English verb *reckon*. Although of course it is not a future marker, the changes which *reckon* has undergone help to shed light on the properties which qualify *zehle* as a source concept for future and which earmark it for grammaticalization. The following reconstruction is based on etymological details in the *Oxford English Dictionary*.

Originally, *reckon* had the meaning 'to ascertain the number'. At the same time, it could also be used more generally to mean more the actual process of mental calculation (i.e. 'estimate'), rather than the simple counting up of individual items. In this way, it could occur with a subordinate clause complement (e.g. . . . *soldiers reckoning how many their enemies were*). From this, the meaning became more intellectual; i.e. 'to consider, judge' (e.g. *We reckon the women to be among the prettiest*). Later it further generalized, invoking more an attitude or personal point of view; i.e. much like the mental verbs 'to suppose/to think' (e.g. *I reckon that no one could accuse me*). Finally, we see the genesis of a new modality expression, *I reckon*, expressing the degree of speaker commitment (e.g. *Neither of us, I reckon, has ever . . .*). Parenthetical *I reckon* can be compared with epistemic particles like *maybe* and the epistemic phrases like *I think* and *I guess* (cf. Wierzbicka 1991: 42–3 on *reckon* and Thompson and Mulac 1991 on *think*). Note that semantically related English verbs like *tell*, *count*, and *figure* are moving along similar paths. They all show the same familiar shift towards increased abstractness and increased speaker-involvement, in particular, speaker commitment to what is being said.

Pennsylvania German *zehle* appears to be travelling along a strikingly similar pathway. I postulate the following set of changes:

'to count (numerically)' > 'calculate' /'estimate' > 'to make the basis for one's calculation' /'plan' (cp. English *count on*) > intention > prediction (i.e. pure future).

Linguists working on grammaticalization have emphasized the importance of inferential reasoning as a stimulus for semantic transfers of this kind (e.g. Bybee, Perkins, and Pagliuca 1994; Traugott 1989; Traugott and König 1991). At the point when *zehle* means something like 'to plan', a hearer might well infer that the subject intends to carry out the proposed plan of action. From this we arrive at intention (compare *reckon* which in some English dialects has come to mean 'to intend'; e.g. *I reckon to leave next week*). From an expression of intention, a hearer is expected to infer that, all being well, the future event described by the utterance will take place—the intentions of the subject will be carried out. This inference is then explicitly coded and prediction becomes part of the general meaning of the verb. The changes involving *zehle* show a loss of semantic complexity and shift to increased abstraction—they follow the expected path from the more concrete world of external fact to the more abstract domain of a future category. They also show the expected increase in pragmatic significance by way of more obvious coding of speaker attitude.

9.4.3.2. Why *zehle*?

Once again it looks like a clear case of grammaticalization. But all this relates more to the 'how' of the change—the question is still why specifically *zehle* was singled out to mark future time. To properly understand this transfer of meaning from 'counting on a future happening' to 'predicting a future happening' we need to take account of aspects of the Anabaptist belief and value system. Mennonite commitment to the subordination of self-will to the will of God means speakers never feel comfortable talking about the future—to talk about future happenings is viewed as arrogance. As one speaker described it to me:

Mer sett net ganz definitely saage—oh mir dien so und so, weil mir wees nie nett. Mer wees nie nett was happene kennt [. . .] Mer saage nett 'we are coming'.

[We shouldn't definitely say—oh we'll do such and such. Because we never know. We never know what will happen [. . .] We don't say 'we are coming.']

Pennsylvania German speakers appear much more comfortable with tentative expressions of future events like those below.

(6)   *Ich figger kumme*
      'I figure on coming.'

(7)   *Ich bin am plaenne fer kumme*
      'I plan on coming.'

(8)   *Ich bin supposed fer kumme*
      'I'm supposed to come.'

(9)   *Ich zehl kumme*
      'I am counting on coming /I will come.'

While it is clear that *zehle* can have a purely prediction meaning (e.g. *Es zehlt gedanst waerre* 'There will be dancing'), it also retains much of the early sense of 'counting on', as found in the more lexical (less grammaticalized) constructions in (6)–(8). The transparent link with its lexical history is appropriate to its relatively new grammaticalized status. Also appropriate is the lack of formal reduction.[4]

There has been a lot of debate about whether or not we can predict the sort of items which qualify as candidates for grammaticalization changes. This Pennsylvania German future is a nice example of the important role which cultural and social factors can play in the selection of a particular lexical item for grammaticalization. Unfortunately, only too often the extralinguistic dynamics of a linguistic situation are overlooked in accounts of change.

9.5. CONCLUSION: 'TODAY'S PRAGMATICS IS TOMORROW'S SEMANTICS'[5]

Pennsylvania German speakers have been able to exploit constructions available to them in the language to express cultural values that are central to the Mennonite belief system. The Germanic 'subjunctive of the modest wish' is well suited to a 'cultural script', to use Wierzbicka's term (1991), that emphasizes subordination of individual will to the will of God—and so too the impressive array of

---

[4] Note that this is not the case in the US variety, however, where phonological reduction is already apparent—*zellen* 'will' shows a short vowel, whereas *zehlen* 'to count' shows a long vowel.

[5] The original slogan (Givón 1971) 'today's morphology is yesterday's syntax' made the point that older syntactic patterns are reflected in synchronic morphology. English compounds like *glue-sniffing* and *gate-crashing*, for example, are relics of older object-verb order.

tentative future expressions that Pennsylvania German has partially calqued from English (examples (6)–(9) above). These examples started life as clear illustrations of what Goddard (this volume) has dubbed ethnosyntax in the 'broad sense', or more particularly 'ethnopragmatics'. But, as Goddard also goes on to describe, 'culture-specific patterns of usage can "harden" into language-specific morphosyntactic constructions'; in other words, they can develop into ethnosyntax in the 'narrow sense'. Through frequency and associated routinization and semantic-pragmatic loss, a tentative expression of future can over time 'harden' into a future auxiliary, as *zehle* has done. But items can take a totally different route too. In the case of *wotte*, routinization of the 'subjunctive of the modest wish' has caused an already grammaticalized modal verb to lexicalize and 'harden' into the ordinary verb of wishing. Although these two outcomes fall at opposite ends of the grammaticalization scale, both illustrate the typical tug-of-war that exists between routinization or idiomatization, on the one hand, and expressivity or creativity, on the other (cf. Hopper and Traugott 1993 and also Enfield's introduction).

Pragmatics-driven changes of this nature are certainly not new to the literature. Over the years a number of researchers working within grammaticalization have focused on the evolution of morphosyntatic structures through the fixing of discourse strategies. Herring (in Traugott and Heine 1991), for example, describes the grammaticalization of Tamil rhetorical questions into markers of subordination. Papers by Givón, Haiman, Shibatani, and Genetti in the same volumes also demonstrate the remodelling of discourse functions into more grammatical ones. In fact, back in 1912, when Meillet first used the term 'grammaticalization', he applied it to changes precisely of this kind; in particular, the fixing of pragmatically determined word orders into syntactic constructions. At first blush, this work seems at odds with work on grammaticalization that emphasizes the lexical source of grammatical elements and the pragmatic strengthening associated with grammaticalization changes, in particular the strengthening of speaker-involvement or 'subjectification'. As discussed earlier, authors like Traugott and König (1991) stress the significant role of inferencing, whereby conversational implicatures become explicitly coded and part of general meaning. (See also Enfield's introduction and Goddard, this volume.) This sort of pragmatic enrichment of lexical items is typical of the early stages of grammaticalization. And this would seem to conflict with these pragmatics-driven changes which show a loss rather than a strengthening of expressiveness, and where pragmatically based meaning is the source not the output of the grammaticalization process. But as pointed out by Traugott and Heine (1991: 5), the two different paths—discourse/pragmatics > morphosyntax and lexical item > grammatical morpheme—are not in conflict, but are part and parcel of the same process. As they describe it, 'discourse uses lexical items in ways that endow them with pragmatic meaning, and if they have the properties salient to grammaticalization . . . and are used more frequently, they may well come to be syntacticized'.

Discourse therefore presupposes the lexicon, but it is cultural values and norms that go to shape discourse. In the Old Order Mennonite community 'cultural scripts' like 'it's more important to be honest than rich', 'to serve rather than be served', 'to yield to others rather than insist on one's own way', and so on give rise to ways of thinking and ways of expression that can then end up embodied in grammar. In the case of *zehle*, the transfer of meaning from 'counting on a future happening' to 'predicting a future happening', I suggested, was stimulated by the promotion of particularly salient pragmatic nuances that then became part of general meaning. But what determined this development from the outset was the cultural queasiness of Pennsylvania German speakers at talking about the future. A tentative expression of future time like *zehle* was made-to-measure and it was speakers' routine use of it that then made the grammaticalization possible. Discourse/pragmatics-driven changes are certainly not new to work in grammaticalization. But what is new is the spotlight that this volume places on the role of culture in the process.

Clearly, in any investigation of the correlation between culture and grammar, we need to determine at the outset, and as objectively as possible, the cultural preoccupations of the group of speakers in question. As Wierzbicka (1979: 313) states, 'It is commonplace to say that every language embodies in its very structure a certain world view, a certain philosophy. To prove it in a rigorous and verifiable way, however, is quite a different matter.' By drawing on the excellent historical and sociological accounts of the Anabaptists produced by scholars like Hostetler, Fretz, and Enninger, I hope I have been able to overcome the sort of arbitrariness which is always a danger in such a study as this. Pennsylvania German presents here two very convincing examples of the important role which cultural factors can play in linguistic development. These factors make it difficult to tell whether or not an item will serve as input to a grammaticalization change, no matter how likely or unlikely a candidate it may appear. Even the unidirectional processes of grammaticalization can be reversed under these special conditions. As 'wild cards' in the game of linguistic change, they also make it difficult to predict the path of change, even one as well trodden as the path towards auxiliariness.

REFERENCES

BUEHLER, ALAN. 1977. *The Pennsylvania German Dialect and the Life of an Old Order Mennonite*. Kitchener: Pennsylvania Folklore Society of Ontario.

BUFFINGTON, ALBERT F., and BARBA, PRESTON A. 1965. *A Pennsylvania German Grammar*. Allentown, Pa.:Schlechter.

BURRIDGE, KATE. 1995. 'Degenerate cases of body-parts in Middle Dutch'. In Hilary Chappell and William McGregor (eds.), *Body-parts in Grammar*. Amsterdam: John Benjamins, 679–710.

——2002. 'Steel tyres or rubber tyres—maintenance or loss: Pennsylvania German in the "horse and buggy" communities of Ontario'. In David Bradley and Maya Bradley (eds.), *Language Maintenance for Endangered Languages: An Active Approach*. London: Curzon Press, 203–29

BYBEE, JOAN, PAGLIUCA, WILLIAM, and PERKINS, REVERE. 1991. 'Back to the future'. In Traugott and Heine 1991: ii.17–58.

——PERKINS, REVERE, and PAGLIUCA, WILLIAM. 1994. *The Evolution of Grammar*. Chicago: University of Chicago Press.

CURME, GEORGE O. 1904. *A Grammar of the German Language*. New York: Frederick Ungar. (Repr. 1970.)

DURRELL, MARTIN. 1991. *Hammer's German Grammar and Usage*. London: Edward Arnold.

ENNINGER, WERNER. 1985. 'Amish by-names'. *Names*, 33.4: 243–58.

——1991. 'Focus on silences across cultures'. *Intercultural Communication Studies*, 1.1: 1–38.

ENFIELD, NICK J. 2002. *Linguistic Epidemiology: Semantics and Grammar of Language Contact in Mainland Southeast Asia*. London: Routledge.

EVANS, NICHOLAS D., and WILKINS, DAVID P. 2000. 'In the mind's ear: the semantic extensions of perception verbs in Australian languages'. *Language*, 76.3: 546–92.

FISHMAN, JOSHUA A. 1982. 'Bilingualism and biculturalism as individual and as societal phenomena'. In Joshua A. Fishman and G. D. Keller (eds.), *Bilingual Education for Hispanic Students in the United States*. New York: Teachers College Press, 23–36.

FRETZ, J. WINFRID. 1989. *The Waterloo Mennonites: A Community in Paradox*. Waterloo: Wilfrid Laurier University Press.

GIVÓN, TALMY. 1971. 'Historical syntax and synchronic morphology: an archeologist's field trip'. *Chicago Linguistics Society*, 7: 394–415.

HEINE, BERND. 1993. *Auxiliaries: Cognitive Forces and Grammaticalization*. New York: Oxford University Press.

HOPPER, PAUL. 1991. 'On some principles of grammaticization'. In Traugott and Heine 1991: i. 17–36.

——and TRAUGOTT, ELIZABETH C. 1993. *Grammaticalization*. Cambridge: Cambridge University Press.

HOSTETLER, JOHN A. 1993. *Amish Society*. Baltimore: John Hopkins University Press.

HUFFINES, LOIS. 1980. 'Pennsylvania German: maintenance and shift'. *International Journal for the Sociology of Language*, 25: 43–57.

LEHMANN, CHRISTIAN. 1982. *Grammaticalization: A Programmatic Sketch*, vol. i. Arbeiten des Kölner Universitäten Projekts 48, Cologne.

PAUL, HERMANN. 1982. *Mittelhochdeutsche Grammatik*, rev. Hugo Mose, Ingeborg Schröbler, and Siegfried Grosse. Tübingen: Max Niemeyer Verlag (first pub. 1881).

PLANK, FRANS. 1984. 'The modals story retold'. *Studies in Language*, 8.3: 305–64.

SWEETSER, EVE E. 1988. 'Grammaticalization and semantic bleaching'. *Berkeley Linguistics Society*, 14: 389–405.

THOMPSON, SANDRA, and MULAC, ANDREW. 1991. 'A quantitative perspective on the grammaticization of epistemic parentheticals in English'. In Traugott and Heine 1991: ii. 313–30.

TRAUGOTT, ELIZABETH C. 1989. 'On the rise of epistemic meanings in English: an example of subjectification in semantic change'. *Language*, 65: 31–55.

——and HEINE, BERND (eds.). 1991. *Approaches to Grammaticalization*, 2 vols. Amsterdam: John Benjamins.

——and KÖNIG, EKKEHARD. 1991. 'The semantics-pragmatics of grammaticalization revisited'. In Traugott and Heine 1991: i. 189–218.

WARNER, ANTHONY R. 1993. *English Auxiliaries: Structure and History*. Cambridge: Cambridge University Press.

WIERZBICKA, ANNA. 1979. 'Ethno-syntax and the philosophy of grammar'. *Studies in Language*, 3.3: 313–83.

——1991. *Cross-Cultural Pragmatics: The Semantics of Human Interaction*. Berlin: Mouton de Gruyter.

——1994. '"Cultural scripts": a new approach to the study of cross-cultural communication'. In Martin Pütz (ed.), *Language Contact and Language Conflict*. Amsterdam: John Benjamins, 67–87.

10

Cultural Logic and Syntactic Productivity: Associated Posture Constructions in Lao

N. J. ENFIELD

Languages with verb serialization provide speakers with a choice between express-ing complex events as tightly cohesive multi-predicate yet single-clause structures, or as looser joinings of separate clauses. Bruce (1988: 25) has argued that the choice to employ one or the other means to describe a particular event is made in a principled way, whereby serial constructions 'are not merely more convenient (shortened) paraphrases' of looser multi-clausal structures. According to Bruce (1988: 28), '[serial constructions] must relate only events which are somehow conceived as notably more commonly associated together in experience or those events which form a culturally important concatenation of events'.

Durie (1997: 322) discusses a number of examples, and himself makes the fol-lowing generalization:

[T]he productivity of verb serialisation is constrained in such a way that a large variety of syntactically well-formed verb combinations will be rejected by native speakers as unacceptable/ungrammatical because they do not correspond to a recognisable event-type, either within the actual experience of speakers, or alternatively within the permitted pat-terns of verb serialisation within a language. This can [. . .] apply even where particular verbs involved in a combination are otherwise able to combine in productive patterns of serialisation.

The issues Durie raises are broad-ranging, and it is my aim here to address and explore some of the problems, namely, (*a*) how we can make sense of a param-

Support and assistance in this research from Tony Diller, Grant Evans, and Syban Khoukham is grate-fully acknowledged. The fieldwork was conducted in Lak Paet, Sisavat, and Saphang Mo villages of Vientiane, Lao PDR, between November 1997 and May 1998. Helpful comments from members of the audience at the 'Ethnosyntax' workshop, Australian Linguistic Institute, Brisbane, July 1998 resulted in improvements. Also helpful were comments on various drafts of this chapter from Avery Andrews, Nick Evans, Cliff Goddard, Chris Manning, and Katherine Travis. My transcription of Lao (Southwest-ern Tai, Laos) is based on IPA convention, except glottal stop /q/, palatal and velar nasals /ñ, ng/, low central vowel /a/, mid front vowel /ê/, mid central vowel /e/, low front vowel /è/, low back vowel /ò/, and high back unrounded vowel /ù/. Tones are marked by superscript numerals: 0: unstressed, atonal; 1: level /33/; 2: high rising /34/; 3: low rising /213/; 4: high falling /51/; 5: low falling /21/. Abbrevia-tions in glosses are as follows: 1/2/3 (1st/2nd/3rd person pronoun); ACHV (achievement marker); C.LNK (clause linker); NEG (negative); PFV (perfective); PL (plural); SG (singular).

eter like 'ready-recognizability of an event', which is a cultural notion more than
it is a 'natural' or purely 'logical' one; (*b*) how we can understand the notion
of 'acceptability/grammaticality' given this view (and I remain sceptical about
Durie's confident assertion of a culture-independent 'syntactic well-formedness'
in these cases); and (*c*) what kinds of grammatical and/or semantic effects related
to this can be observed. I explore these points in turn, examining the last with reference to data from Lao.

I argue that event typicality is a cultural phenomenon, which can be accounted
for and described in terms of *cultural representations*, typifications which are
carried, assumed-to-be-carried, and assumed-to-be-assumed-to-be-carried by all
members of a given group (Enfield 2000). For a complex event to be typical is for it
to have *currency*, i.e. existing status as a cultural representation, readily available
to speakers, in the public conceptual catalogue. Event typicality impacts directly
upon the productive assembly of serial verb (and other) constructions, as well as
the interpretation of the semantics of verb serialization, and of syntactic constructions in general.

This chapter is structured as follows. In Section 10.1, I outline the notion of
'culture' which I assume in subsequent discussion of grammar, pragmatics, and
semantics. The important idea is the existence of *conventions*, which act as premisses in 'cultural logic' for interpreting utterances (and for judging them as 'grammatical' or not). Section 10.2 discusses the notion of *event*, and the relevance of
this notion to the semantics and pragmatics of verb serialization. In Section 10.3,
I turn to the examination of associated posture serial verb constructions in Lao,
which provide a useful range of perspectives from which to focus in more detail on
the observations made by Bruce and Durie, above. Section 10.4 provides a summary discussion of findings, and Section 10.5 concludes.

10.1. CULTURAL LOGIC

Linguistic studies which aim to address ethnographic issues must assume some
view of just how facts of a cultural nature can be worked into the understanding
of linguistic structure and usage. This section presents my own position on the
nature of cultural conventions, and their role in the semantics and pragmatics of
grammar.[1]

10.1.1. *Language and culture*

What we refer to as *language* and *culture* can be viewed as part of a mass of
conceptual categories which are shared, assumed-to-be-shared, and assumed-to-

---

[1] The intention of this section is to describe as simply and briefly as possible my position on culture,
and in the interest of space and clarity, I cannot make extensive reference to literature. The background
is covered in detail in Enfield 2000.

be-assumed-to-be-shared (D'Andrade 1987: 113), and which are formed, aligned, and manipulated via systematic deployment and/or interpretation of signs (in the broadest semiotic sense). This mass of ideas is not necessarily to be regarded as a coherent unitary system, but it does *contain* conceptual systems, with systematic relationships among categories. Beliefs and theories about 'what people do', 'what people think', 'what people say', 'what happens' in the world and why, are represented in this vast semiotic nebula. Therein, we encounter the common ideas which are to be found in the semiotics of symbols, cultural practices, and linguistic structures (Holland and Quinn 1987; Strauss and Quinn 1997).

I assume there are *private representations*, structured in the individual's body, mind, and brain. These are cognitive or sensorimotor in nature, and may take many forms (Enfield 2000: 37 ff.). Despite opposition by some to the notion of 'representations' (Foley 1997: 89), I find it necessary to recognize some kind of individual-specific internal abstractions (cf. Langacker 1994: 26–7), since individuals are clearly able to independently transport and access ideas which serve as premises for cultural logic. Private representations may be internally manipulated by the individual (e.g. they may be recalled, or abstracted upon in various ways), and may include sensorimotor images of how certain practices are performed (e.g. techniques of tool use, posture), sense and emotional impressions, and propositional representations such as the theories, schemas, and norms abstracted from experience of the world (i.e. what people (do not) do, what can happen, what is good, what is bad, and so on).

Private representations are internally formed by individuals on the basis of 'artefactual' material that signifies meanings (i.e. 'mediating structure' such as sounds, Hutchins and Hazlehurst 1995: 56, 64). This includes all kinds of experiential input, from (either performed or observed) instances of complex and structured motor coordination (such as dancing or cooking), to audible phonetic material signifying linguistic expressions. By attending to similar artefactual structure, people jointly construct similar private representations. Prolonged and/or repetitive joint focus on certain mediating artefactual structure (along with mutual regulation, via cooperative discussion, correction, comparison, and internal review) allows us to achieve effectively identical private representations, via ongoing maintenance of conceptual *alignment* or *convergence*.[2] Crucially, private representations are not literally 'passed' on, but are *mediated* by signs in use, and must be separately constructed by individuals in each case, based on the clues and 'instructions' that mediating structure provides (cf. Reddy 1979).

Thus, speakers *effectively* share conceptual/embodied private representations, and may therefore assume common carriage of these representations, across cultural/linguistic communities of arbitrary size (from two people to all people;

---

[2] Hockett's term *intercalibration* is appropriate here, too (Hockett 1987: 106–7, 157–8; cf. Lee 1996: 227–8). Unfortunately, space limitations do not allow a more detailed discussion of *convention* (cf. Lewis 1969; Clark 1996*a*, 1996*b*).

Clark 1996*a*, 1996*b*). Knowledge is thus 'socially distributed' (Schutz 1946, 1970; Salomon 1993; Hutchins 1995). When carriers of a certain private representation know or assume that each other carries the private representation, and also know or assume that they themselves are similarly known or assumed by the other(s) to do so, then the private representation also becomes a *cultural representation* (Enfield 2000: 45), or, better, a *cultural premiss*. It then takes on a crucial role in cultural logic, as a default premiss for working out what is going on in social interaction (see below). Belonging to a certain *carrier group* means not having to overtly introduce the relevant cultural representation, since its presence is cooperatively enforced. It also means that in many cases one *cannot deny* that one carries it, or that one is a member of the said carrier group. Culture (but not necessarily 'a culture') can be defined in this way.

10.1.2. *Use of cultural premisses in interpretation of scenes and events*

Cultural premisses give us a guide to what happens in the world, i.e. what can be, and/or is more or less likely to be, the case. The fact that these ideas can be shared, and be known to be shared, means that human groups can utilize common guiding heuristics in interpreting the world in common ways (Levinson 1995: 240; Clark 1996*a*: ch. 4). Where certain cultural representations have a high level of activatedness and sharedness within a certain group, then individuals' interpretations of certain scenes/events are more likely to converge. Consider Fig. 10.1.

Corresponding to Fig.10.1*a* is a cultural representation associated with situations in which a particular posture indicates acquiescence to discipline, as in school or the military, for which a description *jùùn³ kong³*, literally 'stand straight', is readily selected by Lao speakers. For a Lao, the symbolism of the posture illustrated is unambiguous, and the activity of 'standing to attention' is not unfamiliar for modern Lao people (as for example would be expected in certain situations

(*a*)   (*b*)   (*c*)

Fɪɢ. 10.1

at school). Note that Australian informants generally do not describe Fig. 10.1*a* with the equivalent term *standing to attention*, apparently since the idea of standing to attention is more contextually restricted in Australia (i.e. the feet would not be apart, for example, and the subject would be more obviously uniformed). On the other hand, Figs. 10.1*b* and 10.1*c* do *not* obviously correspond to salient cultural representations for many Lao speakers. The range of responses to Fig. 10.1*b* is revealing. Some informants were not familiar at all with the conventional illustration of the setting/rising sun, or even the conventional graphic perspective depicting receding fields and distant hills. Instead, two informants guessed that the person in the picture was making a fire.[3] Others said that the person was 'watching over their fields', or 'appreciating nature'. The point here is that while Lao people of course appreciate the beauty of the setting/rising sun, there is no salient cultural representation for Lao speakers corresponding to English *watching the sunset/sunrise*. The practice of specifically putting aside time to behold the sight is not categorized as 'something that people do'.

Fig. 10.1*c* also elicited unusual and inconsistent responses from Lao speakers, again due to the lack of a highly salient or current corresponding cultural representation. The artist had been asked to sketch *khon² jùùn³ thaa⁵ lot¹-mêê²* [person stand wait bus] 'people standing, waiting for a bus'. The sketch he produced corresponds to a bus-stop stereotype from a developed country like Australia, where bus stops are signposted places by curbed streets where people wait for buses. But in Laos, few places where people get on buses are signposted in this way. People usually wait at familiar corners or roadheads, where they simply flag a passing bus down. While some people did describe Fig. 10.1*c* as 'people (standing) waiting for a bus', others described the scene as 'people (standing) waiting to cross the road', and one even described it as 'people having their height measured'. This final interpretation is revealing in terms of the heuristic value of cultural representations as inferential premises, and the way in which the relative salience and/or assumed sharedness of cultural representations comes into play in interpreting scenes. The speaker in question saw nothing familiar in the illustration corresponding to a 'bus-stop' scenario, despite the artist's intention. She instead recognized the banded pole as a measuring rule, since she had a pre-existing private representation of this already available (presumably due to her personal experience, perhaps in a community health centre, or the like). And she could assume that this idea/experience was likely to be shared by her interlocutors. For her, it was the idea of the height-measuring scenario that enabled the best solution to the 'coordination problem' (Schelling 1960; Lewis 1969) of interpreting Fig. 10.1*c*. The process of finding that solution involved selection from her catalogue of available cultural representations. Evidently for this speaker, an elderly rural woman, the idea of the modern bus-stop scenario, as illustrated, was not available. In other words, she did not

---

[3] This is a good example of a supposedly 'iconic' sign—the sun setting/rising on the horizon—which is actually not iconic at all, but conventionalized and symbolic; cf. Noble and Davidson 1996: ch. 3 for discussion of the putative iconicity of symbols.

carry (or at least did not assume to be mutually carried) the idea which the artist had assumed would have currency among those who would see his illustrations. It is these principles of reliance on salient and/or current cultural representations which are argued below to play a crucial role in the production and interpretation of syntactic constructions.

10.1.3. *How cultural representations feed into cultural logic*

Available cultural representations are employed as premises in *cultural logic*, the system of reasoning behind our explanations of events, and attributions of intentions to agents and other event participants.[4] Consider the different interpretations a Lao and an Australian would have of a diner drinking water at the last stage of a meal. A Lao normally takes this as a sure sign that the diner has completely finished eating, and indeed this reading regularly compels people to act, for example by clearing away plates, or by (rhetorically) urging one's guest not to stop eating so soon. An Australian, however, would not 'logically' attribute this meaning to the act of drinking water. The difference is that Lao people have a cultural representation in the form of a meal 'script' which reserves the drinking of water for the moment of having finished eating. According to the Lao 'script', people do not drink water *while* they are eating a meal. Of course, Lao people *can* drink water during a meal, and indeed some do. But it is conventionally assumed that they do not, and that the default reading of the act of drinking water towards the end of a meal is that one has finished eating. Exceptions are recognized as such. Australians, on the other hand, have no particular cultural representation or script concerning the timing and/or overlap of water and food consumption.

Another example concerning food and dining is the Lao practice of eating together from communal plates and bowls, rather than serving out meal portions individually. Many foreigners in Laos find this 'impractical'. One Australian, for example, wondered aloud why the Lao do not at least each have their own bowl for *soup*, since transport of hot soup in the spoon is especially prone to spillage. This suggestion to her seemed 'logical'. But for the Lao, any argument that the communal arrangement is 'impractical' is outweighed by local cultural conventions that prioritize personal proximity, camaraderie, and solidarity in day-to-day family-internal activities. Separate personal bowls, even for soup, would create uncomfortable social distance in the normally informal eating situation, since maintenance of *proximity* and *sharing* is culturally important among Lao co-inhabitants. The Lao communal eating arrangement provides important symbolic manifestation of this cultural preoccupation.

---

[4] On cultural logic, see Enfield 2000; cf. Schelling 1960, Garfinkel 1967; Hutchins 1980; Gumperz 1982; Brown and Levinson 1987 (see in particular pp. 8, 64–5, 84–90); Wierzbicka 1991; Levinson 1995 (and other papers in Goody 1995); Clark 1996a.

10.1.4. *How cultural representations and cultural logic feed into 'grammaticality'*

An important area of syntactic research where cultural representations come into play is in the context of eliciting grammaticality judgements as a methodology in syntactic description (cf. Diller and Khanittanan, this volume). One parameter against which people judge the acceptability of utterances is that of event typicality, which is determined, as described above, by cultural conventions. Consider the putative ungrammaticality of the following example (Kay 1996: 112):

(1)   *Sybil had Sidney fall off the couch.

The matrix causative verb *have* requires that its complement verb have an agentive subject. In this case, however, according to Kay, 'the complement verb [*fall*] doesn't allow its subject to express an agent' (Kay 1996: 112), so there is a semantic clash and the sentence is rejected. But then Kay shows that (1) *is* acceptable after all, 'if, for example, Sybil is thought of as a stage director and Sidney's descent represents not real falling but an actor's deliberate simulation' (Kay 1996: 112). So why is (1) deemed ungrammatical? Why would this be 'not real falling'? On what basis are we to make use of this *conditional* grammaticality in syntactic description? In the right context, (1) is a completely normal utterance. I argue that this falling is indeed 'real falling'. It is merely atypical. *Fall* does not *entail* non-agentivity, it only *implies* it (because 'People "don't" fall on purpose').

Adjustment of the context of (1) by invoking the 'theatre direction' context also relies on cultural representations, albeit marked, or less salient, ones. There may come a point where context-adjustment becomes conceptually too demanding.[5] For reasons of what is 'logically possible'—what people would or would not ('ever', let alone 'normally') imagine possible—the utterance may not be accepted, or, indeed, may not even be easily interpreted. Here we find the rejection of marked combinations in verb serialization that Durie describes, for example in an expression like *She took a fish* (*to the market*) *and bought it* (Durie 1997: 326; cf. Sebba 1987: 60). However, even this utterance may be fine given the right context—say, some ritual purchase.[6] Such a case would *not* be an example of 'not real buying', but, again, merely *atypical* buying. It remains unclear to me on what basis one would reject the string on 'logical' grounds, while maintaining the notion of 'syntactic well-formedness' (Durie 1997).[7]

---

[5] Speakers often use the 'heuristics' of cultural typicality to bypass having to resolve interpretations of difficult-to-process structures—hence, for example, the persistent failure of subjects to correctly interpret the meaning of 'verbal illusions' such as *No head injury is too trivial to ignore* (which 'really' means 'All head injuries can be ignored, the most trivial'; Wason and Reich 1979).

[6] Thanks to Nick Evans for pointing this out.

[7] Another important factor in acceptability of such constructions is the culture-specific willingness of informants to indulge in hypothesis about possible situations, especially when these seem unlikely or unconfirmable (cf. Luria 1976: 108 ff.).

10.1.5. *Culture and syntax: discussion*

I have argued that cultural premisses, which provide communities with massive shared backgrounds of common heuristics for convergent cultural logic, come into constant play in all kinds of interaction, and especially in the online interpretation of linguistic utterance meaning. Below, I assume this view of culture and cultural logic, which indeed I see as providing an account for the workings of language itself, whether that concerns the encoded semantics of lexical and grammatical signs, or the context- and assumption-based processes of pragmatic inference and interpretation that pervade our everyday use of language (Grice 1975; Levinson 2000). Both the semantic and the pragmatic in language are at all times cultural.

More specifically, the knowledge required for interpretation and production of syntactic strings is not just knowledge of the structural mechanisms available for combination of meaningful linguistic units, but also, and just as importantly, the possible, and most normal or unmarked, co-occurrences of morphemes in these structures. The claim that cultural typifications can have significant effects on syntactic productivity, and indeed processability, makes ethnosyntax an important field of study even for nativist approaches to syntax. The study of syntax must pay more attention to the productivity of syntactic structures and the combinatorial properties of specific structural elements.[8]

In sum, cultural premisses define what is typical, feeding into cultural logic, guiding and/or constraining the assembly and interpretation of syntactic constructions in context. In Section 10.3, below, we focus on a concrete example, examining the role of event typicality in culture-related constraints on the productivity and interpretation of a type of verb serialization in Lao. But we must first address the notion of *event*, among other aspects of the semantics of verb serialization.

10.2. DESCRIPTION OF COMPLEX EVENTS

The *event* is a fundamental concept in grammatical description and in semantics (cf. Grace 1987; Langacker 1987; Talmy 2000; *inter alia*). Most simply, there has been an event if we can say that something has *happened*.[9] Almost all, if not all, languages contain a formally distinct word class which prototypically denotes events (i.e. the 'verb' class), and many simple events are described by simple single-verb clauses. Of course, no event in the world is *literally* simple, and no event is *literally* bounded, but we can and do abstract away the uniqueness and complexity of given segments of reality, and we find (or imagine) bounded events within the flux of impressions. In describing events, we strip out a great amount of detail,

---

[8] Recent traditions in 'Construction Grammar' (Goldberg 1995; Kay and Fillmore 1999, *inter alia*) focus on issues of syntactic productivity.

[9] I assume that the description of events cannot get any more conceptually basic than the simple categories 'happen' and 'do'; Wierzbicka (1996: 50).

and categorize unlike events in like ways. What is of primary interest here is how events are *conceptualized*, not how they *are*, since it is the former that is embodied in linguistic semantics. Linguistic signs *describe*, but do not necessarily *reflect*, the way of the world.

Important work has been done on the notion of the *conceptual event* (Grace 1987; Pawley 1987; Foley 1997: 37), the idea that events may be conceptualized as unitary and contained, regardless of whether they are obviously made up of component-events, and/or whether their linguistic expression is formally simple or complex. In cases of complex formal structures, this single-event status is often diagnosed with reference to intonational chunking, and other indices of conceptual closure (Chafe 1994: ch. 5). Such conceptually unitary events may be either *simple* or *complex* in terms of their (both conceptual and formal) internal structure. I assume that at least some event descriptions are so simple we would seldom conceptually dismantle them. Consider *Mary opened her eyes* and *John died at 9 o'clock*. Other event descriptions like *John washed the car* and *Mary sold her house*, although conceptually unitary, are at the same time unproblematically and naturally recognized by speakers as consisting of more than one sub-event.

10.2.1. *Description of complex events: alternative fashions of speaking*

The means speakers employ in describing complex events are often determined by convention, as evidenced by the ubiquity of idiomatic metonymy (Lakoff 1987: 78–9; Pawley 1987: 339). Compare American English *go to the bathroom* with Lao *khaw⁵ hòòng⁵-nam⁴* [enter room-water] 'enter the bathroom'. Both refer to essentially the same conceptual event which includes, among other things, the sub-events of 'going' and 'entering'. It so happens that English speakers conventionally refer to the whole event by explicit reference to just the 'going' component, while Lao speakers explicitly mention just the component of 'entering'. In both cases, one sub-event ('going' or 'entering') stands metonymically for the whole complex event. This sub-event metonymy indeed applies productively in the two languages—while in English one also 'goes to' both hospital and prison, in Lao, one 'enters' these institutions. Another example of different metonymies for much the same complex event is English *wash the dishes* versus Lao *laang⁴ thuaj⁵* [wash bowl] 'wash the bowls'—both of these conventionally refer to a category of complex event which involves washing of not only dishes and bowls, but other vessels and utensils, too.

Many events which speakers need to describe of course do not neatly match categories that are already encoded by simple verbs or stock idioms, and one primary function of grammar is to provide speakers with ways to express novel detail in the description of events. Speakers employ a range of resources, including novel predicate-argument combinations, adverbial constructions, adjuncts, particles, strategies of verb subordination and coordination, verb compounding, and verb serialization. We now consider this last strategy.

10.2.2. *Construction of multi-component and multi-facet events via verb
          serialization*

Event descriptions employing verb serialization consist formally of multiple
predicate-like elements, but the predications characterized by these complex
expressions are conceptually unitary. This is an important and often definitive generalization made about serial verb constructions and similar multi-verb sequences
which form structural (and especially intonational) chunks (Pawley 1987; Givón
1991; Lord 1993; Durie 1997). Indeed, it is from work on verb serialization that
the very notion of conceptual event, discussed above, has emerged.

   Events can be complex in at least two ways. First, a conceived event may consist
of multiple separately discernible *component-events*, which can be imagined as
separate, especially in terms of their temporal relationship, with one component-
event following another. Consider (2), a Lao serial construction in which a series
of component-events are predicated, in iconic order:

(2)   *laaw² paj³ talaat⁵ sùù⁴ khùang¹ maa²*
       3SG   go   market buy stuff   come
       'She/he has come (here) from going and buying stuff at the market.'
       (or: 'She/he has been to the market and bought stuff.')

With a single intonation contour, (2) may be regarded as expressing a unitary
conceptual event, while also consisting of easily discernible separate component-
events. Now, a clause linker *lèka⁰* may be inserted between verb phrases, with the
effect of explicitly breaking up those component-events into separated, temporally
sequenced events, each then describing a *separate* conceptual event:

(2′)   *laaw² paj³ talaat⁵ lèka⁰ sùù⁴ khùang¹ lèka⁰ maa²*
       3SG   go   market C.LNK buy stuff   C.LNK come
       'She/he went to the market, and then bought stuff, and then came (here).'

The effect in (2′) is to separate the component-events into distinct events in their
own right, but the basic 'real-world' scenarios described by (2) and (2′), respectively, remain the same. There are still three events which happen one after the other,
namely, those designated by the verbs *paj³* 'go', *sùù⁴* 'buy', and *maa²* 'come'. The
difference in description is one of conceptual closure—in (2) they are *component-
events* of a single conceptual event, while in (2′) they are each separate conceptual
events in themselves.

   Events which are complex in a second, separate sense, may consist of multiple
event-facets, which, again, speakers are willing to recognize as constitutive of a
complete event, but which in this case are *not* separable from other elements of the
event, particularly not in terms of temporal precedence. Rather, event-facets are as
if *overlaid* to form a more detailed and complete event description. Typical multi-
facet events include those which combine manner with direction of motion (*He ran
away, Mary cycled down the hill*), or posture with action (*She slept standing, John
sat writing a letter*).

Consider the following example of a multi-facet event in Lao:

(3)   *laaw² lèèn¹ long²   maa²*
        3SG   run   descend come
        'She/he ran down (here).'

This directional serial verb construction predicates manner, path, and direction, in that order. These facets of the event are conceptually overlaid, and not separable in the same way as the sub-events of (2). Thus, we get a very different result when the clause linker *lèka⁰* is inserted between verbs (cf. (2'), above):

(3')   *laaw² lèèn¹ lèka⁰ long²   lèka⁰ maa²*
        3SG   run   C.LNK descend C.LNK come
        'She/he ran, and (then) came/went down, and (then) came.'

The scenarios described by (3) and (3') are very different. In (3), there is one action, namely 'running', and predicated of that 'running' in addition is that it is downward in path, and towards the speaker (or some transposed 'speaker' locus) in direction. But in (3'), there are three separate events, and there is no entailment that the motion predicated by *lèèn¹* 'run' is downward or towards the speaker, nor is the downward motion predicated by *long²* 'descend' (or the towards-speaker motion predicated by *maa²* 'come') necessarily done in the manner of 'running'.

In Section 10.3 below, we examine serial constructions of this second type—i.e. in which the verbs in combination describe overlaid facets of a single happening.

10.2.3. *How cultural logic constrains the assembly of complex event descriptions*

In the context of the quote given at the start of this chapter, Durie (1997) notes the unacceptability of certain combinations of verbs in serial constructions as 'puzzling'. Consider the following examples (cited in Durie 1997: 329):

(4) White Hmong (Jarkey 1991: 169–70)
  a. nws dhia   tshov qeej
     3SG dance blow bamboo.pipes
     'He dances playing the pipes.'
  *b. *nws dhia   mloog nkauj*
     3SG dance listen song
     (He dances and listens to music.)

(5) Alamblak (Bruce 1988: 29)
  a. miyt ritm   muh-hambray-an-m
     tree insects climb-search.for-1s-3PL
     'I climbed the tree looking for insects.'
  *b. *miyt guñm muh-hëti-an-m*
     tree stars climb-see-1s-3PL
     (I climbed the tree and saw the stars.)

According to Jarkey, while (4a) is a natural, unitary event (whenever the *qeej* pipes are played, the performer dances along with the music), dancing and *listening* (as in (4b)) are 'normally viewed as distinct events' (Durie 1997: 329).[10] Similarly for Alamblak, (5a) is a 'readily recognisable event-type', while (5b) is not (Bruce 1988: 29). Durie (1997: 327) rightly points out that the criteria of 'stereotypical schema for event-types' are very likely to be culture-specific, and that there is thus expected to be some variation across cultures of what 'the normal view' constraining expressions of complex events entails.

In the context of the range of issues raised so far, let us now consider some examples of 'associated posture' serial verb constructions in Lao.

10.3. ASSOCIATED POSTURE CONSTRUCTIONS IN LAO

Lao associated posture constructions are multi-verb sequences in which a posture verb (typically one of *nang¹* 'sit', *jùùn³* 'stand', or *nòòn²* 'lie', which I will refer to hereafter as the *basic postures*) directly precedes a verb denoting some action.[11] The posture verb and the action verb are tightly bound elements of a single verb phrase core, with a single intonation contour. These are verb compounds—there is no obvious reason to consider either the posture verb or the activity verb as head of the predicate to the exclusion of the other—which provide translation equivalents to adverbial or depictive expressions in English (e.g. *John studied [lying down]*). The following sections present cases of syntactic and semantic/pragmatic variation associated with particular combinations of posture and activity in these grammatical constructions. Relevant grammatical details are elucidated where necessary *en route*.

I investigated this problem from two angles. First, I asked speakers to comment on constructed sentences involving various 'posture'+'activity' combinations. Second, I conducted picture-description tasks using a set of sixteen simple sketches, depicting a variety of activities (see Figs. 10.1–10.9). The sketches manipulate two parameters: posture (sitting vs. standing vs. lying), and activity (varying with respect to degrees of typicality in any or all of the basic postures—for example, among the activities depicted, both reading and watching television are normal in all postures, but slightly marked standing, while riding a motorcycle and playing the *lanaat⁴* are almost never done standing or lying down). Other pictures included posture+activity combinations known to have salient cultural/linguistic representations (i.e. they are very typical, such as the combination of 'lying' and 'sleeping', and/or have unique labels, such as 'standing to attention'; cf. discussion in s. 10.1.2,

---

[10] Actually, this seems to be a case, as seen with the example from Kay (1996) above, of the binary nature of grammaticality judgements giving misleading results. My own field investigations with Hmong speakers in Vientiane (in 1999) reveal that (4b) is *odd* because it is so atypical as an event—but it is nevertheless not unacceptable.

[11] For the purpose of this discussion, I ignore subtle differences in meaning between English *sit*, *stand*, *lie*, and Lao expressions glossed herein as 'sit', 'stand', and 'lie'.

above). In some cases, the results of standard elicitation based on extracting grammaticality judgements in response to constructed strings were significantly different from those based on elicitation of posture descriptions.

10.3.1. *An 'activity' typically done lying down: 'sleeping'*

That Lao people typically sleep lying down is not due to anything unique about Lao culture:

FIG. 10.2.

The *fact* of all humans' sleeping lying down is determined, presumably, by 'common phylogenetic inheritance and common terrestrial fate' (Levinson 1997: 281). But the *idea* that 'people typically sleep lying down' is nevertheless a *cultural* one, in the sense of 'cultural' described in Section 10.1.1 above—i.e. everyone carries an idea that 'sleeping is done lying down', everyone knows that everyone carries this idea, and everyone knows they themselves are known to carry it. The conceptual combination of 'lying' and 'sleeping' is not merely logical, but *culturally* logical.

The Lao verbs *nòòn²* 'lie' and *lap²* 'be asleep' combine in describing, most idiomatically, an event in which someone has gone to sleep (e.g. as in Fig. 10. 2):

(6)   *laaw² nòòn² lap²*
         3SG   lie   be.asleep
         'She/he is asleep.'

Example (6) entails that the subject is asleep. It is also common to use *nòòn²* 'lie' alone as a metonymic expression for 'go to bed/go to sleep', but to do so does not *entail* that the person has actually gone to sleep, merely that they are in a lying posture.

Now, it is also possible to refer to other (indeed atypical) cases of sleeping, using *lap²* 'be.asleep' in combination with *nang¹* 'sit' or *jùùn³* 'stand':

(7)   *laaw² nang¹ lap²*
         3SG   sit   be.asleep
         'She/he slept/is asleep sitting.'

(8)   *laaw² jùùn³ lap²*
         3SG   stand be.asleep
         'She/he slept/is asleep standing.'

Clearly, these would only be felicitous in describing unusual circumstances, such as a crowded bus trip, where the sleepy traveller cannot lie down, nor perhaps even sit. While these require more unusual non-default contexts, they nevertheless correspond to readily recognizable situations with an appeal to the shared 'script' of arduous and cramped travelling. In elicitation sessions, examples like (7) and (8) are questioned initially, but are readily accepted as natural once a satisfying context is provided (cf. discussion of example (1) in s. 10.1, above).

The cultural typicality of the combination *nòòn² lap²* 'lie.down'+'be.asleep', illustrated in (6), has significant consequences in terms of morphosyntactic behaviour. The combination has properties of a resultative construction, one of the few V1–V2 combinations in Lao which allows insertion of the negative marker *bòò¹* between the initial and resultative verbs, signifying failure to achieve the result (V2) despite completion of the precipitating action (V1):

(9)   *laaw² nòòn² bòò¹ lap²*
        3SG   lie   NEG be.asleep
        'She/he couldn't/can't get to sleep.' (cf. example (6), above)

The syntactic behaviour of this culturally logical combination is, in contrast, not shared by the *atypical* basic posture compound combinations *nang¹ lap²* [sit be.asleep] 'sleep sitting' and *jùùn³ lap²* [stand be.asleep] 'sleep standing' (cf. examples (7), (8), above):

(10)   ??*laaw² nang¹ bòò¹ lap²*
        3SG   sit   NEG be.asleep
        (Sitting, she/he couldn't get to sleep, i.e. She/he sat, but couldn't sleep.)

(11)   ??*laaw² jùùn³ bòò¹ lap²*
        3SG   stand NEG be.asleep
        (Standing, she/he couldn't get to sleep, i.e. She/he stood, but couldn't sleep.)

Of course, the ideas behind (10) and (11) can be expressed, but this is done with looser, less prosodically integrated grammatical structures, such as the following (suggested by informants as preferred ways of expressing (10) and (11)):

(12)   *laaw² nang¹ maa² bòò¹ lap²   sut²   thaang²*
        3SG   sit   come NEG be.asleep extremity way
        'She/he sat coming here, and didn't sleep the whole journey.'

(13)   *laaw² jùùn³ juu¹ bòò¹ daj⁰ lap²   leej²*
        3SG   stand be.at NEG ACHV be.asleep at.all
        'She/he was standing, and didn't get to sleep at all.'

Both Bruce (1988) and Durie (1997) have similarly observed that less readily recognizable event-types are less likely to be expressible in the tight multi-predicate structures which conventionally express unitary 'conceptual events'.

10.3.2. *Two activities not unusual in any posture: 'reading' and 'watching television'*

The activities of reading and watching television are both typically done either sitting or lying down, and are also not uncommonly done standing up. In neither activity is sitting or lying posture any more typical than the other. But in both cases, to do the activity *standing* is at least marked with respect to the other two. Since watching television and reading are sedentary pastimes, demanding essentially only mental and visual(/aural) attention, and requiring no mobility, one is naturally inclined to rest the body while engaging in these activities. Standing is not a resting posture, but essentially a posture of readiness either to move away or to adopt a more restful posture having just stopped moving.[12]

It is common for people to walk up to a television, turn it on to check what is on, and remain standing, pending a decision to continue watching (in which case one sits or lies down), or walk away and do something else. This is a common scenario, personally embodied and conceptually stored as a cultural typification for members of television-watching human groups, as 'something that people do'. Similarly, to stand and read a book is not particularly unusual, but is marked in that it would only be done when one is perhaps briefly scanning a text, or standing for a particular reason (e.g. as a teacher may stand in front of a class while reading aloud).

Thus, it is not surprising that Lao informants find associated posture constructions involving 'read' and 'watch television' perfectly acceptable with any of the basic postures:

(14) *a. nòòn² beng¹ thoo²lathat¹*
       lie   look television
       'watch television lying down'
   b. nang¹ beng¹ thoo² lathat¹
       sit   look television
       'watch television sitting down'
   c. jùùn³ beng¹ thoo²lathat¹
       stand look   television
       'watch television standing up'

Two interesting effects may be noted here. First, due to the markedness of the standing posture in (14c), informants are apparently compelled—without prompting—to provide further information explaining the more marked circumstances, that is, to activate in their interlocutor's mind the less salient cultural premiss which feeds cultural logic for coherent interpretation of the event. A typical comment was: 'The sentence in (14c) is fine—for example, you might be just checking to see whether there is anything interesting on.'

---

[12] There are also practical and/or cultural reasons to be standing, e.g. while trying to get a view, or while teaching a class, but these do not normally apply while watching television.

Second, when presented with illustrations of possible combinations of the three postures 'sitting', 'standing', and 'lying' with the two activities 'watching television' and 'reading a book', in almost every case speakers used an associated posture construction to explicitly specify the relevant posture in their initial description of each sketch:

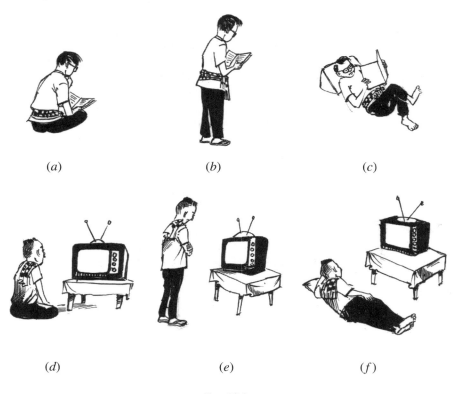

FIG. 10.3.

In these cases, no posture is more typical than the others, and therefore no posture is privileged as a default. The point about defaults is that they do not need to be specified, which is a handy thing in language, since it allows us to economize by leaving out details which we can assume will be 'automatically' understood (Grice 1975: 45; Clark 1996*a*: 70; Levinson 2000: 37). Thus, for example, if shown a scene in which John gives Mary a scarf, in describing it you are unlikely to bother mentioning the fact that he used his *hand* in doing so. On the other hand, if in the scene John uses his *foot* in giving her the scarf, then one would be highly likely to mention this in a description.[13] In the cases of watching television and reading

---

[13] This is borne out by results of recent comparative field research on 'event typicality' by members of the Language and Cognition Group at the Max Planck Institute for Psycholinguistics in Nijmegen.

a book (Fig. 10.3), speakers are virtually obliged to explicitly specify the posture adopted in the given scene, since no single posture is likely to be understood by default.

10.3.3. *Three activities typically done sitting*

10.3.3.1. Playing the *lanaat*⁴

The *lanaat*⁴ is a traditional Lao instrument, a kind of concave xylophone, played on the ground in a seated position, as in Fig. 10.4. To know what the word *lanaat*⁴ means, you need to know, among a number of cultural representations about the instrument, that it is played in a sitting (on the ground) posture. The verb most often used for 'playing' the *lanaat*⁴ is *tii*³ 'hit, beat'. The following constructed examples were supplied to informants for judgement of their acceptability:

(15) *a. tii*³ *lanaat*⁴
      hit lanaat
      'play the *lanaat*⁴'
   *b. nang*¹ *tii*³ *lanaat*⁴
      sit   hit lanaat
      'play the *lanaat*⁴ sitting'
   c. (?)*jùùn*³ *tii*³ *lanaat*⁴
         stand hit lanaat
         'play the *lanaat*⁴ standing'
   d. (??)*nòòn*² *tii*³ *lanaat*⁴
         lie   hit lanaat
         'play the *lanaat*⁴ lying down'

Informants judged examples (15*a*) and (15*b*) as perfectly natural, according directly with cultural representations associated with the *lanaat*⁴. Despite there being no specification of posture, speakers assume that the subject of (15*a*) is seated in the traditional manner. Example (15*c*), on the other hand, was met with

FIG. 10.4

some hesitation, but in most cases judged to be acceptable, usually with a comment to the effect that 'one *could* play a *lanaat⁴* standing up, if it were on a table, say, but people don't do that'. Again, speakers are compelled—consistently, and without prompting—to offer additional information 'explaining' pragmatically marked situations. In interpreting (15c), the informant pauses to search in his catalogue of cultural premises for a sensible interpretation of the unexpected combination. Finally, informants are much less prepared to accept example (15d), in the spirit of the quote from Durie (1997: 322) at the beginning of this chapter. A number of informants actually rejected this string when it was presented out of context. One commented, 'It doesn't make sense—you can't play the *lanaat⁴* lying down.'

These findings on the event combinations in (15a–d) were derived by presenting constructed sentences to informants and asking whether they are possible utterances. Very different results emerge from a methodology which begins with extensional data—i.e. illustrations of real scenes—and asks the informant for a description. The three illustrations of 'playing the *lanaat⁴*' were Figs. 10.4 and 10.5. In the picture-labelling task, the informant no longer has to struggle to imagine the situation actually taking place. Strikingly, in describing Fig. 10.5b, *every* informant spontaneously produced the structure in (15d), a string which most informants in elicitation sessions found difficult to accept, and which some had rejected outright. Fig. 10.5b *gives* the informant the very context in which the atypical combination of 'lying down' and 'playing the *lanaat⁴*' is normal, namely an informal situation in which a musician is practising or playing for fun in the privacy of his own home, and *not* as a normal (public) performance. Given only the sentence (15d), many speakers simply didn't think of a fitting scenario, apparently too fixated on the typical scene of a performer seated in the traditional way (Fig. 4, above). Thus, event typicality apparently restricts the *imagination*, the ability to think laterally, in this case with respect to possible scenes involving the activity

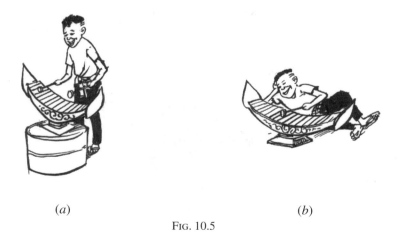

(a)   (b)

Fɪɢ. 10.5

of 'playing the *lanaat⁴*'. Given the sentence (15*d*), once the typical scenario of 'playing the *lanaat⁴*' has become activated in the speaker's mind, the highly salient solution—i.e. that the agent is sitting—is arrived at, and this results in the 'locking off' of further interpretation. Thus, it is hard to imagine someone 'lying down and playing the *lanaat⁴*'. However, seeing the illustration in Fig. 10.5*b*, informants are not forced to search their own conceptual 'store' for a licensing cultural representation (in competition with much more salient combinations). The use of certain morphosyntactic means for description of the scene in a way which had seemed unacceptable out of context becomes completely natural, in fact optimal.

Another issue arising from exposure to the three illustrations of 'playing the *lanaat⁴*' (Figs. 10.4 and 10.5) is the very decision to employ the associated posture construction at all—i.e. to explicitly specify in the description the posture adopted. Recall that in s.10.3.2 above, in response to illustrations of 'watching television' and 'reading a book', speakers spontaneously used associated posture constructions for *all three* basic postures, due to lack of cultural premisses specifying a unique posture as default. By contrast, among scenes of 'playing the *lanaat⁴*', Fig. 10.4 (the stereotypical scene, with the musician seated) almost *never* elicited an associated posture construction. It was not specified that the person playing the *lanaat⁴* was seated—informants just said, 'He's playing the *lanaat⁴*.' The musician's sitting posture in Fig. 10.4 is literally unremarkable. That speakers much more readily omit mention of posture in describing this particular 'posture'+'activity' combination suggests that the factors determining speakers' choice as to whether a certain grammatical construction will be used *at all* may also be essentially cultural.

An important result emerges here concerning a somewhat hazy line in the semantics of verb serialization—namely, the distinction between *compositional* and *idiomatic* semantics. The meaning of a syntactically complex expression may or may not be a neat sum of its constituent semantic parts. In some cases the meaning of the construction may need to be specified as a lexical entry in itself. Of interest here is the verb *tii³*, which literally means 'hit' or 'beat', and may also mean 'play' (a musical instrument). By metonymy, the 'play' reading of *tii³* 'hit' involves not just 'hitting', but *orderly* hitting, resulting in something we recognize as being the proper sound to emerge from a *lanaat⁴*. But one may still use the expression *tii³ lanaat⁴*, literally 'hit the *lanaat⁴*', to describe an event in which someone simply strikes the body of the instrument, perhaps with a stick, in a completely unmusical way. This reading would involve purely compositional semantics. Even so, the expression *tii³ lanaat⁴* out of context is very likely to receive a 'play' reading for *tii³*, not simply 'hit'. Here we observe a window of slippage in 'verb serialization' with respect to the lexicalization/syntax distinction. One informant who rejected (15*d*), which specifies playing the *lanaat⁴* in the atypical lying posture, found the expression perfectly acceptable given the context of a child lying down aimlessly hitting the instrument (i.e. not 'playing' it), in which case *tii³* was interpreted as 'hit' (and the meaning of the overall expression was then purely compositional—

'lying down and hitting a *lanaat⁴*'). The semantic construal of the verb *tii³* in the syntactic combination *tii³ lanaat⁴* as either 'hit' or 'play' can be pushed one way or the other by the particular posture specified in a serial combination. Ultimately, then, the construal of the whole complex syntactic expression can be directly contingent upon cultural representations.

10.3.3.2. *Fang²-thêêt⁴* 'listening-to-sermon'

A second example of an activity typically done sitting is that of *fang²-thêêt⁴* 'listening to (a) sermon'. In Laos, worshippers may visit the temple on *van²-sin³* 'holy days', and partake in a form of worship which involves, among other things, ritually listening to the sermon (referred to as *thêêt⁴*) of Buddhist monks. Like any cultural practice, *fang²-thêêt⁴* is to some extent embodied through personal participation, and to some extent emicized by its conceptualization linked to semiotic material (at the very least involving people's usual ways of talking about the practice). One performs the practice of *fang²-thêêt⁴* in order to *hêt¹ bun³* 'make merit'. One enters the *hòò³ cèèk⁵*, a roofed pavilion within the temple complex, and sits, in the most polite or respectful sitting posture, namely *phap¹-phèèp⁴* (i.e. on the floor, with both legs tucked under and back and to the same side), and with palms pressed together in front of one's chest, in the gesture known as *nop¹* (see Fig. 10.6).

Monks performing the sermon (usually chanted in formulaic Pali) are seated higher than the congregation. These various stipulations are familiar to Lao speakers as cultural representations surrounding the practice of *fang²-thêêt⁴*, regardless of whether one actually engages, or indeed has ever engaged, in the practice. That is, if you know what *fang²-thêêt⁴* is, as an established Lao Buddhist practice associated with the ritual accrual of religious merit, you know that one does it sitting down. The following example shows that specification of the sitting posture in an associated posture construction is optional (as for 'playing the *lanaat⁴*', (15*a*, *b*), above):

FIG. 10.6

(16) *mùù⁴ nii⁴ khòòj⁵ (nang¹) fang²-thêêt⁴ juu¹ vat¹ naak⁴*
day this 1sg (sit) listen-sermon be.at temple N.
'Today I (sat and) listened-to-sermon at Nak Temple.'

The meaning of the combination *fang²-thêêt⁴* in this example is not simply combinatorial, i.e. not semantically merely the sum of *fang²* 'listen' and *thêêt⁴* 'sermon'. While only the 'listening' and the 'sermon' are explicitly mentioned, with
them are imported the complex of culturally defined specifications of the whole
event, including the fact that the subject is intentionally and legitimately participating in a religious ritual performance (with the belief that merit will accrue as a
result), and adopting the standard and legitimate postures, clothing, gestures, and
proxemics defined by relevant cultural representations.

Rather different interpretations emerge from associated posture constructions
combining *fang²-thêêt⁴* with non-sitting postures:

(17) *a. mùù⁴ nii⁴ khòòj⁵ nòòn² fang² thêêt⁴ juu¹ vat¹ naak⁴*
day this 1sg lie listen sermon be.at temple N.
'Today I lay down and listened to a sermon at Nak Temple.'
b. mùù⁴ nii⁴ khòòj⁵ jùùn³ fang² thêêt⁴ juu¹ vat¹ naak⁴
day this 1sg stand listen sermon be.at temple N.
'Today I stood and listened to a sermon at Nak Temple.'

In both (17a) and (17b), the semantic combination of *fang²* 'listen' and *thêêt⁴*
'sermon' is purely compositional, in that there is no entailment or even implication of anything more than 'listening' and 'sermon'. Crucially, the subject in (17a,
b) is understood by informants *not* to be participating in the religious performance known as *fang²-thêêt⁴*, even though *fang² thêêt⁴* [listen sermon] is literally
predicated. If no posture of the subject is predicated, the subject of the predicate
fang²-thêêt⁴ is assumed by default to be seated (as illustrated in Fig. 10.6), and
explicit mention of sitting posture is also perfectly felicitous (if superfluous). But
if a *non*-sitting posture is explicitly predicated, then due to the incompatibility of
a non-sitting posture with cultural premises of the *fang²-thêêt⁴* scenario, the lis-
tener knows that the subject cannot be properly performing the ritual. The 'logical' conclusion is that the person is merely listening to the sound of the sermon, as
is literally predicated, perhaps while waiting in the temple grounds for a friend.
Informants agree that the non-seated subject of (17a) and (17b) cannot be properly
'listening-to-sermon' with the intention to make merit, nor would he be in the *hòò³*
cèèk⁵ itself, where the practice is rightly done.

10.3.3.3. Riding a motorcycle

Motorcycles are designed to accommodate the human body in what is essentially
a sitting position (although not a prototypical one), i.e. one in which the weight of
the body is mainly on the posterior, so that the hands and legs are free and mobile
enough to operate the vehicle (see Fig. 10.7). The unmarked predication of 'rid-

ing a motorcycle' strongly implies this sitting posture. Of the following examples, (18*a*), with no posture specified, is consistently judged by informants to be most natural:

Fig. 10.7.

(18) *a. khii¹ lot¹-cak²*
          ride motorcycle
          'ride a motorcycle'
      b. nang¹ khii¹ lot¹-cak²
          sit   ride motorcycle
          'ride a motorcycle sitting down'
      c. nòòn² khii¹ lot¹-cak²
          lie   ride motorcycle
          'ride a motorcycle lying down'
      d. jùùn³ khii¹ lot¹-cak²
          stand ride   motorcycle
          'ride a motorcycle standing'

Overt specification of sitting posture in (18*b*) was generally considered by informants to be superfluous (more so than in the cases of 'playing the *lanaat⁴*' and '*fang²-thêêt⁴*'), while the specifications of lying and standing posture in (18*c, d*) produced similar results to examples (15*c, d*) and (17*a, b*) discussed above. That is, informants were at first non-accepting, due to a lack of 'ready-recognizability' of these complex events. But they were quickly accepting once fitting contexts were activated.

Other informants were presented with an illustration of someone standing on a moving motorcycle (Fig. 10.8). Some responded with (18*d*), while others omitted mention of the verb *khii¹* 'ride' altogether, giving *jùùn³* 'stand' as a sole main verb, *not* as an associated posture verb:

(19)   *jùùn³ juu¹ theng² lot¹-cak²*
        stand be.at atop   motorcycle
        '(He's) standing on a motorcycle.'

FIG. 10.8.

Others mentioned *khii¹* 'ride' alone as a main verb, but focused on the fact that the rider's hands were not controlling the bike, as in the following:

(20)   *khon²   khii¹ lot¹-cak²   paq²   mùù²*
        person ride motorcycle abandon hand
        '(It's) a person riding a motorcycle with (his) hands free.'

Speakers found the combination of 'lying down' and 'riding a motorcycle' somewhat more difficult to describe in a number of ways (Fig. 10.9). It seems that when *nòòn²* 'lying down', one's weight must be supported along the length of one's body. The area of available supporting upper surface of a motorcycle is too restricted for this, and there was some debate as to whether it was possible to *nòòn²* 'lie down' on a motorcycle at all. A number of informants described Fig. 10.9 with an associated posture construction using the postural verb *mêêp⁵* 'to have one's weight forward on one's chest', as when one falls forward onto the ground:

FIG. 10.9.

(21)   *mêêp⁵*   *khii¹ lot¹-cak²*
       lie.forward.on.chest ride motorcycle
       '(He's) riding a motorcycle with (his) weight forward on (his) chest.'

As described in other cases above—for example with respect to the combination of 'watching television' and 'standing', Section 10.3.2, above—informants presented with the more marked circumstances (in Figs. 10.8 and 10.9) felt independently compelled to offer explanations as to what the circumstances must be. For instance, the most common remark about Fig. 10.8 was that it 'must be a stunt show'. The *stunt-show* cultural representation is less salient among all of those that involve riding a motorcycle, but it is nevertheless one that provides a solution to the coordination problem of interpreting the given complex event, and it has sufficient currency to be evoked in making sense, in this way, of what the illustrator must have intended. The fact that it is marked compels the speaker to activate the idea in the consciousness of his interlocutor, in order to ensure that his interlocutor is sharing the right premises for collective convergence upon the appropriate culturally logical solution.

10.4. DISCUSSION: FIVE FINDINGS

This chapter has examined a number of aspects of event typicality and the semantic and grammatical productivity of verb serialization, with particular reference to data from Lao. This has been based on two complementary methods of investigation—first, constructing example sentences and asking for interpretations and judgements of their acceptability; second, using a picture-description task to elicit spontaneous linguistic descriptions. The results suggest five general observations.

First, the dependence on cultural logic for interpretation of semiotic ('mediating artefactual') structures, including grammatical and morphosyntactic material, entails personal search and retrieval of cultural representations which facilitate the best, most likely, and most 'logical' solutions. When the relevant cultural representations are assumed to be of lower salience and/or lower currency, speakers are compelled to overtly mention their markedness, in order to activate non-default cultural representations in the minds of interlocutors, ensuring convergent culturally logical solutions. This is the essence of Grice's maxim of Manner, or Levinson's 'M-heuristic', whereby 'what's said in an abnormal way isn't normal' (Levinson 2000: 38). What I add to this is to stress that 'what is normal' is culturally defined.

Second, the notion of grammaticality, crucial to standard methodology in grammatical description and analysis, makes constant and direct reference to the heuristics provided by cultural typifications, by which we assess the typicality or plausibility of situations predicated. Research methodology must be revised in this light, not only with respect to verb serialization, but in syntactic research in general (Diller and Khanittanan, this volume). With no satisfying context available, a given sentence may be rejected, and therefore considered by the analyst (or the speaker) to be out of the range of description, i.e. 'not part of the grammar'. Primed with the right context, however, speakers may spontaneously produce such 'unacceptable' utterances. The relevant parameter—event typicality or markedness of conceptual combination—is a cultural one.

Third, the status of possible combinations of conceptual sub-components in complex expressions as more or less 'normal' (as culturally defined) affects the accessibility of such combinations to certain productive morphosyntactic processes (e.g. insertion of various connectors or logical relators, marking of modal and aspectual distinctions, ellipsis, specific intonational properties, prosodic integration, etc.).

Fourth, construal of the semantics of verb serialization, which straddles a blurry line between true syntactic composition and conventionalized/idiomatic meaning (usually involving metonymy), is contingent upon cultural typifications, in that the overall meanings of serial verb constructions will be construed as pragmatically enriched where existing cultural representations encourage or license this, and as purely syntactic/combinatorial elsewhere.

Fifth, the choice as to whether or not to employ a certain syntactic construction *at all* is contingent upon cultural typifications, since the latter provide a measure of plausibility or markedness of the component sub-events of a conceptualized complex event. For example, in Lao, an associated posture construction will be used when the particular 'posture'+'activity' combination in a given scene is pragmatically marked, i.e. requires a less salient or current cultural representation for culturally logical interpretation. When one particular posture is uniquely typical in combination with a certain activity, the associated posture construction is less likely to be used at all, since the relevant posture, being the default, need not be explicitly mentioned.[14] Such constraints on whether a morphosyntactic device will be used at all can be regarded as properly part of the 'rules' of syntax, since these constraints are a crucial part of what it takes for speakers to string utterances together.

10.5. CONCLUSION

The idea that the fine cogs and springwheels of syntax might be guided and/or constrained by the culture of speakers is an intriguing one, self-evident to some, opaque to others, and strongly resistant to clear articulation by anyone. The problem has received little attention in syntactic research relative to other preoccupations, due in part to the descriptive and analytical difficulties of bringing ethnography into the equation. Speakers effortlessly navigate the most delicate yet robust intricacies of linguistic and cultural systems, while almost completely

---

[14] It has long been recognized that there is no need to mention what is already present by default. It is literally unmarked. This is the essence of Grice's second maxim of Quantity: 'Do not make your contribution more informative than is required' (Grice 1975: 45; cf. Levinson's 'I-heuristic', 2000: 37). What I am trying to stress here is that (*a*) what is considered to be already 'automatically' understood by default is to a large extent *culturally* determined, and (*b*) this directly affects syntax, since it determines when and/or whether a certain syntactic construction will be used at all.

unconscious of the systematicity of these semiotic resources. However, the great difficulty of the task is no argument that ethnosyntactic description cannot or should not be undertaken. Despite the difficulties, and the dangers of traversing uncharted terrain, I submit that the unified description of grammar and culture from a broad perspective is a necessary and timely complement to the often narrow concerns of traditional syntactic research.

REFERENCES

BROWN, PENELOPE, and LEVINSON, STEPHEN C. 1987. *Politeness: Some Universals in Language Usage*. Cambridge: Cambridge University Press.

BRUCE, LES. 1988. 'Serialization: from syntax to lexicon'. *Studies in Language*, 12.1: 19–49.

CHAFE, WALLACE. 1994. *Discourse, Consciousness, and Time: The Flow and Displacement of Consciousness in Speech and Writing*. Chicago: Chicago University Press.

CLARK, HERBERT H. 1996a. *Using Language*. Cambridge: Cambridge University Press.

——1996b. 'Communities, commonalities, and communication'. In Gumperz and Levinson 1996: 324–55.

D'ANDRADE, ROY D. 1987. 'A folk model of the mind'. In Holland and Quinn 1987: 112–50.

DURIE, MARK. 1997. 'Grammatical structures in verb serialization'. In Alex Alsina, Joan Bresnan, and Peter Sells (eds.), *Complex Predicates*, Stanford, Calif.: CSLI Publications, 289–354.

ENFIELD, N. J. 2000. 'The theory of cultural logic: how individuals combine social intelligence with semiotics to create and maintain cultural meaning'. *Cultural Dynamics*, 12.1: 35–64.

FOLEY, WILLIAM A. 1997. *Anthropological Linguistics: An Introduction*. London: Blackwell.

GARFINKEL, HAROLD. 1967. *Studies in Ethnomethodology*. Englewood Cliffs, NJ: Prentice-Hall.

GIVÓN, TALMY. 1991. 'Serial verbs and the mental reality of "event": grammatical vs. cognitive packaging'. In Berndt Heine and Elizabeth Traugott (eds.), *Approaches to Grammaticalization*. Amsterdam: John Benjamins, 81–127.

GOLDBERG, ADELE. 1994. *Constructions: A Construction Grammar Approach to Argument Structure*. Chicago: University of Chicago Press.

GOODY, ESTHER N. (ed.). 1995. *Social Intelligence and Interaction: Expressions and Implications of the Social Bias in Human Intelligence*. Cambridge: Cambridge University Press.

GRACE, GEORGE. 1987. *The Linguistic Construction of Reality*. London: Croom Helm.

GRICE, H. P. 1975. 'Logic and conversation'. In Peter Cole and Jerry Morgan (eds.), *Syntax and Semantics*, iii: *Speech Acts*. New York: Academic Press, 41–59.

GUMPERZ, JOHN J. 1982. *Discourse Strategies*. Cambridge: Cambridge University Press.

——and LEVINSON, STEPHEN C. (eds.). 1996. *Rethinking Linguistic Relativity*. Cambridge: Cambridge University Press.

HOCKETT, CHARLES F. 1987. *Refurbishing our Foundations: Elementary Linguistics from an Advanced Point of View*. Amsterdam: John Benjamins.

HOLLAND, DOROTHY, and QUINN, NAOMI (eds.). 1987. *Cultural Models in Language and Thought*. Cambridge: Cambridge University Press.

HUTCHINS, EDWIN. 1980. *Culture and Inference: A Trobriand Case Study*. Cambridge, Mass.: Harvard University Press.

——1995. *Cognition in the Wild*. Cambridge, Mass.: MIT Press.

——and HAZLEHURST, BRIAN. 1995. 'How to invent a shared lexicon: the emergence of shared form-meaning mappings in interaction'. In Goody 1995: 53–67.

JARKEY, NERIDA. 1991. 'Serial verbs in White Hmong: a functional approach'. Doctoral dissertation, University of Sydney.

KAY, PAUL. 1996. 'Intra-speaker relativity'. In Gumperz and Levinson 1996: 97–114.

——and FILLMORE, CHARLES. 1999. 'Grammatical constructions and linguistic generalizations: the *What's X Doing Y?* construction'. *Language*, 75.1: 1–33.

LAKOFF, GEORGE. 1987. *Women, Fire, and Dangerous Things: What Categories Reveal about the Mind*. Chicago: University of Chicago Press.

LANGACKER, RONALD W. 1987. *Foundations of Cognitive Grammar*, i: *Theoretical Prerequisites*. Stanford, Calif.: Stanford University Press.

——1994. 'Culture, cognition, and grammar'. In Martin Pütz (ed.), *Language Contact and Language Conflict*. Amsterdam: John Benjamins, 26–53.

LEE, PENNY. 1996. *The Whorf Theory Complex: A Critical Reconstruction*. Amsterdam: Benjamins.

LEVINSON, STEPHEN C. 1995. 'Interactional biases in human thinking'. In Goody 1995: 221–60.

——1997. 'From outer to inner space: linguistic categories in non-linguistic thinking'. In Jan Nuyts and Eric Pederson (eds.), *Language and Conceptualization*. Cambridge: Cambridge University Press, 13–45.

——2000. *Presumptive Meanings: The Theory of Generalized Conversational Implicature*. Cambridge, Mass.: MIT Press.

LEWIS, DAVID. 1969. *Convention*. Cambridge, Mass.: Harvard University Press.

LORD, CAROL. 1993. *Historical Change in Serial Verb Constructions*. Amsterdam: John Benjamins.

LURIA, A. R. 1976. *Cognitive Development: Its Cultural and Social Foundations*. Cambridge, Mass.: Harvard University Press.

NOBLE, WILLIAM, and DAVIDSON, IAIN. 1996. *Human Evolution, Language, and Mind: A Psychological and Archeological Inquiry*. Cambridge: Cambridge University Press.

PAWLEY, ANDREW. 1987. 'Encoding events in Kalam and English: different logics for reporting experience'. In Russell Tomlin (ed.), *Coherence and Grounding in Discourse*. Amsterdam: John Benjamins, 329–60.

REDDY, MICHAEL. 1979. 'The conduit metaphor: a case of frame conflict in our language about language'. In Andrew Ortony (ed.), *Metaphor and Thought*. Cambridge: Cambridge University Press, 284–324.

SALOMON, GAVRIEL (ed.). 1993. *Distributed Cognitions: Psychological and Educational Considerations*. Cambridge: Cambridge University Press.

SCHELLING, THOMAS C. 1960. *The Strategy of Conflict*. Cambridge, Mass.: Harvard University Press.

SCHUTZ, ALFRED. 1946. 'The well-informed citizen: an essay on the social distribution of knowledge'. *Social Research*, 13.4: 463–78.

SCHUTZ, ALFRED. 1970. *On Phenomenology and Social Relations*. Chicago: University of Chicago Press.

SEBBA, MARK. 1987. *The Syntax of Serial Verbs*. Amsterdam: John Benjamins.

STRAUSS, CLAUDIA, and QUINN, NAOMI. 1997. *A Cognitive Theory of Cultural Meaning*. Cambridge: Cambridge University Press.

TALMY, LEONARD, 2000. *Toward a Cognitive Semantics*, 2 vols. Cambridge, Mass.: MIT Press.

WASON, P. C., and REICH, C. C. 1979. 'A verbal illusion'. *Quarterly Journal of Experimental Psychology*, 31: 591–8.

WIERZBICKA, ANNA. 1991. *Cross-Cultural Pragmatics: The Semantics of Human Interaction*. Berlin: Mouton de Gruyter.

——1996. *Semantics: Primes and Universals*. New York: Oxford University Press.

11

Aspects of Ku Waru Ethnosyntax and Social Life

ALAN RUMSEY

11.1. INTRODUCTION

In this chapter I discuss some relationships between language and other aspects of culture and social life among the Ku Waru people of the Western Highlands of Papua New Guinea, where Francesca Merlan and I have been doing linguistic and anthropological fieldwork on and off since 1981. This leads to some conclusions about the nature of connections we can expect to find between language and culture in general. Before taking up these questions, I provide a brief introduction to some relevant aspects of Ku Waru culture and language.

11.2. ETHNOGRAPHIC BACKGROUND

Ku Waru means 'cliff' (literally 'steep stone'), and is used to designate a loosely bounded dialect and ethnic region of the Western New Guinea Highlands, named after the prominent limestone cliffs abutting it along the eastern slopes of the Tambul Range, near Mt. Hagen. The highlands are by far the most densely populated region of New Guinea, and the last to be contacted by Europeans, which did not happen until the 1930s. The local economy is still largely a subsistence one, based on intensive cultivation of sweet potatoes, taro, and a wide range of other crops.

Despite Ku Waru people's present political encapsulation within the sovereign state of Papua New Guinea, and their increasing involvement with the cash economy, gift exchange still functions among them as what Marcel Mauss (1954) called a 'total social phenomenon', at once economic, political, and religious in its ramifications. The organizing bases of exchange even in this one society are various, and include both what we can gloss as an *interpersonal* dimension and an *intergroup* one. On the interpersonal side, exchange takes place between individual

For their helpful comments on earlier versions of this chapter, I would like to thank Cliff Goddard, Nicholas Enfield, Francesca Merlan, Anna Wierzbicka, and participants at a seminar in the Dept. of Linguistics, RSPAS, Australian National University, where I presented the first draft in 1997. The following abbreviations are used: APL: applicative; COM: comitative; DEF: definite; ERG: ergative; FUT: future; GEN: genitive; HAB: habitual; LOC: locative; NF: non-Final; PL: plural; PP: present progressive; RP: remote past; SG: singular; SJV: subjunctive; 1: first person; 2: second person; 3: third person; 2/3: second or third person; ':' represents a morpheme boundary which is not shown in the interlinear gloss line.

trading partners, who are usually related to each other through ties of matrilateral kinship or affinity—for instance, between a man and his mother's brother's son, or his wife's brother. On the intergroup side, exchange takes place between *talapi*, a kind of segmentary social unit which can for present purposes be roughly glossed as 'tribe' or 'clan'. *Talapi* are, however, unlike some segmentary units found, e.g., in Africa and Polynesia in that there are within them no inherited or otherwise ascribed positions of leadership (see Merlan and Rumsey 1991: ch. 3, for other differences, and further details concerning the nature of *talapi*). Instead of chiefs or chiefly lineages, within each *talapi* there is more-or-less open competition for 'big man' status—a status which is understood to be achieved largely through demonstrating skill in the practice of oratory and ceremonial exchange. These two activities—oratory and gift exchange—are closely interrelated in that exchange transactions between *talapi* are always accompanied by extensive speech-making.

Exchange in its inter-*talapi* aspect cannot be thought of as mutually exclusive with interpersonal exchange. Rather, most exchange transactions between *talapi* consist of, or have an alternate identity as, a set of transactions between individual partners identified with each of the two *talapi*. Thus, for example, a major payment in 1981 by a *talapi* called Kubuka to one called Poika consisted of thirty-three distinct interpersonal payments made by particular members of Kubuka (or small consortia of them) to particular partners in Poika. Now what would-be big men compete at is not so much the maximization of their own 'interpersonal' exchanges, nor their personal contributions to inter-*talapi* ones; rather, they struggle to coordinate their fellow clansmen's interpersonal transactions into an inter-*talapi* one. Or, more generally, as I try to demonstrate below, they struggle for control of the meaning of events for intergroup politics (cf. Lederman 1980).

Transactions among *talapi* are structured in terms of pairing relationships, of three distinct but inter-convertible sorts: compositional pairing, where a pair of social units pairs with another pair to comprise a ramified higher level unit; serial parity whereby units link up in chains, wherein *a* transacts with *b*, *b* with *c*, etc.; and oppositional parity, whereby military allies are recruited in two or more such chains extending outward in opposite directions from a point of conflict (see Merlan and Rumsey 1991 for further details).

Binary structures are a common feature of many social systems around the world and have been extensively explored and compared by anthropologists under the rubric 'dual organization'. In the classic cases of dual organization as found for example in Aboriginal Australia and among the Ge peoples of central Brazil, the whole society is divided 'top down' into two moieties. A person cannot marry within his own moiety but must marry into the other instead. Some anthropologists looking at New Guinea societies from an outsider's comparative perspective (Rubel and Rosman 1978) have attempted to interpret Western Highlands social structures in this way, but this is a mistake, for the following reasons.

Dual organization is based on reciprocity (Lévi-Strauss 1969). Relations of reciprocity are crucial to Ku Waru social life, but are a special case of the more general phenomenon of pairing, of which compositional binarism is another instance. The latter is not dual organization of the classical sort, since units paired in this way do not ordinarily exchange with each other (Merlan and Rumsey 1991: chs. 4, 7). Nor can serial pairing provide the basis for any consistent, overarching dual organization, since pairing relations of this kind are non-transitive and contextually relative. For example, with respect to an important distinction made in the Ku Waru area between the social identities Meam and Kakuyl, we found that these identities were assigned on a sliding scale such that among three tribe clusters A, B, and C, B was identified as Meam relative to A (which was Kakuyl) but as Kakuyl relative to C (which was Meam) (Merlan and Rumsey 1991: 204). We found that the exchange relationships which are so central to Ku Waru social life (as elsewhere in Melanesia) are predicated on relations of difference, which they serve to mediate. But these relations are non-transitive in that, for example, B may be sufficiently different in the relevant way from both A and C without this entailing anything at all about the relation between A and C (Merlan and Rumsey 1991: 204). Another, related feature of these relationships is that:

they presume an ultimate *equivalence* . . . between the two parties. As opposed to systems of [generalized] exchange as modelled by Lévi-Strauss (1969), or hierarchical ones as in Dumont (1970) exchange here is always direct, and does not permit of 'encompassment' of one term in the relationship by another. And unlike some other systems of direct exchange, this one is not underpinned by a dualism of yin and yang—of chronically and essentially opposed orders of being, between which there *must* be exchange because each is incomplete without the other. Rather, this is a system in which it is not only permitted, but for many kinds of transactions positively required that the return prestation be one *of exactly the same order* as what was given.   (Merlan and Rumsey 1991: 204–5)

The Ku Waru emphasis on pairing in the political sphere is one instance of a more general emphasis on pairing in this area of the Highlands, which was noticed by the earliest ethnographers in the region, who worked among the neighbouring Melpa people.

The Lutheran missionary Hermann Strauss, who was one of the first Europeans to learn the local language, noted that the Melpa are disposed toward 'viewing things in pairs' in many different spheres. When speaking of social groups they 'always take the pair as the basic unit' (Strauss 1990: 10; cf. above). And they speak for example of:

mugl möi ragl . . . 'heaven (and) earth, the two of them' . . . 'the sun (and) the moon, the two of them' . . . 'night (and) day, the two of them' . . . 'father (and) mother, the two of them' and so on. Moons (months) are always listed in pairs, taken together as 'an elder brother and younger brother' . . . Animals, birds, objects, types of food, valuables and so on are always seen in pairs.   (Strauss 1990: 11)

Strauss interpreted all this as a 'vital experience of the need for complementation, of the way in which all things, living and dead, require something else, a complement [or] fulfilment without which the individual being or thing is "out of its place" . . . Only the "other half" gives it full validity' (ibid.).

After extensive anthropological fieldwork with the Melpa people later on in the 1960s and 1970s, Andrew Strathern collaborated on a comparative study with cognitive psychologist D. F. Lancy, in which they concluded that pairing among the Melpa functioned as 'an alternative to the taxonomic mode of representation' (Lancy and Strathern 1981). As in Ku Waru, Melpa exhibits relatively few levels of lexicalized superclass–subclass relations (of the type animal–mammal–marsupial, etc.), but many compounds of the type 'marsupial–dog', 'marsupial–bird', and 'pig–dog' (see also Strauss's examples above), which designate classes for which there are no monolexemic labels, and which do not fit into consistent taxonomic hierarchies, since they typically show overlapping or disjunctive membership rather than subclass–superclass relations. I will have more to say below in Section 11.8 about the grammar and semantics of the these pairing compounds.

Let us now consider some of the more general sorts of cultural emphasis with which the nature of these compounds seem to be consonant. In our book *Ku Waru* Merlan and I have described what we consider to be some of the main emphases of Ku Waru people's interactional style or 'set' towards the world (Merlan and Rumsey 1991: 224–42).

One of these emphases, also noted by other ethnographers of the region, is on the interplay of concealment and revelation. There is a widespread scepticism about the possibility of knowing the thoughts and intentions of others ('How should I know? Can I see inside his mind?'). Children are socialized from an early age to expect deceit, for example, by mothers telling them 'Come along now, we're going to eat', and then laughingly announcing to the child after he has come that it was only a 'trick', and that one should not so readily believe what one is told. Yet for all that people expect deceit as normal, there is an equally pervasive interest in trying to bring other people's hidden intentions to the surface (*ak-* 'dig out', as of a sweet potato from the ground). This is one of the main activities pursued, for example, by dispute mediators, whose skills are highly valued, and by 'big men' with respect to the conduct of wealth exchange and intergroup politics.

This aspect of Ku Waru interactional style is also evident in people's attitude toward the unfolding of events. Contrary to the stereotype expectations Westerners have about the 'traditionalism' of 'tribal' peoples, New Guinea highlanders tend to stress contingency and the possibility of dramatic new developments that may negate or supplant their current understanding of how things are.[1] And one of the main ways in which novelty is generated is through what we have called 'contingent juxtaposition', the bringing together of previously isolated entities or categories in a way that brings out something theretofore concealed or latent in each. A prime example would be the first arrival of Europeans in the highlands in the 1930s. This was taken by highlanders not just as a revelation of an outside

---

[1] A particularly striking institutionalized form of this mind set has been reported from the Mountain Ok region to the west, by Fredrik Barth (1975), who describes the system of male initiation among the Baktaman people. Initiands move through seven stages of initiation over the course of many years. At each stage the secret they are let in on is that everything they learned at the previous stage is false or illusory and that the truth is in some important respects the opposite of what they had been taught.

world that they had been unaware of, but as something that placed them in a new relationship that revealed things they had not previously known about themselves (cf. Rumsey 1999*a*). They took the Europeans to be their own ancestors or distant collateral relatives, and all their marvellous wealth and miraculous technology to be something that highlanders themselves had once had, but lost when their white (or as they say 'red') ancestors absconded with them.

11.3. ASPECTS OF THE KU WARU LANGUAGE

Ku Waru is a Papuan language belonging to what Foley (1986) calls the Chimbu family. It is part of a large dialect continuum (one of the largest two in Papua New Guinea), spoken over most of the Western Highlands Province, by well over 100,000 people. Like most Papuan languages, it has strictly verb-final syntax, and makes extensive use of verb- and clause-chaining, non-final verbs being marked for person/number, relative tense, and coreference status of their subject (i.e. whether it is the same as or different from that of the following verb). Ku Waru distinguishes three numbers—singular, dual, and plural—and the usual three person categories, with conflation of second and third person in the non-singular numbers. Table 11.1 shows how these distinctions are made in the personal pronouns. Exactly the same distinctions are shown in all final verbs, which agree with their subject in person and number. For the non-final verbs there is for most Ku Waru speakers a reduced set of number distinctions, with a single ending -*p* used for all three numbers in the first person and a single ending -*k* for second person singular and second and third person plural.

TABLE 11.1. Ku Waru personal pronouns

	Singular	Dual	Plural
First person	na	olto	olyo
Second person	nu	elti	eni
Third person	yu		

Ku Waru has five major clause types (Merlan and Rumsey 1991: 337–40), one of which is regularly used for clauses of 'being'. An example is:

(1)   *lku-yl*   *angalyilym*
      house-DEF be/stand:HAB:3SG
      'There is a house.'

Any such clause can be expanded into a clause expressing possession, by adding a possessor NP at the beginning:

(2)   *na lku-yl*   *angalyilym*
      I   house-DEF be/stand:HAB:3SG
      'I have a house.'

For further details of Ku Waru grammar see Merlan and Rumsey (1991: 322–49).

11.4. METHODOLOGICAL PRELIMINARIES CONCERNING LANGUAGE AND CULTURE

For trying to decide what we might mean by 'ethnosyntax', a useful starting point is provided by Nick Enfield in his introduction to this volume, where he distinguishes between 'broad' senses of the term and 'narrow' ones (see also Goddard, this volume). In the 'narrow' sense it 'refers to the direct encoding of cultural meaning in the semantics of morphosyntax' (p. 7 above). In the broader sense he intends the term to refer to 'culture-specific patterns of distribution and use . . . [of] morphosyntactic categories and constructions which do not themselves encode culture-specific "statements" in their semantics' (ibid.). In what follows I mainly discuss instances of the latter kind of linkage, i.e. culture-specific *uses* of certain cross-linguistically recognizable syntactic devices, among the Ku Waru people. I hope to demonstrate, especially through the examples discussed in Sections 11.6 and 11.8, the precise sense in which the productivity of grammatical resources can be licensed by their use in culturally-specific kinds of contexts. More generally, I hope to show that the relationship is not only one of 'licensing' or 'constraint', but one whereby culture itself is actively reproduced and contested in acts of language use. Before that, however, I briefly summarize some results published elsewhere (Merlan, Roberts, and Rumsey 1997; Rumsey forthcoming) concerning a relationship which is of the more 'narrow' sort, in that the particularities of Ku Waru lexico-grammar are directly tied up with other aspects of culture.

11.5. KU WARU 'CLASSIFICATORY VERBS' AND THEIR CULTURAL CORRELATES

In the discussion of Ku Waru clauses of 'being' and 'having' above, I gave examples with the verb *angaly-* 'stand'/'be'. There are four other verbs that enter into such constructions: *mol-*, *le-*, *pe-*, and *o-*. All of them when used in these clauses are best glossed as 'be', but the choice among them depends on the nature of the subject NP. For example: *no* 'water', *uj* 'tree', and *yab* 'people' usually occur with *mol-* (which in other contexts means 'stay'); *kupulanum* 'road', *on* 'corpse', and *ku moni* 'money' occur with *le-* (which in other contexts means 'put in place'); *numan* 'conscience', *pudumong* 'trouble', and *boni* 'heaviness', 'grievance' with *pe-* (which in other contexts means 'sleep'); *mong* 'eye', *ki* 'arm', and *lku* 'house' with *angaly-* (which in other contexts means 'stand'); and *kumbi* 'nose', *kidipidi* 'whiskers', and *kidipaim* 'fingernail'/'toenail' with *o-* (which in other contexts means 'come'). Some nouns can occur with various of these verbs, for example:

(3) *a. yi   ada-yl   lku   suku   molym*
     man old-DEF house inside *mol*:HAB:3SG
     'The old man is (staying) inside the house.'

   b. yi   ada-yl   lku   suku   pelym
     man old-DEF house inside *pe*:HAB:3SG
     'The old man is lying/sleeping inside the house.'

   c. yi   ada-yl   lku   suku   lelym
     man old-DEF house inside *le*:HAB:3SG
     'The old man is lying prostrate/dead inside the house.'

   d. yi   ada-yl   lku   suku   angalyilym
     man old-DEF house inside *angaly*:HAB:3SG
     'The old man is standing inside the house.'

Pe-, *le*, and *angaly-* do not always mean 'sleep', 'lie dead', and 'stand' respectively. These are contextually specific meanings in clauses with a particular sort of subject. But these verbs do differ consistently in the kinds of states of being which they predicate, as follows.

Angaly- ('stand'/'be') typically predicates states of standing and/or protruding, projecting outward from a surface or ground—thus visibly manifest rather than latent or concealed (e.g. of the body, arms, legs, hair, fingernails, and eyes, but not internal organs). In contrast , *mol-* ('stay'/'be') signals being or existence in a place (also generally visible, not concealed). *Mol-* contrasts with *pe-* ('lie'/'sleep'/'be') in being indeterminate as to the position of an animate being of which existence is predicated, while *pe-* centrally means 'to lie, sleep' (in the latter sense, generally with the preverb *uru*), and thus (often in the Habitual) is used to mean 'live, dwell' via an extension from 'habitually sleeps at' (for examples see Merlan, Roberts, and Rumsey 1997: 77).

Mol- ('stay'/'be') contrasts with *le-* ('be') in that the latter generally expresses existence or being in a place of an inanimate object, and of an animate when the sense is that of an animate being prostrate, lying on the ground, laid out, sick, or otherwise physically impaired (for examples see Merlan, Roberts, and Rumsey 1997: 78). When used of inanimate objects, *pe-* ('lie'/'sleep'/'be') contrasts with *mol-* ('stay'/'be') and *angaly-* ('stand'/'be') in usually entailing the notion that the object is in a subterranean or otherwise concealed position, e.g., sweet potatoes in the garden, sugar in tea, or money in one's pocket (for examples see Merlan, Roberts, and Rumsey 1997: 78).

Le- ('be') is like *pe-* ('lie'/'sleep'/'be') in this respect, in so far as it usually refers to objects which are not in a prominent or highly visible position. When used of money, for example, it simply indicates that the money exists or is possessed by someone. But when the money is tacked to a display board for presentation at a ceremonial exchange event, the verb used of it in existential clauses is *mol-* ('stay'/'be'). But in another respect, the meaning of *le-* has something in common with that of *angaly-* ('stand'/'be') which distinguishes both of them from *mol-*

('stay'/'be') and *pe-* ('lie'/'sleep'/'be'). In order to see what this is, it is important to note that the latter two verbs, *angaly-* and *le-*, occur not only in intransitive (or low transitivity) clauses, but also in certain 'canonical transitive' ones, where they usually can be glossed 'put' or 'put in place' (for examples see Merlan, Roberts, and Rumsey 1997: 79).

As in these canonical transitive clauses, the use of *angaly-* ('stand'/'be') and *le-* ('be') in existential and possessive clauses (as exemplified earlier) usually carries with it a notion that the object (in this case the grammatical 'subject') not only exists, but exists in a specific place or position. Usually the object has been deliberately put there by a conscious agent. For *le-*, we can say that, minimally, the placement is *not* under the conscious control of the object itself. As for *angaly-*, it is obvious that, for example, the existence of a house entails a deliberate 'putting in place'. Less obviously, Ku Waru people also regard the appendages of the human body (arms, legs, hair, fingernails, etc.) not as inevitable developments *in utero*, but as something that has to be formed through repeated acts of intercourse early in the pregnancy and then through massaging the mother's abdomen (see Merlan and Rumsey 1986: lines 426–8, 580–90, 769). This cultural precept accords directly with the grammatical choice made in the language, whereby limbs are linguistically treated as 'put in place'.

To sum up the above discussion, the relevant differences among four[2] out of the five Ku Waru 'classificatory verbs' and their associated existential clauses seem to be analysable in terms of two cross-cutting distinctions, one having to do with existence in a concealed or latent state vs. an openly manifest one, and the other having to do with whether or not the object is in place as a result of intentional human activity (see Merlan, Roberts, and Rumsey 1997: 79–81 and Rumsey forthcoming for further discussion). If so, then, given the Ku Waru cultural emphases discussed in Section 11.2, the grammar of Ku Waru existential clauses would seem to be a possible instance of ethnosyntax in the 'narrow' sense of the term, in so far as it involves a specific clause type which can be defined on formal grounds, the semantics of which involves distinctions of a kind that are highly salient in the culture generally, i.e. between the latent or concealed and the manifest or revealed, and between states of affairs that are the result of intentional action and those that are not. I have called this a 'possible instance' of the 'narrow' sense rather than a definite one, because the semantic distinctions involved are not highly culture-specific. For example, interesting as this particular grammar–culture convergence may be, I think it would probably have been pos-

---

[2] I have left the fifth classificatory verb *o-* out of this discussion because our analysis of its semantics has not progressed as far as for the other four. It is unique among the five in being primarily an active verb (meaning 'to come'), with, as far as we know, no other stative uses outside of these existential clauses. It has by far the smallest inventory of nouns that occur with it, and they are limited mainly to body-parts and qualities (cf. Rumsey forthcoming).

sible for readers with a modicum of linguistic training, but no interest in cultural anthropology, to read and understand Sections 11.3 and 11.5 of this chapter without having read Section 11.2.[3] On the other hand, while perhaps able to understand the semantic basis of the relevant classification, such a reader would not be able to understand all of its applications to specific lexical items without being aware of certain culturally specific premises, such as, for example, the assumed role of Ku Waru parents in actively shaping the body of the developing fetus, as discussed above.[4]

While this may or may not make the Ku Waru classificatory verb system an example of ethnosyntax in the 'narrow' sense, it does involve a connection between specific features of Ku Waru grammar and other aspects of culture.[5] This will become clearer by contrast with the other kinds of examples to which I now turn, which involve formal devices of a kind not at all language-specific, but which are used in culturally specific ways.

11.6. ORATORICAL USES OF KU WARU SINGULAR AND DUAL NUMBER CATEGORIES

In Ku Waru as in English, sociopolitical entities, e.g. the sides in a war, can be referred to in the singular or the plural number (e.g. 'Germany was at war with Poland'/'The Germans fought the Poles'). But unlike in English, in Ku Waru, the singular usages are not limited to the third person, but are also common in the first and second. That is, words which we would otherwise translate as 'I' or 'you' (sg) (and verbs which are marked for 1sg or 2sg subject) can be used to refer not to individual, physically present oratorical 'speaker' and his 'addressee', but to whole segmentary units with which they are identified. This does not necessarily imply that the physically present, speaking individual is included among the referents of his 'I', nor that the referents of his 'you' include individuals present at the speech event, for what are sometimes being referred to are activities which took place well

[3] Contrast this with, for example the Australian Aboriginal cases discussed by Enfield (this volume, p. 6; cf. Hercus and White 1973) where personal pronouns and syntactic agreement rules are sensitive to the moiety membership and generation level of people being referred to. In such cases, one cannot make sense of the grammar without being aware of some specifically Australian Aboriginal principles of kinship and social organization.

[4] I am indebted to Nick Enfield (personal communication) for clarification of the ways in which Ku Waru classificatory verbs may or may not be an instance of ethnosyntax in the narrow sense.

[5] Though there is not the space to go into this matter any further here, I argue elsewhere (Rumsey forthcoming) that the systems of classificatory verbs in Ku Waru and other Papuan languages provide a good example of the way in which the application of abstract grammatical classifications to concrete referents in actual speech-acts is mediated by what I call cultural stereotypes, which are what are taken to be the *typical* attributes of kinds of things that are referred to by a given lexical item: *man* as typically upright, tall, and strong; *woman* as typically squat, short, and weak, etc.

before any of these people were born. For example, 'I' fought with 'you' can mean: 'my ancestors qua segmentary unit fought with yours'.[6] These uses are instances of what Merlan and I (1991: ch. 5) call 'segmentary person'.

An example is the following:

(4) *midipu kujilyi nu-n   yi   kare aki-yl-nga   suku   tekin*
     (man's name) you-ERG man some that-DEF-GEN inside do:NF:2SG
     turun
     hit/kill:RP:2SG
     'Midipu Kujilyi, over that you (sg) have killed some of the men within [this tribe].'

This example shows a segmentary use of the second person singular pronoun *nu*, whereby the leading big man of his tribe, Midipu Kujilyi, is picked out in direct address (he was present at this event) as what we might see as a kind of synecdochic figure for his whole tribe—in fact for a whole congeries of five fairly small tribes, among all of which he is the leading big man. Kujilyi himself could not have actually killed anyone at the war which is here being referred to, as he would have been just a young boy at the time.

Another, textually related example is as follows:

(5) *a. pilyikimil   el   turum-uyl   topa-kin   epola-alya-sil*
        hear/know:PP:2/3PL fight hit:RP:3SG-DEF hit:NF-COM (tribe names)-PAIR
        lyirim-a
        take:RP:3SG
        'You (pl) know that "he" fought, and when he did, Epola-Alya took (sg) it up.'
     b. pi   tepa   oba   na-nga kangi-na nosinsirum
        then do:NF:3SG come:NF:3SG I-GEN skin-LOC put:APL:RP:3SG
        'Then, having done that "he" (i.e. Epola-Alya) came and put it on my skin (i.e., made me liable for it).' ·
     c. jika-kungunuka sirid
        (tribe names)   give:RP:1SG
        'I gave it to Jika-Kungunuka.'

Here the speaking orator is Kujilyi himself (the same man nominated as addressee in the previous example). There are instances of segmentary person references in every line. In the first line, the expression *epola-alya-sil* 'the pair of Epola and Alya' occurs as the singular subject of the verb *lyi-* 'take', describing the recruitment of those tribes into the same war referred to in the first example. In the sec-

---

[6] These usages are also found among the neighbouring Melpa people, and the Huli people in the southern highlands. For textual examples see Strathern 1975: 199 and Goldman 1983: 134, line 294, respectively. Similar usages among Polynesian and African peoples are discussed in Sahlins 1985, Rumsey 1999*b*, and Rumsey 2000.

ond line, this tribe pair becomes the grammatical subject, again referred to with singular number. 'Put it upon my skin' here is an idiom for 'make me liable for', meaning that Kujilyi's tribe pair, Kusika-Midipu, were recruited as allies. Note the grammatically singular form *na-nga* '*my* (skin)'. In the third line, Kujilyi then refers to his own tribe's (or tribe pair's) recruitment of the Jika-Kungunika using a first person singular form (of the verb *si-* 'to give') which translates as though he himself had done the recruiting. But Kujilyi, recall, was a young boy at the time, and cannot himself have played any part in these acts of recruitment (which would have been negotiated by the big men of *that* time).

While in this example it is fairly clear that the individual orator cannot be identified as the sole referent of his 'I', more commonly, in the 'segmentary' uses of these forms, it is ambiguous or a moot point whether the speaker is talking about 'himself' or a whole segmentary unit. This can be illustrated with a more extended example, taken from a transcript of the same exchange event from which the others are taken.

In order for the reader to make sense of the transcript, I need to provide some background information concerning the nature of Ku Waru warfare and this episode of it in particular. Warfare is in a sense the inter-*talapi* transaction par excellence, as *talapi*, or blocs of them, are always involved as the protagonists. One of the *talapi* on each side is always identified as the 'fight source' (*el pul*), the others being recruited in chain-like series such as those shown in the first line of the following:

Chain of Recruitment
A recruits B, then B recruits C

Chain of Compensation Payments
B compensates C, then A compensates B

The acts of recruitment, or the resulting injuries and deaths among allies recruited, must later be compensated for, in a series of transactions which reverses the order of recruitment, as shown in the second row of this figure. In these terms, the players in the present game are as follows

A	B	C
Epola	Kopia	Laulku
Alya	Kubuka	(Mujika)
Lalka		
Kusika		
Midipu		

The war took place in 1982. The five tribes named under A were the 'fight source' on their side, in that it originally broke out as a fight between them and a neighbouring tribe pair, the Tea-Dena (who were thus the 'fight source' among all the tribes on the opposing side). Bloc A then recruited the Kopia-Kubuka, and the Kopia-Kubuka in turn recruited the Laulku (or, arguably, the pair of Mujika and

Laulku—for details see Merlan and Rumsey 1991: 147–52). The exchange event from which all the oratorical examples in this paper are taken is the one at which Kopia-Kubuka (B) were presenting compensation to (Mujika-)Laulku.

As has been widely noted in the highlands, when a segmentary unit is nominally involved in warfare, it is seldom if ever the case that every adult male of that unit joins in the fighting. In general, the further out a tribe is from the 'fight source' along the chain of allies, the lower the proportion of men who participate. Furthermore, some men invariably join in from *talapi* which are not, qua *talapi*, recruited as allies. In general, these men, if recruited at all, are recruited along lines of close matrilateral kinship or affinity. But there is always room for disagreement about the basis of their participation.

This can be illustrated from the transcript with reference to the role of the Poika and Palimi tribes in these proceedings. In the past, these two tribes have been the main allies of the Kopia-Kubuka (B). In the fighting for which compensation is here being paid, by Kopia-Kubuka, several men from these tribes (Poika and Palimi) did participate, and at least two of the Poika were wounded. On the day of compensation, many people from those tribes turned up. A big man from Kubuka called Tamalu gave a speech in which he tried to justify the Poika-Palimi not being paid compensation at this time (for the full context, see Merlan and Rumsey 1991: appendix A, lines 633–8 *et passim*). The speech began as follows:

(6) *a. poika   kang nyikim,   eee!   laulku   kang nyikim*
        (tribe name) lad   say:PP:3SG (exclamation) (tribe name) lad   say:PP:3SG
        'He says "a Poika lad" or "a Laulku lad".'

    b. ilyi nyikin   pel   pora   nyikim   poika   kang-te el
        that say:PP:2SG cousin finished be:PP:3SG (tribe name) lad-DEF arrow
        munsurum aki-yl
        put:RP:3SG that-DEF
        'What you (sg) are talking about, cousin, that's finished, a Poika was wounded by an arrow.'

    c. olto-nga   ung-iyl   kornga pilyipa   lyilym
        we two-GEN word-DEF already hear:3SG:NF get:HAB:3SG
        'As for these words of us two he [the Poika] already understands about that.'

    d. el   ya   naa telybolu   i   kupulanum ilyi,   ime-nga   pansip
        fight here not do:HAB:2/3DU this road   this one these-GEN put:1:NF
        tep   ime-nga   pansip tep
        do:1:NF these-GEN put:1:NF do:1:NF
        'We two do not fight on this "road" [i.e. within the Kopia-Kubuka-Poika-Palimi alliance]; we do it together over and over.'

    e. na nanu   poika-palimi-sil-kin   molup   telyo
        I   I myself (tribe names)-PAIR-COM stay:1:NF do:HAB:1SG
        'I myself stay with Poika and Palimi.'

f. *ya yu-nga ul-uyl   malysip   malysip   modup te midi*
  here he-GEN matter-DEF clean:1:NF clean:1:NF put:1:NF one only
  kim   imituyl-te pirim
  leafy vegetable rotten-DEF lie/be:RP:3SG
  'We've got all of his matters cleaned up except for one old "rotten
  vegetable" [i.e. outstanding debt] that still remains.'

g. *ilyi naa pelka-ja   i   wiylola ilyi-nga pubu*
  that not lie/be:SJV:1/3SG this up there that-GEN go:1SG:FUT
  na mokabu   naa lyibu   nyilka
  I   compensation not get-1SG-FUT say-SJV-1/3SG
  'If it hadn't been for that, I wouldn't be demanding compensation [from
  the Epola *et al.*] so soon.'

In this excerpt (and elsewhere in the speech as well), Tamalu makes subtle use
of segmentary person forms, so as to group the Palimi and Poika together with
the Kopia-Kubuka as relative 'insiders' vis-à-vis the Laulku, so that the Kopia-
Kubuka accept responsibility for compensating the Laulku as a *talapi*, but not for
compensating the Poika as one. Shortly before this speech of Tamalu's someone in
the audience has made an offstage remark about the injury received in the fighting
by one of the Poika participants. Tamalu's first move (line 6a) is to address the general assemblage, telling them about this remark. Starting in line 6b, he addresses
the man who has made the remark, using the first person dual pronoun *olto* (line
6c) to refer not to two individuals, but to whole segmentary units. 'We two' in
this context means 'we Kopia-Kubuka and Laulku'. *Olto-nga ung* 'The word of
us two' means 'the things you Laulku and we Kopia-Kubuka are talking about
between us today'. The implication of line 6c is that these are matters which have
already been thoroughly canvassed between Poika and Kopia-Kubuka before the
payment was given in this form. In line 6d, the reference of the first person dual
category then shifts to another segmentary pair: the pair of Kopia-Kubuka and
Poika-Palimi—just those tribes among whom the matter has purportedly already
been discussed. These are people who fight on the same side as a matter of course.
The first person singular pronoun (*na*) in line 6e can be construed as referring to
Tamalu himself, to the Kubuka tribe, or to the pair of Kopia and Kubuka.

   In any case, the effect is to point to bonds of co-residence which identify Kopia-
Kubuka and Poika-Palimi together in a way that Laulku is not identified with any
of them. But, having made this identification, Tamalu then goes on to explain (in
line 6f) that there is one outstanding debt (metaphorically referred to as a 'rotten
vegetable') that remains to be paid within this alliance. That is a compensation
payment which is owed for the death of a Poika man in a previous war, the one I
mentioned above that was fought about sixty years ago. It was explained to us pri-
vately that this outstanding debt was the reason why the Poika were not recruited
as a talapi to assist the Kopia-Kubuka in the 1982 war. That was presumably one
reason for Tamalu's mentioning it in this context—as an explanation ostensibly

addressed to the Laulku for why the Poika were not now being compensated. But discussion of this transcript with participants in this event, and our own experience of these matters, suggests that the 'private agreement' with Poika on this score was probably not as secure as Tamalu suggests, and his remark was also covertly aimed at the Poika, to pre-empt any claim they might be thinking about pressing at this time. He is presumably also trying to reassure them by suggesting that his tribe, the Kubuka, will later use the compensation they get from those who recruited them into the fight to pay their 'rotten vegetable' debt to Poika, and that he will press for this compensation to be paid soon. Later on in these proceedings, some of the money was in fact presented to some men from Poika. But Tamalu's speech in lines 6*a–c* helped to assure that it could not be construed as having been given to 'Poika' as such. What happened instead was that a relatively small payment was given to particular men from Poika for the role they played in the fighting.

One can see from this example that the question of whether the Poika partici-pated as *talapi* in the fighting—and therefore in the compensation event—is not one which can be addressed independently of how the matter was discursively constructed by those concerned. Particular men identified with a particular *talapi* are agreed to have taken part, and to have incurred injury for which compensation would ordinarily be paid. But from this the conclusions to be drawn for segmentary politics are not self-evident. The men's actions are subjected to various competing constructions using both explicit appeals to a relationship of close identification of 'sameness' among the relevant *talapi*, and the more subtle device of segmentary person to *presuppose* such a relationship. This is a prime example of what I mean by 'struggle for control of the meaning of events for intergroup politics', a strug-gle which has very real material consequences in that it may create or decisively alter the exchange obligations of relevant *talapi*—wealth exchange being canon-ically transacted among segmentary units which are 'different', and requiring joint participation among those which are 'same'. The segmentary first person singular is the ultimate linguistic device for constructing relations of the latter sort, as its use not only presupposes singularity of reference, but directly instantiates singu-larity of social agency in the act of speaking and, by implication, in the act of exchange in which that speaking plays a part. In other words, in its situated use, the segmentary *I* 'personifies' the social unit or units to which it refers.

But equally importantly, in so doing, it 'amplifies' the persona of the would-be 'big man' who uses it. Thus, recall how, in the present example, Tamalu's first per-son references work in such a way as to identify himself totally with his *talapi*, the Kubuka, or with the pair of Kopia and Kubuka, so that it becomes a moot point whether he is *really* talking about himself or his *talapi* (as attested by the frequent exasperation of Ku Waru informants to whom we dutifully persisted in putting such questions, even as we already suspected what their answers confirmed—that our questions had simply missed the point). Thus, even while would-be big men compete to speak as entire *talapi*, in effect they also collaborate to reproduce a social order in which *talapi* figure crucially—often lethally—as relevant agents.

11.7. KU WARU PARALLELISM

As another instance of a culturally specific use of language, let us consider the nature of Ku Waru parallelism—the ordered interplay of repetition and variation (Jakobson 1960; Fox 1977, 1988; cf. Tannen 1989). My first examples of it come from a special, prosodically and paralinguistically marked genre of Ku Waru oratory known as *el ung*, which is used at exchange events such as the one discussed above.

Some of the performance features of *el ung* oratory are as follows. Speakership is self-selected. Competition for the floor is often fierce, but once a speaker has it, he is usually allowed to speak until he is finished, which he usually signals by sitting down or rejoining the surrounding audience. As an orator begins an *el ung* speech, he starts striding briskly in a more or less straight path as he speaks, usually brandishing an axe in one hand and sometimes a spear in the other. After covering a distance of about 10 metres, he pivots around abruptly and returns over the same course. He continues this, back and forth, for the duration of his speech.

The distinctive prosodic features of *el ung* are as follows. The extent of pitch variation from syllable to syllable is much less than in everyday Ku Waru: in *el ung*, sequences of anywhere from one or two to a couple of dozen syllables are pronounced on a single, nearly level pitch contour which terminates with an abrupt fall to an [a:::] or [o:::]. One or the other of these vowels is added to the last word of each line, to which it makes no other lexico-grammatical contribution other than to mark it as *el ung*, and to bound each line as a prosodic unit. There are no pauses within a line of *el ung*, but there are often pauses between lines. The length of the pause, and a change of *el ung* vowel can be significant in marking topical shifts, or otherwise bounding off one section of a speech from another (Merlan and Rumsey 1991: 149).

Apart from the distinctive prosodic and paralinguistic features of *el ung*, there are other features which are not unique to it but highly characteristic of it. One is the special 'segmentary' use of first and second person singular and dual number categories to refer to entire social units, exemplified above.[7] Another is the use of figurative language or 'bent speech' (*ung eke*) such as exemplified by line 6*f* above and lines 18–20 in Noma's speech below (for details see Rumsey 1986; Merlan and Rumsey 1991: 102–9).

Another characteristic of *el ung*, the one most relevant here, is extensive parallelism. These features are illustrated by the speech below, which was given by Noma, the leading 'big man' in the Kailge area where we did our fieldwork, to men who had come to receive a compensation payment from Noma's group.[8] Partial

---

[7] In Merlan and Rumsey (1991: 100–2) we present statistical evidence showing that the incidence of this usage is approximately 3.3 times higher in *el ung* oratory than in other oratory used at the same events.

[8] For the full context of this speech and further exegesis of it, see Merlan and Rumsey 1991: 147–52, 287–8.

or full repetition from line to line is shown on the transcript by braces to the left. Non-identical elements placed in a relation of full lexico-grammatical parallelism by this repetition are shown by underlining them. Pitch and length are shown (by superscripting and repeated vowels) on the first three lines only.

Speech by Kopia Noma, in el ung *oratorical style, 24 July 1983*

⌐ 1 i ^{yi}-ma-ooooooooooooooooooooooo	men!
L 2 i ^{yi}-ma-oooo	men!
3 <u>kunutapie peng kera pe</u>lka-ja-oooo	if there were a plume on the shield
⌐ 4 el adiyl tekir nyib pilyiylka-o	I would really think I'm fighting
5 <u>kera mek bulumingi-na te</u>lka-ja-o	if I fought on the back of a bird of paradise
L 6 el adiyl tekir nyib pilyiylka-o	I would really think I'm fighting
7 yu-nu laimkangi lyip tekir-o	Instead I'm just going around quietly
⌐ 8 <u>kaspis</u>-kiyl tekir-o	I'm just giving [money] for potatoes
L 9 <u>po pubu</u>-kiyl tekir-o	I'm just giving it for sugar cane
10 na-nga yiyl-a	my 'man'
11 mensik pukun pukun-a	you take it for him
⌐ 12 tikiyl kangayl-a	the man from Tikiyl
L 13 tikiyl sokudu pukun-a	you go into to Tikiyl
⌐ 14 idi kani-na-a	there, where, as you know
15 <u>kilkai</u> lelym-kiyl-a	there is a Kilkai spirit-cult place
L 16 idi kani-na-a	there, where, as you know
17 <u>maip</u> lelym-kiyl-a	there is a Maip spirit-cult place
18 idi manya suku kalya-na-a	and there, half sunk into the ground
19 karaip puruyl-te pelym-kiyl-a	there's the rotting trunk of a nothofagous beech tree
20 siyl-topa toba kanakun-a	watch out, lest you slip and fall on it
⌐ 21 mekin pukun kilkai-ne kuyini kanapa-a	if you want to take this [payment] and sacrifice to Kilkai
22 <u>kilkai</u>-ne kuyui-a	then go ahead and sacriface to Kilkai
L 23 maip-ne kuyini kanapa-a	if you want to take it and sacrifice to Maip
24 <u>maip</u>-ne kuyui-a	then go ahead and sacrifice to Maip
25 moni ilyi lepa nyim kanapa-a	this money which is here
⌐ 26 nu lyin kanapa-a	you take it
L 27 nu tid kanapa-a	I gave it to you
⌐ 28 mudika kit pilyiba	the Mudike will feel badly about it
L 29 mudika kasipa-a	Mudike Kasipa [man's name]
30 okun ilyi-nga ena lyirin kanurud kanilyi-a	I saw you come here and stay in the sun
31 adad ilyi koma lensikir-a	I'm carrying this hundred ['pounds', i.e. 200 kina] for you
32 ilyi-nga ok-lyi-o	come and get it

A simple example of full lexico-grammatical parallelism is in lines 8–9 with *kaspis* and *po pubu* as parallel terms. (By contrast, the paired terms in 26–7 and

28–9 are not in grammatically parallel positions; in 26 *nu* 'you' is the grammatical subject, controlling verb agreement, whereas in 27 *nu* is the object, with the verb marked for first person singular subject.) More complex examples are lines 3–6, where the repetition between lines 4 and 6 establishes a parallel between the whole of lines 3 and 5 (parts of which are also placed in a more specific parallel relation by the repeated ending); and 14–17, where the same is true of lines 14 and 16 in relation to lines 15 and 17.

The import of lines 3–7 of Noma's speech is that the fighting for which compensation is being paid was not very serious. No one was killed and only a few people were injured. Noma contrasts this with *real* fighting, which he characterizes by the parallel images in lines 3 and 5, both of which refer to ways of decorating the hardwood shields used by Ku Waru warriors to protect themselves against arrows.

The parallel figures in lines 8–9 are in thematic antithesis to those of lines 3 and 5 in that they present an image of the mundane as opposed to the extraordinary. They trivialize the payment which his group has presented, treating it as something like what we would call 'pocket money', suitable for use on market days to buy the small amounts of purchased food with which Ku Waru and neighbouring peoples supplement their diets of mainly home-grown foods. In lines 14–17 and 21–4 the paired terms are Maip and Kilkai. These refer to ancestral spirits associated with a place called Tikiyl, located along the track through the dense montane forest that lies between Noma's home at Kailge, where the money is being presented, and the recipients' homeland across the Tambul Range.

For other examples of parallelism I now turn to a quite different Ku Waru genre called *tom yaya kange*, a kind of chanted heroic tale. Like *el ung* oratory, *tom yaya kange* are divided into clearly bounded lines, marked both by line-terminating vowels, in this case *e* or *a*, and by intonational features. Unlike in *el ung*, most lines in *tom yaya kange* are not followed by a pause. In the Ku Waru area at least, most *tom yaya* performers use a metrically regular line, with five or six feet of equal measure, but anywhere between one and four syllables to the foot, with syllable length varying accordingly. Pitch patterns vary somewhat from performer to performer, but generally include a pitch rise to the tonic syllable in the third foot of the line and a fall to the last one (which generally consists of only one syllable). There are a small number of standard plots, which are variously elaborated by individual performers, drawing on a set of formulaic phrases and figures, most of which are in parallel form. Many of the tales have as their central character a small boy who defies his parents' admonitions to stay at home, goes out into foreign parts, and single-handedly performs heroic feats, usually including the slaying of enemy clansmen, winning their daughters' hands in marriage, or both. The same stock of tales and formulaic devices are current over a large area of the Western Highlands where Ku Waru and related dialects are spoken.

Here are the first forty-seven lines of a (much longer) *tom yaya* performance, again by Noma, who, in addition to being the leading orator at Kailge, happens also to be its most renowned composer and singer.

Excerpt from Tom Yaya *Chanted Tale by Noma, February 1997*

1 **kang mel we mel kaniyl e**	that small young lad
2 kang <u>mai pup</u> yaka nyirim e	the lad went from rest stop to rest stop
3 kang <u>komunga mong</u> yaka nyirim e	the lad went from mountain top to mountain top
4 <u>ukuni</u> yabu tobu midi nyirim e	he wanted to kill the Ukuni people
5 <u>kobulka</u> yabu tobu midi nyirim	he wanted to kill the Kobulka people
6 **kang mel we mel kaniyl e**	that small young lad
7 kang piditap mel kaniyl e	that neglected young lad
8 <u>pilyini</u> kub nai-ko nyirim e	and who's ever heard such a tale?
9 <u>kanuni</u> kub nai-ko nyirim e	and who's ever seen such a thing?
10 kang mai pup yaka nyirim	that boy strode from perch to perch
11 <u>kobulka</u> yabu tokur midi nyirim e	he wanted to kill the Kobulka people
12 <u>minyabi</u> yabu tokur midi nyirim e	he wanted to kill the Minyabi people
13 **kang mel we mel kaniyl e**	that small young lad
14 <u>pilyini</u> kub nai-ko nyirim e	and who's ever heard such a tale?
15 <u>kanuni</u> kub nai-ko nyirim	and who's ever seen such a thing?
16 <u>dala</u> lyipa kum midi turum e	he packed up his *dala* spear
17 <u>tibun</u> lyipa <u>kum</u> midi turum e	he packed up his *tibun* spear
18 <u>gaima</u> lyipa <u>aipa</u> midi turum	he shouldered his *gaima* axe
19 **kang mel we mel kaniyl e**	that small young lad
20 <u>kumuduka</u> yab tobu midi nyirim e	he wanted to kill the Kumuduka people
21 <u>tamuduka</u> yab tobu midi nyirim e	he wanted to kill the Tamuduka people
22 turum turum turungayl-ko mirim e	he fought till his weapons were blunt
23 gaima lyipa aipa midi turum e	he shouldered his *gaima* axe
24 **kang mel we mel kaniyl e**	that small young lad
25 kang mai komunga mel kaniyl e	was just like a mountain himself
26 kang <u>mai pup</u> yaka nyirim e	the boy went from rest stop to rest stop
27 kang <u>komunga mong</u> yaka nyirim e	the boy went from mountain top to mountain top
28 <u>pilyini-kub</u> nai-ko nyirim	and who's ever heard such a tale?
29 <u>kanuni-mel</u> nai-ko nyirim e	and who's ever seen such a thing?
30 **kang mel we mel kaniyl e**	that small young lad
31 turum turum turungayl-ko mirim e	he fought till his weapons were blunt
32 meba adapa lku-d midi urum e	he carried them around and brought them back to the house
33 <u>pilyini</u> kub nai ko nyirim e	and who's ever heard such a tale?
34 <u>kanuni</u> kub nai ko nyirim e	and who's ever seen such a thing?
35 **kang mel we mel kaniyl e**	that small young lad
36 meba meba lku-d midi urum e	he brought them home
37 *anum ab we mel kaniyl e*	and there stood his substitute mother
38 aba <u>koipa rolipa</u> midi <u>ngurum</u> e	she cooked in the earth oven and fed him
39 aba <u>kalapa kik</u> midi <u>tirim</u> e	she cooked in the hot coals and fed him
40 molupa kanapa kelipa midi purum	staying and seeing, he left
41 **kang mel we mel kaniyl e**	that small young lad
42 kang mel kupada mel mirim e	the boy took a spear
43 mepa ya lku midi urum	and brought it back home
44 nu nanga ama nyib kanakur e	'Can I really regard you as mother?'
45 nu kang nabi teda nyirim e	'Well what kind of a boy are you?' she said

$\begin{bmatrix} 46 & \underline{na}\ \underline{molup}\ \text{kit pilyikir nyirim} \\ 47 & \underline{nu}\ \underline{kanap}\ \text{kit pilyikir nyirim e} \end{bmatrix}$ 'I'm tired of staying here' he said
'I'm tired of you' she said

Like all such performances, Noma's displays a high degree of parallelism at several different levels. As in his *el ung* speech, the majority of lines are paired with one or more others in parallel sets, as shown again by braces and underlinings, at, 2–3, 4–5, 6–7, etc. At a higher level, shown here by boldface, the repetition of the refrain *kang mel we mel kaniyl e* (lines 1, 6, 13, 19, etc.) throughout the text establishes a frame within which the intervening sections are placed in a parallel relation with each other. At an even higher level, shown by boldface and italics, a distinct section of the tale is marked out between lines 37 and 40 by the alteration of the first phrase of this refrain from *kang mel we* 'that small young lad' to *anum ab* 'his mother', which then shifts back to *kang mel we* in line 41.

Now consider the kinds of elements that are brought together by these relations of parallelism. Lines 8–9, which are repeated in lines 14–15, 28–9, and 33–4 (and many more times later in the tale), are a standard refrain in *tom yaya* tales. The paired terms are the roots *pily-* 'to hear'/'to know'/'to sense' and *kan* 'to see'. The pairing highlights what they have in common as ways of knowing (cf. Strathern 1989). Other paired terms are as follows: lines 2–3, 26–7, places one stops at on walking tracks over rugged highland terrain (a *mai pup* is a resting place along a path near the top of a ridge which it crosses); lines 4–5, 11–12, 20–1, pairs of faraway tribes all in the Melpa speaking region to the east; 16–17, two types of hardwood spears used in battle; 38–9, the main ways of cooking, also *ngurum* and *tirim* both of which mean 'give' (remote past-3sg) but in different dialects; lines 46–7, 'you'/'I', and 'stay'/'see' (both non-final, first person).

Based on these two texts and some supplementary examples where appropriate, let me now offer some generalizations about the typical forms and uses of parallelism in Ku Waru.

First, in both texts the sets of parallel terms at the level of contiguous lines are almost always binary, i.e. with two members only. The only exception is in the second text, lines 16–18. This is only a partial exception, in that there is an asymmetrical relation among the three lines: 16 and 17 have one more element in common (*kum*) than either does with 18 (hence my complex bracketing of the three lines). (Note that line 18 is repeated five lines later in 23, this time unpaired with anything else.)

This preference for binary sets in Ku Waru might seem obvious in view of Jakobson's (1960) treatment of parallelism as *essentially* binaristic. But it is by no means universal in verbal traditions of the world. Parallel sets consisting of three or more lines occur regularly in, for example, Finnish folk verse (Steinitz 1934: 104–9, 160–2), the Mayan *Popol Vuh* (Tedlock 1987: 149 ff.; cf. Edmonson 1970: 16–23); and Kuna *ikar* chants (Sherzer 1983: 120 ff.; Howe 1986: 38–42).

Second, unlike in many parallelistic traditions, such as the ancient Hebrew (Lowth 1971), Rotinese (Fox 1971, 1988), or Toda (Emeneau 1937), none of the pairings here is in any way obligatory. While some parallel pairings are more likely than others, in neither of these two genres (nor any other Ku Waru genre, as far as we know) are there any lexical items which *must* be paired at all,[9] much less with some specific pair partner.

The third thing I want to point out about these texts concerns the kinds of semantic relationships there are between the parallel terms. This can be brought out by comparing these two Ku Waru genres with some other poetic traditions from elsewhere in the world. In Kmhmu (a Mon-Khmer language of highland Burma-Thailand-Laos-Vietnam), Proschan (1992) shows that paired terms can be related by hyponymy or synecdoche ('upper body'/'arm' etc.). Proschan notes that this has also been reported from other areas of the world. In some traditions (e.g. Peruvian Quechua, where it is quite typical) the unmarked term regularly precedes the marked (Mannheim 1987: 282); in others the reverse; while in others, including Kmhmu, the order varies freely (Proschan 1992: 3–4). In yet other traditions, hierarchical relations between paired terms are infrequent or unknown. This seems to be true, for example, across much or all of eastern Indonesia, if we may judge from the various reports in Fox (1988) which generally conform to Fox's claim about Rotinese that the relevant 'dyadic sets are essentially neutral pairs; one element is not "superior" to another element' (Fox 1971: 247).

The same is true in Ku Waru. Thus, note that none of the pairings in either text above involves a privative or otherwise asymmetrical relationship between the paired terms. Rather, each of the pairings realizes or suggests a kind of covert class which can be extrapolated from what the two terms have in common. So for example, what *kaspis* (potatoes) and *po pubu* (sugar cane species) have in common is that both are raised in the Tambul district (where the recipients of Noma's compensation payment live) for sale at local and regional markets. Quite a different covert class could be suggested by pairing *kaspis* with, for example, *ka* 'car', as the relevant aspect of *kaspis* would then no longer be that it is a minor cash crop (since it does not share this feature with *ka*), but that it is a European-introduced item. Likewise in the *tom yaya* text quite a different aspect of *komunga mong* 'mountain top' would become relevant if it were paired with *kolya para* 'valley floor' rather than *mai pup* 'resting place'. Compare also the way in which different attributes of *tibun* (spear type) become relevant as it is alternatively paired with *dala* (spear type) (lines 16–17) and *gaima* (axe type) (lines 17–18).

11.8. KU WARU PAIRING COMPOUNDS

The final Ku Waru linguistic device I want to consider is a kind of compound which is formed by putting two nouns together in sequence and adding after them a suffix *-sil*, which can be glossed as 'pair of', e.g. *lapa-mal-sil* 'a/the pair of father

---

[9] The principles of pairing here are distinct from those which apply in the kinds of compounds described in s. 11.8. But as I discuss there, the compounds too are quite open ended in that alternative pairings are possible for a given term.

(*lapa*) and son (*mal*)', *kib-ki-sil* 'the pair of leg (*kib*) and arm (*ki*)', *obi-kebi-sil* 'the pair of penis (*obi*) and vagina (*kebi*)'. These are the kinds of expressions cited from the Melpa language by Strauss in my quote from him in Section 11.2 above.

From the discussion there it should be clear that, based on our fieldwork with the neighbouring Ku Waru people, Merlan and I fully concur in the emphasis placed by Strauss and subsequent ethnographers upon pairing in this area of New Guinea. But if anything, they have underestimated its distinctiveness. To see why, let us consider some more examples of Ku Waru pairings—ones which are harder to interpret than the above in that the meanings do not follow as simply from the sum of their parts, but which in that respect are actually more typical of the range of occurring types.

1. *lopa-kera(-sil)* '(the pair) marsupial–bird', i.e. hunted animals of the forest
2. *owa-lopa(-sil)* '(the pair) dog–marsupial', i.e. chronic antagonists
3. *kung-owa(-sil)* '(the pair) pig–dog', i.e. domestic animals, or people with uncontrolled appetites
4. *kung-langi(-sil)* '(the pair) pork–vegetables', i.e. food
5. *kung-kola koluwa (-sil)* '(the pair) pig–cowrie shell', i.e. valuables, currency
6. *kung-sumuly* 'pig–gold–lipped pearlshell', i.e. major valuables
7. *kung-ab-sil* 'the pair of pig–woman', i.e. domestic wealth
8. *mulu-mai(-sil)* '(the pair of) sky/mountain–ground', i.e. the world
9. *ku-mai(-sil)* '(the pair) stone–ground', i.e. permanent/indestructible things
10. *me-mije(-sil)* '(the pair) taro–yams', i.e. foods eaten on special occasions (grown mainly by men)
11. *kim-ga(-sil)* '(the pair) sweet potatoes–greens', i.e. everyday foods (grown mainly by women)
12. *po-tauwu-sil* 'the pair of sugar cane–bananas', i.e. snack foods (both eaten raw and hence can be picked and offered to guests at short notice)
13. *tok-upiya(-sil)* '(the pair) frog–grasshopper', i.e. small, common things (sometimes eaten, but not highly prized)
14. *temani-kange-sil* 'the pair of *temani* stories–*kange* stories', i.e. stories
15. *mis-man(-sil)* '(the pair) Roman Catholic mass–(Lutheran) prayer/invocation', i.e. Christianity
16. *oma-rais(-sil)* '(the pair) (canned) fish–rice', i.e. imported foods obtainable only with money
17. *gu-pengi-sil* 'the pair of tooth–head', i.e. inalienable parts of oneself (expression used, for example, of one's land, which is not to be given away lightly)
18. *uj-ku-sil* 'the pair of wood–stone', i.e. things used to cook in an earth oven; *uj-ku teamiyl*, lit. 'Let's do wood and stone', i.e. Let's cook in an earth oven
19. *tepi-keri-sil* 'the pair of fire–mouth', i.e. things which 'eat' (NB Like many other New Guinea languages, Ku Waru has a single verb which means both 'burn' and 'eat'.)

What these kinds of pairings do is construct a kind of covert superclass by juxtaposing two terms which share some common characteristic on the basis of which the larger class can be inferred (rather like our use of the phrase 'et cetera' or 'and so on'). For example, the Ku Waru phrase (1) above, *lopa-kera(-sil)*, glossed literally as '(the pair of) marsupial and bird', actually serves as a cover term for all hunted creatures of the forest, of which these two are prototypical instances.

Now consider this pairing in relation to (2) *owa-lopa(-sil)* and (3) *kung-owa-(-sil)*. There can be no fixed, taxonomic relationships among the three classes associated with each of these pairings, not only because a single term may enter into more than one pairing, but because the relevant semantic features of a single such term can vary freely from one pairing to another, this or that feature becoming relevant by association with the other term. So while what is relevant about *lopa* in (1) is its arboreal habitat and desirability as game, these characteristics become irrelevant in (2), where what matters is the chronic antagonism between marsupials and dogs, this being an expression for any pair or set of actors who, as we say, 'fight like cats and dogs'. The same kind of potential openness of possible pairings of a single term is further illustrated by (3)–(7), which show *kung* 'pig' in five different combinations, and by (8)–(9) which show *mai* 'ground, soil' in two. As we have remarked elsewhere:

The various semantic characteristics that become relevant for such pairings are usually not what Western theorists would consider *definitional* or *denotative* features but rather, contingent or 'connotative' ones. They are not fixed specifications within some abstract, formal structure that we can call *the* Ku Waru (or Melpa) language.[10] Rather, they are aspects of people's myriad common experiences of the two sorts of things which are paired—common, that is, to people who share in a particular form of life—one in which, for example, pigs and dogs sleep indoors [albeit not both at the fire], birds and marsupials live mainly in uncultivated areas, where they are hunted by men, etc. Given a particular set of lexical forms (linguistic 'types') and a shared range of experiences of typical applications of them (contextualized 'tokens'), almost any aspect of that shared experience can become relevant, according to what is common to both of the paired types . . .

Thus, unlike the lexical categories themselves (and the grammatical structures of compounding which they employ), these pairings are not necessarily elements of linguistic structure per se. They range from fully standard 'lexicalized' ones such as /*yi-ab*/ 'man–woman' for 'person' (widespread in Papuan languages) to highly innovative ones arising from particular historical circumstances, or even made up for particular occasions. (Merlan and Rumsey 1991: 115–16)

11.9. CONCLUSIONS

In Sections 11.5–11.8 above I have discussed, respectively:

1. the grammar of Ku Waru existential clauses;

[10] I note here, however, that many of the aspects of lexical meaning which most linguists would consider connotative are treated as definitional by Wierzbicka (e.g. 1985), who includes much more information in her definitions than most other linguists. The same is true of Langacker (1987–91) whose model of 'cognitive grammar' effaces the distinction between dictionary and encyclopedia.

2. some uses of the first and second person singular and dual person/number categories among the Ku Waru people;
3. some aspects of Ku Waru people's use of parallelism;
4. some facts about the form and meaning of Ku Waru pairing compounds.

What can we conclude from all this about the relation between language structure and other aspects of Ku Waru culture?

As I have already discussed (in 11.5) regarding point 1, and as the comparison with 2–4 should make clear, 1 is the best candidate (and probably the only one) for being considered an instance of 'ethnosyntax' in the 'narrow' sense of the term (Enfield, Introduction; Goddard, this volume). While pattern-consistency of this kind between grammar and (the rest of) culture is interesting to find, I am rather inclined to agree with Ken Hale that it is 'a matter of luck, a chance happening' when such a 'neat correspondence' is found (Hale 1986: 237).[11] For as Boas, Sapir, and even Whorf realized, grammar is a relatively autonomous system with functional prerequisites (and perhaps universal underlying 'parameters') of its own that tend to favour the development and reproduction of certain broadly similar structural features even among historically unrelated languages spoken in very different cultural settings.

What I think we can expect to find far more often are instances of ethnosyntax in the 'broad' sense, such as in the examples discussed in Sections 11.6–11.8 above, where certain cross-linguistically recognizable formal devices get *used* in culture-specific ways. And in order to understand what is going on in such cases, one needs to recognize along with Sapir that 'all grammars leak' and take account of other aspects of the sociocultural contexts in which the language is used.

Consider for example the Ku Waru person–number categories as used in the contexts discussed above. The meanings of the first and second person singular and dual categories as used in oratorical contexts differ from their everyday meanings, in ways that cannot be accounted for without allowing for the kinds of segmentary social identities in terms of which Ku Waru people conduct the events at which the oratory is performed. As I have shown above (cf. Rumsey 1986; Merlan and Rumsey 1991: ch. 5) this oratory has a number of prosodic and paralinguistic features which serve as cues, or 'keying devices', which mark a shift from the everyday values of the relevant person–number categories to their segmentary ones. So there is a kind of systematic polysemy here, but it is not a kind of polysemy that can be disambiguated by the linguistic context alone (like the one, for example, between ergative and instrumental case in some languages, or between the two senses of 'Flying planes can be dangerous'). Rather, it is disambiguated (if at all) by the occurrence of the group-personifying usages in very specific social contexts where the relevant interacting parties are understood to be segmentary social groupings (*talapi*) and 'big men' (*yi nuim*) who personify them.

---

[11] I also agree with the qualification Hale immediately adds, that 'This could, however, be wrong, and the search for such correlations should never be abandoned' (Hale 1986: 237).

For understanding what goes on at those events, it is best to study the forms of person reference, and speech in general, as an aspect of social action, in which it plays an integral part along with other non-discursive aspects of social practice. The relevant person/number categories are of course also integral to the Ku Waru language, its system of verb agreement, clause chaining, switch-reference marking, etc. as discussed above in Section 11.3, and formally comparable to the person–number systems of languages around the world. This thoroughgoing two-facedness is characteristic of indexical categories, which sit, Janus-like, at the interface between language and the rest of the world. Or, as David Wilkins (personal communication) has put it, they are especially likely to be an area of grammar where 'language meets culture' in the form of 'constructions with general semantics' being used in 'culture-specific ways'.

Roughly the same is true, I would say, of parallelism. If Jakobson (1960) was right that parallelism is a universal feature of language in its poetic function, its mere presence is unlikely to reveal anything very specific about the societies and cultures in which it is used. But from the examples I have discussed above I think we can conclude that there can be highly culture-specific aspects to the *way* in which parallelism is used. I have tried to show that Ku Waru parallelism in two otherwise very different discourse genres can be characterized by the conjunction of at least the following three features: (1) a strong preference for sets of parallel lines to consist of two only as opposed to three or more; (2) for any given lexeme, relatively great latitude as to what other lexemes can occur in parallel position with it; (3) a strong dispreference for privative or otherwise asymmetrical semantic relations between terms occurring in parallel positions. None of these features is logically intrinsic to parallelism nor universally present in parallelistic traditions around the world, as shown by counter-examples I have cited along the way.[12] And each is just one manifestation of a characteristic Ku Waru form of pairing which is evident in a wide range of other domains, as discussed above.

One of the other ways in which this mode of pairing is evident is in the form and semantics of the Ku Waru compounds I have discussed above. As will be evident from my discussion there, the typical patterning of these corresponds closely to that of Ku Waru parallelism in each of the three respects: (1) they are strictly binary; (2) nouns are not restricted to a single fixed pairing but productively recombinable into alternative ones; (3) the relation between the two terms is generally a symmetrical one rather than privative or hierarchical. And as should be clear from Section 11.2, precisely analogous characteristics to these also pertain to the main forms of social relationship among Ku Waru tribes and exchange partners, which are strictly binary, non-transitive, and non-hierarchical.

Although pairing as a social practice is highly durable, we found that many of the actual pairings of *talapi*, especially of the serial and oppositional types, were regarded as recent and potentially short-lived creations. Over the long run, what

---

[12] For further details see Rumsey 1995.

gets reproduced most effectively is not specific pairings, but rather the practice of pairing itself, which is embodied both linguistically and in other ways—for example within the *el ung* performance genre by back and forth striding of the orator as he speaks, the stepwise alternation between two pitches within each line, and the alternation at a higher level between the two different line-terminating vowels. All of these are iconic of each other, and all together comprise, in Peircean terms, a 'diagram' of pairing qua social relationship (cf. Urban 1986: 35–6, 39). So too does extensive parallelism of the kinds exemplified in the texts above.

Merlan and I have argued that the features of pairing as a form of social relationship are consistent with the way pairing works as a classificatory trope in Ku Waru (Merlan and Rumsey 1991: chs. 8–9). The classes which one constructs in this way have a kind of open-endedness to them which cannot be captured by any taxonomic analogue we might construct for them, for the paired terms typically do not by themselves exhaust the potential membership of the class. Rather, the pairing of just those two serves to suggest a common feature on the basis of which the class can be extrapolated.

Dennis Tedlock has come close to capturing what is going on here with the phrase 'complementary metonyms', by which he describes the operation of similar tropes in Quiché (Tedlock 1987: 148), where, for example, the expression *caj-ulew* 'sky-earth' (just as in Ku Waru example 8 among the pairings listed in Section 11.8 above) has the abstract sense something like 'world', of which each of the paired terms is a (synecdochic) metonym. But the notion of 'complementarity' does not appropriately describe the nature of Ku Waru pairing in general (*pace* Strauss 1990, quoted above) as it implies that the complementary terms together comprise a well-bounded whole, whereas the trope of pairing instead provides reference points for potentially open ended and innovatory extrapolation. See, for example, Merlan and Rumsey (1991: 156–97, 210–14) where we describe how a local women's work cooperative drew upon their 'in-between' status with respect to men's segmentary politics to identify themselves with the avowedly trans-segmentary regime of 'government law' and intervene on the battlefield between two opposing alliances, effectively pacifying them where armed police would not intervene (Merlan and Rumsey 1991: ch. 7).

To return once more to the notion of ethnosyntax in the 'broad' sense, both Ku Waru parallelism and the Ku Waru pairing construction are linguistic devices which are more or less comparable to ones found elsewhere around the world, but which are used by Ku Waru people in culturally specific ways. This is not a matter of absolute determination, where linguistic form exerts a stranglehold on people's ways of thinking or acting. The three features by which I have characterized Ku Waru parallelism are strong tendencies, not categorical constraints: Ku Waru speakers do occasionally construct parallel sets with three or more parallel terms, and some of the same sets of parallel terms crop up rather often notwithstanding the overall productivity of the system. And with respect to the pairing compounds, there is a wide range of occurring semantic types, notwithstanding the strong preference for the open-ended sort. What is most interesting though is that, given the many ways in which these two distinct formal devices *can* be used without violating any categorical rules of Ku Waru grammar or poetics, the ways in which the two devices actually *are* used tend to be channelled in exactly the same culture-specific directions—or, as Whorf (1956: 158) would have put it, 'co-ordinated in a certain framework of consistency', of the kind that he called 'fashions of speaking'.

But one of the main points I hope to have demonstrated here is that these are not only fashions of *speaking*, or even of thinking. From a Ku Waru perspective, there is no reason to separate parallelism or pairing as specifically linguistic phenomena from the wider social field in which the activity of what they call 'making twos' is practised. Just as we have seen above for the oratorical uses of *na* 'I', *nu* 'thou', *olto* 'we two', and *eni* 'you (pl)', it is not so much the linguistic resources themselves, but the patterning in what is *done* with them that is of most interest for understanding how grammar meets (the rest of) culture.

REFERENCES

BARTH, FREDRIK. 1975. *Ritual and Knowledge among the Baktaman of New Guinea*. New Haven: Yale University Press.

DUMONT, LOUIS. 1970. *Homo Hierarchicus*. Chicago: University of Chicago Press.

EDMONSON, MUNRO. 1970. 'Notes on a new translation of the Popol Vuh'. *Alcheringa*, 1: 14–23.

EMENEAU, MURRAY B. 1937. 'The songs of the Todas'. *Proceedings of the American Philosophical Society*, 77: 543–60.

FOLEY, WILLIAM. 1986. *Papuan Languages of New Guinea*. Cambridge: Cambridge University Press.

FOX, JAMES J. 1971. 'Semantic parallelism in Rotinese ritual language'. *Bijdragen tot de Taal-, Land- en Volkenkunde*, 127: 215–55.

——1977. 'Roman Jakobson and the comparative study of parallelism'. In C. H. van Schooneveld and D. Armstrong (eds.), *Roman Jakobson: Echoes of his Scholarship*. Lisse: Peter de Ridder Press, 59–90.

——1988. *To Speak in Pairs: Essays on the Ritual Languages of Eastern Indonesia*. Cambridge: Cambridge University Press.

GOLDMAN, LAURENCE. 1983. *Talk Never Dies: The Language of Huli Disputes*. London: Tavistock.

HALE, KENNETH. 1986. 'Notes on world view and semantic categories: some Warlpiri examples'. In Pieter Muysken and Henk van Riemsdijk (eds.), *Features and Projections*. Dortrecht: Foris, 233–54.

HERCUS, LUISE, and WHITE, ISOBEL. 1973. 'Perception of kinship structure reflected in the Adnjamathanha pronouns'. In *Papers in Australian Linguistics*, 6. Canberra: Pacific Linguistics, 47–72.

HOWE, JAMES. 1986. *The Kuna Gathering: Contemporary Village Politics in Panama*. Austin: University of Texas Press.

JAKOBSON, ROMAN. 1960. 'Closing statement: linguistics and poetics'. In T. A. Sebeok (ed.), *Style in Language*. Cambridge, Mass.: MIT Press, 350–77.

LANCY, DAVID. F., and STRATHERN, ANDREW. 1981. '"Making twos": pairing as an alternative to the taxonomic mode of representation'. *American Anthropologist*, 83: 773–95.
LANGACKER, RONALD W. 1987–91. *Foundations of Cognitive Grammar*, 2 vols. Stanford, Calif.: Stanford University Press.
LEDERMAN, RENA. 1980. 'Who speaks here? Formality and the concept of gender in Mendi, Highland Papua New Guinea'. *Journal of the Polynesian Society*, 89: 479–98.
LÉVI-STRAUSS, CLAUDE. 1969. *The Elementary Structures of Kinship*. Boston: Beacon Press (first pub. 1947).
LOWTH, ROBERT. 1971. *Lectures on the Sacred Poetry of the Hebrews*, 2 vols. New York: Garland (first pub. 1753).
MANNHEIM, BRUCE. 1987. 'Couplets and oblique contexts: the social organization of a folksong'. *Text*, 7: 265–88.
MAUSS, MARCEL. 1954. *The Gift: Forms and Functions of Exchange in Archaic Societies*, trans. I. Cunnison. London: Cohen and West (first pub. 1925).
MERLAN, FRANCESCA, ROBERTS, STEVEN, and RUMSEY, ALAN. 1997. 'New Guinea "classificatory verbs" and Australian noun classification: a typological comparison'. In Mark Harvey and Nicholas Reid (eds.), *Noun Classification in Australian Languages*. Amsterdam: John Benjamins, 163–203.
——and RUMSEY, ALAN. 1986. 'A marriage dispute in the Nebilyer Valley, Western Highlands Province, Papua New Guinea'. *Pacific Linguistics*, A74: 69–180.
————1991. *Ku Waru: Language and Segmentary Politics in the Western Nebilyer Valley, Papua New Guinea*. Cambridge: Cambridge University Press.
PROSCHAN, FRANK. 1992. 'Poetic parallelism in Kmhmu verbal arts: from texts to performances'. *University of California at Los Angeles Selected Reports in Ethnomusicology*, 9: 1–31.
RUBEL, PAULA, and ROSMAN, ABRAHAM. 1978. *Your Own Pigs You May Not Eat: A Comparative Study of New Guinea Societies*. Chicago: University of Chicago Press.
RUMSEY, ALAN. 1986. 'Oratory and the politics of metaphor in the New Guinea Highlands'. In T. Threadgold, E. A. Grosz, G. Kress, and M. A. K. Halliday (eds.), *Language, Semiotics, Ideology*. Sydney: Sydney Association for Studies in Society and Culture, 283–96.
——1989. 'Grammatical person and social agency in the New Guinea Highlands'. In B. Music, R. Graczyk, and C. Wiltshire (eds.), *Papers from the 25th Annual Regional Meeting of the Chicago Linguistic Society; Part Two; Parasession on Language in Context*. Chicago: Chicago Linguistic Society, 242–53.
——1990. 'Wording, meaning, and linguistic ideology'. *American Anthropologist*, 92: 346–61.
——1995. 'Pairing and parallelism in the New Guinea Highlands'. In P. Silberman and J. Loftlin (eds.), *SALSA II: Proceedings of the Second Annual Symposium about Language and Society Austin* (*Texas Linguistic Forum*, 34), 108–18.
——1999a. 'The white man as cannibal in the New Guinea Highlands'. In Laurence Goldman (ed.), *The Anthropology of Cannibalism*. Westport, Conn.: Bergin & Garvey, pp. 105–21.
——1999b. 'The personification of social totalities in the Pacific'. *Journal of Pacific Studies*, 23: 48–70.
——2000. 'Agency, personhood and the "I" of discourse in the Pacific and beyond'. *Journal of the Royal Anthropological Institute*, 6: 101–15.

RUMSEY, ALAN. Forthcoming. 'Men stand, women sit: on the grammaticalization of posture verbs in Papuan languages, its bodily basis and cultural correlates'. In J. Newman (ed.) *The Linguistics of Sitting, Standing, and Lying*. Amsterdam: John Benjamins.

SAHLINS, MARSHALL. 1985. *Islands of History*. Chicago: University of Chicago Press.

SHERZER, JOEL. 1983. *Kuna Ways of Speaking*. Austin: University of Texas Press.

STEINITZ, WOLFGANG. 1934. *Der Parallelismus in der Finnisch-karelischen Volksdichtung*. Folklore Fellows' Communications 115. Helsinki: Suomalainen Tiedeakatemia, Academia Scientarum Fennica.

STRATHERN, ANDREW. 1971. *The Rope of Moka*. Cambridge: Cambridge University Press.

——1975. 'Veiled speech in Mount Hagen'. In Maurice Bloch (ed.), *Political Language and Oratory in Traditional Society*. London: Academic Press, 185–203.

——1989. 'Melpa dream interpretation and the concept of hidden truth'. *Ethnology*, 28: 301–16.

STRAUSS, HERMANN. 1990. *The Mi-Culture of the Mount Hagen People, Papua New Guinea*. Ethnology Monographs 13. Pittsburgh: University of Pittsburgh (first pub. 1962).

TANNEN, DEBORAH. 1989. *Talking Voices: Repetition, Dialogue, and Imagery in Conversational Discourse*. Cambridge: Cambridge University Press.

TEDLOCK, DENNIS. 1987. 'Hearing a voice in an ancient text'. In Joel Sherzer and Anthony Woodbury (eds.), *Native North American Discourse*. Cambridge: Cambridge University Press, 140–75.

URBAN, GREG. 1986. 'The Semiotic functions of Macro-parallelism in the Shokleng origin myth'. In Joel Sherzer and Greg Urban (eds.), *Native South American Discourse*. Berlin: Mouton de Gruyter, 15–57.

WHORF, BENJAMIN LEE. 1956. *Language, Thought, and Reality*. New York: Wiley.

WIERZBICKA, ANNA. 1985. *Lexicography and Conceptual Analysis*. Ann Arbor: Karoma.

12

From Common Ground to Syntactic Construction: Associated Path in Warlpiri

JANE SIMPSON

12.1. INTRODUCTION

It is widely assumed that both words and grammatical structure can signal meanings (semantic or pragmatic). As Fillmore, Kay, and O'Connor (1988: 534) write:

A language can associate semantic information with structures larger than elementary lexical items and can associate semantic interpretation principles with syntactic configurations larger and more complex than those definable by means of single phrase-structure rules.

Most work on the semantics of syntax has concentrated on idiomatic constructions, such as the 'let alone' construction (Fillmore, Kay, and O'Connor 1988), whose meanings cannot be easily computed from the meanings of their parts plus a simple rule of composition, or on constructions which appear to have semantic restrictions on which members of a category can appear in the construction, such as the Japanese adversative passive (Wierzbicka 1988), or constructions whose meaning is paralleled by that of some morpheme in another language, such as the *it*-cleft construction (Mohanan and Mohanan 1999).

Wierzbicka takes further the idea that constructions have meaning, and argues, along with Goddard (this volume), that constructions can embody in their semantics 'a culture-specific "message"'. That is, not only can they have meaning, but that meaning is linked in an interesting way to the cultural practices of the speakers. Goddard calls this ethnosyntax in the narrow sense, the study of how syntactic constructions express certain culture-specific meanings and ways of thinking. This is to be distinguished from ethnosyntax in the 'broad' sense, as in Enfield's claim (this volume) that cultural practices can constrain implications arising from realizations of certain constructions (for example, a particular realization of a serial verb construction in Lao, *fang²-thêêt⁴* 'listen-sermon', implicates for the Lao hearer sitting as part of the typical religious performance of *fang²-thêêt⁴*). This

I thank David Wilkins and Felix Ameka who started this chapter off, Nick Enfield for critical editing, and Barry Alpher, David Nash, Franca Tamisari, Anna Wierzbicka, Eve Sweetser, and participants at the Ethnosyntax Workshop, Australian Linguistics Institute, 1998, for helpful comments.

implication is cancellable by adding a stance verb 'lie', which furthermore indicates that the person lying is not performing the proper ritual.

I regard as uncontroversial both the claim that constructions (at least idiomatic ones) have meanings, and the claim that cultural practice may be involved in the implications of a particular realization of a construction (as sitting is implied by $fang^2\text{-}th\hat{e}\hat{e}t^4$). However, the claim that it is possible to carry out ethnosyntax in the narrow sense is not uncontroversial. It is a twofold claim: a claim that the meanings of some syntactic constructions involve cultural concerns, and a claim that it is possible to find out what the cultural concerns underlying a syntactic construction are. This 'narrow ethnosyntax hypothesis' accords with Wierzbicka's claim that one can examine a culture through examining the meanings of key words used by the speakers (Wierzbicka 1997). It is an important hypothesis, because finding a link between cultural concerns and syntactic constructions has implications for theories of the relation between language and society, since syntactic constructions can permeate a language to a greater extent than particular lexical items can, and since speakers are less conscious of the meanings of syntactic constructions than of words.

If ethnosyntax is a field of study distinct from the study of the semantics of syntactic constructions, then there must be some way of distinguishing 'culture' from language. If they cannot be distinguished, then any attempt to describe the meaning of a construction is 'ethnosyntax', and so the 'semantics of syntax' is always 'ethnosyntax' (see Enfield 2000a). It is then hard to falsify the claim that 'Speakers of language X share value Y because we can find a component relating to that value in several words and constructions of their language.'

Both parts of the Narrow Ethnosyntax Hypothesis require notions of sharing language, and of 'culture'. I discuss these first, pointing at the same time to difficulties in determining 'culture'. Suppose we start by looking at language at the level of the individual. I take it for granted that no two individuals speak alike, that is, have wholly identical vocabulary and syntactic constructions, assign identical meanings to them, and use them in identical ways. Thus A and B may both use the word *tiger* with the same denotation, some similar connotations, and some different connotations, depending on how they learned the word, who they learned it from, what associations they have with tigers, and so on. However, speakers of the same language do understand each other, more or less, and so usually assign similar meanings (senses) to words and constructions. Grammars and dictionaries contain approximations of these shared meanings. Thus we have a notion of shared language, without assuming that all speakers assign identical meanings to words and constructions. The approximations of shared meanings of constructions are the province of the semantics of syntax. The hypothesized connection between these shared meanings and the practices and concerns of a social network of speakers is the province of ethnosyntax in the narrow sense.

If there is a real connection between the language of a people and their non-linguistic concerns and cultural practices, then we must show how people's non-linguistic concerns and practices could get embodied in the linguistic constructions they use (Wierzbicka 1992: 375). We do not expect people's 'culture' to appear magically in their language. Now, the domain of what is taken to be 'culture' is enormous: all human activity in, and understandings of, the world. A promising starting point for the path from non-linguistic concerns to language is likely to be what people talk about, common topics of conversation. Following that come shared expectations and assumptions about how people will or should behave (Enfield 2000*b*), how the world is, and shared assumptions about building conversations. These represent the aspect of 'culture'[1] that is probably most relevant to the Narrow Ethnosyntax Hypothesis. Following Clark (1996) I call them 'common ground', rather than 'culture', to avoid the essentialism associated with the word 'culture' (Fabian 1991). The syntactic construction-meaning pairs which we share are, as linguistic constructs, part of common ground, but I assume for the moment that we can distinguish linguistic constructs from the other parts of common ground. I discuss the three parts of this non-linguistic common ground briefly, and will refer to it simply as 'common ground'.

12.2. COMMON GROUND

12.2.1. *Common topics of conversation*

If people talk about something a lot, then it has some importance to them. Knowledge of that thing is likely to form a part of common ground between members of a social network. Moreover, the more people talk about something, the more likely that they will need mnemonics, shorthand ways of referring to it, which will lead to forming new words and perhaps to new constructions, as Polivanov (1974*a*: 195–6) showed for Standard Russian after the Bolshevik revolution. Likewise if people engage in a particular activity a lot, then it has some importance to them. Usually, people will tend to talk a lot about shared activities. What people talk about will be observable in records of the language of the time.

12.2.2. *Shared expectations and assumptions*

Members of a social network share some expectations of how people behave, or should behave in certain situations, and how the world is. To some extent such expectations are based on experience, on how, say, a bus conductor will behave when offered a bus fare. In such clear exchanges of goods and services, the need for speed and efficiency of exchange leads to routine ways of asking, accepting, and so on. These routines are important and relatively easy for outsiders to learn

---

[1] While other cultural practices are relevant to ethnosyntax in the broad sense (such as patterns used in art, ways of cooking, approaches to birth and death), I do not see how to propose a direct route from these to the evolution of a syntactic construction, except indirectly as topics of conversation and sources of metaphors.

(often featuring in language-learning textbooks), from a combination of observation and general principles (inference formation, relevance, the idea that people have wants and thoughts; in this case 'I want something. I believe this person can give me what I want'). Again, such routines may result in new mnemonics: words and syntactic constructions. However, most of our interactions are not routines with well-defined content, but are rather casual conversation, pleasantries, gossip, plans, reminiscences, which contain some routines, some new content, and involve shared assumptions about what is interesting, funny, or appropriate. Such shared assumptions are much harder to learn by observation than how to buy a bus ticket. Outsiders tend to infer them from conversations and subsequent actions.

12.2.3. *Shared assumptions of how to build conversations*

Carrying out conversations also involves information like: how one coordinates the conversation, how one holds oneself and gestures, where one looks, when one can interrupt, what turn-taking involves. Conversation-structuring devices could enter the regular lexicon as words and syntactic constructions. Again, these are learned from participation (except perhaps for the explicit teaching of conversational practice to autistic people).

Topics of conversation, routines for carrying out certain activities (including conversations), assumptions and expectations of how people behave, are learned throughout childhood and adulthood. We are constantly faced with new situations, and we adapt our behaviour according to our experience, our routines, our knowledge, and general principles of reasoning. That is, common ground is constantly changing.

12.3. A PROCEDURE FOR CARRYING OUT ETHNOSYNTAX?

I now move to the second part of the Narrow Ethnosyntax Hypothesis, that it is possible to determine the structure–meaning pairs and the cultural practices connected to them. The need for some sort of procedure is well illustrated by the danger of circularity in characterizing the grammar–culture connection (see Enfield, Introduction to this volume, s. 1.3.5). To avoid this, I propose a procedure for carrying out ethnosyntax in the narrow sense:

1. identify the construction (syntactic or morphological);
2. identify a meaning (or a pragmatic inference or function) associated with the construction;
3. propose a relationship between this meaning and some shared topic of conversation, assumption, or expectation of the speakers;
4. provide evidence that this shared topic of conversation, assumption, or expectation is, or has been, highly salient for the speakers (i.e. something they often mention or do, or which often seems to inform their actions);

5. provide an explanation based in conversational practice as to how the construction came to exist and bear the proposed meaning (or pragmatic inference or function);
6. look at similar constructions in other languages and check to see if the proposed connection between conversational practice and grammatical construction holds. In the strongest case the connection would be causal.

I now discuss the steps of the procedure, focusing on likely difficulties.

12.4. STEPS 1 AND 2: IDENTIFYING A CONSTRUCTION AND ITS MEANING

We must start by looking for particular constructions (Wierzbicka 1992: 373), not at the language as a whole. Reasons for dismissing the claim that '*language as a whole given system* is conditioned by *contemporary* social factors' were given by Polivanov in his critique of a simplistic linking of societal evolution and language evolution:

In language we depend more than elsewhere (for example, in material and spiritual culture, art, literature, etc.) on tradition obediently reflecting in our words the facts of the linguistic consciousness of long-past generations, the majority of which are strange to us even in their ethnic names. To speak of the full adequacy of the language for a given epoch for its social life or cultural content, with the intention of *explaining* from them all the language facts existing synchronically in this period, means, in the first place, forgetting that the same sentence *moj brat umer* 'my brother died' can be understood by us in the 20th century as well as by a speaker of Russian in the 12th century; forgetting, in the second place, that two groups can be found with remarkable similarities in the area of social life and with completely different languages; and forgetting, in the third place, that two related languages, even with maximal differences in the facts of the social life of their groups, usually continue the system received by them from the common source and introduce individual modifications only in gradual succession and, moreover, each time only on the scale of parts of this system (otherwise the danger of losing a common language for two contiguous generations would arise). (Polivanov 1974a: 199)

Polivanov did not intend his argument to preclude the possibility of particular words and constructions having meanings that relate to the common ground of contemporary speakers; indeed he considers 'the study of causal connections between socioeconomic and linguistic phenomena' as part of 'sociological linguistics' (1974b: 177). But his argument does make four important points. First, the words and grammatical constructions that we use are by and large those that our parents and grandparents used. Their continued existence merely shows that those meanings were highly salient to speakers when they were introduced, not that they continue to be highly salient, although obviously if a word is of no use, it will disappear. For example English speakers learn all sorts of arbitrary facts, that *pork* is the meat of *pigs*. We continue to make a distinction that was important to the English speakers who first used the word *pork*, even though the French/English vocabulary distinction does not have the pragmatic effect that it had in diglossic twelfth-century England.

Second, languages are complex systems. Grammatical constructions may change in response to changes in other parts of the system and lose the meaning first associated with them. Thus the English dative experiencer construction has disappeared from the language; we no longer say *Her likes . . .* We cannot attribute the loss of the experiencer construction entirely to a change in English speakers' assumptions about the causes of emotions, because the loss is part of a wider change in English as to how grammatical functions are realized (Allen 1995).

Third, the links between languages and societies are often not directly observable. Related to this is the fourth point, that languages and societies do not change in tandem. Common ground may change faster than language. Hence, we should not expect to find direct reflections of present-day common ground in words and constructions inherited from previous centuries. Rather, we should look for reflections of present-day common ground in constructions that are likely to relate to the present-day speakers' common ground. As Wierzbicka (1992: 373–5) points out, profitable sources of data would be change and variation, frequency, and productivity. I look at each in turn.

12.4.1. *Change and variation*

If speakers choose to adopt new words and constructions, or adopt new uses for old words and old constructions, or show variation and choices in uses of words and constructions, then it is likely that the concepts expressed by those words and constructions are salient to those speakers.

However, even in areas where there is great change, caution must be exercised. Take an example from English. English, like many Indo-European languages, has many lexicalizations of ways of qualifying the attribution of properties, including class membership, to entities or actions or states. At one end of the range are intensifiers, ways in which the speaker strongly asserts his or her commitment to the belief that, say, an entity has a certain property: *The book launch was very/really/bloody/ incredibly/terribly/terrifically/stunningly/sickeningly/disgustingly/extremely/ amazingly/outrageously . . . good.*

We also have syntactic constructions for expressing intensity, the comparative and superlative. These may be analytic (English *the most exciting, most exciting of all, there's nothing so exciting as . . .*), suppletive (English *best*), or transparent suffixal (English *-est*). We have other ways of intensifying, using comparison: *The food was stone-cold, His feet were as cold as ice*, or using negative polarity items: *it isn't worth a damn/straw/red cent*. While comparisons are understandably specific to lexical items: *stone-cold*, but not *stone-angry*, intensifiers often have collocational restrictions (Apresjan 1974: 45). *Intensely* works better with feelings, *intensely satisfying*, than it does with currents, *?an intense wind.*

This profusion of intensifying expressions has been a feature of English for a long time; cf. the fourteenth-century *Confessio Amantis* by John Gower (Macaulay 1969): <u>gret</u> *desputeisoun* 1. 1440, <u>*mochel*</u> *thoght* 1. 1568, *he lay ded* <u>*as eny ston*</u> 2. 2741, <u>*Welmore*</u> *whyt* <u>*than eny Swan*</u> 3. 797, *The day was* <u>*wonder*</u> *hot withalle* 1. 2307, <u>*so*</u> *foule yit syh he* <u>*nevere non*</u> 1. 1532. In fact many Indo-European languages have superlative constructions, and a superlative is reconstructible for proto-Indo-European (Harold Koch, personal communication). The grammaticalization inherent in the superlative construction suggests that, at some time in the past of Indo-European, it was conversationally common to express the idea that something possesses some attribute to a greater extent that any other thing in the domain of comparison.

We not only have a vast number of such intensifiers; we also keep on creating new ones, e.g. in 1998 Manchester English *It's way good, It's well good* (Kersti Börjars, personal communication). Likewise people are constantly making new similes to intensify a property: *mad as a meataxe, useless as a screen door on a submarine.* We do this for intensifiers. But we do not do it, for say, toasters. The English-speaking child learns that there are domains in which they can expect to learn new ways of saying much the same thing, like intensifiers, and many domains in which they can relax, thinking they will not need to learn new words.

The Central Australian language Warlpiri, on the other hand, has no morphological or syntactically marked superlative or comparative construction, or intensifying negative polarity constructions like *don't give a damn.* It has one intensifying clitic -*nyayirni* which can attach to different parts of speech, and a clitic -*piya* 'like' which can attach to different parts of speech to make a comparison, but not commonly for intensifier similes like English *run like the wind*.

The difference between Warlpiri and Indo-European languages with respect to qualifying the attribution of properties extends further than intensifiers. English has several ways of denying attribution of properties, including the use of intensional predicates, and they have been productive for centuries. I list them below, coarsely grouped into categories:

X is not Y, but one might think it was Y
artificial/imitation silk, synthetic fabric, false teeth, fake ID, bogus credentials, sham leather, spurious counter-example, apparent/seeming concern, virtual reality, counterfeit money, faux marble, ersatz coffee, mock-turtle, play money, toy gun, pretend fur, pseudo-intellectual

X is not what people would normally think of as Y, but is closer to Y than it is to anything else: *greenish, kinda, sorta.*

X is not Y, but once was Y: *former, previous, earlier, ci-devant, quondam, ex-, defrocked*

X is not Y: *a non-existent dinosaur, a hypothetical question, an imaginary animal, an un-person, a non-event*

X may not be Y: *hypothetical, alleged, supposed, so-called*

Warlpiri has particles *kulanganta*, *nganta*, and *mayi* which cover much of the semantic range of the English forms given above.

To sum up:

(i) English and other Indo-European languages have many more words and constructions for qualifying property attribution and class membership than languages like Warlpiri.

(ii) Similar forms have been salient in the distant past, resulting in grammaticalization and a range of syntactic constructions.

(iii) New forms are being invented or borrowed with great frequency. The language learner has to learn that intensifiers and 'fake'-type words are areas where new words can be coined.

So, these semantic categories are certainly salient, and are in present use. The productivity of intensifiers is often attributed to the expressive meaning component which they bear, but it is doubtful that such an explanation will work for the productivity of the related class of 'fake'-type words, which are not as emotionally laden. Moreover, it does not explain their absence in languages such as Warlpiri. Could the semantic categories represented by intensifiers and 'fake'-type words express some meaning or meanings related to the common ground of speakers of Indo-European languages? It is hard to make this argument, for the reasons Polivanov gives: the use of intensifiers and superlatives dates back probably to proto-Indo-European, and the cultural practices of speakers of Indo-European languages have diverged over time and space.

An alternative explanation for the productivity of intensifiers may lie in language play and language art. Figures of speech related to qualifying property attribution, such as hyperbole and simile, have been around in the Western European oral and written tradition for a long time. They represent long accepted ways of embellishing speech. It may be then that the productiveness of the category has more to do with maintaining traditions of verbal art, and less to do with specific meanings. The teenagers who invent 'way good' may not be doing so because the meaning of intensifiers is particularly important to them. Instead, they want to mark themselves out as different. But they do so by inventing a new word within a category where English speakers have had licence to invent new words for a long time.

Warlpiri speakers have not traditionally had the licence to embellish their speech by inventing new intensifiers. However, they have other strategies for displaying verbal art. The existence of auxiliary vocabularies, styles and the possibilities afforded by multilingualism may represent the language embellishments that English speakers perform in domains with lots of partial synonyms.

So, to conclude, new words and constructions are good areas to look for reflections of a social network's interests. However, if they occur in a domain where there is a long tradition of inventing new words or constructions, then we cannot assume that the invention of a new word reflects the importance of the meaning of the category in the social network. It could just as well indicate the importance of the category as one where speakers are licensed to invent new words, and so display their verbal art, their identity as members of a group, and so on. Such a claim could be tested by an examination of the vocabulary of the language over time, considering in which domains new words appear.

12.4.2. *Frequency and productivity of morphosyntactic constructions*

A second area to look for clues to reflections of common ground in languages are *frequency* of words, and *frequency* and *productivity* of constructions, as Wierzbicka (1992: 374) notes. If speakers use a word or morphosyntactic construction a great deal, then one can argue that the meaning of that construction, the way for creating new meanings that it represents, is one that people find useful.

Some constructions, like Subject Verb Object in English, are very frequent and highly productive. But of course much, maybe all, of the meaning of the SVO construction, 'who does what to whom', is both abstract and readily expressible in every other language. Hence, this kind of construction does not embody a 'culture-specific message', and so will not tell us much about the common ground of speakers of English. Ethnosyntax can profitably focus on new or emerging constructions. An example that Wierzbicka (1992) gives is the increasing Australian English use of *-ie* and *-o* to form hypocoristics, words with the same denotation as another word related to it in shape, but different connotations, as *mozzie:mosquito* and *garbo:garbage-collector*. While the *-ie* and, to a lesser extent, the *-o* are found in other English dialects, they are quite productive in Australian English (Simpson 2001*b*), and strike speakers of other dialects of English visiting Australia; thus the common remark about Australians speaking babytalk. This in turn can give rise to the emblematic use of words like *mozzie*. Speakers may use them unself-consciously, unaware that outsiders consider *mozzie* an Australianism. But once they do learn that, they may use *mozzie* as an emblem, in a more or less conscious attempt to seem Australian.[2]

12.4.3. *Frequency*

The presence of a word or construction in the language is not of itself evidence that the idea which that word or construction denotes is salient for the speakers of

---

[2] Both the realization (*form*) and the *structure* can be group identifiers (Enfield, Introduction to this volume), and are used as emblems depending on user and hearer. The *form Ersko:Erskineville* may be an in-group emblem in Sydney, meaning for its users something like 'We're the kind of people who are familiar with the suburb Erskineville.' The same speakers, familiar with many similar diminutives of suburb names—*Paddo:Paddington* and *Chippo:Chippendale*—may see the *structure* 'first syllable plus -*o*' to form a hypocoristic of a place name as normal, and not as an emblem at all. By contrast a person from Adelaide may see the use of the structure as an in-group emblem, 'that is the kind of word they use in New South Wales'. A Welsh English speaker may see the structure as an in-group emblem for Australians in general.

the language. However if a word or a construction is frequently used, then it may represent something that people want to talk about, or a marker of an identity that they wish to assert.

Establishing frequency can only be ascertained by searches of large corpora containing representative examples of different spoken language genres, from a random sample, and checking for variables such as geography, age, sex, educational, socioeconomic, and ethnic background. If these variables do not affect greatly the active use of -*ie* and -*o* diminutives, then they may be a construction shared by speakers of Australian English. If, however, these variables are relevant to whether a person uses these diminutives, then a stronger case has to be made for these diminutives reflecting concerns of Australian English speakers, rather than of a subgroup (there is some evidence that the -*o* structure is more productive in the eastern states; Simpson in press). Unfortunately, while corpora for determining frequency may be attainable in the future, the existing corpora are neither random nor representative enough to use as a basis for asserting that a construction is used by most speakers of a language with lots of speakers.

To conclude this discussion, seeking evidence for constructions shared by social networks of speakers from innovation, frequency, and productivity of constructions is important for the Narrow Ethnosyntax Hypothesis, but is also fraught with difficulties of generalizability when dealing with large and diverse communities. Better testing grounds for the Narrow Ethnosyntax Hypothesis are languages spoken by small numbers of speakers.

12.4.4. *Grammaticalization*

An inviting window into the way constructions reflect concerns of the speakers is provided by the initial stages of grammaticalization (the changing of a word with richer content into a morpheme with a more specific grammatical meaning). I assume that grammaticalization has as a precondition frequency, especially frequency of co-occurrence (Sweetser 1990; Wilkins 1991; Bybee, Perkins, and Pagliuca 1994; Burridge, this volume). Why bother to grammaticalize something that you do not say very often? On this point Wilkins has argued that:

[I]t *is* cultural interests and concerns which determine what are common topics, themes, and relevant information in discourse, and it is these factors which set the stage for, and constrain the nature of, possible grammaticalization. This is not to say such factors will definitely lead to grammaticalization, but they constitute prerequisites for it.   (Wilkins 1991: 213)

The relevance to the Narrow Ethnosyntax Hypothesis of grammaticalization is thus clear. It comes from the start of the grammaticalization process. Once a category has become grammaticalized and become, say, an inflection, the idea it denotes may or may not remain important for speakers.

An instance of grammaticalization which seems a good candidate for ethnosyntactic investigation is the associated motion construction in Central Australian languages discussed by Wilkins (1991, 1996), who argues that it is a grammatical category in Arrernte. This construction, which I shall call 'associated path', involves a single complex verb expressing both an action or event and another event involving motion or direction of one of the participants (see Enfield, this volume, for similar associated posture constructions in Lao). The examples in (1) are from the Central Australian language Warumungu:

(1) *a. Kiwari ama kakan.*
　　　　child   it   cry-PRES³
　　　　·'The child is crying.'
　　 b. Kiwari ama apan.
　　　　child   it   move-PRES
　　　　'The child is going/moving.'
　　 c. Amanya-arnpa kiwari kakirrapan.
　　　　that.same-still child   cry-hither.PRES
　　　　'That same child is coming crying.'

For activity verbs such as 'cry' in Warumungu the associated path affix introduces both motion and orientation. For motion verbs the affix introduces orientation (to or away from the speaker). For stance verbs the affix introduces either motion and orientation (go along sitting, as in the back of a car) or just orientation:

(2)　　*Ngalanya yuwaji **ngunjjirranta** kajunu.*
　　　　this　　　road   lie-away.PRES north
　　　　'This road goes north.'

The time of this movement is concurrent or overlapping with the main event ('do on the way, do while going along'). In Warumungu, this category is so deeply embedded in the language that it has become inflectional. Tense, aspect, and associated path form portmanteau affixes. In (1c) *kaki-rr-apan* consists of root plus an augment /rr/ plus a form resembling the present tense of 'go', *apan*. The presence of *apan* is a historical vestige—compare the same tense with 'thither' *kakijirranta*, with an augment *-jirr*. No verb-form *anta* has been discovered (Simpson 2001a). Historically, many of these forms appear to have developed from the compounding of a participle with a finite motion verb but they cannot be so analysed synchronically. We cannot assert that the category of associated path is currently highly salient to the speakers, because it forms part of an inflectional paradigm, and thus there is little choice in its use.

Fortunately, we can see the start of a similar process of grammaticalization of participle plus motion verb in a neighbouring language, Warlpiri. Warlpiri allows motion verbs (and only motion verbs) to be compounded with participles. The form of the participle and of the motion verb are clear, but the participle cannot

---

³ Abbreviations: away: away from deictic centre; ERG: ergative; hither: to deictic centre; IMPERF: imperfect; NPAST: nonpast; PPL: participle; PRES: present; SEQ: sequential complementizer; 333: third person plural subject; 122: first person inclusive subject.

occur on its own. Example (3) contains the verb *yani* 'move' which on its own
describes motion. But in combination with the stance verbs its meaning alters—(3)
involves path and not actual motion:

(3)   *Pirli ka   **parnta-parntarri-nja**-mpa-ya-ni.*
         hill PRES crouch-crouch-PPL-along-go-NPAST
         'The hills stretch out in front.'

Compounding with *yani* is defined in the *Warlpiri Dictionary* (Laughren, Hale,
and Hoogenraad in preparation) as 'x perform action or be in state designated by
V, and move along PATH or be arrayed along PATH or be arrayed over period of
time'.[4] This process is productive and frequently used, but has not yet reached the
obligatory inflectional status that associated path has in neighbouring Warumungu.

Thus we have a candidate for the first two steps of the suggested ethnosyntax
procedure—a construction and a meaning proposed for it.

12.5. STEPS 3 AND 4

The third and fourth steps revolve around finding a relation between this meaning
and some concern of the speakers, part of their common ground. We could argue,
as Wilkins (1991) does for the Arrernte (southern neighbours of the Warlpiri),
that the relation between the associated path constructions and the speakers' common ground has to do with people's concern for motion and travel, and orienting
events.

It is a truism that, as Central Australian peoples live in semi-desert country, and
were in the past nomadic peoples, travelling, way-finding, and location of places
were of great importance in traditional life. Munn writes:

In Walbiri symbolism this nomadic patterning of life—the movement from water hole to
water hole—takes precedence as an organising focus over other large-scale rhythmic cycles
such as that of the rainy and dry season. The small-scale concomitant of this pattern—the
daily departure from the camp for hunting and food gathering and the nightly return to the
camp—is also of importance.   (Munn 1973: 7)

Today the Warlpiri are superficially sedentary, living in towns, settlements, and
outstations in the best-watered parts of their country. People still visit other parts
of their traditional land for hunting and gathering, for religious reasons, and travelling through to other communities. But most of Warlpiri traditional country is not
occupied on the scale that it was before the British invasion.

While by the standards of the past people do not travel much, travelling still
plays a much larger part in their lives than in those of their non-Aboriginal neigh-

---

[4] The disjunction between motion and orientation is of concern for a good semantic representation.
While in (3) the hills are not moving, the same construction could be used of a person crouching down
in a truck as it moved along. This is why I prefer to call it 'associated path', with motion inferred
pragmatically.

bours.[5] Indeed, Stotz argues for eastern Warlpiri that the primary social unit is as much the 'car-hold', the group that travels together, as it is the 'household' (Stotz 1993). What has changed is the *mode of transport* (from foot to car except for short distances), the *reasons for travelling* (continued travelling is no longer essential for finding food and water), the *places that people travel to* (other towns and settlements where related families live, apart from the forays mentioned earlier), and the *kind of routes* that people use (graded roads rather than walking across sand without defined footpaths).

Thus, from the point of view of European Australians, travel appears to be an important shared activity for Warlpiri people. How does it relate to conversational practice and thus to the associated path meaning? Nash (1998) discusses the importance to the Warlpiri of 'topographical gossip', conversations about country, trips, navigation. Wilkins (1991) shows for the Arrernte how common associated motion constructions are in some texts, and he argues that Arrernte adults build more complex descriptions of motion events than English speakers do (Wilkins 1996). He also points out the importance of travel in ancestral myths which are usually travel stories emphasizing the creation of places, and thus their location. The same is true for the Warlpiri; for example, Napaljarri and Cataldi (1994) consists of fifteen stories illustrating the *jukurrpa* (law) told by people considered good story-tellers. All but one of the stories have travel to and from named places as a central part of the action. Clauses headed by motion verbs start the action in about half the stories, and end it for most of the stories.

We have thus put up the hypothesis required for Step 3 (i.e. proposing a relationship between a grammaticalized meaning and some shared concern of speakers), and we have made a start on Step 4, finding independent evidence for this shared cultural concern. But Step 4 raises serious methodological considerations. How do we determine what is (non-linguistic) common ground; how do we provide evidence that the shared topic of conversation, assumption, or expectation of behaviour mentioned in Step 3 is, or has been, highly salient for some social network?

12.5.1. *Determining common ground*

In trying to find out what is common ground, the linguist is acting as ethnographer. Three questions arise at once:

- What are the social networks to which the speakers belong?
- What is the position of the observer-linguist?
- What differences and interactions are there between what people say their common ground is and how they act?

I discuss each in turn.

---

[5] Warchivker, Tjapangati, and Wakerman (2000) observed a mobility rate of about 35% over the period of one year in one remote Aboriginal community with close ties to Warlpiri people.

12.5.1.1. What are the social networks to which the speakers belong?

Anthropologists are increasingly sceptical of notions of a single culture, recognizing that people share different topics of conversations, assumptions, and expectations with different people, and that their common ground is constantly being updated and changing (Steeding 1999). Consider the many people who speak an English variety as their first language. They may grow up in such differing communities as Australian Aboriginal fringe camps, Indian Muslim households, Scottish fishing villages, Australian suburbs. All these people can understand each other talking English to some extent, and certainly far better than they can understand a monolingual Warlpiri speaker. We can produce evidence of the linguistic structures shared among English speakers much more easily than we can produce evidence of non-linguistic common ground shared by all English speakers.

So, suppose we take a smaller unit of English speakers, determined by geography and history: Australia. These speakers in turn may belong to more than one network, differing as to what common ground they share, what routines they have evolved, what expectations they have of how people behave. Thus, I share different common ground, and will engage in different conversations, with teachers, cyclists, visitors to Alice Springs, residents of Canberra. No one would expect a single ethnography to cover all these networks. The more diverse the range of occupations and living conditions in a society, the less plausible a single ethnography becomes, the more difficult defining their common ground becomes, and the less likely we are to be able to test hypotheses about what constitutes common ground.

We then require ethnographies for each of the groups within Australia. To find out what is common to Australians, we should look at the ethnographies for each of the groups and find what is common between them, a bottom-up approach. But that of course is a great deal of work. As a result, it seems sensible to test the feasibility of ethnosyntactic description by restricting ourselves to small-scale societies with relatively simple economies, most of the members of which know of each other, and so can be assumed to share a lot of common ground. The Warlpiri might still be thought of as such a society, although the effect of colonization has resulted in speakers' involvement in other networks.

12.5.1.2. What is the position of the observer-linguist?

Having restricted ourselves to a small-scale society, we must then consider the sources of information on the common ground shared by speakers.

As humans, we engage in ethnography much as we engage in language learning. First language/culture acquisition differs from second language/culture acquisition in kind. When, as untrained adult observers, we visit another country, we learn a few words of the language, and we learn a few basic things about the way locals behave. Our perceptions are, naturally enough, largely determined by our chance experiences. However, as soon as one reads a good ethnography of the community, one sees how fragmented and partial one's first impressions of a place and a people can be. The casual observer (linguist included) does not have the training or the long-term knowledge of the people's ways of behaving in order to fit observations into more general patterns. The temptation for a linguist in looking at the meaning of a construction is to focus on just those aspects of the ethnography which may relate to the construction under investigation. But unless we look at the ethnography as a whole, we may miss important patterns.

Fortunately, in the case of the Warlpiri, we have at least fourteen ethnographies,[6] several collections of narratives (e.g. Napaljarri and Cataldi 1994), and the largest dictionary of an Australian language (Laughren, Hale, and Hoogenraad in preparation). Even with this wealth of information, it is hard to find descriptions of 'common topics of conversation' or even transcripts of conversation, let alone 'shared expectations of how people behave'.

Ideally, data on the common ground of a community would come from at least three sources: members of the community, and observers from at least two different societies. This will lessen the problems of ethnocentrism (Holy and Stuchlik 1983: 33 ff.). Even the best ethnographers tend to notice those things that are different from their own culture, and ignore those things that seem similar (because they seem natural). Thus, to a European Australian, the amount of time Warlpiri people spend travelling, and discussing travelling, seems considerable, and so we readily think of it as a common topic/activity for them. A Warlpiri person producing an ethnography of the Warlpiri would write it in the light of the sedentarism of their European Australian neighbours, and so might also highlight travelling. However, if a Haillom (Bushman) speaker were to write an ethnography of the Warlpiri, the travelling might seem too normal to comment on. There might be other things in common between the Warlpiri and European Australian communities which seem unremarkable to us and the Warlpiri, but which the Haillom ethnographer finds strange and worth describing. We have ethnographies of the Warlpiri from American, Australian, Austrian, British, and French ethnographers (although not yet from Warlpiri speakers), so some triangulation is possible.

12.5.1.3. What differences and interactions are there between what people say their common ground is and how they act?

Holy and Stuchlik (1983: 56) suggest that what ethnographers observe falls roughly into two types of data which represent different realms of social reality: actions (observed patterns) and 'notions' (the subjects' ideas and statements about actions and behaviour). For example, observed patterns could include determining 'common topics of conversation' and 'common activities', by measuring frequency of occurrence among a representative sample of people, thus increasing the reliability of the data, and the chance of recording diversity and negative data that do not fit the ethnographer's hypothesis (Johnson 1978). But 'notions', in this case 'shared expectations and assumptions', do not exist apart from people and the situations those people find themselves in. They are in people's heads, and are less directly knowable than language.

---

[6] See the bibliography maintained by David Nash, at http://www.anu.edu.au/linguistics/nash/aust/wlp/wlp-eth-ref.html.

One source of information about people's 'notions' is what they say about their ideas, but this must be treated with caution. Because a group professes a stereotype of themselves as egalitarian, say, this does not mean that a concern with egalitarianism is actually part of their common ground, and so is able to filter into their language. Both the content of the stereotype and the point of view involved determine the likelihood that the content of the stereotype is actually part of people's common ground. 'Content' involves not only how much actual people differ from the stereotype, but also what group the stereotypes are true of. For example, more than half the Australian population is excluded from the denotation of the stereotype Australian as a bushman supporting his mate, a hard-drinking, swearing, gambling larrikin, an uneducated working-class man. 'Point of view' raises such questions as: who does the stereotype benefit, and where do the stereotypes come from? Nineteenth-century European Australian stereotypes of Aborigines as lazy and untrustworthy helped the European Australians justify taking land from the Aborigines and treating them as second-class citizens. Stereotypes, like the emblematic uses of *mozzie* mentioned earlier, are likely to arise when groups define themselves in opposition to each other. For example, some Warlpiri have an image of themselves as people who live on the ground (Munn 1973: 58), in contrast to house-dwelling European Australians. European Australians may have similar stereotypes of the Warlpiri. Thus the Warlpiri and European Australians to some extent define what is characteristically Warlpiri, and what is characteristically European Australian, with relation to each other.

These stereotypes are powerful; they linger long after the observable patterns that gave rise to them has changed (most Warlpiri now live in houses). They are historical artefacts that develop in response to historical pressures, and then are passed on to succeeding generations. Thus the stereotype of an Australian appears to have developed late in the nineteenth century, as part of defining Australians as members of a new country shaking off its status as British colony (Campbell 1989). It was strongly promoted by influential writers, mostly men. At the same time, Australian women made great headway in gaining education and legal equality,[7] but this did not make its way into current stereotypes of Australians (except indirectly through egalitarianism). The stereotype was strengthened in the First World War by the desire of the Australian Imperial Forces troops (mostly young men) to differentiate themselves from the British. Opposition to a stereotype of the English as ignorant of the bush, over-polite, interested in culture, obsessed with hierarchy, may explain many of the characteristics of the stereotypical Australian. This stereotype lingers on, linked to words like 'mate', 'bush', 'outback', 'battler', regardless of the facts that women have outnumbered men for a long time and that most Australians live in cities.

---

[7] In South Australia women gained the right to take university degrees in 1881, property rights for married women in 1883, and suffrage in 1894 (Jones 1985).

Stereotypes, words and constructions associated with them, and emblematic words and constructions represent ideas that have been taken as important to a particular group of Australians, and involve expressions used by an overlapping group. In turn the group of Australians using those words and holding those ideas have been taken (or promoted) as typical of Australians, and then as stereotypical Australians. Stereotypes of what Australians are like are part of common ground for many Australians, at different levels of remove—close: *I think that people like me value X*; distant: *I know that some people think people like me value X*. But the X of the stereotype may not in fact be part of the common ground of contemporary Australians. Thus the shared expectations of behaviour that the stereotypical Australian 'fair go' and 'mateship' evoke may have been part of the common ground of nineteenth-century Australians, and may be reflected in words, phrases, and constructions inherited from that time. But we cannot deduce from this that those expectations are still current in Australian society, although we know that the stereotype is widely held, and so now can be invoked in debate by politicians, appealing to different interpretations of *fair go* to urge their cause. The seduction for linguists is that stereotypes are easy to find and discuss; observing patterns and determining what actually are important aspects of common ground are not easy.

Likewise, replicability of linguistic data is somewhat easier than replicability of data about common ground. Consider the case of an ethnographic fieldworker recording the last speaker of a language on videotape. On the basis of the transcription of the language on the tapes, the fieldworker can come up with language patterns and can generalize them to produce a dictionary and grammar. They are incomplete approximations. But the hypotheses about language patterns can be tested, say by another person creating a new text, giving it to the speaker, and seeing if they give it roughly the same interpretation as the hypothesis predicts. We can even do this on the basis of written texts of dead languages. Moreover, translations can be achieved even by people who have developmental social difficulties, as Smith and Tsimpli (1994) show. We have thus a replicability test for linguistic analyses.

Can we from the same material deduce what the common ground of the speakers was, on the basis of the activities and reflections of one member? It is surely more difficult than the linguistic task. Ethnographers can, and do, take another ethnographer's description, say, of how to join in a group in a particular community, and attempt to replicate it in that community. But there are many more complicating factors: people may not accept that outsiders know how to behave and can claim common ground; one's common ground is continually being updated, whereas one's language is much slower to change. Thus descriptions of linguistic constructions appear to be more easily falsifiable than descriptions of 'shared expectations and assumptions'.

To finish with Steps 3 and 4, we have some reason to be hopeful about looking for evidence of reflections of common ground in syntactic constructions in Warlpiri because the community is relatively small and homogeneous, and because there are a number of ethnographies. However, against this must be balanced the fact that we do not have ethnographies from Warlpiri native speakers, or from observers from widely differing societies. Nor do we have a large body of conversation (as opposed to narrative) to look at. And finally, the task of determining what is common ground for speakers is far from easy.

12.6. STEP 5: PROPOSING A PATH

Let us assume that we can overcome the difficulties faced in trying to find out what is common ground among Warlpiri speakers. The fifth step is to show how travel and orientation as topics of conversation and social practice could be linked to particular constructions. We need to propose a plausible way of linking them (Lehmann 1995). This seems possible for Warlpiri: assume that people talk a lot about actions and accompanying motion or orientation using periphrastic participial constructions. Assume these periphrastic constructions frequently occur next to the main verb. As Enfield (this volume) suggests, if the ideas expressed by the verb and the participle are easily construed as a complex idea that is conversationally common, this provides fertile ground for the verb and participle to be reanalysed as a single word. Then a periphrastic construction *Participle Finite-motion verb* develops into a compound structure *Participle+Finite-motion verb* (Koch 1984; Simpson 2001*a*).

For this to happen, the word order of the earlier stage must not only allow the participle to precede the finite verb but also must make this common enough that compounding is likely to happen. Now, Warlpiri is a free word order language. So how can this happen? Synchronically, Warlpiri has a periphrastic construction for expressing prior events which resembles the periphrastic construction posited for the first stage of associated path. The construction is illustrated in (4) (examples from Simpson 2001*a*):

(4) *a. Yinga-lpa-lu   nga-rnu. Nga-rninja-rla ya-nu   wirlinyi-lki.*
         SO-IMPERF-333 eat-PAST eat-PPL-SEQ   go-PAST hunting-now
         'So they'd eat it. Having eaten it he'd go off hunting now.'

     b. Yujuku-pu-ngu-lpa,   nya-ngu-lpa.   Yujuku-pi-nja-rla-lpa
         nest-make-PAST-IMPERF see-PAST-IMPERF nest-make-PPL-SEQ-IMPERF
         parnka-ja.
         move.quickly-PAST
         'He would make a nest, he'd have a look. After making the nest he'd fly off.'

     c. Kuja-ka-rnalu   nga-rni   jalangu-rlu-lku paji-rninja-rla
         which-PRES-111 eat-NPAST today-ERG-now cut-PPL-SEQ
         'which we cut and eat today still.'

The words in boldface are inflected participles consisting of the verb stem followed by a non-finite suffix, followed by a complementizer suffix -*rla*. The complementizer suffix indicates that the event denoted by the participle clause takes place before the event denoted by the finite verb clause, and that the subjects of the two clauses are the same. The order of the participle and the finite verb is free, and the participle usually heads a subordinate clause. Either event can involve motion (4a, b), or neither (4c).

When the participle directly precedes the main verb, there is 'an effect which is more closely akin to coordination than to subordination' (Hale 1982: 226). The participle appearing next to a verb is interpreted as modifying that verb, whereas when it appears next to the sentence it modifies the whole event.

Assume that, in the past, people often talked about activity events and motion events together, using sentences like those in (4). Since these constructions are popular today, it is not implausible that speakers used similar constructions in the past. With frequency would come phonological coalescence, and then the change from a phrasal structure to a morphological structure representing associated path. Such semantic shifts would allow the biclausal constructions to merge their argument structures, and thus become the monoclausal constructions of associated path.

This then illustrates Step 5, providing a path to relate use in conversation to a syntactic structure.

12.7. STEP 6: TESTING PROPOSED LINKS

Step 6 involves checking the proposed path between conversational practice and grammatical construction. This has to be done if we are to achieve anything more than the assertion of a link between a structure, a proposed meaning, and a claimed property of the common ground of the speakers, and if we are to convince sceptics that we have constrained the natural desire to find what one is looking for. Other geographically distant and genetically unrelated languages with similar structure–meaning pairs and evidence for similar common ground would give some supporting evidence. A first pass at this for associated path is not rewarding; there are plenty of societies in Australia similar to the Warlpiri without associated path constructions, and there are languages with associated path constructions (such as the Mayan languages described by Zavala Maldonado 1993) whose speakers live differently from the Warlpiri. I return to Polivanov; we can find groups with remarkable social similarities but speaking languages structured so differently that comparable constructions could not evolve. A group can be bilingual, speaking two languages with radically different structures. Likewise, two groups can speak approximately the same language, but differ greatly in social life. Finding comparable situations to test the proposed connection is a challenge, and hence the connection between construction–meaning pair and common ground proposed by the Narrow Ethnosyntax Hypothesis is difficult to falsify.

12.8. CONCLUSION

This chapter has discussed how one might examine the Narrow Ethnosyntax Hypothesis. I have expanded on Wierzbicka's (1992) suggestions for finding likely constructions, and discussed pitfalls to be avoided, such as alternative possible explanations for the frequency and productivity of intensifiers. I have suggested and illustrated a procedure for carrying out ethnosyntax using as an example the incipient grammaticalization of associated path in a language whose speakers form a relatively homogeneous group, and about whom a number of ethnographies have been written (by outsiders from a range of backgrounds). And even for this good case, challenges remain—in establishing what is common ground for speakers, in creating a testable description of that common ground, and in justifying a path between the common ground and the word or syntactic construction.

REFERENCES

ALLEN, CYNTHIA L. 1995. *Case Marking and Reanalysis: Grammatical Relations from Old to Early Modern English*. Oxford: Oxford University Press.

APRESJAN, JURIJ D. 1974. *Leksicheskaja semantika: sinonimicheskije sredstva jazyka*. Moscow: Nauka.

BYBEE, JOAN, PERKINS, REVERE, and PAGLIUCA, WILLIAM. 1994. *The Evolution of Grammar: Tense, Aspect, and Modality in the Languages of the World*. Chicago: University of Chicago Press.

CAMPBELL, ROSEMARY. 1989. *Heroes and Lovers: A Question of National Identity*. Sydney: Allen & Unwin.

CLARK, HERBERT H. 1996. *Using Language*. Cambridge: Cambridge University Press.

ENFIELD, N. J. 2000a. 'On linguocentrism'. In Martin Pütz and Marjolijn H. Verspoor (eds.), *Explorations in Linguistic Relativity*. Amsterdam: John Benjamins, 125–57.

——2000b. 'The theory of cultural logic: how individuals combine social intelligence with semiotics to create and maintain cultural meaning'. *Cultural Dynamics*, 12.1: 35–64.

FABIAN, JOHANNES. 1991. *Time and the Work of Anthropology*. Chur: Harwood Academic Publishers.

FILLMORE, CHARLES J., KAY, PAUL, and O'CONNOR, MARY CATHERINE. 1988. 'Regularity and idiomaticity in grammatical constructions: the case of "let alone"'. *Language*, 64.3: 501–38.

HALE, KENNETH L. 1982. 'Some essential features of Warlpiri main clauses'. In Stephen Swartz (ed.), *Papers in Warlpiri Grammar: In Memory of Lothar Jagst*. Berrimah: Summer Institute of Linguistics, 217–315.

HOLY, LADISLAV, and STUCHLIK, MILAN. 1983. *Actions, Notions and Representations: Foundations of Anthropological Inquiry*. Cambridge: Cambridge University Press.

JOHNSON, ALLEN W. 1978. *Quantification in Cultural Anthropology: An Introduction to Research Design*. Stanford, Calif.: Stanford University Press.

JONES, HELEN. 1985. *Nothing Seemed Impossible: Women's Education and Social Change in South Australia 1875–1915*. St Lucia: University of Queensland Press.

KOCH, HAROLD. 1984. 'The category of "associated motion" in Kaytej'. *Language in Central Australia*, 1: 23–34.

LAUGHREN, MARY, HALE, KEN, and HOOGENRAAD, ROBERT. In preparation. *Warlpiri Dictionary*. Electronic data files. Department of English, University of Queensland.

LEHMANN, CHRISTIAN. 1995. *Thoughts on Grammaticalization*. LINCOM studies in theoretical linguistics 01. Munich: Lincom-Europa.

LEONT'EV, A. A. (COMP.). 1974. *E. D. Polivanov: Selected Works: Articles on General Linguistics*. The Hague: Mouton.

MACAULAY, G. C. (ed.). 1969. *The English Works of John Gower*, vol. i. The Early English Text Society. Oxford: Oxford University Press.

MOHANAN, K.P., and MOHANAN, TARA. 1999. 'Representing presuppositions'. In Tara Mohanan and Lionel Wee (eds.), *Grammatical Semantics: Evidence for Structure in Meaning*. Stanford, Calif.: CSLI Publications, 217–59.

MUNN, NANCY. 1973. *Walbiri Iconography: Graphic Representation and Cultural Symbolism in a Central Australian Society*. Ithaca, NY: Cornell University Press.

NAPALJARRI, PEGGY ROCKMAN, and CATALDI, LEE (eds.). 1994. *Warlpiri Dreamings and Histories: Yimikirli*. The Sacred Literature Series. San Francisco: Harper Collins.

NASH, DAVID. 1998. 'Ethnocartography: understanding central Australian geographic literacy'. Paper presented to the Australian Anthropological Society Annual Conference. Canberra, 2 October 1998.

POLIVANOV, EVGENIJ D. 1974*a*. 'On the phonetic features of the dialects of social groups and, in particular, of standard Russian', in Leont'ev 1974: 195–210.

——1974*b*. 'The sphere of immediate problems in contemporary linguistics', in Leont'ev 1974: 171–8.

SIMPSON, JANE. 2001*a*. 'Preferred word order and grammaticalization of associated path in Warlpiri', in Miriam Butt and Tracy H. King (eds.), *Time over Matter: Diachronic Perspectives on Morphosyntax*. Stanford, Calif.: CSLI Publications, 127–63.

——2001*b*. 'Hypocoristics of place-names in Australian English', in Peter Collins and David Blair (eds.), *Varieties of English: Australian English*. Amsterdam: John Benjamins, 89–112.

SMITH, NEIL, and TSIMPLI, IANTHI-MARIA. 1994. *The Mind of a Savant: Language Learning and Modularity*. Oxford: Blackwell.

STEEDING, MARY MARGARET. 1999. 'The state of culture theory in the anthropology of South East Asia'. *Annual Review of Anthropology*, 28: 431–54.

STOTZ, GERTRUDE. 1993. 'Kurdungurlu got to drive toyota: differential colonizing process among the Warlpiri'. Ph.D. dissertation, Deakin University.

SWEETSER, EVE. 1990. *From Etymology to Pragmatics: Metaphorical and Cultural Aspects of Semantic Structure*. Cambridge: Cambridge University Press.

WARCHIVKER, ILAN, TJAPANGATI, T., and WAKERMAN, JOHN. 2000. 'The turmoil of Aboriginal enumeration: mobility and service population analysis in a Central Australian community'. *Australian and New Zealand Journal of Public Health*, 24.4: 444–9.

WIERZBICKA, ANNA. 1988. *The Semantics of Grammar*. Amsterdam: John Benjamins.

——1992. *Semantics, Culture, and Cognition: Universal Human Concepts in Culture-Specific Configurations*. New York: Oxford University Press.

——1997. *Understanding Cultures through their Key Words: English, Russian, German and Japanese*. New York: Oxford University Press.

WILKINS, DAVID P. 1991. 'The semantics, pragmatics and diachronic development of "Associated Motion" in Mparntwe Arrernte'. *Buffalo Working Papers in Linguistics*, 207–57.

——1996. 'A near accident at the semantics-pragmatics interface'. Intended for Bert Peeters (ed.), *The Lexicon/Encyclopaedia Interface*.

ZAVALA MALDONADO, ROBERTO. 1993. 'Clause integration with verbs of motion in Mayan languages: some facts without fiction'. MA dissertation, University of Oregon.

GENERAL INDEX

INDEX OF NAMES

35550813